LESSONS FROM
CHILDHOOD

LESSONS FROM CHILDHOOD

Some Aspects of the Early Life of Unusual Men and Women

BY

R. S. ILLINGWORTH

M.D. (Leeds), F.R.C.P., D.P.H., D.C.H.

Professor of Child Health, University of Sheffield

AND

C. M. ILLINGWORTH

M.B., B.S. (Durham), M.R.C.P.

Formerly Tutor in Child Health, University of Sheffield

BALTIMORE

THE WILLIAM AND WILKINS COMPANY

1966

Printed in Great Britain

PREFACE

WE are not biographers. We are paediatricians and as such are interested in the way children grow up, in their personality and behaviour, in the normal variations which occur in the pattern of their development—variations such as mental inferiority and mental superiority, or lateness or precocity in certain fields of development such as speech. We are particularly interested in the early signs of genius—and in failure to recognise the early signs of unusual talents. We are very much concerned with the effect of the early management and environment—at home and at school. It is this sort of subject which we have tried to explore in this book. We have, in short, described those subjects in which we, as paediatricians, are particularly interested. We make no pretence at all to have covered all aspects of the childhood of the 450 men and women mentioned in our book.

Our concern is the lessons which can be learnt from the childhood of interesting and unusual men and women, good and bad, famous and infamous. We have tried to bring together information which will be of interest and value to all who are concerned with children—whether with their own, or with the children of others. Our greatest difficulty in so doing, and a difficulty of which we were acutely conscious throughout, was that of welding together the innumerable scraps of information which we felt were interesting, useful and important to the subject.

Not being biographers, we have made no attempt to refer to all the original documents on which biographies are based. It would obviously be an impossible task for anyone, in view of the number of men and women included in the book.

Instead we have obtained our material from the many accepted biographies, and wish to express our thanks to all the very many authors and publishers who have given permission to quote from their books. In every instance we have given the source of our information at the end of the book, in order that those interested may read the original biographies. Our quotations are direct verbatim ones or indirect.

We have read innumerable other biographies of the individuals described in this book; but we have not quoted from them because they did not contain material concerning childhood which interested us. Whenever possible we have read more than one biography of an individual, and have often been impressed by the disagreement between biographers as to the interpretation of events in childhood, and the emphasis which should be placed on them.

We hope that we have not committed many errors. As for autobiographies, we remembered George Bernard Shaw's comments that 'all autobiographies are lies. I do not mean unconscious unintentional lies. I mean deliberate lies. No one is bad enough to tell the truth about himself during his lifetime, involving as it must the truth about his family and friends and colleagues.' We agree with Pascal that autobiographers tend to overdramatise themselves. Biographers, on the other hand, may conceal the truth, in an attempt to propound their own point of view: and the information about the childhood of the subject of the biography may be severely limited or even non-existent.

With only two or three exceptions, we have confined our study to the lives of men and women who are no longer living.

We can obviously be criticised for having excluded many famous people. The omission may be due to accident or ignorance because we did not know books about them; or it may have been deliberate, either because little is known about their childhood, or because there was little of interest to us in the books which we read. For instance, little is known about the childhood of Chaucer, Lavoisier, Rabelais, Shakespeare and Stalin; and we were unable to find many items of interest in the childhood of Erasmus, Nelson, Pavlov and Samuel Pepys. Concerning Guy Fawkes, all we could gather was that he came from an ordinary middle-class family, and that 'No one thought it worthwhile to record his early words, to notice his progress at school (St Peters, York) or to keep copies of his correspondence'. Moore, in his life of Oliver Goldsmith, wrote as follows: 'It is greatly to be regretted that there is no means for determining by certain birth marks when a child is destined to achieve greatness in after life, so that the people around it may begin to make notes of its lispings for future biographers.'

Omissions there are in plenty: but it is inevitable that we were limited by the availability of biographies and of interesting information relevant to our theme.

We owe a great debt to our friend Dr John Apley, of Bristol, who laboriously read every word of the script, and made innumerable criticisms and suggestions for its improvement.

Finally, we thank the Librarians of more than twenty libraries which we have consulted, including the British Museum. The excellent libraries of the University of Sheffield and the City of Sheffield have been particularly helpful.

SHEFFIELD, 1966   R. S. I.
                                                   C. M. I.

ACKNOWLEDGMENTS

The authors wish to acknowledge their thanks to the following publishers for permission to quote extracts from their books:

ALLEN & UNWIN, London (1924) Schweitzer, A. *Memoirs of Childhood and Youth.*
(1957) Jean-Aubry, G. *The Sea Dreams.*
(1960) Murray, Gilbert *An Unfinished Autobiography.*
ARNOLD, London (1961) Green, V. H. H. *The Young Wesley.*
BARRIE & ROCKLIFF, London (1956) Bulman, Joan *Jenny Lind.*
BELL, London (1937) Bishop, M. *Pascal. The Life of Genius.*
(1963) Young, K. *Arthur James Balfour.*
BENN, London (1927) Peck, W. E. *Shelley.*
(1928) Earl of Ronaldshay *The Life of Lord Curzon*
(1930) Belloc, H. *Richelieu.*
BURKE, London (1956) Franks, A. H. *Pavlova.*
CAMBRIDGE UNIVERSITY PRESS, London (1955) Ketton-Cremor, R. W. *Thomas Gray.*
CASSELL, London (1934) Rasputin, Maria *My Father.*
(1959) Pound, R. and Harmsworth, G. *Northcliffe.*
CLARENDON PRESS, Oxford (1962) Ridley, J. *Thomas Cranmer.*
COLLINS, London (1963) Jaffe, A. *Carl Jung, Memories, Dreams and Reflections.*
COLUMBIA UNIVERSITY PRESS, New York (1958) Simon, L. *Shaw on Education.*
CONSTABLE, London (1950) Woodham-Smith, C. *Florence Nightingale.*
CURTIS BROWN, London (1954) Lord Elton *General Gordon.*
CURTIS BROWN, London (1938) Monrad-Johansen, D. *Edward Greig.*
DAVIES, London (1932) Bryant, A. *Macaulay.*
DENT, London (1940) Saunders, W. *Weber.*
DOUBLEDAY, London (1929) Leonard, J. N. *The Life of Charles Proteus Steinmetz.*
ELEK, London (1953) Gorky, M. *Autobiography.*
FABER & FABER, London (1936) Sexton, Sir James *Agitator, The Life of the Dockers' M.P. Autobiography.*
(1948) Nash, Paul *Outline—an Autobiography.*
(1958) Barker, R. H. *Marcel Proust.*
(1962) Magarschack, D. *Chekhov.*
GOLLANCZ, London (1936) Stravinsky, Igor *Chronical of my Life.*
GOLLANCZ, London and Executors of late H. G. Wells (1934) Wells, H. G. *An Experiment in Autobiography.*
HAMILTON, London (1946) Vallentin, A. *Mirabeau.*
HARCOURT, BRACE & WORLD INC., New York (1942) Padover, S. *Jefferson.*
HARRAP, London (1943) Van Loon, H. W. *Lives.*
HEINEMANN, London (1958) Parson, H. *Johnson and Boswell.*
(1962) Mack, M. P. *Jeremy Bentham.*

ix

ACKNOWLEDGEMENTS

HEINMANN, London (1964) Hillcourt, W. with Olave, Lady Baden-Powell *The Two Lives of a Hero*.
HODDER & STOUGHTON, London (1925) King, A. G. *Kelvin the Man*.
(1931) Lodge, Sir Oliver *Past Years—an Autobiography*.
(1964) Harrity, R. and Martin, *R. Helen Keller*.
HOME & VAN THAL, London (1947) Cole, G. D. H. *Samuel Butler and the Way of all Flesh*.
HUTCHINSON, London (1957) Minney, R. J. *Clive of India*.
(1962) Roosevelt, Eleanor *Autobiography*.
KIMBER, London (1963) Murray, Margaret *My First Hundred Years*.
LONGMANS, GREEN, Harlow (1932) Trevelyan, G. M. *The Life and Letters of Lord Macaulay*.
MACGIBBON & KEE, London (1962) Foot, Michael *Aneurin Bevan*.
MACMILLAN, London (1920) Begbie, H. *The Life of William Booth*.
(1946) Feiling, K. *The Life of Neville Chamberlain*.
(1961) Brook-Shepherd, G. *Dollfuss*.
MACMILLAN, New York (1956) Moraes, F. *Jawaharlal Nehru*.
(1961) Freehill, M. F. *Gifted Children*.
METHUEN, London (1949) Pearson, H. *The Life of Oscar Wilde*.
(1957) Lea, F. A. *The Tragic Philosopher*.
(1959) Mortimer, E. *Blaise Pascal*.
MASSIE, London (1959) The Earl of Birkenhead *The Life of F. E. Smith, First Earl of Birkenhead*.
MURRAY, London (1926) Clarke, E. *Benjamin Disraeli*.
NELSON, London (1961) Gerin, Winifred *Branwell Brontë*.
ODHAMS, London (1959) Churchill, Winston S. *My Early Life*.
ORION PRESS, New York (1959) Yarmolinsky, A. *Turgenev*.
OXFORD UNIVERSITY PRESS, London (1932) Trevelyan, G. O. *Lord Macaulay*.
OXFORD UNIVERSITY PRESS, New York (1936) Eaton, H. A. *Thomas De Quincey*.
PETERS, London (1946) Blunden, E. *Shelley*.
(1959) Sykes, C. *Orde Wingate*.
ROCHE PRODUCTS, London (1964) Roche *Famous People and their Illnesses*.
ROUTLEDGE & KEGAN PAUL, London (1956) Reid, J. C. *Francis Thompson, Man and Poet*.
SCRIBNER, New York (1954) Nevins, A. *Ford, The Times, The Man and The Company*.
SIMON & SCHUSTER, New York (1937) Bell, E. T. *Men of Mathematics*.
SECKER & WARBURG, London (1954) Packe, M. St. J. *John Stuart Mill*.
(1956) Hanson, L. and E. *The Tragic Life of Toulouse-Lautrec*.
SHEED & WARD, London (1944) Ward, M. *Gilbert Keith Chesterton*.
SIDGWICK & JACKSON, London (1958) Villers, Jean *T. E. Lawrence*.
SOCIETY OF AUTHORS, London (1949) Shaw, G. B. *Sixteen Self Sketches*.
UNIVERSITY OF CALIFORNIA PRESS, Los Angeles (1947) Trollope, A. *An Autobiography*.
WINGATE, London (1954) Kubizek, A. *Young Hitler*.
WORLD DISTRIBUTORS, Manchester (1960) Clarke, C. *Eichmann. The Savage Truth*.

CONTENTS

CHAPTER I

HOME AND UPBRINGING

WE felt that it would be natural and reasonable to begin our study of the childhood of the famous and infamous with the environment at home, because it is of such vital importance for the child's emotional development, character formation and whole future. Most people would agree that the most important psychological needs for a young child are love and security, the feeling that he is accepted, wanted and approved, wise loving discipline, so that he learns the difference between right and wrong, encouragement in his interests and aptitudes; the implanting of a desire to learn; the setting of a good example; and the gradual equipment for and acquisition of independence. Children need not only to be loved, but to feel that they are loved.

Psychiatrists are agreed that children most need their mother in the first three or four years of their life. Children also need a firm loving father, who takes an active part in their upbringing.

From the parents, children demand time, tolerance, a sense of humour, sympathetic guidance without overdomination and overprotection, and an understanding of their developing personality and emotional needs.

Insecurity, with its chain of resulting behaviour problems, results from the deprivation of love, from separation from the parents by death or other reason; from unkindness, constant criticism, sarcasm, ridicule, favouritism, and perfectionism.

This chapter gives an idea of how these needs were met—or not met—in some famous people. We have discussed several facets of the environment under the headings of religious upbringing, order and discipline, punishment and its effects, insecurity and emotional deprivation, and the loss of parents.

RELIGIOUS UPBRINGING

In this section we describe some of the more interesting features of the religious background of some eminent men.

Gogol, the Russian writer, was the son of an obscure and rather poor Ukrainian land-owner. Both parents showed literary and dramatic ability. The father gave very little time to his son, but the mother was a deeply religious woman who had married when she was fourteen, and who implanted in her son the fear of the devil and hell-fire. In a letter he wrote: 'I went to church because I was told to, and was taken there, but as I stood there I saw nothing except the chasuble of the priest, and heard nothing except the horrible howling of the deacon. I crossed myself because I saw everyone crossing himself. Only once—I remember this occasion very clearly— I asked you to tell me about the Last Judgment, and you told me, a child, so well, so intelligibly, so movingly about the bliss that awaits the people who live virtuous lives—that it awakened all my sensibilities and afterwards aroused in me the most lofty thoughts.'

One of the most remarkable stories of childhood management, including religious upbringing, is that of *John Ruskin*. He describes it himself in *Praeterita*. His mother was a strict evangelical puritan, who herself had had an unhappy childhood. She regarded all pleasure as sin, and denied John the pleasure of toys. When an aunt brought him a Punch and Judy from a Soho bazaar, they were immediately put away and were never seen again. At first a bunch of keys was the only toy he was allowed. Later he was allowed a cart and a ball, and finally a box of bricks. No other toys were permitted. John Ruskin described how he would pass his days contentedly tracing the squares and comparing the colours of his carpet, examining the knots in the wood of the floor, or counting the bricks in houses opposite. His chief resources, he said, were the carpet, and the patterns in the bedcovers, dresses and wallpapers.

On Sunday mornings all story books were taken away. 'A lurid shade was cast', he said, 'over the whole of Friday and Saturday by the horrible sense that Sunday was coming', and 'all the glory of Monday, with church six days removed again, was no compensation.' Only cold meat was allowed for dinner. Even at thirty-three he apologised for writing a letter on Sunday. Not till he was thirty-nine did he even make a sketch on a Sunday.

Before he was three, he repeated to his mother the whole of the 119th psalm. His mother read the Bible to him for hours, beginning with Genesis, going through to the last verse of the Apocalypse, and beginning again at Genesis next day. Wilenski, in his biography, wrote that: 'Into his brain his mother forced, brutally, the text of the Bible day by day, and then his father made him listen to long extracts from the Poets. From the earliest childhood to manhood he had to read two or three chapters of the Bible word by word to his mother every day, with all the genealogies and long names.'

Ruskin wrote: 'It is only by deliberate effort that I recall the long morning hours of toil, as regular as sunrise, by which, year after year, my mother forced me to learn these paraphrases and chapters (the eighth of the first of Kings being one —try it, good reader, in a leisure hour!) allowing not so much as a syllable to be missed or misplaced; while every sentence was required to be said over and over again till she was satisfied with the accent of it. I recollect a struggle between us of about three weeks concerning the accent on the "of" in the lines "Shall any following spring revive—the ashes of the urn?" I, insisting, partly in childish obstinacy, and partly in true instinct for rhythm (being wholly careless on the subject both of urns and their contents) on reciting it with an accented "of". It was not, I say, till after three weeks' labour, that my mother got the accent lightened on the "of" and laid on the ashes, to her mind. But had it taken three years she would have done it, having once undertaken to do it. And assuredly, had we not done it, well, there's no knowing what would have happened: but I'm very thankful she did.'

He had a lonely solitary childhood. His parents kept themselves to themselves, and expected John to behave likewise. All his early education was at home, except for a few months at school. Almost all his early years were spent without companions.

His mother's principles, he said, were to guard him with steady watchfulness from all avoidable pain or danger: and for the rest to let him amuse himself as he liked, provided that he was neither fretful nor troublesome. The family law was that he should find his own amusement, without toys. He was always summarily whipped if he cried, did not do as he was told, or tumbled down the stairs. 'Whenever I did anything wrong, stupid or hard hearted', he said, 'my mother always said "It is because you have been too much indulged".'

In *Praeterita* he wrote: 'I had been taught the perfect meaning of Peace, in thought, act and word. I never had heard my father's or mother's voice once raised in any question with each other: nor seen an angry, or even slightly hurt or offended glance in the eyes of either. I had never heard a servant scolded; nor even suddenly, passionately, or in any severe manner blamed. I had never seen a moment's trouble or disorder in any household matter; nor anything whatever either done in a hurry, or undone in due time. I had no conception of such a feeling as anxiety. I had never done any wrong that I knew of—beyond occasionally delaying the commitment to heart of some improving sentence, that I might watch a wasp on the window pane, or a bird in the cherry tree: and I had never seen any grief.

'Next to this quite priceless gift of Peace, I had received the perfect understanding of the nature of obedience and faith. I obeyed word or lifted finger, of father or mother, simply as a ship her helm: not only without idea of resistance, but receiving the direction as a part of my own life and force, a helpful

law, as necessary to me in every moral action as the law of
gravity in leaping. My practice in Faith was soon complete:
nothing was ever promised to me that was not given: nothing
ever threatened to me that was not inflicted, and nothing ever
told me that was not true.

'Lastly, an all round perfection in palate and other bodily
senses, given by the utter prohibition of cake, wine, comfits,
or except in carefullest restriction, fruit.'

Ruskin then went on to recount the equally dominant
calamities. Firstly, he had nothing to love. 'My parents were
visible powers of nature to me, no more loved than the sun
and the moon.' He said that he had no companions to quarrel
with, nobody to assist, nobody to thank. Everything was
done for him. Secondly, he had nothing to endure. 'Danger
or pain of any kind I knew not: my strength was never exercised, my patience never tried, and my courage never forti-
fied.' Thirdly, he never learnt etiquette or manners: he just
had to remain unobtrusive; and saw no other children. Lastly,
the chief evil, he said, was the fact that his judgment of right
and wrong, and powers of independent action, were left
entirely undeveloped, because 'the bridle and blinkers were
never taken off me'. 'My present verdict on the general tenor
of my education must be that it was at once too formal and
too luxurious: leaving my character, at the most important
moment for its construction, cramped indeed, but not disciplined: and only by protection innocent, instead of by
practice virtuous.'

When he went to Oxford, at eighteen, his mother insisted
on taking rooms there, so that she could watch over him. She
stayed during the whole three years of his residence, leaving
her husband in London, and insisted that John should have
tea with her every day of the week at seven.

His upbringing left him unable to enjoy sex. He never
consummated his marriage and was divorced by his wife—
who then married Millais, the painter. 'Surely', Millais wrote,

'such a quiet scoundrel as this man never existed?' 'He is an undeniable giant as an author, but a poor weak creature in everything else, bland, and unheartless and unworthy.'

Looking back from his old age, Ruskin wrote of 'the general mistake, mismanagement and misfortune of all my education, mind and heart, which characterised it'. He had bouts of madness in adult life and for the last eleven years was virtually insane.

General Gordon was taught to believe that every word of the Bible was literally true. For institutional religion, as practised by his family in his childhood, he acquired a hearty distaste. 'The regular churchgoing, the interminable sermons, for which the only compensation was the curtained pews "where you could have made your toilet and no one would have been any the wiser"—to the end of his life he remembered it all with a shudder.' 'What husks,' he would write, 'the evangelical religion is.' He stoutly refused to be confirmed.

The parents of *Edmund Gosse*, poet and critic, were Plymouth Brethren. They found pleasure nowhere but in the word of God, and endless discussions of the scriptures. His father was a zoologist and his mother a writer. They scarcely ever had visitors, and never had a meal away from home. At night they discussed theology. 'My parents founded every action, every attitude,' he said, 'upon their interpretation of the scriptures and upon the guidance of Divine Will as revealed to them by direct answer to prayer.'

'My father', he wrote, 'said positively that if I worshipped a thing made of wood or stone, God would manifest his anger.' In order to test his father's statement, Gosse said his prayers to a chair. 'The result of this ridiculous act was not to make me question the existence and power of God; those were forces which I did not dream of ignoring: but what it did was to lessen my confidence in my father's knowledge of the divine mind. I had worshipped a chair made of wood, and God had made no sign whatsoever.'

Edmund found great pleasure in books, but their range was limited, for story books of every kind were excluded. No fiction of any kind, religious or secular, was permitted in the home. 'Never in all my childhood', he said, 'did anyone use the expression "once upon a time".' 'I was told about missionaries, but never about pirates. I had never heard of fairies and though I understood about wolves, little Red Riding Hood was a stranger even by name.' 'So far as my dedication was concerned, I can but think that my parents were in error thus to exclude the imaginary from my outlook upon facts. They desired to make me truthful, the tendency was to make me positive and sceptical. Had they wrapped me in the soft folds of supernatural fancy, my mind might have been longer content to follow their traditions in unquestioning spirit.'

The peculiarities of a family life founded upon such principles had an obvious effect. 'Here was perfect purity, perfect intrepidity, perfect abrogation: yet there was also narrowness, isolation, an absence of perspective; let it be boldly admitted, an absence of humanity.'

Edmund Gosse had a very lonely childhood. He had no young friends. He wrote: 'The mere fact that I had no young companions, no story books, no outdoor amusements, none of the thousand and one employments provided for other children in more conventional surroundings, did not make me discontented or fretful, because I did not know the existence of such entertainments. I have no recollection of any curiosity about other children, nor of any desire to speak to them or play with them. They did not enter into my dreams, which were occupied entirely with grown up people and animals. I am unable to recollect exchanging two words with another child till after my mother's death' (when he was eight).

When she became ill, he said, 'I was my mother's sole and ceaseless companion; the silent witness of her sufferings, of her patience, of her vain and delusive attempts to obtain alleviation of her anguish. For nearly three months I breathed the atmosphere of pain, saw no other light, heard no other sound, thought no other thoughts than those which accompany physical suffering and weariness. I read the Bible every day at much length: also—with I cannot but think some praiseworthy patience—a book of incommunicable dreariness called Newton's *Thoughts on the Apocalypse*.

'My childhood was long, long with interminable hours, hours with the pale cheeks pressed against the window pane, hours of mechanical and repeated lonely "games" which had lost their savour and were kept going by sheer inertness. Not unhappy, but long, long.'

Robert Louis Stevenson wrote: 'I had an extreme terror of Hell implanted in me, I suppose, by my good nurse, which used to haunt me terribly on stormy nights when the wind had broken loose and was going about the town like a bedlamite.'

The parents of *Orde Wingate* were Plymouth Brethren. He was brought up in an atmosphere of extraordinary puritanism. A feature was its insularity: the children were segregated from all other children. They had no outings, they were not allowed to mix with others, there were no parties, no dances, no football or cricket. They were deliberately isolated, so that they would not be corrupted.

Paul Nash, the artist, wrote that he was not allowed to paint on Sundays. 'This was to ensure that Sunday should be different from other days, an idea adhered to by my father throughout his life. In later years he deplored my working on Sundays for another reason. While sanctioning the re-creation as legitimate, there remained for him the disquieting thought that the picture I painted that day might sell.'

ORDER AND DISCIPLINE

Young *John Wesley* was brought up in an orderly strictly disciplined environment. He was the second surviving son, though the fifteenth child of his parents. (His mother was the twenty-fifth child of her father.) His mother was a highly intelligent capable woman, who had not only to look after her brood, but had to keep accounts for a household half rectory half farm, find time for religion and reading, and cope with her husband who was in and out of debt. Neighbours were hostile. Her husband was a 'High Church' Rector, and most of her neighbours were 'Low Church'. The villagers stabbed his cows, fired his crops and beat drums below the windows to annoy the occupants of the vicarage. They twice set fire to the rectory, and on the second occasion John, then aged five, was rescued at the last moment. The children were sent to relatives, where they thoroughly enjoyed themselves away from the strict discipline of home. Their mother was horrified by their bad behaviour, slipshod speech and vulgarity on their return.

Green wrote in his biography that Mrs Wesley had amazing powers of concentration. She could read or write or instruct one of the children while the rest were playing on her knee: every moment of the day was carefully mapped out, so that she was never hurried, and always seemed to have time.

Mrs Wesley was a firm believer in discipline. She said: 'When turned a year old (and some before) they (the children) were taught to fear the rod, and to cry softly, by which means they escaped abundance of correction which they might otherwise have had.' 'At meal-times if they wanted anything they were allowed to whisper their requirements to the maid. They were not allowed to be finicky or greedy over their food. They were absolutely forbidden to eat anything between meals, and if one of them dared to go into the kitchen to ask anything of the servants, they were certainly beat.'

Mrs Wesley believed that the fundamental factor in a child's development was obedience. 'The first thing to be done is to conquer their will and bring them to an obedient temper—the subjecting of the will is a thing which must be done at once, and the sooner the better. When the will of the child is totally subdued, and it is brought to revere and stand in awe of their parents, then a great many childish follies and misadventures may be passed by.' Self-will was regarded as the evident root of all sin and misery.

It was a loving home. Quarrelling was almost unknown. Nevertheless, it is interesting to note that the married lives of the girls were almost uniformly disastrous, as was John's own. John married a widow who had four children. She had an ungovernable temper, and eventually left him.

Elizabeth Barrett Browning said that her father treated his twelve children like slaves. 'In his vocabulary there were two words that stood out above all the others—command, obey. His was the mission to command: his children's, the duty to obey' (Thomas).

The Earl of Birkenhead (F. E. Smith) was brought up with the strictest discipline. His mother was a domineering character, who ruled the household. His father demanded absolute obedience, but nevertheless treated the children as equals, and never lost his temper with them or raised his voice in anger. 'My ambition', he said, 'is to be the friend of my children.'

Lord Beaverbrook's mother was a strict disciplinarian. His father was a Presbyterian minister, described by Driberg as 'a formidable man of God. He seemed to his children as remote from their everyday pleasures and tragedies as the Old Testament deity on whose behalf he thundered every Sabbathday.' The children were forbidden to play cards in the Manse, though they were allowed to play at the homes of their friends. Max devised a game with home-made cards that 'looked innocent but differed little from the forbidden whist'.

DISORDER

In contrast to the orderly discipline in the home of John Wesley and others, *Sir Patrick Hastings'* home was one of chaos. Patricia Hastings, Sir Patricks' daughter, wrote that it would be hard to think of a worse upbringing for a little boy.

He never enjoyed a settled home or any sense of security.
'Sometimes his family was rich, and sometimes poor: sometimes his parents were happy and united, sometimes divided
and despairing. His father was frequently on the verge of
bankruptcy, often drunk, and made the habit of leaving his
family for long periods: his mother was an artist, utterly
oblivious of the conventions of a rigid society. From an early
life his companions alternated between the most brilliant wits
of London and the bailiff's men. By all the tenets of psychiatry,
one would think that the result of such a childhood would be
a man with no moral values, unstable, neurotic and introverted. But my father was none of these things.'

She went on: 'As a mother, she was quite hopeless. She
had no idea of how to look after children. When she read a
book, she couldn't be bothered to turn the pages over and
mark the place: she simply tore each page out as she finished
reading it and dropped it on the floor.'

Nevertheless, she loved her children, and they adored her.

George Bernard Shaw's home was in some ways similar. He
emphasised that he was in no way maltreated. His father,
George Shaw, was a 'soft easy going man with a squint and a
taste for the bottle'. His mother was twenty years younger
than her husband. She left the children largely to the care of
the servants. 'We children were abandoned', he said, 'entirely
to servants who were utterly unfit to be trusted with the
charge of three cats, much less of three children.' The children
spent almost all their time in the basement kitchen. He said
that he would have been much more decently brought up if
his parents had been too poor to afford servants. He hated
the servants, who thumped him on the head when he was
troublesome. 'I was taken and took myself for what I was, a
disagreeable little beast.' The nurse took him into slum public
houses and started 'a lifelong hatred of poverty and the devotion of all my public life to the task of exterminating the poor
and rendering their resurrection forever impossible'.

He described the conditions at his home in Dublin as 'eccentric to the point of anarchy'. Mrs Shaw 'went her own way with so complete a disregard and even unconsciousness of convention and scandal and prejudice that it was impossible to doubt her good faith and innocence, but it never occurred to her that other people, especially children, needed guidance and training, nor that it mattered in the least what they ate or drank or what they did so long as they were not actively mischievous.' He wrote: 'I should say that she was the worst mother conceivable, always, however, within the limits of the fact that she was incapable of unkindness to any child, animal or flower. She did not hate, but she did not love.' He never forgot the misery of his childhood, or her responsibility for it.

As a result of his childhood he developed a loathing for respectability and religion. 'Being drugged in low church and chapel, and forbidden to play with the tradesmen's children, gave him complexes from which he has never recovered, and made him utter loud outcries against custom-made morality —and the tame conformity of the genteel.'

LACK OF DISCIPLINE

The life of *Lord Clive* provides an interesting and amusing story of indiscipline in child management—and the far reaching consequences. At two-and-a-half he was sent to his aunt's home in Manchester, to be away from 'the irascible stormings of his gouty father, from whom he had derived more in heredity than it appeared good for environment to augment', to use Minney's words. Almost immediately after arrival the boy had a serious illness, and after his unexpected recovery was thoroughly spoilt. Minney added: 'Every act of mischief or burst of anger was taken as a sign of returning health. He did with his guardians as he pleased. The mature pair were forced into all sorts of antics for his amusement. For hours the grave yet kindly uncle sat by the cot endeavouring to

conduct from there as much of his business and correspondence
as the boy would allow. The uncle exulted in the boy's increasing ill temper as a good omen of his mending.' Within
a month neither uncle nor aunt was able to leave the home
without the boy's consent. He completely dominated the
pair and became 'fierce and imperious'. 'For this reason', said
the uncle, 'I do what I can to suppress the heroic, that I may
help forward the more valuable qualities of meekness, bene-
volence and patience.' The couple frequently attempted to
bribe him, though without success. The boy became 'impetuous, spirited and intractable to discipline'. He had to be
sent from one school to another because of his bad behaviour.
Minney added: 'At Market Drayton the whole town were up
in arms about his exploits. The tradesmen and distressed
parents of other children besought the headmaster to remove
Clive. He had organised a band of urchins, armed them with
stones, and threatened to destroy shop windows if they were
not given money and apples. After a dispute with one of the
traders Clive lay in the gutter and dammed the water with his
body until the shop was flooded.' He was moved to the
Merchant Taylor's School in London and later to a private
school in Hemel Hempstead. His biographer added: 'he had
a ready inventiveness in strategy and displayed a fearlessness
and daring that made one of his schoolmasters declare that in
the unlikely event of his reaching manhood alive, he would
inscribe a name on the pages of history than which there
would be few greater'.

He made poor progress in his work, and in despair his father
despatched him at the age of seventeen to India, 'to die of a
fever for all it mattered'.

The author concluded: 'A neglected rod altered the fate of
three nations.'

John Hunter, famous surgeon, was a problem child, largely
because of lack of parental discipline. The father was too ill
to exert control, and the mother spoilt him, the youngest of

the family. He became a stubborn, wilful, disobedient boy, and a great trial to everyone.

Branwell Brontë was spoilt by his father and his aunt. He was removed from Haworth Grammar School because it was thought that he was not suited to the rough and tumble of village school life. He had violent temper tantrums, and these were ascribed to his having been bitten by a mad dog, and to the wound not having been cauterised. He was given much more liberty than his sisters. Charlotte and Anne said 'his freedom wasn't coupled with any of the necessary warnings against the temptations and vices of the world from which they as girls were so sedulously shrouded—as though girls were something very frail and silly indeed, while boys are turned loose on the world as if they, of all beings in existence, were the wisest and least liable to be led astray'.

Not one of the Brontës was at any time allowed any pocket money, not even the price of a stamp. This did not trouble the girls, but it had a bad effect on Branwell. Early in life he got into debt, at first trivially, but later seriously.

He eventually became an alcoholic and an opium addict.

PUNISHMENT

Both parents of *Martin Luther* were cruel and despotic. They both regarded thrashings as essential, just as much as eating or drinking. According to Erikson, Martin's father, who was a miner, 'showed the greatest temper in his attempt to drive temper out of his children'. On one occasion his father beat him so much that Martin ran away. On another occasion his mother caned him until the blood came, for stealing a nut. Martin felt a permanent grudge against his father for his treatment; his thrashings at home left a deep impression of injustice. He lived a boyhood 'without joy or beauty or love'. From his terrible childhood experience he always retained a jealousy never free from suspicion, and a contempt for all women.

A most remarkable story of sheer blind hatred and rejection is that of *Gabriel Mirabeau*. He was the victim of conjugal dysharmony—and of the unfortunate fact that he was the image of his maternal grandfather. His father, the Comte de Mirabeau, was himself the product of an unhappy childhood with harsh restraint, and had married an heiress, the daughter of a Marquis, an uneducated woman with no trace of good breeding, and little trace of beauty. The Comte had intense pride in his own family, and loathed and despised his wife. He wrote later, after separation from her, 'that the twenty years I lived with that woman were twenty years of renal colic'. He added that 'my true cross is her son'. He had a second son later—his favourite.

Vallentin, in her biography, wrote 'all that was perverse in the Comte de Mirabeau' (Gabriel) 'all his extravagance in revolt, his reckless pursuit of his aims in precocious self-confidence, the sullen obduracy that took pleasure in providing justification for the mistrust that surrounded him, all this may be traced back to that poisoned source in his childhood. The father's bitterness reproached young Mirabeau almost from birth, as a low-class child.'

Gabriel was an ugly child, born with two teeth and a large head. His father told him incessantly how ugly he was. 'My son, whose body grows, whose prattle increases, and whose face grows incredibly ugly', he wrote, 'is moreover ugly by choice and predilection.' He searched hard for faults in the boy, feeling a deep physical repugnance for him. In a letter to his brother, the Marquis wrote: 'He is of an utterly unheard of type of baseness, absolutely commonplace and of the quality of the rough and muddled caterpillar that will never be a chrysalis.' Another time he wrote: 'he is cross grained, fantastic, fiery, awkward, with a drift to evil before he knows of it or is capable of it', and referred to 'This fiery wrongheaded eldest son of mine, everyday more troublesome and insane.'

He deliberately chose tutors who would be cruel and vicious

to the boy, and urged them to beat him. The Comte dismissed them if they showed any sign of kindness. When Gabriel was seven, the Marquis wrote: 'he is never out of his succession of punishments' at the hand of the Tutor Poisson. The boy tried to disarm his father by docility, but only succeeded in infuriating him further. The Marquis wrote: 'he seems to me, so far at least, to have the makings of nothing but an incurable maniac, on top of all his vile qualities. I see in him an animal nature, and I do not think it will ever be possible to make anything of him.' He could see nothing in the boy but the faults of his mother.

The father could not fail to recognise Gabriel's intelligence and capacious memory, but was furious when his tutors remarked about it. He sent him to a stern school, the Abbé Choquard's College, but removed him, intending to send him to a reformatory. For a time he would not allow the boy to use his family name at school, giving him the name of a property of his wife—Pierre Buffière. He sent him to a military school, with instructions to his teachers to be exceedingly strict and rigorous with him. Gabriel said that everything which he did there had excessive repercussions. 'I can do nothing right', he complained, 'my slightest slips have more fearful results than the worst ones of my fellows.' The Marquis had him put into prison at eighteen because of a love affair, and was on the point of sending him to a penal settlement.

The childhood of *Ivan Turgenev*, the novelist, was hardly much better than that of Mirabeau, though Ivan's sufferings were at the hand of his mother. She herself had suffered dreadful cruelties and humiliations because of the cruelty of her stepfather. They burnt themselves into her mind and left a hideous scar there. She too had an unhappy marriage, and later warned her friends never to marry on a Friday, as she had, because the day was fatal to married happiness.

Turgenev's biographer, Yarmolinsky, wrote that the serfs and sons 'lived in an atmosphere of feudalism not tempered by the chivalric ideal of the West. The mother felt herself authorised to inflict anything on them, from a flogging to a forced marriage. She ruled her serfs with a rod of iron. She was so utterly convinced that she had a right to do anything that pleased her with her serfs that any suggestion that they ought not to be flogged or sent to Siberia or pressed into the army merely aroused incredulous amazement in her.'

Ivan said: 'I have not a single happy memory of my childhood. I used to be birched almost daily for all sorts of trifles. One day one of my mother's companions, an old woman, seemed to have caught me doing something, what it was I do not know to this day, and told my mother about it. She thrashed me herself with her own hands, and in reply to my entreaty to tell me why I was being punished, kept saying "You know very well why I am thrashing you". When on the following morning the boy was still at a loss to know what crime he had committed, the punishment was repeated by his mother, who threatened to go on thrashing him until he confessed. He was ten at this time, and in terror decided to run away. He set off in the middle of the night, but was intercepted by his tutor. His mother evidently received sexual satisfaction from her thrashings, for once when thrashing her eldest boy she nearly fainted with excitement, and the boy howled for water (for his mother) at the top of his voice.'

Ivan spoke of being flogged daily. He told how, because of some trivial misdeed, he would be lectured first by his tutor, then whipped and deprived of his dinner, finally wandering out, hungry and sore, into the park, 'drinking with a kind of bitter pleasure the salt water which streamed from my eyes down my cheeks into my mouth'.

His father never interfered with his wife's treatment of her children, but when one of the German tutors tried to emulate her example, hearing Nicholas' screams in the nursery, he rushed in and threw the German tutor down two flights of stairs.

Yarmolinsky wrote that 'the whole course of her second son's life was to bear witness to the crushing effect of her over-bearing manner. It sapped his initiative in the conduct of his affairs, and his dislike of her self-assertiveness made him in-capable of standing up for his own rights. The flabbiness of will which afflicted Turgenev to the end of his life may have been in part due to the cramping atmosphere of arbitrary out-bursts which prevailed in the household. So strong was her passion for regularity and labelling that her house was run with the strictness of a military establishment. She insisted upon certain formalities of speech and gesture in the children's approach to their parents and their deity.' 'The hatred of injustice which warms so many of his papers must have been kindled again and again in the heart of a tormented and furious boy who not only suffered himself, but constantly saw his brothers and his playmates, the familiar household serfs, undergo disproportionate punishment for trivial misde-meanours.'

He was a clever boy. After a serious illness, necessitating some months in bed, during which he developed an interest in literature, he went to the University of Moscow at the age of fourteen.

The father of *Anton Chekhov*, dramatist and writer, was described by Magarshack as a badly educated and foolish man of little ability, with a woeful ignorance of child management and discipline. He was a brutal despot, who ruled his children with a rod of iron. In his writings Chekhov constantly refers to the despotism of his father as the cause of his unhappiness. 'Despotism and lies so disfigured our childhood that it makes me sick and horrified to think of it.' He remembers 'the dis-gust and horror which he felt every time his father made a scene at dinner because there was too much salt in the soup or called mother a fool'. He added: 'I remember father began to teach me, or to put it more plainly, whip me, when I was only five years old. He whipped me, boxed my ears, hit me over the head, and the first question I asked myself on awakening every morning was "Will I be whipped again today?" I was forbidden to play games or romp. I had to attend the morning and evening Church services, kiss the hands of priests and monks, read psalms at home.' When he was eight he worked as an errand boy, and was beaten every day on various pretexts. He found it impossible to believe that his schoolfriends were never birched. His mother said that her husband possessed an inborn and inveterate spite. Anton at the age of seven was so used to beatings at home that he was not at all upset by the grosser brutalities at school.

His father had a special interest in church music, and organised a choir composed of his own children and townspeople. Anton often cried bitterly during the choir practices, which went on until the late hours, depriving him of sleep.

If the choir was to sing at morning mass, his father would wake his children at two or three in the morning and go to church with them, regardless of the weather. Chekhov wrote: 'when, as a child, I was given a religious education, and made to read the lesson at church or sing in the church choir, and the whole congregation gazed admiringly at me, I felt like a little convict, and now I have no religion. Generally speaking, so-called religious education can never do without, as it were, a little screen, behind which no stranger is allowed to peep. Behind that screen, the children are tortured, but in front of it people smile and are deeply moved. It is not for nothing that many divinity students become atheists.'

In later years he said that as a boy he was treated with so little kindness that even when grown up, he accepted kindness as something unusual, something of which he had little experience. 'That is why', he said, 'I should like to be kind to people, but don't know how. I have grown callous and lazy, though I realise very well that people like us cannot carry on without kindness.'

His father hoped that Anton would follow a career in

business, and sent him to the Greek School at the Church of St Constantine. His examination results were poor, however, and he was transferred to the local secondary school.

During a serious illness he thought of taking up medicine. He developed an interest in acting. His talent as an actor showed itself when he was thirteen, and visited the Taganrog theatre. Only later did he develop an interest in writing.

Lord Curzon suffered when seven at the hands of a governess, one Miss Paraman. The Earl of Ronaldshay, in his biography, wrote: 'there were frequent occasions on which she acted with all the savagery of a brutal and vindictive tyrant. The many ingenious forms of punishment which she devised were such that, in after years, he declared that he doubted if any children well born and well placed cried so much and so justly. There can be little doubt that this ferocious discipline to which she subjected her unfortunate charges did much to foster that rebellious spirit of the existence of which, sometimes latent, at other times disastrously active, George Curzon was himself aware throughout his life.'

Frederick Delius, one of twelve surviving children, had an unhappy childhood. Sir Thomas Beecham wrote that home was an abode of fear, and all the children alike went in terror of a tyrant who ruled his little flock with a heavy rod of iron. The father was proud, unbending and intolerant, a cruel punitive man. Frederick's mother was a dogmatic bitter woman. She never showed any interest or pride in her son's rise to fame. She never once went anywhere to hear a note of his music. Frederick made one or two unsuccessful attempts to run away from home.

Rudyard Kipling was brought to England from India when he was five years old and left in lodgings in Southsea without any warning of impending separation. He was left as paying guest in a retired naval officer's home. The parents returned to India, leaving Rudyard for some five years. The officer

died, leaving his wife in charge of Rudyard. Both she and her
son beat him constantly.

He began to read avidly, but as soon as it was realised that
he was reading for enjoyment, he was deprived of books. He
was made to learn long portions of the Bible and many
collects.

His eyesight deteriorated, but for a long time this was not
recognised. He began to receive bad reports from school. He
destroyed one report because it was so bad, and said that he
had never received it. He was found out and beaten, and sent
to school with a placard saying 'liar' on his back. Eventually
the defective eyesight was discovered, and for some weeks he
was forbidden to read.

He never complained of the bad treatment which he was
receiving when he wrote to his parents. Finally his mother
returned from India unexpectedly, and, discovering the state
of affairs, took him back to India.

He never forgot the unhappiness of his early years.

Maxim Gorky lived in a house of strife. He wrote that 'my
grandfather's house was filled with hot vapours of hostility—
the hostility of each towards all. From this space of time, as I
go back to it, I find it a strain to believe that such things
actually took place. My impulse is to dispute and disown the
reality—such dull savagery on the part of one's own tribe is
too wounding to acknowledge. An endemic plague of
hostility festered in my grandfather's home.' He constantly
received severe beatings himself, but he was even more upset
by the hostility between his relatives. He saw his uncles and
grandfather fighting during dinner—hitting each other and
wrestling. 'Horrible curses were uttered from Uncle Mike,
as he twisted his head, soiling his wispy black beard in the
dirt.'

In none of the three following cases was there persistent
cruelty. *Edison*, at the age of six, had deliberately set fire to
his father's barn, in order to observe the effect. His father,

having publicly advertised his intention, whipped him in the square near his home at Milan (Ohio).

Lord Beaverbrook's mother was strict, and frequently beat Max after his scrapes. A neighbour said that she often remembered seeing Max, with his hand in front of his face, sobbing after being punished by his mother.

Nehru at the age of six found two fountain pens on his father's table, and took one. His father discovered the loss, but Nehru was too terrified to confess. He was severely beaten by his father. Nehru wrote: 'almost blind with pain and mortification at my disgrace, I rushed to my mother, and for several days various creams and ointments were applied to my aching and quivering little body'.

His father had a considerable temper. 'Even in after years', wrote Nehru, 'I do not think I ever came across anything to match it in its own line.' His father was somewhat feudal in his treatment of his servants. 'When moved to wrath by a domestic's ineptitude, he thought nothing of rising from the table and there and then thrashing the unfortunate man with his bare hand.'

He had a lonely childhood, and Moraes wrote that 'some at least of the brooding melancholy which was part of his nature might be traced to his solitary boyhood. With no companion of his own age at home he sought instinctively the company of his mother and other sympathetic elders. He was left very much to himself, and this isolation sharpened his thought and imagination.'

SOME EFFECTS OF PUNISHMENT

George Bernard Shaw once wrote 'to punish is to injure'. We have described some of the effects of punishment in the preceding section. These effects sometimes persisted throughout life.

In the case of *Rousseau* a memorable beating by Uncle Bernard had a lasting effect. Wrongly accused of having broken a cane, he was chastised, despite his denials. He then conceived his first idea of injustice. He claims that from that moment there was a marked and general deterioration in his behaviour and general character. The idea of injustice was in-eradicably planted in his mind. Ever afterwards the spectacle of any unjust action brought him to a state of ungovernable fury.

In his *Confessions*, he talked of the sexual pleasure which he derived from the smackings administered to him by the pastor's sister. He said that they exercised a determining and lasting influence on his sex life.

Jean Marat, of the French Revolution, wrote that his moral sense was well developed when he was eight. 'Docile and diligent, my masters obtained everything from me by gentle-ness. I was only chastised once, and the resentment at that unjust humiliation made such an impression upon me that it was found impossible to bring me again under my instructor's authority. I remained two whole days without taking nourish-ment. I was then eleven years old, and the strength of my character may be estimated from this single trait. My parents not having been able to bend me and the paternal authority believing itself compromised, I was locked up in a room. Unable to resist the indignation that choked me, I opened the casement and flung myself out into the street.'

Edmund Gosse described how he did something naughty when he was six and his father, after a solemn sermon, whipped him. His father justified this by reference to the Book of Proverbs which stated: 'spare the rod and spoil the child'. Edmund said that he was made furiously angry by this caning, and for some days he went about the house with a murderous hatred for his father. He added: 'I do not regard physical punishment as a wise element in the education of proud and sensitive children.'

INSECURITY AND EMOTIONAL DEPRIVATION

Leonardo da Vinci, an illegitimate child, was brought up by a stepmother, and was carefully kept away from his real mother. Vallentin, in his biography, wrote that 'His development was permanently influenced by the fact that he grew up a motherless child, bereft of the primitive irreplaceable tenderness and natural warmth of mother love. Incomplete acceptance coloured his whole personal development and outlook on life.'

Richelieu was brought up in an atmosphere of insecurity of another kind. Belloc wrote that 'Richelieu passed the first years of his life in a community that was in constant apprehension of arson and pillage, in a land where famine and pestilence were frequent visitors, and where these conditions existed because the law was not strong enough to repress the violent and protect the orderly.' 'These early impressions were as deeply implanted in his mind as the lessons he conned from his tutor, and formed quite as important a part of his education.'

Before *Jonathan Swift's* birth, his father died leaving his wife penniless. The boy was separated from his mother and brought up by a wet nurse. He did not see his mother for three years. He was miserably poor at school and university, depending entirely on the charity of his relatives. His life, to use his biographer's words, was 'poisoned from the very start'. He was most unhappy at school and university.

Though *Samuel Johnson* did not suffer from emotional deprivation, it is true to say that there was much conflict in the home, which arose partly because his mother thought herself socially superior to her husband, and constantly reminded him of the fact. There was frequent nagging, his mother constantly scolding the boys without telling them how they should behave. His experience of home left an indelible impression on Samuel, who never ceased to inveigh against parental authority, and always sympathised with sons and daughters in their conflicts with their parents. He ridiculed the idea that they should respect their parents' opinions when opposed to their own. Nevertheless he loved his mother.

Thomas Gray, the poet, was the product of a most unhappy marriage. Edmund Gosse described Thomas' father as violent, jealous and probably mad. Ketton-Cremer describing the father as a man of bad temper and a corroding jealousy, wrote that 'at times his gloom would give place to moods of uncontrollable fury, when he would attack his wife in the most inhuman manner, by beating, kicking or punching, and with the most vile and abusive language'. Thomas was terrified of him, but adored his mother.

Rousseau suffered from insecurity even more than did Samuel Johnson. His mother died a few days after his birth, and his father deserted his family and went to Constantinople for five years. Jean was left with an uncle. His eldest brother disappeared from his employment as apprentice to a watch-maker not long after his father's disappearance. Nevertheless, Jean Jacques was happy with his uncle and aunt.

Dr *Edward Jenner* lost both parents when a young child, and was greatly upset as a result. He wrote later: 'I have been through life, almost from the earliest period of my recollection, haunted by melancholy.' The early loss of his parents may well have been a cause of this.

Talleyrand, the statesman, said that during his whole life he never spent one week under the same roof as his mother and father.

Froebel's mother died before he reached his first birthday. His father, a parson, left him largely to the care of the servants, who neglected him. Throughout his life he was practically a stranger to his father. His father remarried when Froebel was four, but contrived to neglect the boy, though he did teach him to read—with great difficulty.

Chateaubriand, author and statesman, was the son of a Breton nobleman, and lived in a castle. He wrote that 'I was acquainted with suffering from my earliest childhood: I bore a germ of suffering within me, as a tree bears the germ of its fruit. A strange poison mingled itself with all my feelings.'

He was not allowed to mix with children outside the castle, and was thrown in to the company of his sister Lucille—an eccentric odd child who gradually became insane and died, possibly by suicide. She was a melancholy girl, who was convinced that the whole world was against her.

His mother was a devout woman who spent hours a day in the castle chapel. His father spent many hours alone every day in his study. It was an unhappy childhood for Chateaubriand. He attempted suicide, but the musket misfired at the critical moment (Sieburg).

De Quincey's father died when Thomas was seven, and he was left in charge of his domineering and forceful mother. A few months before his father's death a sister died of hydrocephalus, and another sister died following brutal treatment by a servant. His grandmother died when he was five. Eaton describes the mother as a strict disciplinarian, with no sense of humour and no adaptability. She became more and more rigid in her religious feeling, with a corresponding increase in the severity of her judgment. Thomas wrote: 'A peculiarity there was about my mother which is not found in one mother out of five hundred. Usually mothers defend their own cubs, right or wrong; not so my mother. Trial by jury, English laws of evidence, were all forgotten. We were found guilty on the bare affidavit of the angry accuser. Did a sister say some flattering thing of a talent or accomplishment by one of us? My mother protested so solemnly against the possibility that we could possess either one or the other that we children held it a point of filial duty to believe ourselves the very scum and refuse of the Universe.' Every morning of the year all the children had to parade in the mother's dressing room for inspection.

He describes her as 'austere in the degree which fitted her for the lady president of rebellious nunneries'. She was a rigid woman, expecting the highest standards of herself and everyone else, strongly conscientious and pure minded. Thomas could never confide in her. Her apparent hardness and lack of sympathy left a permanent mark on him. His elder brother William constantly bullied and maltreated him. He enjoyed little happiness at home.

In view of his mother's attitude, it is interesting to read about an episode which occurred at Bath Grammar School, when he was thirteen. He was accidentally hit on the head by a cane, and when he returned home, although he had not been hurt, his head was shaved, leeches were applied and re-applied next day. He was not allowed to read, write, talk or eat meat, and was kept in bed for three weeks. His mother took him away from the school and kept him at home with tutors for two years. Psychiatrists regard such overprotection as one of the features of rejection.

The early years of *Branwell Brontë* were marred by bereavements. His mother died when he was four, and his aunt took over the running of the parsonage. She loved Branwell, but never really won his affection. Winifred Gerin wrote that 'the absence of all such tender relationship between parent and child might be found to be at the origin of the Brontës' unsatisfied hunger for love which brought such turbulence upon at least three of them in after life'.

Three years after the mother's death, Branwell's much loved sister, Maria, died. Gerin wrote: 'the attendant pathos, injustice and terror was indelibly to mark the surviving children. In the case of Branwell it may not be too much to say that the death of Maria was the chief cause of his mental instability and of the consequent disasters that dogged his days. She had had a great influence on Branwell, taking him for walks, putting him to bed, listening to his prayers. Her death when he was seven had a profound effect on him.' Soon afterwards his aunt died.

Jenny Lind was a rejected illegitimate child, who presented an embarrassment and financial problem to the parents. Her mother at the age of seventeen married an army officer, and later divorced him on the grounds of unfaithfulness. Under the terms of the divorce he was forbidden to remarry during her lifetime. She had a baby by the marriage. She set up a girls' school. She then met Niclas Lind, five years her junior and had a child, Jenny, marrying the man when Jenny was fifteen. Jenny was quite fond of her father, a gay irresponsible feckless youth with no fixed occupation, who was more than once in a debtor's prison. When Jenny was a few months old she was sent to live with a friend of the mother near Stockholm, living there for four years, and being visited from time to time by her mother. Jenny had then to be taken home on account of illness of the fostermother. This involved a change from a comfortable home to the squalor of her mother's home. There were to be many more moves. At eight, when her mother closed her school, Jenny was sent to live with another fostermother for a year. She returned home, and there was constant friction between Jenny and her mother. For a time she then lived with her grandmother.

Her mother was a soured and bitter woman. The drudgery, the dreariness, the endless company of tiresome children, undernourishment and eternal financial anxiety had worn her out, and her ill humour always seemed to be directed at Jenny.

Jenny and her mother were similar in personality, and, as often happens, this led to considerable friction. Jenny had inherited her mother's obstinacy and narrow prejudice, her morbid sensitivity, her easily inflamed temper—as well as her energy, will-power, and boundless capacity for work. She was forced to attend her mother's school. Jenny was far younger than the other girls, and it was on her that her mother always vented her anger. Her sister Amelia, and the other girls, tried in vain to protect Jenny from her mother's ire. Jenny was miserable at home. As her mother grew older, she coarsened, and her ill temper and aggressiveness constantly embarrassed the girl. Finally at eighteen she left home for good. Jenny grew introspective and lost her natural gaiety. Joan Bulman, her biographer, wrote: 'The seeds were sown of an instability in later age, a self distrust which alternated with a compensating, sometimes overcompensating, self assertiveness when pressed too far. All through her life she kept something of the wistfulness of an unwanted child—an indefinable quality which tore at the heart, and constituted, according to some observers, a large part of her charm.' Throughout her stage career, she suffered agonies from lack of self-confidence. 'From each European capital in turn she nearly fled before her première because she feared that her reputation would be destroyed.' 'She was left with a deep longing for home and security, a need for affection that was like a constant craving appetite, and that expressed itself in her incessant appeals to her friends not to forget her, not to be angry with her, never to turn their love away from her.'

Samuel Butler was highly critical of his father. In his biography, Cole discusses fully the difficulty of assessing the truth of Samuel Butler's criticisms of his father. The father was a canon who eventually became a bishop. In his novel *The Way of All Flesh* Samuel Butler described his own father.

Samuel thought that his father treated him very badly, tried to keep him in subjection from childhood onwards, and did his best to thwart him on every occasion. Cole wrote that 'it is perfectly possible for a father to present every appearance of loving his son, and indeed to feel sure that he does love him, and yet to be continually at loggerheads with him in private life'. 'It is perfectly possible for a man', he wrote, 'and especially for a clergyman, to appear to himself and to others to be activated by the highest moral principles and the most kindly sentiments, and yet to be domestically an oppressor, mistaking his own preferences and predilections for the Will of God, and his own impulse to exact unquestioning obedience for the voice of duty.'

Canon Butler regarded children as a nuisance, and his son's ways cut right across his father's conceptions of right and wrong, and of the dutifulness to be expected from children.

Samuel's sense of justice was again and again outraged. He became obsessed with the idea that his father was an unkind, unjust, unaccountable power that continually thwarted him without giving the reasons why, and he wrongly concluded that his father had no love for him, and always disliked him.

Cole wrote: 'if love there was, it was strongly mixed with disapproval, for the canon was narrow minded, and Butler's tastes and questionings frightened him. In his fright he attempted to drive out by force those of his son's qualities that he disliked; and in doing this he gave Samuel the impression of a severity wholly untempered by affection. Butler felt that his father had done his best to knock clean out of him everything that was most characteristically his own, and had thus turned him from a naturally joyous person, with an ardent will to live and be happy, into a crabbed and unhappy rebel, always expecting to be snubbed and put down. To a great extent this is what did happen, and the mark of it stayed on Butler to the end of his life.'

He loved his mother, though she always took sides against the children when her husband was involved in arguments.

Mark Twain very soon became acquainted with poverty, tragedy and the seamy side of life. He was brought up in a midwestern village of poor whites. He saw slaves flogged and men killed in the streets. His friends were desperately poor vagrants. His father was a morose and discouraged derelict who hardly ever played with his children or showed them any love. He died when Mark was eleven. He left Mark 'an unruly, ragged, undersized, sickly and neurotic little roughneck', who was taken out of school and put to work as a 'printer's devil'. His employer described him as 'a youngster with a huge head, an ink smudged face, and an infinite capacity for laziness'. He fell in with the idlers of the village and became acquainted with every phase of human aberration (Thomas).

Joseph Conrad had a most disturbed and unhappy childhood, largely because of his father's political activities. His father was one of many who wanted to liberate Poland from Russian oppression, and he had been in touch with Ukrainian leaders who were trying to co-ordinate peasant insurrectionist movements. He was arrested in Warsaw and deported to a distant province. His wife begged to go with him, and her request was granted provided that she went as a political prisoner. Joseph went with her, and became seriously ill on the way to Moscow. They reached the place of exile, but his mother then became ill, when Joseph was six years old. Owing to her illness she was given three months' leave from exile, to stay with relatives. This was Joseph's first contact with children. His mother died when he was eight. Joseph tried to find solace in books—and read widely, in Polish and French. At nine he was sent to live with his brother-in-law. His father then became ill. As soon as he had finished school Joseph took to his books. He said: 'I don't know what would have become of me if I had not been a reading boy. My prep finished I would have had nothing to do but sit and watch the awful stillness of the sick room flow through the closed door and coldly enfold my scared heart. I suppose that in a futile childish way I would have gone crazy. Often, not always, I cried myself into a good sound sleep.' When Joseph was eleven his father died.

Toulouse Lautrec was brought up in a house full of hate. His mother and father had no love; their relationships were thoroughly bad, and they lived as far as possible as strangers. His father was an eccentric person, his mother a devout catholic. As often happens when a mother is unhappy in marriage, she devoted all her attention to her son, and concentrated all her hopes on him. As Hanson wrote, he was to give her half a lifetime of anxiety, and worse than anxiety.

Eleanor Roosevelt had good reason for feeling insecure as a child. At five she was sent to a convent school (as a non-catholic), and was very unhappy there. In her autobiography she described how a girl swallowed a penny. Eleanor was very impressed by the fuss which this occasioned, and so went to the Sister and said that she had swallowed one too. Her mother was sent for, and took her away in disgrace. 'Understanding as I do my mother's character, I realise how terrible it must have seemed to her to have a child who could lie. I remember the drive home as one of utter misery: for I could bear swift punishment far better than long scoldings. I could cheerfully lie at any time to escape a scolding, whereas if I had known that I would simply be put to bed or be spanked I probably would have told the truth.'

Her father, who drank too much, had to go to hospital for a prolonged period, and Eleanor described how worried she was, because she could not find out what was wrong. When Eleanor was seven, her mother died of diphtheria, and she was sent to live with her grandmother. Her father visited her at intervals, without warning, and she describes her great delight at those visits. When she was nine, he died. When she was fifteen she was sent to a school in England, near Wimbledon.

She was told by her aunt that she was the ugly duckling of the family. Eleanor described how ashamed she was of this. It was made clear to her that she must not expect to get as far as the others would, because of her lack of good looks.

Lawrence of Arabia was an illegitimate child, a fact which directly and indirectly led to a great deal of insecurity. His father was a baronet, who had married a woman so cantankerous that she was known in Irish Society as the 'Vinegar Queen'. He fell in love with the childrens' nurse from Skye, and eloped with her, changing his name to Lawrence. This woman, a person of a strictly calvinistic upbringing, was Lawrence's real mother. His father had five daughters by his wife, and five sons by the nurse.

Because of the real mother's sense of guilt and sin, she tried to atone by making her sons intensely religious. Determined that her guilty secret should not be discovered, she forbade her children to mix with neighbours, and kept them very much isolated, so that they had a lonely childhood—which was to leave its mark in later years.

T. E. Lawrence discovered the secret of his illegitimacy and was 'deeply wounded to discover that his parents, pious and austere to the point of ostentation, did not practise what they preached, that many of their postures were hypocritical, and in fact that the desires of the flesh played a major part in the lives of people whom till then he had idolised. From the day of those revelations he was to conceive a horror of physical love and an obsession with social pretences' (Villars).

No doubt another cause of insecurity was the many moves from home to home. The family moved from Kirkcudbright to the Isle of Man, then to Jersey, Dinard, the New Forest and Oxford. Such moves may cause much emotional disturbance in children.

LOSS OF PARENTS

A surprisingly large number of children destined for fame lost one or both parents during childhood. Even when one bears in mind the fact that the expectation of life was shorter in days gone by than it is today, it still seems that the number of parental deaths is excessive. It will be noted that five of them, Nero, Ivan the Terrible, Danton, Robespierre and Eichmann, are included in the group whom we have termed 'Some evil men'. It may be that the early loss of a parent was a factor in their subsequent undesirable behaviour.

On pp. 34-35 is a list of such children who lost their parents in the first ten years. It may not be complete, but we have included all those of whom we are aware.

HAPPY HOMES

It must be obvious that innumerable children destined for

fame had entirely happy homes, and it would be tedious to recount their experiences. One or two examples will be mentioned below.

Linnaeus of Uppsala, the botanist and naturalist, always remembered his happy childhood. His father was a rector.

Loss of Parents in first ten years	Age of Child in years when Parent died Mother	Father
Nero	2	2
Confucius		3
Mohammed	6	first year
Dante	5	
Fra Lippi	first year	2
Copernicus		10
Michaelangelo	6	
Raphael	? by 10	? by 10
Ivan	8	5
Ben Jonson		first year
Rubens		first year
Richelieu		5
René Descartes	first year	
Murillo	10	10
Pascal	3	
Isaac Newton		first year
Leibnitz		6
Jonathan Swift		first year
Swedenborg	4	
Lady Mary Wortley Montagu	4	
Abraham Cowley		first year
Voltaire	7	
David Hume		first year
Rousseau	first year	first year
Lawrence Sterne		
William Cowper	6	
Antoine Lavoisier	5	
Pestalozzi		5
Thomas Telford		first year
Danton		2½
Sir William Jones		3
Jenner	early	early

Loss of Parents in first ten years	Age of Child in years when Parent died	
	Mother	Father
Thomas Chatterton	first year	
Robespierre	7	
Fourier	8	8
John Rennie		5
Humboldt		8
De Quincey		7
Wordsworth	8	
Froebel	first year	
Byron		3
Abraham Lincoln	9	
Charles Darwin	8	
Chang and Eng		8
Thackeray		5
Alexandre Dumas		4
Edward Bulwer Lytton		early
Nathaniel Hawthorne		early
Charlotte Brontë	5	
Wagner		first year
Eddy	early	
Branwell Brontë	4	
Balfour		8
Kelvin	6	
Nietzsche		3
Tolstoy	2	9
Gosse	?8	
Baden-Powell		3
Conrad	8	
Paderewski	first year	
Steinmetz	1	
Sibelius		$2\frac{1}{2}$
Curie		10
Somerset Maugham	8	10
Ernest Bevin	8	
Eleanor Roosevelt		10
Ronald Knox	3	
Stafford Cripps	4	
Anna Pavlova		2
Norman Birkett	3	
Eichmann	4	

The home was one of 'complete affection, simple habits and sincere piety'. No father was more honest or trustworthy.

The father of *Jane Austen* was a rector. The rector and his wife were not strict or domineering parents, 'guiding by example and personality rather than rule and precept'. It was a happy peaceful home, with much entertaining and an atmosphere of classical learning. Jane had a 'serene, loving happy childhood'.

Gandhi had a loving peaceful home. He was tremendously impressed by his father's sublime forgiveness when at the age of fifteen he had to confess to his father a petty theft. There was no scolding, no reprimand, no punishment. Both wept.

William Temple had a particularly happy home. His parents were happy in marriage. His father, the Archbishop, 'won complete devotion from his children, unaffected reverence and absolute confidence'. A chaplain wrote: 'It was a wonderful and beautiful family life, the old Archbishop sitting in the evening at a small card table in the drawing room, writing his judgment on "Incense and lights" and the boys in no way awed to silence.'

Franklin Roosevelt, an only child, had an entirely happy childhood. He was in no way pampered. 'He knew nothing of family strife, physical want, contemptuous glances.' His father never ridiculed him. He adored both his mother and father.

When *Lord Balfour* wrote of his indebtedness to many men, statesmen, philosophers and friends, he added: 'But all my debts to them, compute them how you will, are as nothing to what I owe to her (his mother's) love, her teaching and her example.' At school he was regarded as a namby-pamby, and a bit effeminate. He never married.

Robert Louis Stevenson had a happy childhood. In his biography, Balfour wrote of Robert's mother that 'She had in the highest degree that readiness for enjoyment which makes light of discomfort, and turns into holiday any break of settled routine. Her desire to be pleased, her prompt interest in any experience, however new or unexpected, her resolute refusal to see the unpleasant side of things, all had their counterpart in her son, enabling him to pass through the many dark hours that would have borne far more heavily on his father's temperament.'

Aneurin Bevan's home was very different from the wealth of those of the Temples, Roosevelts and Balfours—but there was no less love there. Michael Foot wrote that the family background was one of self reliance, resource, music and nurture, through its own logic and past struggles, of the richest soil for the cultivation of new heresies. The father on most days left home at 5.30 a.m. and was rarely home before dark, yet he had a full life in the community. He was a crafts- man, a book lover, and fond of music. Aneurin's mother was 'the organiser and disciplinarian, stern but just, dominating but not domineering, guarding her brood against all comers, but determined that nothing she could give or inflict would be withheld if it could help them to get on in the world'. 'She cooked, cleaned and kept house with tireless efficiency. None went hungry even in the harshest times.' 'She was up before five to get her husband's breakfast ready. At nine she started her own work as tailoress. She had to count every penny to make ends meet for her ten children. All had to be present promptly at mealtimes; they must sit down together formally and not gossip about their neighbours.' The children all adored her.

STIMULATION AND INHIBITION

Innumerable were the homes in which the children who were to become famous were given every help and encourage- ment, particularly with regard to literature and music.

Thomas Arnold remembered receiving from his father a copy of Smollett's history of England in twenty-four volumes, when only three years of age, as a reward for the exactness with which he repeated all the little tales and anecdotes relating to successive reigns.

Dante Gabriel Rossetti lived in a stimulating atmosphere of intelligent conversation between his family and the many visitors. He read freely in his father's extensive library. 'It was a household in which artistic expression was not a freak or a hobby but a normal activity of man.'

Chevalier Jackson, the surgeon, had a similar home. Everyone was busy. Both his parents read extensively. 'A standing joke at home', he said, 'was a regular page in the American Agriculturalist devoted to the subject of the Long Winter Evenings', or the 'Interminable Winter Evenings'. Chevalier found the evenings far too short, for there was always so much to do.

The home of *Robert Baden-Powell* was the scene of social gatherings of many famous men—Thackeray, Ruskin, Thomas Huxley and many others. His mother, twenty-eight years younger than her husband, who died when Stephen was three, was left with seven children and two stepchildren to bring up. She spent much of her time with them teaching them reading and writing, implanting in them her ideals of honour and duty, self-reliance and perseverence. There was a communal cash box, from which the children drew pocket money as they required it, depositing a note of the amounts they withdrew—a good lesson in honesty. She encouraged them to take an interest in natural history and in her husband's library and scientific instruments.

Hillcourt described how Stephen disliked being sent to bed when a party was to begin. Only once did the temptation prove too great. He got out of bed and sneaked downstairs. Thackeray, sitting nearest to the door, saw him. Sensing trouble, the author held up a warning finger, pulled out a shilling, slipped it into Stephen's hand, then pointed his thumb biddingly upstairs. Without a murmur Stephen went back to bed.

Beatrice Webb's home was in many ways similar, though here there was an element of rejection. Men of eminence frequently visited the home. Her father, a flourishing business man, encouraged his daughters to read anything they wished, even advising them to buy a book in which they were interested but which happened to be banned by the circulating libraries. 'A nice minded girl', he said, 'can read anything, and the more she knows about human nature the better for her and for all the men connected with her.'

OVERANXIETY

When *Horace Walpole* went to Eton, at the age of nine and a half, his anxious mother tried to watch over his precarious health from a distance, and sent him medicines of her own manufacture, which he was expected to take.

When *William Pitt* went to Cambridge, he was accompanied by a nurse because of his ill health.

Feodor Dostoevsky and his brothers were never allowed by their father, a physician, to go out alone. Even when they went to school they were taken there and brought back in their father's carriage. They could walk and play in the grounds of the hospital, in which the father worked, but they were not allowed to talk to the patients or to associate with anyone outside the family.

Dostoevsky grew up to be almost a recluse. His father had said 'Build a wall round yourself. Keep away from the contamination of your fellows.' When he entered the school of engineering at St Petersburg he was thought to be a snob, because he would not mix with other students. His biographer wrote that 'his only companions were his dreams'. 'I dream of the great and beautiful', he said, 'I live in a world of dreams.' His biographer added that 'he lived in the abstract because his father never allowed him to live in the concrete'. His father had taught him never to mention women except in dramatic verse—and he was greatly teased by other members of the engineering school for his attitude to the opposite sex.

Alfred Nobel, the third of three boys, was deeply attached to his mother—as were his brothers. His father, an engineer, had become bankrupt in the year in which Alfred was born, and was always working feverishly on new inventions, in the hope of recouping his fortunes. He was particularly anxious to discover an explosive which would be useful in the building of canals and roads. In one experiment he made such a loud explosion that a hostile crowd gathered and he was forbidden to carry out any more experiments with explosives in the city. He thereupon went to Finland to continue his work, leaving his family.

Alfred shared a bedroom with his mother, the brothers sharing another room. Alfred and his mother were mutually dependent on each other. When he went to school at eight he found it difficult to make friends. He had frequent illnesses, and was devotedly looked after by his mother. His father complained that his mother was making him more susceptible to illness. His intense love for his mother led to a revulsion against normal sexual relationships with women. (He had a love affair with a woman for eighteen years, but did not marry her.)

Oscar Wilde's parents were an eccentric pair. The father was an Irish Ear, Nose and Throat surgeon with archaeological interests, short of stature and excitable in nature. He was described as garrulous, quick tempered and addicted to alcohol. The mother was a highly intelligent woman, tall, stately and aloof, dignified and handsome. The dress and manners of both were extraordinary. There was a public scandal over an affair of the father with one Mary Travers.

Oscar's mother had longed for a daughter, and was disappointed when the boy was born. There is a story of Oscar being dressed in girl's clothes when a small child. If this is true, it would have an important bearing on his future sexual life.

Marcel Proust's father was a physician near Chartres: Marcel's mother was an intelligent woman of means. The story of his childhood is one of excessive parental anxiety about his health, with associated psychogenic disease. Marcel was so delicate as a child that he was not expected to live. He clung to his parents more than the other children, and demanded affection from morning to night. When he did his lessons he insisted that his mother should stay at his side. When he went to bed he caused her to lie down in his room, so that he could feel the comfort of her presence as long as he was awake.

He had indigestion, and his parents were continually cautioning him about his diet. He had hay fever in the early summer, and at nine developed asthma. Asthma troubled him for the rest of his life. As a child, it was precipitated by anxiety, by over exertion, or by a sleepless night. His indigestion and his asthma were accompanied by psychological disturbances. 'More emotional than other children, he was also more completely the plaything of his emotions.' He was an unstable child—too easily elated and angered, heartbroken and depressed. He wept hysterically when his mother left him for a few days. He had temper tantrums when she refused him anything that he wanted. His parents dare not exert normal discipline because of his precarious health. His biographer wrote: 'when he was well, his mother watched over him, and when he was ill, she nursed him, so that he became even more dependent upon her. Once at least when he was kept indoors she slept in his room to console him. He was indeed consoled; he began to wish that he might always live so, shut up with his mother, secure in the warmth of her affection.'

When he was eleven he went to the Lycée. He did well there, but was frequently kept at home on account of ill health. His associates at the Lycée were suspicious of him. He was ill at ease with the other boys, who seemed insensitive and rude. 'When he showed his good will by flattering them or writing sonnets on their beauty, their response was disconcerting.

One boy, whose hand he seized in a moment of impulsive ardour, shrank away in fear: others drove him off with insults or threatened to give him a thrashing.' He did not know why they disliked him. He was too girlish for their taste. He even looked like a girl, with small frail delicate limbs. The boys felt that he was different from them. He found consolation in the society of older women.

At nineteen he studied law and political science at the University in order to please his parents, but turned over to his real interest, writing, in later years.

H. G. Wells was overprotected in a different way, and not one which was calculated to lead to an abnormal sexual outlook—as happened in the case of Nobel and Proust, and to some extent in the case of Dostoevsky. The father of H. G. Wells was a gardener, and his mother was a snob whose interest in appearances was very well developed. Wells wrote that 'whatever the realities of our situation, she was resolved that to the very last moment we should keep up the appearance of very comfortable members of that upper servant tenant class for which her imagination had been moulded. She believed that it was a secret to all the world that she had no servant and did all the household drudgery herself. I was enjoined never to answer questions about that or let it out when I went abroad. Nor was I to take my coat off carelessly, because my underclothing was never quite up to the promise of my exterior garments. It was never ragged, but it abounded in compromises. This hindered my playing games. I was never to mix with common children, who might teach me naughty words. The greengrocer's children over the way were considered to be rough. People who were not beneath us were apt to be stuck up and unapproachable in the other direction. So my Universe of discourse was limited.'

DISPLAYING THE PRODIGY

Some parents, with natural pride, make the mistake of dis-

playing in public the supposed prowess of their offspring—
often to the detriment and annoyance of the child, and the
boredom of the audience.

The father of *Carl Weber* was obsessed with the idea that
Carl was a prodigy, like Mozart. Saunders remarked that
'Not content with allowing any talent the child might possess
to develop of its own accord, he immediately introduced a
forcing process which caused the boy untold misery and
nervous derangement. During the parents' wanderings
throughout Germany no stone was left unturned to make him
the prodigy his father had set his mind upon.' He added that
the boy shrank almost in disgust from the process of showing
himself off. He was put through an intensive musical training,
which caused him many tears: the training was not easy, and
his elder brother, after trying to teach him, once said: 'Carl,
you may become anything else you like, but a musician
you will never be.' When he was about twelve, however,
the boy began to realise himself that success was within his
grasp.

Jeremy Bentham's father constantly tried to show others his
boy's genius. Jeremy absolutely refused to perform, much to
the annoyance of his father who was 'left to complain of his
son's weakness and impudence in keeping wrapt up in a napkin
the talents it had pleased God to confer on him'.

The father of *Samuel Johnson* caused a great deal of friction
by trying to show off his precocious child. It is said that at
every opportunity he forced him to perform before admiring
neighbours and relatives, and constantly bragged about the
boy's literary talents. Pearson wrote that Samuel had little
love for his father, who had little time for the instruction or
entertainment of his children, and that his real objection to his
father was the fact that the child had to entertain the parents.
'After some petting and kissing he was expected to show off
on social occasions: and at last he came to loathe his father's
caresses because they preluded a displaying of his mental

alertness in one form or another.' He often tried to avoid the displays by climbing a tree and hiding until the danger was over. 'That is the great misery of late marriages', he said, 'the unhappy product of them becomes the plaything of dotage: an old man's child leads such a life as a little boy's dog with awkward fondness and forced to sit up and beg to divert a company, who at last go away complaining of their disagreeable entertainment.'

Beethoven's father was determined that Ludwig should become a prodigy, like Mozart. The alcoholic father forced his boy to practise, insisting on daily lessons on the pianoforte and violin in spite of his tears. He would return late at night after drinking and haul Ludwig out of bed, to keep him at the piano all night. Ludwig was made to play in a concert when he was eight.

Brockway wrote that 'the childhood of *Mozart* is one of the masterpieces of the Rococo. His loving but ambitious father raised him in the principle that he was a performing bear. From his sixth year he was dragged over the map of Europe and exhibited as a marvel. Great monarchs made much of him, and by the time he was fourteen he had seen the interior of every palace from London to Naples.'

Whittier had a precocious memory and at seven could recite entire chapters of the Bible by heart. His father made him display his ability at the quarterly meetings of the Quakers.

In contrast to the above, the behaviour of *Macaulay's* parents was exemplary. According to Trevelyan, 'they never bandied his productions about, or encouraged him to parade his powers of conversation or memory. They abstained from any word or act which might foster in him a perception of his own genius with as much care as a wise millionaire expends on keeping his son ignorant of the fact that he is destined to be richer than his comrades. It was scarcely ever that the consciousness was expressed by either of his parents of the superiority of their son over other children.'

COMMENT

We feel that the most striking fact which emerges from this chapter is the widely diverse home backgrounds of the men and women who were destined for fame. The contrasts were extreme. Some, like Jane Austen, William Temple and Franklin Roosevelt, had the most secure and happy home possible; others, like Mirabeau, Turgenev, Chekhov and Jenny Lind could hardly have had to endure greater misery in their home life. The cruelty experienced by some was to leave a permanent sense of injustice, which was to be of great importance in their future careers, actions and stability of character. Some were brought up with excessive strictness, and some like Clive, without discipline at all. It is well known that in many ways the results of lack of discipline and excessive discipline may be similar—and include such results as accident proneness and any of the many results of insecurity. In the case of Clive the lack of discipline, as his biographer remarked, was to affect three countries.

It is interesting to contrast the effects of strictness with love and those of excessive strictness without love, or even with frank hate. The story of Sir Patrick Hastings' early years shows that a childhood spent in chaotic surroundings does not necessarily presage an unstable future. In his case a factor of great importance was probably his mother's love for the children and their love for her. The chaotic home of George Bernard Shaw may well have had a different effect, and greatly influenced his future writings and thinkings, for there was little love to temper the chaos of his home. In the case of John Wesley, the upbringing, though strict, was tempered by love, and yet the Wesley children grew up to experience disaster in marriage.

We have also shown how some children, such as Thomas Arnold, Baden-Powell, Chevalier Jackson and Beatrice Webb, were brought up in a background of learning and of intellectual stimulation. We shall show elsewhere in this book how other people of eminence were brought up in homes of exactly the opposite kind—homes without any books or learning of any sort at all.

It is always a temptation for the parents of an unusually intelligent child, of whom they are greatly proud, to show him off. Examples of this are to be found in the childhood of Carl Weber, Jeremy Bentham, Samuel Johnson and Beethoven. It is bad for the child, and it is interesting to note how Jeremy Bentham and Samuel Johnson rebelled against this practice.

Most parents hope that their children will grow up to have a normal happy sex life. In the case of homosexuality, the most common features found in the home background are a weak, passive, ineffective or hostile father, who takes little part in the upbringing of the boy, together with an unusually dominating mother, resulting in an abnormally strong mother-son relationship. The seeds of an unhappy sex life were thoroughly sown by the parents of John Ruskin, Alfred Nobel, Dostoevsky, Marcel Proust and perhaps of Oscar Wilde.

John Ruskin was isolated from contact with all other children and brought up without any stress at all—with the most undesirable results, as John Ruskin wrote himself. Children need to learn to face difficulties and disappointments; if they never meet them in childhood, they are likely to find it more difficult to deal adequately with them in later years, when they lack the guiding hand of loving parents.

It may be argued that many of the persons mentioned in this chapter achieved their fame because of the peculiar family background, because of the insecurity of their childhood, because of the loss of a parent, with all that it meant to them. Samuel Smiles, as we shall note in our final chapter, had something to say about this—about the value of difficulties in life. What we can never say, however, is how many potential geniuses were nipped in the bud, and never allowed to develop their real potential, just because of the difficulties which we have mentioned. Some may surmount difficulties, and some may be stimulated by them to greater endeavour. Others will just give in and abandon the struggle.

CHAPTER 2

EDUCATION AT HOME

IN days gone by, it was in no way unusual for a child to receive all or much of his education at home, either from his parents or from tutors. In many cases the child would begin school at a much older age than is customary at the present day, but with an extensive general knowledge acquired mainly from his parents. The fantastic home education received by Sir William Hamilton is described in Chapter 8. In this chapter we shall describe some of the other stories of home education which we found in our reading, with some notes about the psychological consequences which arose from boys not being able to mix with others of their own age in the rough and tumble of school life. We shall note the remarkable precocity achieved by some of the children as a result of this method of intensive individual instruction.

The type of home education to which *Blaise Pascal* was subjected has been described by several writers. We have obtained most of our information from the biographies by Morris Bishop and Mortimer, and the book by Terman and Cox.

The father of Blaise Pascal was a member of a well-to-do family, and was one of the most important government officials in Central France. He was well known as a mathematician, and an expert in mechanics. He was described by Bishop as a 'competent executive, an imperious father, sacrificing himself for his children, and requiring their sacrifices as his right, utterly honest, but demanding all his due, jealously proud of his achievement, of his family, of his small nobility.' He had four children, of whom three survived—two girls and a boy, Blaise. He found in the rapid and extraordinary development of his children's intelligence an interest more absorbing than all his worldly success. When Blaise was seven his father relinquished his post in order to devote all his time to his children's education. The boy's mother had died when he was three.

Étienne, the father of Blaise, had unorthodox views on education, considering that the exercise of reason was more important than the routine of Latin grammar. He wanted the boy to learn reason and judgment, and to learn the nature of a fact and its value. 'Information was to come to him', wrote Bishop, 'as an answer to curiosity, as a reward for the desire to know.' He taught history, geography and philosophy during meals, and devised games to illustrate the principles. His principle maxim was to keep the boy superior to his tasks—that he should never let the work get him down, by being rushed or overloaded with knowledge. It was for this reason that he wanted his children to learn classics before mathematics. The whole course of education was carefully planned in advance.

'He showed him what languages are, their organisation and purpose, how they have been reduced to grammar in the form of rules, how these rules came to have exceptions, and how the correspondences of the languages have permitted men to transfer their thoughts from one linguistic conglomerate to another. He showed him the reason for grammatical rules, so that when he came to learn grammar, he knew why he was doing so, and applied himself precisely to those things which needed the most application.'

The curriculum included civic and canon law as well as religious and ecclesiastical history. In science the boy learned insensibly the principles of the experimental method, observing, classifying and proposing generalisations from his evidence. 'From his childhood', says Gilberte, 'he could not surrender except to what seemed to him evidently true, so that when he was not given good reasons, he sought them out himself, and when he had become interested in something, he would not quit it until he had found a reason which could satisfy him.' Mortimer wrote that 'always and in everything the truth was the one goal of his mind, and nothing short of it contented him'. 'From his childhood he would only believe what seemed to him plainly true, so that where people failed to supply him with sound reasons for things he sought them out himself, and when he was on the trail of a reason he would not stop until he had tracked it down. On one occasion some-one at table accidentally struck a porcelain plate with a knife and it made a sound. Blaise noticed this and saw that when the plate was touched the sound stopped. At once he wanted to know why, and this led him to make other experiments in sound.'

Bishop added that Blaise's precocity upset his father's edu-cational scheme. When Blaise heard friends talk about geo-metry, he asked what geometry was. His father replied that it was the noblest and highest form of a man's knowledge. Blaise felt ill-used because he had not been taught this, and begged and pleaded for instruction, 'whining for mathematics as another would whine for candy'. His father refused, for he thought that the mathematics would distract him from classics, and forbade his son to think or speak of it again. He promised him mathematics as soon as he knew Latin and Greek. He locked up his textbooks and cautioned his friends not to mention mathematics in the boy's presence. All that Blaise could gather was that geometry was the science of making true diagrams, and of finding the proportions between them. Thinking about this, he began to make charcoal diagrams on the floor. He noted certain evident truths and axioms. He set himself problems and devised satisfactory methods of proof or demonstrations. He proceeded from step to step until he reached the thirty-second proposition of Euclid that the angles in a triangle together equal two right angles. His father chanced to enter the room and stood and watched for a time without Blaise knowing that he was there. On questioning,

Blaise explained the structure of his logic with his own terminology. His father, Étienne, did not say a word: he left the room and wept tears of joy to a friend. He unlocked the Euclid and gave it to the boy. The boy learned Latin and geometry together, mastering the science in his playtime. Four years later (at sixteen) he produced his essay on conic sections, in which he progressed beyond the mathematical knowledge of his century, and heralded modern projective geometry.

Étienne was a member of the Academie Libre which met weekly to discuss scientific matters. He introduced Blaise to this body, and Blaise absorbed ideas and teachings there. At nineteen he invented and constructed the first calculating machine. He gave Pascal's law to physics, proved the existence of the vacuum, and helped to establish the science of hydro-dynamics. He created the mathematical theory of probability. His prose style influenced French literary language. Subse-quently he wrote his Pensées, thoughts which 'affected the mental cast of three centuries'. He died at thirty-nine, after a life of invalidism. He once told his sister that from the age of eighteen, he had not passed a day without suffering.

Bishop wrote that Blaise was never inside a school. There is no record of his ever having had dealings with boys of his own age, to learn his place in the group, to gain a sense of what humans consider human realities, to be subjected to physical and psychological as well as intellectual rivalries. He always had a sense of apartness from the world. His view of humanity was that of an observant god-like visitor, not of a man among his fellows. It may be that the physical and nervous disorders, the hypersensitiveness of his later years, had their origin in the regime of genius and disregard of physical training.

Mortimer, in his biography, described the father's education as 'remarkable for its paternal self-denial, its eccentricity, vigour, patience and success, where failure might almost have been predicted'.

John Wesley's education took place largely at home.

Mrs Wesley had an unusual educational system for her large family of children. It was described by James Laver, in his biography. Her eldest son, Samuel, had not learned to talk until he was five years old. In consequence she made no attempt to teach the others even the alphabet until they reached the same age. When they did, however, she expected them to learn it in one day, and all except two succeeded. They were taught to read almost as quickly, and even though the rector himself was responsible for teaching the boys Latin and Greek, his wife took charge of the other subjects in her children's education, devoting to them three hours in the morning and three in the afternoon.

She got the family up at 5 a.m. to read the psalm of the day and a chapter of the New Testament. At 5 p.m. she had a serious talk with each of her children in turn.

The elder children had to help the younger ones with lessons.

John was sent to Charterhouse when ten and a half years old.

The father of *Jeremy Bentham* was a lawyer. Mack, in his biography, described how this man, with meticulous thoroughness, drew up a detailed plan for Jeremy's education. He had been ambitious himself, but somewhat thwarted, and he transferred his ambitions to his boy. He had not been able himself to go to Westminster and Oxford, and he was determined that his son should. He bought his boy a Latin Grammar when he was three, and by four or five the boy was able to write Greek and Latin. He submitted the boy to intensive home education until he went to Westminster School at seven. He was not permitted to mix with other boys. As Mack put it, his father wanted to 'keep the boy pure for the Lord Chancellorship, a model of social graces uncontaminated by the local artisans and tradesmen's sons'. 'He wanted him to be pious; instead he was terrified and repelled by religion; he could never understand why it must be painful to be good.'

He censored the books available for the boy to read in the family library. 'Whatever books were made for laughter, whatever was irreverent or not obviously instructive, was locked away—only the heavy depressing volumes were left.'

Terman and Oden wrote that other children were treated as dunces in his presence, and he learned to feel scorn and contempt for less acute minds. At college there was scarcely a companion in whose society he could discover any pleasure; he thought all his contemporaries stupid. Terman and Oden wrote that at school he nursed a feeling of his own inferiority, hated all social pleasures, and was for the most part solitary in his play as in his work. 'I was a child without a guide', he recalled, 'idling, trembling and hiding myself.'

Goethe received almost all his education at home—either from his father or from tutors. He missed the influence of schoolfellows of his own age.

Gibson, in his biography of *Pitt*, wrote that Lord Chatham applied himself to train his son for public speaking, to read well, to be careful in elocution, to translate—always using and sometimes pausing for the right word—and to cultivate the power of rapid and appropriate arrangements of thoughts and topics. He made him constantly recite from Shakespeare and Milton and directed him to study the style and language of Barrow and Bolingbroke.

John Keble, one of the pioneers of the Oxford Movement, after whom Keble College, Oxford, was named, came from a good family at Fairford. There is nothing of special note about his mother, and her five children loved her. The father was a cleric. All five of their children were highly intelligent.

Battiscombe, in his biography, wrote that John's father had original views on education. He taught the two boys at home and sent his three daughters away to school—mainly, it is thought, for 'finishing', and even they received their main education at home. He made his children learn their lessons in the middle of all the hurly-burly of a large family in a rather small house. They had to work in the room in which their brothers and sisters were reciting, reading aloud or practising the piano, and at any moment the father would call on them to shut the Latin grammar or arithmetic book and answer questions on a totally different subject.

His pupils were under no compulsion; he taught them only when they were willing and anxious to learn. The two boys learned four languages, the girls Latin, French and Italian, and all of them were well read in English literature and history. He was able to take the boys well up to and beyond the level reached by Eton and Winchester.

It was a happy closely-knit family, entirely self-sufficient. In the many family letters there is little or no mention of other friends or playmates of their own age. The family formed an affectionate, intellectual and very small circle, whose members seldom if ever moved beyond the bounds of Oxfordshire and Gloucestershire. For amusements and hobbies they enjoyed gardening, walks, and the annual fair at Fairford.

As a result of this isolation from others, John was prevented from going to a Public School. It made it difficult for him later to anticipate the reaction of an average person to any idea or proposal: he was never in touch with the man in the street. Although he himself never regretted his home up-bringing, he felt his lack of a Public School education as a real limitation in practical affairs.

John applied for a scholarship at Corpus Christi College at fourteen and succeeded. He thoroughly enjoyed the company of others and the new experience of friendships. He had given the impression to his friends that he was not doing sufficient work. He was shy about admitting his presumption in trying for both mathematical and classical honours, and worked secretly at his mathematical books, rapidly concealing them in his cupboard when an unexpected visitor came to see him. His father, however, had no doubt about his probable success. His friend Coleridge, educated at Eton, could never bring himself to believe that a man like Keble, with merely a home education, could compete on even terms with men from the great Public Schools; but in fact John Keble obtained a double first—in classics and mathematics—an achievement confined in the past to one person only—Robert Peel.

One of the most fantastic stories of intensive home teaching concerns the childhood of *Karl Witte*, who was born in Germany in 1800. Over 1,000 pages were devoted by his father to details of his education, but our information is obtained principally from a one volume abbreviated edition translated into English. Witte's father was a clergyman in a German village, and possessed strong and unusual views on education. He held that a child's education should begin from birth, and that the instruction which he received in his first five or six years was vital to his future. 'My whole work', he wrote, 'is intended to prove to the intelligent person that the schoolmaster, no matter how well endowed with knowledge and the ability to teach, is, in spite of his best wishes, unable to accomplish anything if others have previously worked against him, or still continue to work against him.' 'This view came into direct collision with the accepted pedagogical policy of refraining from anything in the way of formal education until the child reached school age.' He held that 'Since children are essentially thinking animals, they are certain, from the moment they first use their own minds, to draw inferences and arrive at conclusions regarding everything they see, hear and touch; but if left to themselves will inevitably, because of their inability to form sound critical judgments, acquire wrong interests and thought habits which all the education of later life may not be able wholly to overcome.' It was Witte's aim to direct and develop his son's reasoning powers in the plastic formative years of childhood. 'I say "Woe to the Father or educator who is so foolish as to say my son shall do up to his eighth year as he pleases".'

He felt that too much stress is put on man's natural aptitudes. He wrote: 'The natural aptitudes have less to do with it than the child's education in his first five or six years. Of course there is a difference in regard to the aptitudes, but as a rule, that is, with such as most men are born with, infinitely more depends on education than is usually believed. I hope to prove in fact that I am right. If God grants me a son, and if he, in your opinion, is not to be called stupid, which Heaven forbid, I have long ago decided to educate him to be a superior man, without knowing in advance what his aptitudes may be.' He said that he did not want to make a savant of him, much less a precocious scholar. He wanted to educate him to be a strong, healthy, active young man. 'It would have been in the highest degree unpleasant for me', he said, 'to have made of him pre-eminently a Latin or Greek scholar, or a mathematician.' 'All I wanted to accomplish with my son was that in his seventeenth or eighteenth year he should be mature for the University, but that he should have such a many sided and thorough education as to be able to compete with any graduate, with the tacit conviction of his power to surpass them.'

It was essential for him to resign from his parish, in order to give his whole time to the education of his son, and he persuaded the City and University of Leipzig to give him a considerable stipend for this express purpose. The French Westphalian Government and subsequently the German monarchy continued the stipend. The Government examined the boy repeatedly, and with suspicion, but paid the money regularly.

Preparation for the child's development had to begin before conception. 'A man should train himself as much as possible, and should choose for himself a healthy, mentally well developed and well intentioned wife, and then the children will be healthy, mentally strong and well intentioned. After everything possible has been done for one's children before their procreation, one should double the precautions during the mother's pregnancy. Moderation and simplicity in food, drink and the enjoyment of corporal love, much exercise in the open, pure drinking water, the most scrupulous bodily cleanliness, strict execution of duties, contentment, joyfulness and faith in God. If the father sweetens her life by thinking, feeling and acting in the same way, both may be assured that the Deity will, as a rule, give them a healthy child that is at the very least, provided with average capacities of body and mind. Nothing more is required.'

Karl's instruction began when he was a baby in arms. His parents named parts of the body, the objects in the room and in the garden. 'For example, we held one finger close to Karl's eyes and moved them, now singly, now several at a time. He soon noticed them and grabbed at them, but in the beginning usually missed them. We did not mind this, but brought one hand nearer to his or his nearer to ours. He seized it, happy to have succeeded, and drew a finger into his mouth and sucked it. Then we pronounced the word "finger" slowly, distinctly and repeatedly. After a few minutes we withdrew our finger from his mouth and held it once more before his eyes, first one, saying "one finger", then two, in the same way saying "two fingers", and so forth. If he grabbed the thumb, we should have said, as above, "thumb". When he actually knew the fingers we gave him the thumb, pronouncing the word at the same time. We slowly differentiated the pointer, the middle finger, the little finger. In every case the road was properly prepared, and the words were enunciated loudly, clearly, slowly and repeatedly. Keys and other objects were used to show him simple arithmetic and reason—comparing the size of trees, the breaking of an object into two, and so on. Everything was frequently shown and clearly and plainly named to him. Later when he spoke correctly he was fondled and praised: when he failed, we said in a decidedly cooler manner: "Mother, or Father, Karl cannot yet pronounce this or that word." "There was no danger of stammering because he had to speak very slowly and was never intimidated." ' They absolutely avoided 'baby-talk'. 'In this way Karl learned easily to know and name correctly everything surrounding him and what he could pronounce he always spoke in pure German as though he had read it in a well written book especially prepared for children. This prepared him for learning foreign languages.'

The father laid down rules to be observed strictly by all in the household in their dealings with Karl. The whole family life was regulated with a view to suggesting to the child ideas which, taking root in the subconscious region of his mind, would tend to affect his moral outlook and exercise a lasting influence on his conduct. Hasty words, disputes, discussion of unpleasant topics, all such things were studiously avoided. Witte and his wife displayed only those characteristics with which they wished to imbue their son. They were unfailingly genial, courteous, considerate and sympathetic. Over and above this, they set Karl a constant example of diligence, in itself a most valuable form of moral discipline.

'I tolerated nothing in my home, yard, garden etc. which was not tasteful, especially nothing that did not harmonise with its surroundings.' In every room there was but little furniture, 'but such as there was was carefully selected. On all the walls hung paintings or etchings, but none that was in tastelessly glowing colours or represented an unpleasant subject. His attention was drawn frequently to things of artistic merit.

'Karl was but sparingly praised by us. Some other stimuli were employed. For example, small rewards, with which, however, charitable purposes were invariably connected; the noting down of his conduct in a book which Dr Funk had presented to him. Karl had to have done something extraordinary for his age before he was patted or kissed. But nothing had such an effect with him as the assurance I gave him especially at a noteworthy moment of his life that he, no doubt, was standing higher than ever in the eyes of God. Usually Karl after such a conversation evinced still more docility, more industry, more goodness of health than heretofore.

'If my wife or I was dissatisfied with Karl, they (the neighbours or friends) never defended him, but on the contrary, treated him with some coolness. If we gave a friendly utterance about him he was heartily fondled by them, but they did not overflow with praise.

'When visiting a neighbouring Pastor, at coffee drinking, Karl carelessly spilled some of his milk on the table. The law was that in such a case he was to be punished by getting nothing more to eat or drink except bread or salt.

'If there was any food which he did not like, we made this concession that we did not force him to eat much of it. At the same time we directed his attention by representations or a story invented for the occasion to the fact that by his dislike he deprived himself of a great enjoyment since the particular food was very much liked by us, and by all other men. We rejoice every time it comes, we would say, and you feel aggrieved. Get used to eating it, and you will not be aggrieved, but will rejoice with us. Since we, as parents, ate anything, we could so much the more easily get him to do likewise, by directing his attention to our example.

'Frequently he would do without butter, because our stories had taught him the usefulness of reducing one's wants. In regard to sugar and all sweetmeats, we had taught him from the start to eat little or nothing at all of them.'

His parents carefully rationed his food. 'We noted every day, often more than once a day, Karl's complexion, appetite, activity and spirits, and also, later, the ease with which his mind worked, but more especially his growth. His height was marked on a doorpost. He was measured the first of each month, and as a rule the increase in height was noticeable every time. If it were greater than usual, we gave him a little more meat.' 'By means of careful treatment and diet, Karl in his third year, as ever afterwards, was neither too violent nor too meek.'

They had strong views about discipline. His father wrote: 'Implicit obedience is infinitely more important than one would usually think, for a child is again and again on the point of doing something by which he may hurt himself. To the obedient child you need only call out "Do not do that, my child", or simply call out his name, and he will stop at once, will stand still, will pay attention. Then you can impart to him the reasons for the prohibition, in order to safeguard the child in a future similar situation.

'If one of us had overlooked something in him, or had too easily forgiven him, the other considered that to be as great a fault as to have been too stern or too vehement, for, at bottom, both are equally bad.

'Karl was allowed to ask for anything that was natural that was not unjust, that was good. It was generally granted to him, even if we had to add the remark that, for this or that, it was no longer proper for him. If he asked for anything else, he was flatly refused it without giving him any further reasons; if he could know them himself; with sound and comprehensible reasons, if they were still unknown to him. If he seemed to have forgotten those which he knew, we quizzed him, to bring them back to his memory.

'From the third to the fourth years he was introduced into every kind of society. He became acquainted with the concert, drama and opera, as well as with watermills, windmills, lions, ostriches and elephants, as with moles and bats, with salt mines as with steam engines, with the village market as with the Leipzig fair. He was frequently asked whether he had taken good notice of this and that.'

He had few toys. 'I hardly ever bought toys in the ordinary sense of the word. This experience I was spared. Everything was a plaything to him. One of the most profitable toys was a box of building blocks.'

The father went on: 'since I was repeatedly informed that Karl should have a playmate, I finally gave in and chose two somewhat grown girls who at that time were apparently the best behaved children in the community. They sang, danced and played with him, and he naturally was happy; but the same child that heretofore had never been stubborn and had never told an untruth, now learned both. He also became accustomed to coarse expressions, and grew arbitrary and domineering, because those girls did not oppose him. In the end we had to banish them. It is indeed a foolish and highly injurious idea that children cannot be merry without other children. One need only be a child with them, need only take part in many jests, let the children now and then get the upper hand and be more clever, by allowing them to occupy a place of greater dignity and so forth, and they will feel just as happy playing with older persons, will learn to avoid naughty things, and will not so easily take any harm. Worst of all it is to make playmates out of uneducated children, especially without any close observation. It is rank stupidity to imagine that children cannot be agreeable and sociable unless they all the time go around with other children. Naturally the opportunity for coming together with children is not excluded, but their commingling should occur only now and then and under supervision.'

He encouraged the child to ask questions, and in his replies he went as fully as he could into the whys and the wherefores of whatever was under discussion. Above all he avoided giving superficial answers, for it was his chief object to impress upon Karl the desirability of thoroughness, of appreciating analogies, dissimilarities, relationships and also of being able to reason logically from cause to effect. He insisted that all others who talked to the child should be careful how they talked in his presence.

He described in detail the method he used to teach him to read and write. 'One of Karl's favourite amusements was to look at pictures. We naturally explained to him everything worth knowing in a picture and afterwards we had him describe it to us. So long as he could not read, we used to say regretfully, "Oh, if you only knew how to read. It is a most interesting story, but I have no time to tell it to you." If we then went away, he looked at the story in the picture book as at a talisman whose secret powers were useless to him, because he lacked the magic wand with which to unlock it. Thus we roused in him by degrees the desire for reading. (He was then three to four years old.) I brought ten sets of German printed letters, and ten sets of the Latin alphabet, and of the numbers 0 to 9. I threw the whole into a box and showed it to him as a new game. (They picked out letters in turn and named them for him.) If he recognised it we fondled him. If he did not recognise it, we would laughingly say "Oh, you silly child, it is an 'a' or 'e' " etc. It took him but a few days for Karl to know all the letters. As soon as he had learned the letters, we began to put together syllables or words.'

When his father went away on a visit, his wife tried to teach him to read. 'What I had feared, actually happened. He became embarrassed and discouraged when he had to busy himself with mere printed words.' (He felt that Karl was not ready for it, because he had not shown a lively desire to read in books.) He went on: 'I was thus induced to search for all kinds of means for making reading agreeable to Karl, so that he would be able quickly and with pleasure to enjoy the fruits of his endeavours. He became fonder and fonder of it.' The father's aims were to instil in him love for his study, to teach him the most necessary things, and to make the instruction as comprehensive and easy as possible.

'I did not formally teach Karl writing. We frequently gave him inducements for the desire to write. But we did not help him out, at least for any length of time and only after his repeated requests. At first he drew printed letters. When, after a while, we jested him about them, and at his request gave him the written letters, he began to draw these too and finally was able to do easily what others attain only after laborious study.'

He began to introduce formal work—at first fifteen minutes a day. 'During those fifteen minutes he had to collect all his mental powers. He had to perform everything that was in his power to perform. Karl soon became accustomed to look upon his worktime as something sacred.'

He began to teach him languages when he was six, starting with French. He aimed at making him want to learn it, and enjoy it, and getting him to understand the exact meaning of every word. Within a year he was so far advanced that he could read an easy French book with pleasure. He began to teach him Italian, and in six months he could read Italian books. He then introduced English, Latin and Greek. By the time he was eight Karl read without great effort and with enthusiasm, Homer, Plutarch, Virgil, Cicero, Ossian, Fenelon, Florian, Metastasio and Schiller.

'We frequently referred in his presence to what he would have developed into if he had grown up without careful training and instruction, and what many a child would have developed into if he had been brought to our house at his birth and we had accepted and educated him as our own child. We also explained to Karl how much more advanced in every respect he would be if he had always been attentive and industrious. But he knew only too well how often he had failed in one respect or another. His memory and his Book of Conduct told him that.'

At seven and a half he was tested in his knowledge by various well known men and achieved public fame as a result. When seven he gave a public demonstration of his ability to read Italian, French, German and Latin.

He displayed a love of knowledge rarely seen in a boy of

his age. Most impressive were his logical habits of mind, the fulness and accuracy of the information he possessed, and his linguistic proficiency.

At nine his father sent him to the University of Leipzig, to which he was admitted by a special dispensation, after matriculation. He was given his Ph.D. when he was thirteen. At sixteen he was made Doctor of Laws and appointed to the teaching staff of the University of Berlin as professor. He was sent abroad, however, before taking up his duties, and became an expert on Dante. He then took up his career in jurisprudence.

He led a long and active life, and was happy in his domestic and social relationships. He was devoted to the community, and acquired high honour and distinction. He died at the age of eighty-three.

Born six years after Karl Witte, *John Stuart Mill* had a very similar education at home, though in many ways Mill's father, James, showed less wisdom than did the father of Karl Witte, particularly with regard to motivation. Mill's eventual achievements, however, were the greater. The story is told by Packe.

James Mill had strong views on education, and was the author of a book entitled *The Analysis of the Human Mind*. He was strongly influenced by his friend Jeremy Bentham. 'They both felt that an academic education was overrated, and that a close supervision of a boy's learning in his own home was both cheaper and of much greater value. James Mill felt that an intensive home education thoroughly under his control would not only be an interesting experiment, but would vindicate his views. He was no believer in the genetic factor in intelligence. He thought that all minds started as much alike as stomachs, or hands or any other physical organs. They were all blank sheets, forced to record every experience which the senses introduced to them.' 'Whoever had power to regulate the sequence and the strength of the experiences which flowed in upon a young mind, decided the habits of association it would form, and to that extent determined both the character and the ability of the later man. The process of regulation was what was known as education. The sovereign rulers of men's actions were the pursuit of pleasure and the avoidance of pain. The educator should, therefore, by a judicious use of the pleasures and pains at his disposal, not only build up a chain of associations which could induce the child to act as he desired, but also encourage it to develop by experience and knowledge of what caused what, a faculty of reason, enabling it to ensure that its actions were those likely to produce ultimately pleasurable results. In short, all that an educator need hope to do was to help the child to reason accurately.'

James Mill taught his son Greek when he was three, using a novel method. He wrote out a number of common words on cards, with their English meaning, and John was required to recognise them by comparing them with the articles which they represented. He did not at first expect him to understand the intricacies of grammar, or to know what he was reading about. He had to identify the Greek words which he had learnt and apply their general meaning. Beginning with Aesop's Fables, by the age of six he had read the entire works of Herodotus, and was reading Xenophon, Plato and Lucian. When John had mastered Greek, his father set aside an extra portion of the evenings to teach the elements of arithmetic, much to the boy's distaste. Until he was eight, apart from reading and writing, which were taken for granted, Greek and arithmetic were the only subjects which he was made to learn. In mathematics he soon outran his father, for the latter could not spare the time necessary to keep ahead of him. He was therefore left to solve his own problems, his father merely exhorting him to work faster. Unlike Pastor Witte, John's father had to earn his living, and was writing his *History of India* and articles for the press, while teaching his children.

Jeremy Bentham made his extensive library available to the boy. At five the boy was able to engage Lady Spencer in an animated comparison of Wellington and Marlborough. At six and a half he compiled from his own reading a history of Rome in 1,500 words.

At eight he was required to teach his young sister Wilhelmina Greek and arithmetic, and subsequently the other children. At eight he was now taught Latin in the same way as he had been taught Greek, and by the age of twelve he could read Cicero, Ovid, Livy, Virgil, Horace, Lucretius, Tacitus and Juvenal. Algebra and geometry were now added to the curriculum, followed at nine by conic sections, spheres and Newton's arithmetic. Astronomy and physics were in his curriculum at ten and he began to study philosophy and logic at twelve, with differential calculus. At twelve he could read Greek and Latin as easily as English. Political economy was added at thirteen.

By way of introducing him to poetry, his father used a new method. While John was struggling with a passage of the *Iliad*, he drew his attention to Pope's translation. John became devoted to it, reading it repeatedly, and trying to improve upon it himself. He was not required to waste his time in the composition of classical verses; instead he was encouraged to write English verse.

From Plato he learnt the Socratic method of enquiry, and so grew to recognise a fallacious argument. His father endeavoured to teach him oratory, by making him read aloud, and criticising his diction. 'He drew John's attention to the skill with which Athenian orators insinuated their ideas into the minds of their hearers at the moment when a gradual and persuasive preparation had ripened them for an acceptance of the unpalatable.' 'He also pressed him remorselessly with problems still beyond him, such as the syllogism, berating and taunting him for his incapacity, and never supplying him with the right answer until he was exhausted in trying to find it himself. In this way he contrived to make the understanding precede the fact, and avoid parrot knowledge even in this whirlwind syllabus. Precise thoughts were all Ten Commandments to James Mill. He strictly catechised his son for remarking that something was true in theory but required correction in practice: if the theory were true, he said, the practice was so inevitably true as to require no demonstration.'

It was, John wrote, 'a severe school; but,' he added, 'a pupil from whom nothing is ever demanded which he cannot do, never does all he can.'

When John was thirteen, his father decided that the boy had learnt all he could from lessons: the only thing left for him to learn was how to take his place with other boys. Prior to this John had been protected from all contact with other children. The only two boys who met John before this time are said to have recoiled from John in horror because of his lack of religious views. In his world 'there were no companions; it consisted entirely of principles, reasons and conclusions'.

At this stage his father decided that the boy should go to France. He took the boy for a walk and told him that on going into the world, there was something important for him to know; if it should appear to him that he was in some respects ahead of other boys, he must attribute it not to any virtue in himself, but to his good fortune in having a father to teach him so devotedly and well. When he was fourteen he went to Paris, to stay with Jeremy Bentham's brother. The change was a tremendous shock to John. He was bewildered by the lack of books. He was introduced to swimming, fencing and dancing. The time available for him to study his mathematics, classics and logics was whittled down, so that he could no longer study all of them on the same day. He clung desperately to his nine hour daily study period, and had to get up earlier and go to bed later. 'Lovingly, like a miser, he counted the fragmentary periods, dividing them up minute by minute between subjects, switching abruptly from one to another, resenting even the moments lost in changing over books. Gradually, he succumbed, and lessons stopped.'

At fifteen he returned to his family in Marlow.

Packe remarked: 'John Mill had been brought up on a definite plan, based on a psychological theory, intended to make him not merely a reasoning machine, but a machine that reasoned in a radical way. To that end he had been subjected to certain influences both intellectual and personal, and to that end he had been protected from all others. Up to his eighteenth birthday, the experiment was a complete success. His mental activity was enormous, and he delighted in it; his corporal pleasures had been severely limited to what was necessary for his life. Any display of emotion had been ruthlessly stamped out. Like a machine, he had no ideas of his own, not even a conscience of his own, and his intellect was all the stronger for being narrow. His brothers and sisters apart, he knew scarcely anyone of his own age or younger. He had never had a friend. From his autobiography his childhood emerges as a weary drudgery, and his home as cheerless, godless, silent and afraid.'

John himself believed that though the experiment achieved astonishing results in the intellectual part of his mind, at the same time it cramped other equally valuable facets of his nature. It is possible to suppose that the wholeness of the later man was reached because of, not in spite of, his beginnings.

Freehill, in writing about mentally superior children, remarked: 'It is interesting that after such a remarkable childhood environment, he [Mill] used his prodigious learning for such aims as the popular vote, women's rights, Universal education, proportional representation and free discussion. He was described as the strenuous advocate of warm and compassionate political theory dedicated to the elimination of human exploitation and despotism.'

Lord Tennyson was largely educated by his father—though

he later went to the school at Louth (Chapter 9). Before his father would pronounce him fit for going to school, he had to repeat by heart on successive mornings the four books of the *Odes of Horace*.

In his autobiography, *Anthony Trollope* wrote: 'My father constantly had an eye to my scholastic improvement. From my very babyhood, before those first days at Harrow, I had to take my place alongside of him as he shaved at six o'clock in the morning, and say my early rules from the Latin Grammar, or repeat the Greek alphabet; and was obliged at those early lessons to hold my head inclined towards him, so that in the event of guilty fault he might be able to pull my hair without stopping his razor or dropping his shaving brush. No father was ever more anxious for the education of his children. Of amusement he never recognised the need—though for our welfare he was willing to make any sacrifice.'

When the *Brontës'* mother was ill, Maria took over much of the early education of the other children. Winifred Gérin, in her biography of Branwell Brontë, tells how Branwell went to Haworth Grammar School for a short time, but was thought ill-suited for the rough and tumble of a village school and was removed. He did not lose much by leaving school, for his father was a better classical coach than the headmaster and had a passion for learning and a gift for teaching. By the time Branwell was ten he had assimilated the Homeric and Virgilian epics; Greek and Latin history, contemporary history; exploits of eighteenth- and nineteenth-century explorers; contemporary politics; and the whole field of English literature. Mr Brontë's great virtue lay in encouraging his children to read for themselves and in never restricting their reading, for they had absolute liberty to browse where they willed.

Dostoevsky's father was a doctor at a Moscow hospital. Coulson described the father as an exacting, impatient and irascible man. When he taught his sons Latin, they were not allowed to sit at the table or even lean against it, but had to stand for an hour or more. They dreaded the lessons because of their father's frequent and violent outbursts of anger. Eventually Dostoevsky was sent to a school of military engineering.

Lord Kelvin and his elder brother, James, received intensive home education by their father, formerly mathematics master at the Belfast Academy, and subsequently Professor of mathematics in the University of Glasgow. Kelvin's mother died when he was six. King, in his biography, described how young Kelvin's father then devoted all possible time to his sons' education; he literally lived with the boys, even sharing the same bedroom. He taught them to spell almost as soon as they could speak. He taught Kelvin geography when he was three, and then mathematics, history, and natural science. He rose at 4 a.m. to write books and prepare his lectures, so that he would have time to teach his children. When Kelvin was eight (and his brother ten) his father obtained permission for them to attend his own and other lectures at the University, and Kelvin was admitted as a regular student when he was ten, having matriculated. At this age he received two prizes for the Humanities, and next year the prize in Greek. Subsequently, he won prizes in mathematics, logic and astronomy. When twelve he won a prize for translating Lucian's dialogues of the gods with full parsing of the first three dialogues. He wrote shortly before his death in 1907: 'A boy should have learned by the age of twelve to write his own language with accuracy and some elegance. He should have a reading knowledge of French, should be able to translate Latin and easy Greek authors, and should have some acquaintance with German; having thus learned the meaning of words the boy should study logic.'

He was appointed to the Chair of Natural Philosophy at Glasgow at the age of twenty-two, subsequently becoming a great physicist.

Edmund Gosse, in his book *Father and Son*, described how

he was taught geography by his father. 'I was to climb upon a chair; while standing at my side with a pencil and a sheet of paper he was to draw a chart of the markings on the carpet. Then when I understood the system, another chart on a smaller scale of the furniture in the room, then of a floor of the house, then of the back garden, then of a section of the street. The result of all this was that geography came to me of itself, as a perfectly natural miniature arrangement of objects, and to this day has always been the science which gives me least difficulty.'

He was taught to read when he was four, together with the simple rules of arithmetic, natural history and drawing. 'He laboured long and unsuccessfully to make me learn by heart hymns, psalms and chapters of scripture, in which I always failed ignominiously and with tears.'

Although *Patrick Geddes*, future philosopher, teacher and scientist, went to the Perth Academy when he was eight, his father had taught him to read and write, and he supplemented his formal instruction by talks indoors and walks outside. Boardman, in his biography, wrote that every supper-time the father read aloud to the family from the Bible, or recited old Scottish ballads. It was these readings which first stirred Patrick's imagination; he was thrilled by the stories of Ezra and Nehemiah, of the building of Solomon's temple, and by many other Old Testament stories. One day his father took him to Perth to join the Mechanics' Library, which had a small but well chosen selection of books. To Patrick this was one of the greatest excitements and most enduring joys of his whole boyhood and youth; he was staggered by an impression of limitless riches when he first saw the shelves upon shelves of books. He immediately began to read at the outstanding rate of nine or ten books a week, in addition to doing all his school work. He kept this pace up for years, until, in his own words, he had devoured the home library and soaked up the public ones.

The whole of his boyhood can be summed up as an un-usually complete introduction to the worlds of action and thought under the intelligent guidance of the best teacher he ever had, his father.

At fifteen he was the recognised leader among the boys at the academy.

The father of the *Earl of Birkenhead* (F. E. Smith), was tire-less in his education of his son. He would challenge his son to give a completely accurate definition of some common English word, ruthlessly criticising any inaccuracy. F. E. Smith found that the more common the word, the more exacting became the task of dissection. In his biography of his famous father, the lawyer, the Earl of Birkenhead (Junior) wrote that the wonderful clarity of his father's later judgments were probably erected upon this sure foundation.

Nehru was educated entirely at home until he went to Harrow at the age of sixteen. He had a series of English governesses and tutors, an Irish tutor called Ferdinand Brookes, who developed in him a taste for reading and science, and an Indian tutor who taught him Hindi and Sanskrit.

Orde Wingate's father was a colonel and a member of the Plymouth Brethren. Sykes, in his interesting biography, described the early background and education.

'The home was a very bookish one, in which the pressure of work and learning was such as we read of in the early life of Macaulay or John Stuart Mill. The life of a public school-boy was in comparison one of leisure. Mrs Wingate taught the four eldest children the rudiments of reading, writing and elementary knowledge; they in turn taught those younger than themselves; while a governess was imported to advance matters onward from a primitive stage. In addition, school-masters and mistresses from the local grammar school called at the home to teach music, drawing, mathematics, French, Latin and Greek.

'The Colonel's brother, Sir Andrew Wingate, had strong

views, insisting that large maps be hung in the rooms where
the children worked. The children worked full school hours
every day, and though Sunday was very much set apart, it
was not a day of idle repose.

'The morning of Sunday was taken up with religious devo-
tions, and the afternoon with one of the main family interests,
the study of the Bible. The children would assemble round
a table for sacred reading and doctrinal exposition by the
parents, followed by lighter readings from such publications
as *The War Cry* (the magazine of the Salvation Army). Later
in the day they were allowed to colour black and white drawings depicting episodes of Bible history. From these pious
Sunday afternoons a family custom grew; part solemn, part
play, for the children to master a chapter of the Old Testament in the Authorised Version sufficiently well to be able to
read it through and recite some of it by heart. When the test
was passed to the satisfaction of the parents a copy of the Bible
was presented.

'Orde had already dislocated the educational regime of the
household by his inability to learn reading from his mother,
and he again showed himself behind the others in his slowness
with the scriptures. He remained perversely slow at his books.
Then suddenly he learnt to read.

'It is difficult to know whether this was a happy home or
the reverse. The children certainly groaned at the long hours
of study to which they were condemned, at the excessive
church going, and the forbidding of all luxuries of food.

'The most extraordinary feature of the Wingate family life,
which in its merits and defects belonged so entirely to the
19th century, was its insularity, and especially the segregation
of the children from others. It has been calculated by one of
them that for six years, from 1909 to 1915, they met hardly
more than half a dozen other persons of their own age. There
were no outings with others who were not of their family,
no football and cricket, no sight of the human world beyond

the family gates. This segregation was carefully planned, it being the belief of the parents that contact with people outside the family would exert a corrupting effect on the souls of their teaching.

'It is not fanciful to see in this circumstance some of the beginning of his lifelong rebelliousness.'

When he was eleven the family moved to Godalming so that they could be near Orde when at school. The aim was that he should have the best education without the dangers attaching to residence in a Public School away from the brethren; and at twelve he went to Charterhouse as a day boy.

COMMENT

Perhaps the most remarkable feature of many of these accounts is the erudition of the parents, and their tireless devotion in teaching their children. They were able to teach their children to an advanced stage in a wide variety of subjects, so that they were able to surpass, often by a wide margin, those who had been educated in the more usual way at school. Such methods may lead to intellectual advancement, but one feels that the cost in terms of loss of the joy, happiness and adaptability derived from play and association with other children must have been enormous, and irreparable. John Stuart Mill, John Ruskin (Chapter 1), John Keble, and Orde Wingate, were all isolated from their fellows, and were unable to learn the rough and tumble of everyday life, the pleasures of childhood and of play with children of their own age.

Nevertheless, one should not be too critical of some of these parents. It would certainly seem to have been wrong of Jeremy Bentham's father to deprive his son of all books except those of an 'edifying nature'. It would seem to be more reasonable to bring children up in such a way that they know the difference between good and bad literature, and that because of their tastes and interests, which have been fostered by the home environment, they will prefer the good to the bad.

On the other hand, it is wrong to deprive a highly intelligent child of the material for learning, such as books. Many parents fear that a child may learn to read too soon. There is no truth in this, provided that he is developmentally ready to learn to read, and that he wants to read. To deprive him of the opportunity to read is to deprive him of a great pleasure. In Chapter 7 we have given several examples of children who were reading well at the age of three, and enjoying it. It would be mistaken to criticise the father of Blaise Pascal, or the guardian of William Hamilton (Chapter 8) for enabling their charges to learn unusually early.

It is important that children should be encouraged to want to learn. Bloom, in the United States, has adduced evidence that much of the pattern of learning is established in the pre-school years. Madame Montessori long ago realised the importance of teaching children at the time when they were interested in learning, and before they have lost interest. Learning should be a pleasure and not a duty. The father of Edmund Gosse made geography interesting. Carl Witte's father took care to make Carl enjoy what he was learning; he understood well the meaning of motivation. The same cannot be said of the teaching which John Ruskin or John Stuart Mill had to endure; they hated much of the home instruction which they received. There is something seriously wrong when learning becomes a painful duty.

It is a truism that if too little is expected of a child, little is likely to be achieved; if too much is expected of him, he is likely to be frustrated, to feel worried because he cannot live up to the expectations and aspirations of his parents, and to feel a sense of defeat. We have given examples of both degrees of expectation. Somewhere in between is the right amount of stimulation needed for each individual child. This must depend on his intelligence, personality, aptitudes and abilities, and on the way in which he is taught, the interest which the teacher can arouse in his pupil, and the interest which the teacher himself feels in imparting his knowledge and implanting in his charges the pleasure of learning and the desire to learn.

CHAPTER 3

UNRECOGNISED ABILITY

THOUGH many of the children who were destined to be famous showed obvious ability in the early years, impressing their parents and teachers alike, many others showed no outstanding qualities at all—or at least their talents and promise went unnoticed, or their significance was unrecognised. Some were thought to be positively backward at school—some merely in certain subjects, some in every-thing. Some were quite good in some subjects, or even out-standingly good, but they were so outstandingly bad in other subjects that it was never thought that their overall prospects were bright. Some of the derogatory opinions described below may have been expressed in moments of pique, and not really meant, though it is probable that most of the opinions to be described were sincere. We are not quite sure whether the father of Ralph Emerson was really serious when he com-plained that his son was 'rather a dull scholar' and 'was not reading very well' when he was a mere two years old.

We think it is true to say that with the exception of musicians, mathematicians and perhaps artists, the majority of children destined to become eminent were not thought to show un-usual promise at school. It may be argued that as the training of teachers is so much better now than it used to be, such failures to recognise future genius are likely to be less frequent now than formerly. That may be, but we suspect that many boys and girls, destined to reach positions of eminence, will continue to be thought by their teachers and parents to be backward or no better than ordinary.

In many cases, it was not just the poor performance at school which made it appear unlikely that certain children would ever achieve renown: it was partly their humble beginnings; the lowly nature of the work which they were doing, or their general behaviour, which made the outlook for these children look so bleak.

Samuel Smiles, discussing the unpromising childhood of some famous men, wrote: 'One wouldn't expect the ill-used sickly boy, serving beer in a German Cabaret, to become the philosopher and astronomer Kepler, one of the greatest men of his time; or the young soldier, who spent his youth in battles and sieges, to be the great Descartes, one of the most original of thinkers; or that Clive, that "Leader of rapscallions, robber of orchards, climber of church steeples"—would achieve such fame, and become founder of the Indian Empire.' He added that two of the most reckless young gamblers in France eventually became the greatest cardinals and statesmen of their time—Cardinal Richelieu and Mazarin.

We are going to describe the unpromising childhood of many famous men and women under the subjects in which they later acquired eminence—art, music, science, writing, politics, and the art of war, with an unclassified section. We have enumerated some famous men who were expelled from their University, much to the dismay of their parents: and concluded with a brief section which describes the unfavourable opinions expressed by some parents about their children who were destined to be famous.

ARTISTS

Leonardo da Vinci neglected his school studies, partly because of his interest in nature, and partly because his father was away a great deal and was not able to supervise him. Vallentin wrote that Leonardo was to suffer throughout his life from the defective educational grounding due to his failure to take what opportunities there were in the local school. He wrote that the immense store of knowledge which he accumulated later was self taught, and he had painfully to acquire first elements at a time when he was more concerned with final results. He did not know what he was losing (or gaining!) when he neglected his wearisome and unintelligible school books for the sake of direct observation and experience.

From an early age he refused to permit anyone of his family to enter his room—a foible which remained with him all his life.

The childhood drawings of *Sir Joshua Reynolds* were regarded as the least promising of the family. All the Reynolds children were fond of drawing and painting. They used to draw with burnt sticks on the walls of a long passage. In his ordinary school work Joshua was no scholar. He neglected his studies, and took no trouble to learn spelling and grammar. *Gauguin* did not start painting until adult life. In his school work he was inclined to dream, and was completely indifferent to what was being taught. He was a poor pupil and his progress was slow. Of *Turner* it was said that 'It is much to be doubted whether the finest education would have entirely freed him from a liability to incoherency. His brain was naturally misty.' His education was inadequate, and this was to cause him much embarrassment in later years.

Edouard Manet caused his father, a judge, considerable anxiety because he was not working hard enough at school and appeared to be making no progress whatever. He was a well behaved boy, but was deplorably inattentive. He was moved to an aristocratic boarding school at Paris. There his teacher wrote: 'The boy is backward, but he is showing zeal, and we have great hopes of him.' He was near the bottom in every subject, however. In Latin prose he was never higher than forty-second out of sixty-two and sometimes as low as fifty-seventh. He showed very little interest in his studies. Another teacher described him as being altogether a little slow, and needing more application and drive, though he had shown himself willing. He was not moved up into the next form with the other boys.

Van Gogh provided no evidence of genius at his school at

Zevenbergen. He was remembered only by one peculiarity —his refusal to sit at the table at mealtimes. He always wanted to go into a corner by himself and eat a piece of bread.

Picasso's father was worried by Pablo's backwardness, especially in arithmetic. The boy had to confess to an examiner that he knew absolutely nothing. He had a peculiar difficulty in remembering the sequence of the alphabet—a difficulty which he never lost.

MUSICIANS

Musical genius was not always recognised in the early years.

Beethoven's tutor, Albrechtsberger, who was trying to teach him composition, said: 'Beethoven never has learned anything and never will learn anything. As a composer he is hopeless.' Haydn taught him for a time, but was unable to see any talent in him.

Rossini was described as a lazy little boy, who preferred doing nothing to any definite pursuits. *Verdi* was rejected by the Conservatoire at Milan, to which he applied for entry.

Though *Paderewski* was fond of music, he showed no particular promise in the early years. It was said that at school the only thing he did not care for was work. When he was twelve he went to Warsaw to complete his musical education, but his masters were not impressed by his talent.

In his general work, *Sir Edward Elgar* did not show any early signs of unusual ability. There seemed to be nothing which singled him out from the rest of the family as being worthy of special attention. *Sibelius* was inattentive. A teacher said: 'Janne found it difficult to sit still during lessons and listen to things that did not interest him in the least. He sat, buried in thought, and would be quite absent-minded when questioned suddenly.' *Sir Henry Wood* wrote that at school he learned very little, for he was not a brilliant scholar—though he did carry off every prize for painting, drawing and music. *Frederick Delius* was an indifferent scholar at the Grammar School,

Bradford. He learnt little, spending all his available time reading tales of the Wild West and crime thrillers.

SCIENTISTS

Many of the world's greatest scientists showed little or no promise at school.

Sir Isaac Newton was for a time bottom in the lowest form but one at the Grammar School at Grantham. He was inattentive and a bad scholar, but in later years he improved and worked his way to the top of his class.

James Watt excelled neither in lessons nor in games, and was described as being 'dull and inept'. Some of his teachers thought that he was backward for his age, though others recognised some ability. He began to show definite signs of ability at school when he was thirteen. Nevertheless, his early interests in drawing, described in Chapter 7, showed definite indications of his real quality.

Humboldt, the naturalist, made little progress at school, and was slow in learning, though his great interest in collecting and cataloguing flowers, butterflies, beetles and shells was a pointer to his future career.

Fresnel, the natural philosopher, was a dull boy at school. It was with difficulty that he could be taught to read. He showed no ability until he was twenty-five, when he made his great discoveries on light.

Johann Berzelius, the Swedish chemist, showed no promise at school and was in no way outstanding in his medical studies at Uppsala: yet at twenty-three he had acquired fame for his chemical researches.

Charles Darwin wrote: 'I was considered by all my masters and by my father as a very ordinary boy, rather below the common standard in intellect.' He was slower than his sister in learning. Slow maturation was in fact a feature of the Darwin family, which produced Fellows of the Royal Society in five successive generations; they were late developers, and tended to show no real distinction until the postgraduate stage at the University, into which they had found entry difficult.

Thomas Huxley wrote: 'I worked extremely hard when it pleased me, and when it did not, which was a very frequent case, I was extremely idle.'

Edison was always at the bottom of his class, and his father thought that he was stupid. One day his teacher said that his mind was addled. The boy heard it, stormed out of the class and refused to return. His mother fortunately did not believe that he was as dull as the teacher said, and taught him herself. He was, in fact, a clever boy. It is said that when he was eleven or twelve he could refer to the exact page of a book describing anything which he had read.

Marconi said that he was not a clever boy at school, and that his early school days were not marked by any brilliance; but his obvious mechanical ability, described in Chapter 7, showed that he had some aptitude.

Albert Einstein at the age of nine was regarded by his classmates as an amiable dreamer. He had not shown any evidence of special talent. His father was distressed by the teacher's reports that the boy was 'mentally slow, unsociable and adrift forever in his foolish dreams'. He was good at literature and arithmetic, because he found them interesting, but he sat through his language and history lessons without learning anything. He did not even pretend to be learning, and his inattentiveness infuriated his teachers. They called him 'Herr Langwill', Mr Dullard. Nevertheless, he had mastered Euclid, Newton, Spinoza and Descartes before he was fifteen. 'He had', he said, 'a furious impulse to understand and to be informed.' It is surprising that his ability was not recognised.

It seems that many world famous medical men were particularly unpromising at school.

William Smellie, the famous obstretician, wrote that he was very idle and dull at school, and was much more interested in carving and painting than in books.

John Hunter was described at Kilbride as being impenetrable to anything in the way of book learning. This was probably due largely to his special difficulty in learning to read (Chapter 4). His exasperated teachers 'finally wrote him off as an idle surly dullard, irredeemable by punishment or reward'. When he was taken away from school at the age of thirteen, at the end of his formal education, he could barely write coherent English, and he had acquired a considerable distaste for work. A niece said that 'he would do nothing but what he liked, and neither liked to be taught reading nor writing nor any kind of learning'. He had his own views on his future, saying: 'When I am dead, you will not soon meet with another John Hunter.'

Sir Astley Cooper was an idle boy. The teaching of his mother, his father and the village schoolmaster, who taught him mathematics, made little impression on him.

Claude Bernard, the physiologist, was described by his teacher as only an average student, who never liked to read. Reading seemed to him to be a waste of valuable time.

Louis Pasteur was conscientious and worked hard but learnt slowly. He was only a mediocre pupil. In the Baccalaureat at Dijon when twenty years old, he was fifteenth out of twenty-two in chemistry.

Röntgen was not a bright pupil. There was nothing in the youth which pointed to future genius, though he did show an aptitude for mechanical contrivances.

The famous Spanish neurohistologist, *Ramon Y. Cajal*, the son of a country physician, was a source of great anxiety to his father, who feared that his artistically inclined son would never earn his living. Haymaker, in his book on the Founders of Neurology, wrote: 'A wandering artist said he had no talent, A barber and shoemaker, to whom he was finally apprenticed, said he was crazy. Salvation came through his love of drawing, which first led him to anatomy and then to medicine.'

Sir James Mackenzie wrote: 'The things that I remember most clearly about my school education were that I was considered a dunce at most of my classes, and that the subjects in which I did well were those in which my understanding, rather than my memory, was called into play.' He was undistinguished at school. At the University he had difficulty in passing his examinations.

Sir Ronald Ross was an idle medical student at Barts, qualifying with difficulty, and passing low in the list. He wrote: 'I must confess that the medical profession and all its associates and associations were little to my taste or inclination.' When he should have been studying medicine, he was writing poetry, stories, plays, composing music, painting or doing sculpture. He went into the Indian Medical Service on qualifying.

Carl Jung wrote: 'most of my teachers thought me stupid and crafty'. He was extremely upset when a teacher said that his essay was the best, but that he must have copied it from someone. Jung said that he was less intelligent, less hardworking, attentive, decent and clean than many of the other boys. He complained that whenever anything went wrong in school he was the one on whom suspicion rested. 'If there was a row somewhere, I was thought to be the instigator.' In reality he was only once involved in a brawl.

WRITERS AND POETS

Jean de la Fontaine was described by his teachers as a 'well disposed but hopeless dunce'. His mental qualities were slow to develop, and his gifts lay dormant. He seemed to find a melancholy pleasure in idling away his time. He was not unintelligent, but he had peculiar interests, and no amount of discipline succeeded in making him like other boys. He was virtually unknown until he was forty-four.

Jonathan Swift entered Trinity College Dublin when he was fifteen. He turned a deaf ear to his teachers, neglected his studies, and reading as whim and accident directed, was not ready to take his final examination, which he failed at the age of eighteen. He was allowed to resume his studies, but when he proceeded to absent himself from Chapel and roll call, to neglect his lectures, and to associate with a gang of dissolute and idle youths, he was publicly censured for his behaviour. He was described by his examiners as dull and inefficient. His *Tale of a Tub*, published when he was thirty-seven, made him famous.

Oliver Goldsmith was described by his teachers as impenetrably stupid, and a 'stupid heavy blockhead, little better than a fool, whom everybody made fun of'. 'There never was such a dull boy.' Nevertheless, he showed his interest early, for he was constantly writing verses. Johnson described him as 'a plant that flowered late'—and added that there was nothing remarkable about him when he was young. His ungainly appearance made him the butt of his school. He went to Trinity College at seventeen, but made little progress, and graduated lowest in the list of B.A.s in the year. He then went to Edinburgh to study medicine. At twenty-eight he was employed by an apothecary in London, and then went to teach in a school. At thirty he sat an examination of the Royal College of Surgeons and failed. Finally at thirty-six he wrote his *Vicar of Wakefield*—and became famous.

Thomas Chatterton, the poet, was sent to school at the age of five, but was soon sent home as a 'confirmed dullard'. He did well, however, at another school when older.

Wordsworth alone of the four sons gave his guardians anxiety about his scholastic progress. Even at Cambridge, when seventeen years old, his genius was not suspected by himself or by others.

Sheridan was 'by common consent of both parents and preceptor pronounced to be a most impenetrable dunce'.

Sir Walter Scott did not give a good impression at school. He was unmanageable, and attended infrequently. His school performance was below average, but a discerning teacher would have noted the fact that he was intensely interested in reading.

Lord Byron found little to interest him at Harrow, apart from sport. He declared that his pursuits at school were cricketing, rebelling, rowing and mischief. He attended irregularly, but when he did attend he did well. He was clearly intelligent.

Honoré de Balzac was given up by his teachers as a failure, and abandoned to his dreams. One of them said: 'This fat little fellow goes around in a state of intellectual coma.' He was idle and disobedient, and was sent to another school, where his behaviour was no better.

Thomas Carlyle left the University at eighteen without a degree.

John Keats was just an ordinary happy school boy, with no evidence of unusual ability until his later years. At the age of fifteen or sixteen he suddenly developed a passion for books. He published his first poetry when twenty-one and his last at twenty-four, the year of his death.

George Borrow was said to be 'slow of comprehension and almost dull witted'. He was not interested in books. When he was six, he was very observant of things which interested him, but showed no interest in other things. When he was thirteen he went to the Grammar School at Norwich, where he was idle and made poor progress.

Hans Andersen was the despair of his teachers because of his propensity for day dreaming; he paid very little attention to them.

Charles Thackeray was 'less than mediocre' and showed no distinction in either work or sport. At Charterhouse, his teachers constantly nagged at him, calling him an idle, profligate shuffling boy. A teacher remarked: 'If only somebody could stir him out of his laziness. Why, this fellow could do anything, if he chose, but he never chooses.' In his letters from Charterhouse he always confessed how lazy he was, and promised to be industrious tomorrow. He never settled down to anything at school or University, so that he never became good at anything. After two years at the University he was expelled because of unsatisfactory work.

Conrad Ferdinand Meyer, the Swiss poet, was unique with regard to his early development. Unfortunately there is no biography in English about him. We are indebted to Kretschmer, for the following details of his career, and to Dr Heinz Herzka of Zürich for translating various biographies from the German.

Conrad Meyer was born at Kilchberg, near Zürich. His father taught history at the local college, and had very little time for his children. Five years after his birth his sister Betsy was born—and he became very closely attached to her. There was also an adopted mentally defective child. Conrad's mother was a neurotic, overprotective, fanatically religious woman, with strict Calvinistic beliefs. She had a nervous breakdown after giving birth to him. She had severe headaches every day with fits of depression and melancholy, and declared that her bad nerves could not be cured by the consolation of religion. She would not allow any of her children to kiss her. Frey, in his biography, wrote that Meyer was only delivered from his mother when she committed suicide—when he was thirty-one years old. Other biographies emphasised the abnormality of this mother-child relationship. His father died when Conrad was fifteen.

At first Conrad did well at school, and was nearly top of the class. At six, however, he developed what was said to be rubella (German measles). Whether or not he had encephalitis as a complication of this, we do not know, but he was seriously ill, given numerous medicines, lost weight, and became completely different in personality, losing his previous joyous and carefree behaviour, becoming silent, morose, introverted and melancholic. His work at school seriously deteriorated. He could not concentrate, persistently day-dreamed, and indulged in excessive fantasy thinking. When six or seven he said to his mother: 'I often think who am I? What is the world? But I can find no answer.' If he started a task and found it difficult, he would immediately give it up. Consequently he rarely completed his homework, or read a book through. When he was eight, many wondered that a boy from such a good family should act so strangely.

When fifteen, he took up law, but soon gave it up, not knowing what he really wanted to do.

Meyer had a peculiar disturbance of skull growth with an unusually broad head, and his bodily development was retarded. Until his fortieth year he was stunted and thin, and it was not until he was forty that his beard began to grow and his figure acquired normal proportions. It was only then that his poems appeared. As Kretschmer put it: 'A paradoxical functioning of the endocrine glands turned the whole course of his development topsy-turvy, for his youth was the deepest winter of his life, and spring came to him only in the later years of manhood.' Meyer wrote:

> I was as one bound by a heavy spell
> Life had not reached me; I lay stiffly in dream.
> And now a thousand unused hours
> Swirl boisterously around me.

Kretschmer wrote: 'Up to forty he was an ungifted eccentric son of a highly respected family.' At one time his mother wrote: 'My poor son remains always in practically the same condition. He retains his melancholy disposition and his incorrigible incapacity to take up any regular work. He suffers much from his inability to aim at any goal or take up any career, or in any way make up his mind. I am compelled to admit that I have come to expect nothing more of him in this world.'

Shy of human beings, dejected, wrapped in dreams and bitterly confined within himself, he wandered here and there, tried this and that, all to no avail. He wanted to be a painter, then a poet and a lawyer, but in no field did he show real talent.

'Friends of the family had to look after him, and his mother was much concerned to provide the cost of his living. He had a large lonely garden in which he used to walk alone, always threading the same snake-like path around the lawns, disappearing deep within the shrubbery and taking to flight instantly if he unexpectedly encountered anyone. In the end people took him for dead, for he never showed himself and only went out at night on lonely wanderings through the empty streets.'

Even in times of momentary happiness he would be suddenly seized by an acute nervous anxiety; he would burst into tears and be unable to answer any questions. He disliked having any bodily contact with people and when anyone greeted him he would offer only two fingers of the right hand.

He was admitted to a lunatic asylum for the first time in his twenty-seventh year. There he suffered from melancholy, hypochondria and insane delusions, in which he believed, for example, that 'all people found him disgusting and afflicted with noisome breath'. 'The feeling took hold of him', said a friend, 'that he lived in the midst of emptiness. He had actually no real contact with life but floated about in the web of his own brain, having no duties, no social life and no order in his daily life. He despaired of himself and came near to making a deliberate end to his life.'

'Then suddenly, at forty, all was changed, and he blossomed forth into poetry, writing for the next twenty-seven years.' 'Never was any mother more justified in thinking that her boy would never achieve anything; nothing seemed more unlikely than that he would acquire such fame in the world.'

Dante Gabriel Rossetti, according to Waugh, did not leave any particular impression on King's College School. He was said to be dreamy, timid and bored there. Waugh wrote that 'with his imagination captured by the richer education of his

home, he regarded his work and play as a tiresome inter-
ruption'. He learned some Latin and a little Greek. He
already knew Italian, French, and German. He abhorred
mathematics and science. He left at fourteen and went to
Cary's Academy. Here he spent four years of 'irregular
application, often wasting days in fits of idleness, writing a
great deal of verse, reading and translating the Italian poets,
picking up odd prints cheap, visiting art exhibitions, scheming
to buy an easel, and, between times working hard at the pro-
bationary drawing necessary to secure admission to the
academy school'.

Christina Rossetti had little interest in books or work, and
was regarded as less intelligent than her three siblings. Her
brother said that of science and philosophy she knew nothing,
and for history she had no inclination.

Anthony Trollope said that from the first to the last there was
nothing satisfactory about his school career—except the way
he defeated a bully in a fight and caused him to be taken home
for treatment.

Leo Tolstoy had many troubles at school. His teacher said
of the three brothers that 'Sergei is willing and able, Dimitri
is willing, but not able and Leo is both unwilling and unable'
(to learn). He would not concentrate on anything but poetry.

Émile Zola was a poor student at his school at Aix, and he
was no better at the École Normale in Paris. He cut his
classes, and refused to recite when called upon. He devoted
all his time to writing poetry and reading, but in his final
examination he scored zero for literature.

Yeats was thought to be mentally subnormal, largely because
of his special difficulty in reading. He said: 'because I had
found it hard to attend to anything less interesting than my
thoughts, I was difficult to teach'.

Chekhov made poor progress at school, and failed his
terminal examinations in the third and fifth forms.

It was said of *Rudyard Kipling* that he was distinguished only for his precocious moustache, 'an early spring growth of black hair that had sprouted on his upper lip at the age of twelve. Otherwise he showed nothing, either physically or mentally, which singled him out from the other students.' Nevertheless, he was an omnivorous reader—a clue to intelligence.

G. K. Chesterton achieved no distinction at school. One of his teachers said 'we thought him the most curious thing that ever was'. His chief occupation consisted of drawing all over his books, making caricatures of his masters and colleagues. His schoolfellows at St Pauls would see him 'striding along, apparently muttering poetry, breaking into inane laughter'. Ward wrote: 'perhaps most surprising is that all this does not seem to have made clear to either masters or parents the true nature of Gilbert's vocation. He suffered at this date from having too many talents. For he still went on drawing and his drawings seemed to many the most remarkable thing about him, and were certainly the thing he most enjoyed doing.' When he was eighteen a teacher wrote that 'his compositions were mostly futile'. He was grossly obese, bit his nails, consistently had dirty hands and a running nose. His teacher declared that if anyone were to open Chesterton's head, he would find nothing but a lump of fat.

POLITICIANS, STATESMEN, SOLDIERS

Hernando Cortez, the conqueror of Mexico, was a poor student. At the University of Salamanca, where he was studying law, he showed himself to be unsuited for the career which his parents had chosen for him, and he was threatened with expulsion. As for *Robert Clive*, Macaulay said that the general opinion of him was that he was a dunce. There can be no doubt, however, that in later childhood he did show his true ability. *Mirabeau* achieved practically nothing at school except in mathematics, for most of his regular school work did not appeal to his imagination.

Napoleon Bonaparte was in no way outstanding at school, and left forty-second in placing. At the age of sixteen, his certificate gave the following report: 'Reserved and laborious, he is more fond of study than of any pleasure. He likes to read good authors. He is very diligent in abstract sciences, but makes little inquiry into others. He knows thoroughly mathematics and geography; he is silent, loves solitude, obstinate, haughty, exceptionally given to egoism, talks little, is energetic in his answers, prompt in action, and severe in meeting opposition; he has much self esteem, and is ambitious. This young man is worthy of being favoured' (Terman and Oden).

The Duke of Wellington made only slow progress at school. In one examination he was fifty-third out of seventy-nine.

Gladstone made no special impression in his first three years at Eton. He described himself as a slow developer. He said: 'There was more in me perhaps than in the average boy, but it required greatly more time to set itself in order. I have no recollection of being a loving or a winning child, or an earnest or diligent or knowledge-loving child. I cannot in truth have been an interesting child. I was not a devotional child. Neither was I a popular boy though not egregiously otherwise. If I was not a bad boy, I think I was a boy with a great absence of goodness.'

Joseph Chamberlain was a hard worker at school and did well, without being in any way remarkable or exceptional. A teacher said that he did not care much for games. He was industrious and intelligent, but rather too anxious about his lessons. He left school at sixteen. At eighteen, he was a member of a debating society at Birmingham. It is said that his speeches were not particularly good, and his delivery was bad. He did not become a good speaker by natural facility or anything else but an unfailing systematic determination to learn.

Earl Baldwin obtained a third class in his degree at Trinity.

He had not been distinguished at school. This poor performance was ascribed indirectly to a grievance at Harrow, where he got into trouble over some boyish pranks and as a result was not made a prefect. Stanley Baldwin felt that this was most unjust, and when he went up to Cambridge and found that the headmaster had become Master there, he dropped classics and took up history, slacking in it, and doing badly as a result.

The story of *Winston Churchill's* school days is well known. When his Latin entrance examination paper was handed in at Harrow it was found to contain nothing but a figure one in brackets, two smudges and a blot. The headmaster accepted him because he did not think that Lord Randolph's son could be so stupid. He passed into Harrow at the bottom of the lowest form, and never moved out of the lower school for the whole of the five years he was there. He remained perpetually bottom of the class, and did not excel in sport. At his former school he had been described by his teacher, Miss Moore, as 'a small red headed pupil, the naughtiest boy in his class. I used to think he was the naughtiest boy in the world.' Churchill wrote, concerning his days at Harrow: 'my teachers saw me at once backward and precocious, reading books beyond my years and yet at the bottom of the form. They were offended.' It is interesting to read that although he was in the lowest form, he won the first prize open to the whole school for reciting 1,200 lines of Macaulay's *Lays of Ancient Rome*.

Franklin Roosevelt was undistinguished at school. He was liked by his teachers, and thought to be quite intelligent, but not brilliant. He was not particularly successful in sport.

Concerning *Ernest Bevin*, it was said that no one at school would have thought that he would become any more than a manual labourer, or at most a shop assistant.

Nehru was just an ordinary boy at Harrow. He was described as a 'well behaved quiet boy, who gave no trouble', although he was never an exact fit there.

Aneurin Bevan was not thought to show promise. His headmaster called him lazy and kept him down for a year with younger boys. At Sunday School he was a disturbing element, and one teacher is said to have threatened to resign if he stayed on as a pupil.

Orde Wingate showed no signs of exceptional gifts or unusual qualities. He was said to be 'just an ordinary difficult little boy'. His biographer wrote: 'Throughout his childhood and youth he showed no extraordinary proficiency, no unusual alertness of mind, no exceptional gifts. None of his friends had reason to guess he was to be anyone outstanding. He seemed to be one of hundreds of difficult little boys, singular only in the very singular circumstances of the family life from which he came' (Chapter 1). At Charterhouse he was undistinguished in work, sport and the Officers Training Corps. His biographer wrote that there is now a memorial to him in the Chapel Porch. 'It must have seemed as probable then that marble trophies or princely monuments were to be created to celebrate the man who mowed the lawn or the boy who blacked the boots.' One of his contemporaries recalls him as being 'a small uncommunicative scalliwag with a stooping gate'.

SOME OTHER LEADERS

Thomas Cranmer, Archbishop of Canterbury, was thirty-second in place out of forty-two in the B.A. examination in Cambridge, after an undistinguished career.

Bishop Warburton, critic and divine, was regarded at school as a really stupid boy, and one of his teachers described him as 'the dullest of all dull scholars'. Smiles records that when taxed by a friend as being dull and inattentive, Warburton said: 'I know very well what you and others think of me, but I believe that I shall, one day or other, convince the world that I am not so ignorant or so great a fool as I am believed to be.'

When he wrote his *Divine Legation*, his former teacher found it difficult to believe that 'so great a work could proceed from so thick a skull'.

Heinrich Pestalozzi was an awkward clumsy boy at school, with little promise. He came from a good home, but his mother was left in great poverty by the death of her husband when the boy was only five. Heinrich was not allowed to play in the street, in case his clothes should be damaged. He was a weakling, and behaved awkwardly when he met other boys, and was laughed at by them. He was constantly the butt of practical jokes, and when he was nine or ten he was nicknamed 'Harry Queer of Foolstown'.

His spelling was bad, his writing poor, and he had no head for arithmetic. His teachers predicted that he would be a failure. Little did they realise that his name would live on for generations after his death, and that his fame would arise from his revolutionary ideas of teaching—which included the modern idea of motivation, making the work interesting and relating it to everyday life. He also did a great deal towards the teaching of the poor.

Dr Alexander Murray, the son of a shepherd near Kirkcudbright, was considered by his father to be both stupid and lazy. Smiles wrote that he was always committing some blunder or other when sent to herd the sheep or bring the cattle home. In his first seventeen years he had not received more than thirteen months' formal education in all. His father had taught him the alphabet, and then, by the age of fifteen the boy had taught himself Latin, Greek, French and Hebrew, and was soon able to read Caesar, Ovid and Livy. He left the farm, and learned German, Anglo-Saxon, Abyssinian, Visigothic and Welsh, and subsequently the whole of the European languages. He then began research into the more recondite dialects of the East, and at thirty he was the most accomplished linguist of his time. He became Professor of Oriental Languages in Edinburgh at thirty-six.

Karl Marx was a competent but not brilliant pupil. He was said in his report to be very satisfactory in ancient languages, German and History, satisfactory in mathematics, but only moderate in French.

Baden-Powell was popular at school, but did not stand out in work or sport. He managed occasionally to be twelfth in a class of fifteen, but also succeeded in being nineteenth out of nineteen. The headmaster reassured Mrs Baden-Powell that 'your son's ability is greater than would appear by the results of the quarter. I am well satisfied with his conduct and hope that he will work enough to ensure himself against super-annuation at sixteen.' His reports continued to deteriorate and comments such as the following were mentioned by his biographer: 'In classics—seems to me to take very little interest in his work. Mathematics—has to all intents given up the study of mathematics. Natural science—paid not the slightest attention except in one week at the beginning of the quarter. French—could do well but has become very lazy. He often sleeps in school.'

When he applied to Balliol College, Oxford, he was rejected as being unsuitable. He tried at Christchurch, with the same result. His examiner in mathematics was Professor Dodgson (Lewis Carroll). Baden-Powell wrote: 'he found out what I could already have told him, but what I hoped he would not discover for himself, that it was a subject about which I knew little or nothing'.

There was consternation at home when he was refused admission at Oxford. His father had been professor there, his brother George had won the Chancellor's prize, and his brother Frank had won a scholarship to Balliol. He thereupon decided to take the open examination for commissions in the army, and out of 718 examined, was placed fifth for infantry, and second in cavalry. His mother was delighted, and wrote to Oxford to tell them of the opportunity which they had missed.

Lord Beaverbrook, because of his inability to concentrate, was never expected by his teacher to make any great success of life.

Margaret Murray, famous Egyptologist, and one of the first woman dons, wrote in her autobiography that she did badly at school, while her sister was always top. 'I never got through any examination in my life', she wrote, 'until I took the full doctorate.' 'May, of course, distinguished herself by passing with honours all the examinations in the courses of lectures that we attended, while I equally failed to get even the minimum number of marks for a pass.'

EXPULSION—FROM SCHOOL AND UNIVERSITY

Hernando Cortez was probably sent down from the University of Salamanca on account of poor work in his law studies.

William Penn was expelled from Christchurch, Oxford, because of his religious beliefs, his refusal to conform with the religious practices of the college, and because of the religious meetings which he held in his rooms.

Some 150 years later *Shelley* was to be expelled from Oxford on account of militant atheism.

Samuel Johnson, on returning to Lichfield Grammar School six months late, after having had a pleasant and interesting time with friends, was refused readmission and went to Stourbridge School.

Edgar Allen Poe was expelled from West Point Military Academy.

James Whistler was expelled from West Point because of failure in chemistry.

Charles Makepeace Thackeray, after two years at Cambridge was sent down without a degree.

William Röntgen was expelled from school in Utrecht at sixteen for a harmless prank. Before class one of his friends had drawn a caricature of the teacher. The teacher arrived unexpectedly, saw the picture, and was very angry. He asked

Röntgen to name the culprit, but Röntgen refused to do so. The teacher threatened him with expulsion, and eventually had him expelled. Röntgen realised that this would make it difficult for him to obtain entrance to a University, and he worked hard at home for the purpose. On the day before the entrance examination the teacher who was in charge and who was favourable to Röntgen became ill, and was replaced by a teacher who had taken part in the suspension proceedings. Admission was therefore refused. At seventeen, however, he gained entrance to the Technical School at Utrecht, and later to the University there.

Guy de Maupassant was expelled from a clerical seminary at Yvetot after a drinking bout in which he drank the Father Superior's wine.

Sickert was expelled from University College School, London, after he was said to have sold doughnuts to other boys at a profit—a heinous sin which was denied by Sickert. He went to the Bayswater Collegiate School, Notting Hill, instead.

Albert Einstein was sent for one day and told it would be desirable if he were to leave school. When Albert asked what offence he had committed, he was told that his presence in the class was having a disruptive effect on the other students.

Of the evil men, described in Chapter 13, *Mussolini* was expelled from school for stabbing a boy; and *Titus Oates* was expelled from the Merchant Taylor's School, London, from Cambridge University, from the Royal Navy, from a religious college in Spain, and from a religious college in France.

Sir William Osler was expelled from school after a series of pranks. Harvey Cushing declared that the expulsion was due either to unscrewing all the desks and benches from the school floor in the weekend and hoisting them through a trap door into the garret, so that the room was bare when the school assembled on the Monday; or to shouting disparaging remarks about the headmaster through a keyhole; or to locking a flock of geese in the school-room.

George Gissing was expelled from Owen's College, Manchester, at the age of nineteen because he had stolen books, money and coats from his fellows. He received a prison sentence, was sent to Liverpool to work as a clerk, and thence to Boston, U.S.A.

SOME OTHER DISAPPOINTMENTS

Galileo was refused the doctor's diploma at Pisa, and left.

Verdi was rejected by the conservatoire at Milan.

Anthony Trollope tried three times for exhibitions or scholarships at Oxford and Cambridge, without avail.

Gregor Mendel twice failed his examination in Vienna which would have enabled him to become a qualified teacher.

The Earl of Birkenhead was greatly disturbed at his failure to win a scholarship at Harrow.

Winston Churchill was unable to go to Oxford or Cambridge because of his weakness in classics.

Albert Einstein at sixteen applied for entrance to the Swiss Federal Polytechnic School at Zürich, but was rejected, because of inadequate knowledge of modern languages, zoology and botany.

DISAPPOINTED PARENTS

It is interesting to read about the opinions expressed by parents concerning the capabilities and difficulties of their children. We have mentioned many of those in passing.

Chatterton was thought by his mother to be an absolute fool, and she often told him so.

Wellington was regarded by his mother as the dunce of the family, and at times she felt almost aversion for him. His parents were greatly disappointed when he had to leave school because of his failure in classics.

Napoleon, because of his badly shaped head, was thought to be the member of the family of whom greatness was the least to be expected.

Charles Darwin's father told his boy that 'You care for nothing but shooting, dogs and rat-catching. You will be a disgrace to yourself and all your family.' Dr Robert Darwin thought that the boy was a good-for-nothing, whose only mission in life was to mess up the house with his rubbish.

Louis Pasteur was thought by his father to be just mediocre. His father was concerned about his future.

Mrs Shaw never expected anything of *George Bernard*. She had a low opinion of his capabilities.

Beatrice Webb was the 'odd man out' in her family. Her parents were wealthy, and the father was engaged in numerous profitable financial enterprises. Her mother was the daughter of a Liverpool merchant. They had nine daughters, and Margaret Cole, in her biography, tells how eight of them made socially successful marriages. Beatrice had no particular friends among her other sisters. Her father never showed to her quite the same affection that he showed to the others, and her mother had very little sympathy for her. She said, in fact, that 'Beatrice is the only one of my children who is below the general level of intelligence'.

COMMENT

The disappointments and anxieties of other parents about their children are described elsewhere. (See John Hunter, Cortez, Yeats, William Wordsworth, Richard Wagner, Schubert, Mirabeau, Toulouse-Lautrec, Edouard Manet, Flaubert, Samuel Butler, and Eleanor Roosevelt, amongst others.) Little did they realise the fame which these disappointing children were destined to acquire! How wrong they were in their estimate of these children! How completely did they fail to anticipate that it was these very disappointing and perhaps difficult children who were going to bring fame to the family name—not the brothers or sisters, and certainly not they themselves!

We believe that many parents and teachers would profit by reading about the childhood of the men and women of fame mentioned in this chapter. They would be reminded that there are many diverse routes to success in life, and that it is not at all easy to predict what a child will do with his talents —but that it is easy to be blind to the talents which he possesses.

Because these children were to achieve eminence in later years, it would be profitable to speculate as to why their superiority and potential was not recognised. It is a good general principle that if an intelligent child does not achieve his best at school, or even does badly at school or University, the fault is likely to lie in one of four places—the teacher, the child, the parent, or the method of assessment, such as the examinations.

No teacher is likely to get the best out of a child unless he likes the child and the child likes him and wants his approval. It is not unnatural that a teacher may dislike a child who is spiteful, rebellious, ostentatious, or antagonistic, and may well underestimate a child who stutters, dissolves into tears when spoken to, regularly arrives late, or will not open his mouth at all. He may well underestimate the child who thinks slowly, who thinks so carefully round a problem that he cannot see the obvious and expected (but possibly incorrect) answer, and is thought to be dull as a result. If a teacher shouts at children, uses the weapons of threats, sarcasm, or actual punishment, he cannot expect the children to achieve their best. If he constantly tries to make them work faster, they may suffer an emotional block and a panic reaction and appear to be dull as a result. Nevertheless, one cannot help but feel sympathy for the teachers who had to deal with such characters as George Bernard Shaw, Curzon (Chapter 6), or Galois (Chapter 8). Teachers who accept their charges more as equals, who respect the children (as Madame Montessori advocated), and accept their parents as helpers rather than as foes, are much more likely to get the best out of children. One disadvantage of large classes must be the difficulty of getting to know the children, their personalities and their emotional needs.

It is not unnatural that the ability of children tends to be assessed by their success in the subjects of the curriculum—or in subjects as they are taught. Failure in these subjects is apt to blind the teacher and parent to the child's ability in other directions.

It is well known now that motivation is essential—that the subject must be made interesting, if the child is to achieve his best. Efforts are now being made to relate mathematics to everyday life—so that the child is interested in the subject. Very many of the children described in this chapter may have done badly because of the way in which the subjects were taught.

In retrospect it must have been obvious that James Watt was an able boy, because of his interest in mechanical matters; that Edouard Manet, Marconi, Einstein, Oliver Goldsmith, Edward Elgar, Henry Wood and Frederick Delius, had talent, but not in the subjects in the curriculum.

The child's lack of success at school may be due to slow maturation. Slow starters are not rare. In this chapter we have mentioned several examples. They probably included Berzelius, Charles Darwin, Faraday, Fresnel, Gladstone and Isaac Newton, amongst others.

It is well known that certain physical or sensory defects, such as poor vision or hearing, or difficulties in reading (Chapter 4) may give the impression of mental slowness. A good example of the latter was John Hunter, who was thought to be impenetrable to learning, and who had a special difficulty in learning to read—a difficulty which would affect so much of his school work.

Children may do badly at school because of insecurity and unhappiness at home or school. Constant friction at home, emotional deprivation and lack of love, excessive expectations up to which the child cannot live, and the mere effect of failure at school, of constantly being at the bottom of the class, all reduce the standard of a child's school performance.

Poor concentration, unwillingness to work because of lack of interest, and sheer laziness, whatever that is due to, are important causes of the underestimation of a child's ability. Laziness must have been an important cause of the failure to recognise the ability of Jonathan Swift and Charles Thackeray —though in Thackeray's case it is only fair to say that some ability was recognised. Excessive fantasy-thinking and day-dreaming led to the underestimation of many children—such as Balzac and Hans Christian Andersen.

Just as a good home is of the greatest importance in enabling a child to achieve his best at school, so a poor home will retard his progress. Boys from good homes can keep up with much more intelligent boys from poor homes. The qualities of a good home which help a child to do well at school include love and security, the aspirations of the parents, the stimulation to do well, praise and approval for good work and interest in what they achieve, the example of working and of reading, the intellectual interests and activities of the home, the material for learning in the way of books and equipment, the opportunity to learn outside home and school, and many other factors. Many parents fail to recognise the importance of education, and keep their children away from school totally unnecessarily; some positively discourage them from work.

Finally, the examination system is another possible cause of the failure to assess a child's real ability. No examination is perfect. Not all clever children do well in examinations—perhaps because they think slowly, write slowly, or are poor in marshalling and expressing their knowledge. Furthermore, examinations may assess the child's knowledge of the subjects in the curriculum, but not the subjects in which he happens to be interested and gifted. Very many children must fail to develop their real potential, because they have taken up the wrong subjects, through faulty advice or just lack of advice, or because of the requirements of the curriculum.

We believe that these many examples of unrecognised ability in children who were to be famous are important and provide much food for thought. The accurate assessment of a child's potential is no easy matter, and it behoves us to know something of the reason for poor performance in intelligent children.

CHAPTER 4

SOME LEARNING DIFFICULTIES

IT is interesting and instructive to read about learning
difficulties experienced by children who were going to
become men of fame and renown. There are still many
who fail to realise that all children are different—not only in
their personality and intelligence, but in their aptitudes and
abilities. Some children are slow starters, and seem to show
no promise in anything during the early months or years.
Some are average or superior in some subjects, but seriously
backward in others. This backwardness may be related to
poor teaching, or to mere lack of interest in a subject. It may
be due to a special learning difficulty, which may resolve itself
as the child grows older—as if he were late in maturing in that
particular subject—or leave him weak in that subject throughout his life.

Just as some children are later than others of comparable
intelligence in learning to sit, walk, and acquire control of the
bladder, so others are late in learning to talk, to read and to
spell. Sometimes this sort of difficulty runs in the family. The
subject which perhaps gives more trouble to children than any
other is mathematics. Some children find mathematics easy,
but are unable to master any foreign language.

In the pages to follow it is probable that many of the difficulties to be described were not serious ones; in some cases it
is clear that the difficulties were really troublesome, and caused
much distress.

We feel that this chapter may provide some consolation to
parents of otherwise intelligent children with learning difficulties in certain subjects, and that it may encourage teachers
who feel that they are fighting a losing battle in their efforts
to implant knowledge of their subjects in some otherwise

intelligent children; for in all the cases to be described the difficulties were experienced by children destined for fame.

We have divided our material up into mathematics, languages, reading and spelling, grammar and composition, speech and spatial appreciation, and concluded with a section on clumsiness.

MATHEMATICS

Many famous men in their childhood had a special aversion to mathematics. They included *Benjamin Franklin*, *Schubert*, *Emerson*, *Gogol*, *Wagner* and *Conan Doyle*. *Lord Lytton* at fifteen was described as 'probably the best classical scholar, but the worst calligrapher and the most blundering mathematician'. *Henry James* 'couldn't tackle the smallest problem in mechanics or face without dismay the simplest geometric challenge'. *Conan Doyle* loathed arithmetic.

Lord Northcliffe was poor at mathematics. Pound and Harmsworth wrote that 'to the point almost of mental distress he could not then or after, give his mind to matters which did not interest him. Arithmetic, for example, bored him exceedingly, and he would allow himself to be defeated by the simplest exercises and problems, cheerfully risking the consequences. All maths were a sore trial to him.' His headmaster, though recognising his intelligence, thought that his poor performance in mathematics would debar him from any form of professional career.

Gandhi had 'more difficulty in mastering his multiplication tables than in learning naughty words for his teachers'.

Alfred Adler was so poor at mathematics that he had to repeat the work of his form. According to his biographer, Orgler, his teacher advised his father to remove him from the school and apprentice him to a shoemaker, because he was not fit for anything else. Adler later remarked that if his father had taken the advice and let him become a cobbler, he would probably have done the work well, but he would have be-

lieved all his life that there is such a thing as having no gift for
mathematics. His father let him stay at school, and Alfred
worked hard at mathematics when at home. Orgler tells how
subsequently, when the teacher wrote a problem on the
blackboard, which none of the pupils or the teacher could
solve, Adler stood up and said 'I can solve it!' The teacher
made sarcastic remarks, but let him try, amidst the laughter
of his schoolmates, and he solved the problem successfully.
Thereafter he was the best in the form at the subject.

  Jung, in his book *Memories, Dreams and Reflections*, wrote that
school bored him. It took up time which he would rather
have spent playing and drawing. Divinity classes, he said,
were unspeakably dull, and he felt a downright fear of the
mathematics class. 'The teacher pretended that algebra was a
perfectly natural affair, to be taken for granted, whereas I
didn't even know what numbers really were. They were not
flowers, nor animals, nor fossils; they were nothing that could
be imagined, mere quantities that resulted from counting. To
my confusion those quantities were now represented by letters,
which signified sounds so that it became possible to hear
them, so to speak. Oddly enough my classmates could handle
these things and found them self-evident. No one could tell
me what numbers were, and I was unable even to formulate
the question. I thought the whole business was entirely
arbitrary. All my life it remained a puzzle to me why it was
that I never managed to get my bearings in mathematics when
there was no doubt whatever that I could calculate properly.
Mathematics classes became sheer terror and torture to me. I
was so intimidated by my incomprehension that I did not dare
to ask any questions.'

  He said that he found other subjects easy, and that he contrived for a long time, thanks to a good visual memory, to
swindle his way through mathematics. 'But my fear of failure
created in me a kind of silent despair which completely ruined
school for me. In addition, I was exempted from drawing

classes on grounds of utter incapacity.' 'To my defects in maths and drawing was now added a third: from the first I hated gymnastics. I was going to school in order to learn something, not to practise useless and senseless acrobatics.'

Epstein found mathematics difficult, but his teachers closed their eyes to it, because of his excellent drawings. *Picasso* was backward in arithmetic. On taking an entrance examination to a new school, the master wrote a sum on the board, and Pablo could not solve it. The master had written the answer on a piece of blotting paper, and Pablo, seeing it, got the answer right and as a result was admitted to the school.

Paul Nash, in his interesting autobiography, wrote: 'Although I appeared to possess a good average intelligence, I was extremely deficient in mathematical calculation. Every examination showed the same result; my total suffered by the scores of marks lost in arithmetic, algebra and geometry. Actually I was capable of quite complicated methods of computation to prove my sums. But the answers were fantastically wrong. It was as if, instinctively, I argued that 2 and 2 make 5, or on other occasions, no more than 3. My unfortunate masters were in despair. I think almost from the first, all those who attempted to teach me mathematics were baffled, and how I was able to progress at all I do not know. I think, sometimes, I must have been given marks for sheer perverse ingenuity. I have seen mathematical teachers reduced to a sort of awe by my imbecility.'

LANGUAGES

Linnaeus was amongst the worst in his school at Greek, Hebrew and theology, but was one of the best at mathematics and physics.

The *Duke of Wellington* had to be removed from Eton on account of his failure in classics—and was sent to a military academy in France as a result. His failure occasioned his parents the greatest distress.

Thomas Carlyle at Edinburgh University made practically no headway in classics and philosophy, but did well in mathematics. Nevertheless, he left the University at eighteen without a degree.

Lord Lytton, though in fact he did well in classics, regarded Latin and Greek as 'mere inventions of some enemy of youthful happiness, involving certain special ordeals of torture in the way of construing, parsing, learning by heart and other such exercises'.

Gogol learnt little at school, his French and German being as bad as his Latin, and his mathematics were even worse. *Charles Darwin*, with a little exaggeration, one suspects, said: 'during my whole life I have been singularly incapable of mastering any language'. *Thackeray's* difficulty with classics, however, was genuine and troublesome.

Richard Wagner was moved down a form at his Leipzig school, and was infuriated and disappointed. As a result he lost all interest in classical studies, idled, and threw away all chances of academic advancement. Subsequently his mother received a note that the boy had not attended school for six months.

Lord Balfour, according to Young, had no gift for languages; he disliked grammar, and the weekly task of writing Latin prose he detested almost as strongly as he detested the weekly task of writing Latin verse. His teachers were displeased with his progress in classics.

Frith, in his autobiography, wrote: 'I found copying Dutch prints much easier than geography, to say nothing of Latin, for a very slight experience of that language led me to feel that life would be unendurable if I were compelled to learn it; so that beyond a little of the grammar, and the acquisition of a few quotations, which I find useful to this day when I desire to create an impression that they are but samples of a wealth of the classical knowledge that I possess—I know nothing about it.'

Sir Oliver Lodge wrote that 'Latin grammar was a nightmare; especially when later I came to the syntax part of it, where a lot of rules had to be learned by heart, without any genuine meaning attaching to any of them'.

Winston Churchill found Latin particularly troublesome at Harrow. It was because he had not learnt Greek that he was never able to go the University of Oxford or Cambridge.

Nehru confessed that after many years of effort his knowledge of Sanskrit was about as small as his subsequent knowledge of Latin at Harrow.

READING AND SPELLING

Sir Joshua Reynolds was weak at spelling and grammar, but it was probably due to laziness more than a special difficulty in these subjects. It is said that throughout his life his letters showed constant evidence of this defect in his education. *Dr John Hunter*, on the other hand, probably had a specific reading disability. In spite of all efforts to teach him, he learnt to read only with the greatest difficulty, when he was seventeen years old.

Napoleon never learned to spell correctly, and his writing was abominable.

George Stephenson as an adult could read only with difficulty, and his writing and spelling were bad: but this is probably due to the fact that he had had no education, and at eighteen could neither read nor write.

George Bernard Shaw always found spelling difficult. He tended to spell in the phonetic manner.

Henry Ford never learned to spell, to write a good hand, to read easily, or to express himself in the simplest written sentence.

Jan Smuts did not learn to read until he was twelve.

Yeats had particular difficulty in learning to read, despite the efforts of his aunts to teach him. They supposed that his intelligence was defective. He fared no better at school, and his father then tried to teach him—but finished by flinging the reading book at his head. His spelling and mathematics were also weak.

GRAMMAR AND COMPOSITION

Turner was always hampered by a difficulty in expressing himself in speech and writing. *Beethoven* throughout his life had the same difficulty, but this was due more to his education finishing at eleven, than to any specific learning problem.

Paul Ehrlich was a highly intelligent boy. At Breslau College he excelled in Latin and mathematics, but was very weak in German composition. Marquardt, in his biography, described how when faced with this Paul would 'bite his pen-holder, scratch behind his ear, run all five fingers through his blond tuft of hair, and finally rub it down with the palm of his hand until it was entirely flat'. Paul hated examinations of any kind, and all his life pitied everybody who had to take one. In his school leaving examination he was given very good in Latin, and satisfactory in all other subjects, except German composition. He very nearly failed the whole examination because of this, but after careful consideration and discussion the headmaster decided to let him pass.

SPEECH

Alessandro Volta, pioneer of the development of electricity, from whose name the word 'voltage' is derived, caused much concern to his family because he seemed dull witted and was slow in learning to talk. He could not say a word until he was four. At four he suddenly developed, and by the age of seven he was regarded at school as being exceptionally bright. In an article in the *Scientific American*, Giorgio de Santillana described how the father, after Alessandro had become famous, remarked that 'We had a jewel in the home but did not know it.'

Albert Einstein was very late in learning to talk and his

parents began to be afraid when he was four that he might be mentally backward. He still lacked fluency of speech when he was nine. He hated learning classical languages.

Stuttering

This is a complex problem and it is not correct to say that it is purely and simply a learning disorder, though it may legitimately be considered to be partly so. Amongst well known people who stuttered were Moses, Aristotle, Aesop, Demosthenes, Virgil, King Charles the First, Robert Boyle, Charles Lamb and Charles Darwin.

Aneurin Bevan had a troublesome stutter when at school. His mother thought that Aneurin had begun to stutter in imitation of his uncle, who had the same problem. It caused Aneurin much embarrassment. He used poetry to help him to speak without stuttering, and at times would look up synonyms for words which he knew would cause him difficulty.

Somerset Maugham suffered from a stammer throughout his life. His unhappiness at King's School, Canterbury, was partly due to this handicap, the other boys laughing at him on account of his speech difficulties and making him worse. It is said that his stammer embittered his whole life.

Indistinctness of speech is often in part related to delayed maturation. It may consist of the substitution of letters, such as that which occurs in the lisp, in which 'th' is substituted for 's' because of protrusion of the tongue between the teeth on attempting to pronounce the 's'.

Emile Zola suffered from an embarrassing lisp. It is recorded that on starting school he was asked his name, and he stammered 'Thola'. This became his nickname for the rest of his school days.

Michael Faraday's period at school came to a sudden and abrupt end because of his speech. He pronounced the r's as w's. His teacher tried to ridicule him out of the defect, and then decided to resort to force. She gave his older brother a halfpenny to go to a shop to buy a cane, in order that she could give Michael a public flogging. The boy threw the halfpenny over the wall and ran home to tell his mother, who promptly withdrew Michael from the school.

SPATIAL APPRECIATION

Henri Poincaré, the mathematical genius, had an interesting difficulty in spatial appreciation—the recognition of space and form. He was utterly unable to make drawings that 'represented anything in heaven or earth'. His score of zero in the school entrance examination in drawing almost made him fail the entrance test.

CLUMSINESS

Some children and some adults are more skilled in the use of their hands than are others of the same intelligence. In some children the awkwardness in the use of the hands leads to trouble with the teacher. Some children are awkward in all their movements, and never learn to dance, or to achieve any success in the gymnasium. They may be truly clumsy and awkward. There are many causes of this, some of them dating from birth or before birth. It may even run in the family.

In our reading we came across several examples of this clumsiness in children who were to achieve renown in widely differing fields.

Napoleon was remarkably clumsy and awkward as a boy. He could never throw a stone in the right direction. He was a very poor shot with a gun. He never learned to ride well. He was described as being not only awkward, but in many instances helpless. He was unable to do his hair in the arrangement of pigtails and side curls which was the fashion of the day.

Beethoven was said to be clumsy in all his movements. Nothing fragile was safe in his hands.

LFC I

Henri Poincaré suffered considerably from clumsiness, and he never outgrew it. He had difficulties in spatial appreciation, and in particular with geometry. He was awkward in the use of his fingers. When he learned to write, it was found that he was ambidextrous, and wrote or drew equally well (or rather badly) with each hand.

Oscar Wilde was an awkward clumsy boy, who was continuously knocking things over—much to the amusement of his schoolfellows.

G. K. Chesterton was described as being tall, untidy and incredibly clumsy and absent-minded. Ward describes how in the later part of Chesterton's school life physical exercises were made compulsory, and the boys would form parties to watch his strange efforts on the trapeze or parallel bars. He was perfectly good humoured about the tricks which were played on him.

The classical example of laterality problems was that of *Leonardo da Vinci*. He was left handed and wrote from right to left, reversing letters (strephosymbolia).

Branwell Brontë wrote equally fluently with both hands—and at times with both hands at once. He would write Greek with his right hand and at the same time Latin with his left.

Baden-Powell worried his mother because he used both hands, shifting pencil or brush from his right hand to his left and back again indiscriminately. Hillcourt described the anxiety experienced by his parents on this account. She discussed the problem with John Ruskin. Ruskin studied the boy at work, painting with equal ease with either hand. He concluded that there was no cause for alarm.

Later, when Baden-Powell was eighteen, the other boys were fascinated by his ability to dash off recognisable portraits of school personalities, now with the right hand, now with the left, and sometimes two at a time, using both hands together.

Sometimes as a trick he would draw the picture with the right hand and shade it with the left hand at the same time.

COMMENT

There must have been very many other examples of such problems. They are commonly seen in schools today. There are numerous books devoted to many of these difficulties, particularly in reading difficulties (dyslexia) and in speech. There is much which we do not understand about them even now. One can well imagine how much trouble some of those difficulties caused in days gone by. It is important to note that the occurrence of those difficulties in childhood did not prevent the sufferers from eventually reaching positions of the greatest eminence.

It is probable that in many of these cases the child's poor performance in a particular subject was due more than anything else to his dislike of or lack of interest in it. This may have been due to his dislike of the teacher, or of the method by which the subject was taught, or to a learning difficulty. It is essential to realise that some children will never be interested in some subjects, however well they are taught. It is unfortunate if attempts are made to force them, perhaps because of some examination requirements, to study the subjects which do not interest them. They are apt to do badly and to feel resentment at being forced to study them. They do badly, and failure leads to more failure. The effect of such failure may be long lasting. It is far better, where possible, to give all possible encouragement in those subjects which really interest a child, and to avoid discouraging him by insisting on his learning subjects which really trouble him—unless they are really essential for his future.

CHAPTER 5

SOME PHYSICAL DIFFICULTIES

BIOGRAPHIES of eminent men frequently refer to 'delicacy' in childhood. We have referred to some of them in this chapter, but we have little doubt that many more could be added. The term 'delicate' is a vague one, not referring to any particular disease or any specific medical condition. It is not a term which would be likely to find a place in a medical textbook. Nevertheless, it is well known that some children seem to be more susceptible than others to infections. The picture of the 'delicate child', however, is not just a picture of frequent lung or other infections—it conjures up the anxious parent, who considers that the child is different from other children, and more 'delicate', when in fact there is nothing wrong with him. The term 'delicate', in fact, is more often a reflection of the parents' attitude than a feature of the child's health. In some cases the child, particularly in adolescence, regards himself as 'delicate' when there is nothing physically wrong with him.

In this chapter we have put together some of the stories of 'delicate' children. It is obvious that they represent a wide variety of medical and psychological conditions, and that in many of them we shall never know what if anything was really wrong with the child.

As for the newborn period, it must be remembered that in the period under discussion many more died in infancy than now and it would not be surprising if there was great anxiety about many of the children during the first days and weeks of life. There was very good reason for it.

Other sections of the chapter include diseases of bones and joints, convulsive disorders, and defects of eyesight and hearing, with a section on the famous Siamese twins, Chang and

Eng. We have also included a section on physical ugliness—
a source of much unhappiness in some of the children concerned.

THE NEWBORN PERIOD

Amongst famous premature babies were Isaac Newton,
Voltaire, Charles Wesley, Keats, Victor Hugo, Anna Pavlova
and Winston Churchill. Isaac Newton said that his mother
often told him that he was so small when he was born that
he could have been put into a quart mug. He was so weak
later that he had to wear a bolster round his neck to support
his head.

Voltaire was born half dead, and was 'slapped to life' by
nurses. They gave him not more than four days to live, but
he lived for eighty-four years. Almost every day for several
months it was reported to his mother that he was dying, but
at the end of a year he gained strength. *Jeremy Bentham*, very
weak and delicate as a child, lived to the same age.

Neither *Joseph Addison* nor *John Constable* was expected to
survive infancy.

Samuel Johnson was born more dead than alive after a
difficult labour. He was christened within a few hours and
handed over to a wet nurse to feed. It was thought that 'the
bad humour of the nurse might have given him the scrofula
(the King's Evil), the blindness in one eye and deafness in
one ear'.

Rousseau said that he was brought into the world in an
almost dying condition, and there was little hope of saving
his life. He wrote: 'I carried with me the germs of a complaint
which the course of time has strengthened, and which at times
allows me a respite only to make me suffer more cruelly in
another manner.'

Chateaubriand was born at St Malo, a puny infant, showing
little inclination to live.

Robert Stephenson was such a weak and sickly baby that

when he was christened at Willington in the school-room, his early death was confidently predicted.

Thomas Hardy was thought to be stillborn, or to have died immediately after birth. The midwife, however, brought him to life with a good slapping.

Picasso was thought to be stillborn, and was abandoned on the table by the midwife. His uncle, a doctor, resuscitated him.

Anna Pavlova was so weak and puny that her parents had her baptised three days after birth: she spent most of her time in the next few months literally wrapped in cotton wool.

MISCELLANEOUS AILMENTS

Cortez, conqueror of Mexico, was a delicate child, growing up 'so ill that he was often on the verge of death'. According to Salvador de Madariaga, the family sought a cure in their devotion to St Peter. They were pious and devout people, and drew lots to see which of the twelve Apostles should be the boy's patron saint. The lot fell to St Peter, and the recovery of his health was ascribed to St Peter's intercession.

René Descartes, mathematician and philosopher, was regarded as so delicate that the rector of the school, thinking that he needed much more rest than other boys, told him to lie in bed as late as he wished in the mornings, and not to leave the room until he felt like it. Thereafter, all through his life, according to Bell, he spent his mornings in bed when he wanted to think. Looking back in later years, he said that these long quiet mornings in bed, with silent meditation, were the real source of his philosophy and mathematics.

Blaise Pascal had a serious but obscure illness when he was one year old. It could have been tuberculous peritonitis, for it was chronic, growing worse for a year, and there was abdominal distension. Bishop tells the story of how gossip at Clermont diagnosed the malady as the result of a sorcerer's spell. Some suspected a poor woman who lived near. At first Pascal's father ridiculed the story, but eventually the story became so persistent that he sent for the woman and threatened to have her hanged if she did not confess. She said that in vengeance for his refusal to plead a case for her, she had put a spell on the child, which could only be broken by transference to an animal. The father suggested a horse, but the woman preferred a cat, and threw a cat out of the window. She then demanded that a poultice be applied to the boy's abdomen: it was to be made of nine leaves of three herbs gathered by a seven year old child before sunrise, and it had to be applied at 7 a.m. This was done, and at midday the father was told that his son was dead. He seemed to be dead, and in grief the father struck the witch; she said that the boy would continue in the death-like state until midnight, and then recover. Between midnight and 1 a.m. he began to yawn and at 6 a.m. he recovered consciousness.

From the age of eighteen he was a semi-invalid, not passing a day without suffering.

Christopher Wren had poor health as a child, and caused great anxiety, but he lived to the age of eighty-nine.

Thomas Gray was the only survivor of twelve children. It is not clear what caused their death, but Ketton-Cremer, in his biography of Gray, wrote as follows: 'There is a story that his little brothers and sisters had died of suffocation, owing to too great a fulness of blood, and that he (Thomas) would certainly have been cut off as early, had not his mother, with a courage remarkable for one of her sex and withal so very tender a parent, ventured to open a vein with her own hand, which instantly removed the paroxysm.' We know of no medical condition for which such treatment is necessary.

Jonathan Swift was a delicate sickly boy, who later became a hypochondriac. From early childhood he had recurring spells of dizziness.

Horace Walpole was delicate from infancy. When he was a baby his mother, Lady Walpole, was told that 'that baby cannot possibly live'.

James Watt, *Edmund Burke* and *William Pitt* were all delicate children, occasioning much anxiety to their parents.

Rousseau and *Wilberforce* were delicate, and not expected to survive childhood.

Edward Gibbon describes his own ailment in an interesting manner. He wrote: 'So feeble was my constitution, so precarious my life, that in the baptism of my brothers my father's prudence successively repeated my christian name of Edward, that in case of the departure of the eldest son, this patronymic appellation might still be perpetuated in the family. To preserve and to rear so frail a boy the most tender assiduity was scarcely sufficient: only my mother's attention was somewhat diverted by her frequent pregnancies, by an exclusive passion for her husband, and by the dissipation of the world. But the maternal office was supplied by my aunt. My weakness excited her pity. Many wakeful nights did she sit by my bedside in trembling expectation that each hour would be my last. Of the various and frequent disorders of my childhood, my own recollection is dark: nor do I wish to expatiate on so disgusting a topic. Suffice it to say that while every practitioner, from Sloane and Ward to the Chevalier Taylor, was successively summoned to torture or relieve me, the care of my mind was too frequently neglected for that of my health. The chain of my education was broken as often as I was recalled from the school of learning to the bed of sickness.'

He referred to the violence and variety of his complaints. 'A strange nervous affection, which alternately contracted my legs, and produced the most excruciating pain, was ineffectually opposed by the various methods of bathing and purging.' He tried the waters of Bath, and had to leave school because of his health. His condition improved at sixteen, 'since when few persons have been more exempt from real or imaginary ills'.

The *Earl of Chatham* suffered severely from gout while at Eton, and it prevented his taking part in sport. He had such severe gout at Oxford that he had to leave the University after a year, without obtaining a degree.

Sir William Herschel, astronomer, at five started with asthma and 'rheumatism', and suffered from them for the rest of his life.

Mozart had a series of illnesses during his childhood. He had scarlet fever at six, and was ill for four weeks, convalescing slowly. He then had constant lung infections. At nine he was dangerously ill with tonsillitis and delirium. His father wrote that Wolfgang was scarcely recognisable after four weeks' illness, being reduced to skin and bone. Two years later he had severe smallpox, and at sixteen another severe illness, possibly acute nephritis.

Sir Walter Scott, when a young child, suffered an attack of poliomyelitis which left him permanently lame, and had a severe bowel haemorrhage, from which he nearly died.

Conrad Meyer's remarkable delay in the onset of puberty is so bound up with his equally remarkable psychological problems, that we have discussed both together in Chapter 3.

Mazzini, at eleven, was said to have trouble with his digestion, and his mother 'Whenever she found it was irregular or weak, was to see that he rested his brain so that the blood could return to his stomach.'

Gregor Mendel had a mysterious illness in childhood, repeated in adolescence, which was probably psychological in origin.

Gogol was never a healthy child. As a baby there was doubt whether he would survive. He suffered from 'scrofula', and was deaf in one ear. He was round shouldered as a boy, and short-sighted.

Lord Lytton was away from school for two years on account of his health.

Chopin and *Liszt* were delicate children. Liszt had a cramp, and his father, certain that he was going to die, ordered a coffin from the village carpenter.

Charles Dickens was a weak child, and had violent attacks of spasm (? asthma) which prevented active exertion. His father prophesied that he would never live to experience the bitterness of maturity.

Christina Rossetti was not expected to reach adulthood.

Cecil Rhodes, Albert Roussel and *Toscanini* were delicate children. The latter had one illness after another. He was pitifully thin, and kept on a rigid diet of soup and cereal paps. The sea air was thought to be upsetting him, and he was sent to live with his grandparents.

Alfred Nobel had numerous illnesses as a child, and there was great anxiety about his life. He had indigestion, with violent spasms of sickness, which kept him in bed. He also had some spinal ailment, for which he was advised to lie flat on his back as much as possible. It is said that his mother spent so much time nursing him that he became excessively attached to her and developed a revulsion against normal sexual relationships with women.

Lord Balfour was regarded as a very delicate child, though he said later that what exactly the ailment was supposed to be, he did not know. He had frequent colds from the age of two to eleven, and for several years he was kept indoors throughout the winter. Young, in his biography, wrote that Balfour said 'For many winters I never crossed the threshold, but used to lie on my face on the nursery floor, chalking or painting in water colours pictures in the illustrated newspapers. My ill health principally chronicles itself by the terrible long nights that I lay awake, troubled continually with a hacking exhausting cough, and praying for sleep or morning from the bottom of my shaken little body.'

He started regular schooling at nine, but there were in-numerable absences. At school he had to lie down in the after-noons whenever he felt tired, and was excused early school on doctor's orders. At Eton he was not thought to be strong enough to play football.

Robert Louis Stevenson was constantly troubled by chest infections from the age of two to eleven.

Beatrice Webb had almost continuous illnesses as a child, with 'neuralgia', indigestion, lung infections and other troubles, which frequently kept her in bed and away from school, isolating her from her friends.

Jacob Epstein was known as 'the sick one'. He had a serious illness, lasting for two years, as a young child.

Albert Schweitzer was a delicate sickly child. He wrote: 'On one occasion they actually thought I was dead, but the milk from neighbour Leopold's cow, together with the excellent Gunsbach air, worked wonders for me: from my second year I improved marvellously, and became a strong and healthy boy.'

Alfred Adler was delicate as child, and was said to have rickets with attacks of spasm of the glottis (presumably laryngismus stridulus, which used to be a common symptom of rickets). He would suddenly find it extremely difficult to breathe in, and he was terrified by the attacks. They occurred particularly when he was crying, and at the age of three he decided never to cry or scream again. He grew out of them shortly afterwards.

CONVULSIVE DISORDERS

Lennox, in his book on epilepsy, gives a long list of scores of eminent men who had epileptic convulsions. They include Alexander the Great, Petrarch, Pythagoras, Empedocles, Democritus, Julius Caesar, Alfred the Great, William the Third, Peter the Great, Charles the Fifth of Spain, Louis the Thirteenth, Napoleon, Archduke Charles of Austria, Pascal, Swedenborg, Paganini, Swinburne, William Morris, Van Gogh and many others. Richelieu in his fits believed himself to be a horse, and would run round the room, neighing and kicking in hippic fashion.

It is uncertain how many famous men first had fits in childhood. *Mohammed* had fits from the age of two. *Lord Byron* had a fit at birth and others later. *Dostoevsky* had his first fit at school when he learnt that his father had been murdered. *Molière*, *Charles Dickens* and *Nobel* had fits as children. *Flaubert's* first major fit occurred when he heard that he had failed an examination.

Edward Lear would have up to eighteen fits a day. He was greatly burdened by them, and marked them as a cross in his diary. Davidson wrote in his biography that 'his whole subconscious life was coloured by it (epilepsy), and it is equally certain that it was largely responsible for the deep melancholy which constantly beset him and for those fits of irritability of which no one was more guiltily conscious than himself'.

ORTHOPAEDIC CONDITIONS

Alexander Pope was a life-long cripple. He had a severe humpback. He was 4 ft. 6 in. in height, and had rickets as a child. He found it difficult to stand upright except in a canvas corset. Johnson said that Alexander was so weak that he had to be helped to dress, and so small that he had to have a special chair at the table.

He always suffered from ill health, and referred to it as 'that long disease, my life'.

Talleyrand was lame for life as a result of an injury which befell him at the age of three when boarded out with a poor woman in Paris. He fell from a chest of drawers and injured his foot. His parents thought that his lameness rendered him unfit to inherit his father's titles, and these were therefore bestowed on Talleyrand's younger brother.

Sir Walter Scott developed poliomyelitis in his second year, and was left with a weak right leg. Nevertheless, he learnt to ride and run. He was at first teased by his schoolfellows, but won their respect for his gameness in spite of the lame leg.

Karl Weber, musician, was permanently lame as a result of a hip disease, and could not walk until he was four. Long before he was able to walk, however, he could play the clavier.

Lord Byron was lame as the result of a congenital deformity of the foot. He did not allow it to interfere with sport, however, for he took part in many of the active sports of his schoolfellows. Nevertheless, he was sensitive about his lameness, and at times his mother upbraided him for it.

Henry James, as an adolescent, had an ill-defined disease of the spine causing back pain.

Sir Patrick Manson developed spinal curvature as a child, with an obscure condition of his right arm, associated with tremor. He had to lie on his back for six months. The disability persisted throughout his life.

Much has been written about the disability of *Toulouse-Lautrec*, but its nature remains uncertain. He was small in stature, with narrow sloping shoulders, and a pigeon chest. At ten he began to tire easily, but his real trouble began at fourteen when he had to lie down for a prolonged period. He broke a leg, and was very frail. His biographer, Perruchot, described the remarkable change which came about in the appearance of Toulouse-Lautrec at about the age of fifteen. 'He was growing uglier every day. His nose was broadening, his lips were swelling and becoming puffy, forming a sort of roll above his retreating chin. The words that issued from his pendulous lips were deformed by a lisp and a curious rolling of the r's and fell over each other, while many of the syllables were drowned in a flood of saliva. His whole body seemed to be swelling, thickening, growing rickety and out of proportion. His tiny forearms ended in hugely fingered hands.' His arms and legs were short, while his trunk was normally proportioned. He was strikingly ugly. At seventeen he realised that his health would never improve and that he would always be handicapped.

It is suggested that he had an inherited bone disease, resulting from his parents' first cousin marriage. He died at thirty-seven.

Steinmetz, the scientist, had an inherited spine and bone disease, like his father. When he was born, the midwife reported that he had a humpback, the same as his father, and that his left leg was not straight. He was permanently deformed.

SENSORY HANDICAPS

Kepler, the astronomer, had a severe attack of smallpox when he was four and was left with crippled hands and defective eyesight.

Samuel Johnson was deaf in his left ear, and almost blind in his left eye as the result of ophthalmia. He was said to have tuberculous glands in the neck.

William Cowper at the age of eight was in danger of losing his sight on account of punctate keratitis, a serious eye infection.

Beethoven became deaf as a result, it was thought, of congenital syphilis.

Edison became deaf at twelve because of inflammation of the ear.

The trouble experienced by *Rudyard Kipling* as a result of his defective eyesight is described in Chapter 2.

The most remarkable story of a combination of blindness and deafness which itself led to fame is that of *Helen Keller*.

Helen Keller was the daughter of a newspaper man in Alabama. At eighteen to twenty months of age she became ill and lost her sight and hearing. The story is well told by Harrity and Martin. She had an illness, probably encephalitis, with a high temperature. On the day after the temperature settled, her mother suddenly noted that the child's lids did not close when her hand approached her. She screamed, and Helen did not seem to hear.

The parents took the girl to one doctor after another, without receiving help. Mrs Keller then read Charles Dickens' *American Notes* and read about a deaf and blind girl, Laura Bridgman, who had been taught in the Perkins Institution in

Boston to communicate. The Kellers got in touch with Alexander Graham Bell, who had a deaf mother and wife, and had invented the telephone to help his deaf pupils. He advised a visit to the Perkins Institute. Her mother's brother, however, told Mrs Keller to put the child away, because, he said, she was mentally defective. It was found that there was only one teacher available at the Institute—a twenty-one year old girl, Anne Sullivan, who had been a patient herself on account of defective eyesight. She began to teach Helen when she was seven, and taught her by patient perseverance to understand the meaning of words and how to talk and express her thoughts by her fingers. When Helen was seventy-five, she told a reporter: 'My birthday can never mean so much to me as the arrival of Anne Sullivan on 3rd March 1887: that was my soul's birthday.'

The authors of the biography wrote that after the first contact had been made, Anne Sullivan largely guided Helen Keller into leading a normal life. She took her for walks in the woods, and through the countryside, describing the beauties and wonders of nature and animals, taught her to swim and ride and play with other children, and to share the joys of her devoted family. Then began the formal training that eventually made Helen Keller one of the best educated women in the world.

Helen would scream with frustration, pounding the floor because she could not make herself understood.

'I had a battle royal with Helen this morning', wrote Anne Sullivan shortly after she arrived at the Keller home. Anne had insisted on Helen using her spoon at breakfast, for Helen had dreadful table manners, grabbing food off other people's plates and eating with her hands.

'Naturally the family was much disturbed and left the room', Anne Sullivan reported. 'I locked the dining room door and proceeded to eat my breakfast, though the food almost choked me. Helen was crying on the floor kicking and screaming and trying to pull my chair from under me. She kept this up for half an hour, then got up to see what I was doing. I let her know I was eating, but did not let her put her hand in the plate. She pinched me as I slapped her every time she did it. Then she went all round the table to see who was there and finding no one but me she seemed bewildered. After a few minutes, she came back to her plate and began to eat her breakfast with her fingers. I gave her a spoon, which she threw on the floor. I forced her out of the chair and made her pick it up. Finally I succeeded in getting her back in her chair again, and held the spoon in her hand, compelling her to take up the food with it and put it in her mouth. In a few minutes she yielded and finished her breakfast peaceably. Then we had another tussle over folding her napkin. When she had finished, she threw it on the floor and ran toward the door. Finding it locked, she began to kick and scream all over again. It was another hour before I succeeded in getting the napkin folded. Then I let her out into the warm sunshine and went up to my room and threw myself on the bed, exhausted. I had a good cry and felt better. I suppose I shall have many such battles with the little woman before she learns the only two essential things I can teach her, obedience and love.'

Anne and Helen moved into a garden house, some distance from the main house. There Anne spent hour after hour trying to break down the barriers, tapping words endlessly into the child's hand, hoping and praying that she would learn just one. She could tap the words back correctly, but they had no meaning. Then on 5th April 1887, Anne wrote: 'This morning, while she was washing, she wanted to know the name for water: when she wants to know the name for anything, she points to it, and pats my hand. I spelled "water" and thought no more about it till after breakfast. We went to the pump-house and I made Helen hold her mug under the spout while I pumped. As the cold water gushed forth, filling the mug, I spelled "water" with Helen's free hand. The word, coming so close upon the sensation of cold water rushing over her hand, seemed to startle her. She dropped the mug and stood as one transfixed. A new light came over her face. She spelled "water" several times. Then she dropped on the ground and asked for its name and pointed to the pump and the trellis, and suddenly turning round she asked for my name. I spelled "Teacher".'

She soon learned Braille, reading every book she could obtain, while Anne ceaselessly tapped out answers to questions.

As she ran the forefinger of her left hand along the line of the book, she would spell out the word with the other hand. Asked why she loved books so much, Helen said: 'Because they tell me so much that is interesting about things I cannot see, and they are never tired or troubled like people. They tell me over and over what I want to know.'

Helen was then taken to the Horace Mann School for the Deaf, in Boston, at the age of ten, and was taught by Miss Fuller. Miss Fuller wrote: 'I began by familiarising her with the position and condition of the mouth parts and with the trachea.' Helen soon learned six letters M P A S T I. After ten lessons, she could tell teacher 'I am not dumb now'. A cousin said: 'Many times it was necessary to put her sensitive fingers in teacher's mouth, sometimes far down into her throat until teacher would be nauseated.'

When Helen was twelve she wrote a story on her Braille slate. She later went to New York for advanced lessons in oral speech and lip reading, and entered the Cambridge School for young ladies at sixteen. The teacher sat with her in class, spelling the lectures with her hand.

Louis Braille was born in the village of Coupvray, in the department of the Seine and Marne. His father was the village saddler. When Louis was three years old he picked up a piece of leather, when his father's back was turned, and tried to cut it. The leather was tough and elastic, and his knife slipped, penetrating the left eye. The boy screamed with pain, and blood poured from the wound. There was no doctor in the village, and no expert treatment was available. A few months later the other eye gradually lost its sight (presumably as a result of sympathetic ophthalmia, whereby an injury to one eye is followed by blindness in the other). He became totally blind by the age of five.

Louis was taught a little by the village schoolmaster, and according to Roblin, in his biography, the boy's father tried to teach the boy the alphabet by touch, having driven a number of upholsterer's nails into a wooden plank to form the letters. When Louis was ten, he was granted a scholarship to the Royal Institute for Blind Children in Paris. The Principal, Dr Guillié, used thin cardboard sheets pressed upon lead types to produce raised letters.

Louis won several prizes at the Institute, learning history, geography and mathematics. Pignier, who taught him from the age of twelve, wrote that 'possessed of a lively intelligence, he soon came to the fore through the progress he made and the success he gained in his lessons. Whether literary or scientific, his essays were models of exact thinking, remarkable for their precision of thought and for the clarity and correct language in which it was expressed. He had a fertile imagination, but it was always controlled by reason' (Roblin).

When Louis was twelve, a retired artillery captain, Charles Barbier de la Serre, visited the chairman of the Board of Governors of the school, and claimed to have invented an improved method of teaching the blind, by using a punched out pattern of dots on the surface of a sheet of cardboard, the dots being grouped to form words and phrases. When Louis was twelve, he met the captain, and being greatly impressed with the method, set about improving it. He worked at his lessons by day, and at night spent many hours devising a new system on the same principle, with individual letters, including accents and punctuation, which could also be used for mathematical symbols and musical notes, and which were a suitable size for the finger tip of the blind person. He largely perfected the method when he was fifteen.

When he was nineteen, he was appointed to the staff of the Institute, teaching geography and algebra, and subsequently became professor. When he was twenty-four he became organist of the Church of Saint Nicholas-des-Champs.

He had a long fight to persuade others outside the school to use the method, suffering much thwarting and annoyance in the process. His health was poor, and when he was twenty-six he developed symptoms of pulmonary tuberculosis. He died of this when he was forty-two.

UGLINESS

Confucius had huge ears. It was a Chinese tradition that large ears portended great wisdom, and for that reason his father called him Kung-Fu-Tse, the wise Mr King.

Socrates was said by both Plato and Xenophon to have notably broad nostrils with a snub nose, with a peculiarity of his eyes, either prominence or an unusual width between them. He looked grotesque, and Aristophanes compared his walk to the strut of a wild fowl.

Michelangelo had a fight with a fellow apprentice who criticised one of his paintings, and his face and nose were permanently disfigured as a result.

Goldsmith was left severely scarred by smallpox, and *William Penn* lost all his hair in an attack of smallpox and thereafter had to wear a wig.

Mirabeau was born with two teeth. He had an unusually large head, and was notably ugly.

Napoleon had sunken cheeks and a large aquiline nose with enormous eyes.

Turner was said to resemble an adolescent monkey.

Anthony Trollope was described as big, awkward, ugly, ill dressed and dirty.

According to Halasz, *Alfred Nobel*, because he loathed his own appearance and believed that it denied him the happiness of being loved, decided while still young to compensate by dedicating his life to mankind. His brother said 'Alfred Nobel's miserable existence should have been terminated at birth by a humane doctor as he drew his first howling breath'.

Leo Tolstoy was acutely conscious of his ugliness, and feeling that there was no possibility of happiness for one as ugly as he, resolved to end his life. A contributory factor was probably his loss of faith in religion; he had drifted from religion to agnosticism and from agnosticism to nihilism and despair. He was extremely worried about his ugliness. It is said that his face was as ugly as that of a gorilla, with small sunken eyes, low forehead, thick lips, large bulbous nose, and enormous ears.

Claude Debussy was self-conscious about an osteoma (a bone tumour) on his forehead.

Mirabeau, Napoleon, Thackeray, Mark Twain, Swinburne and *Thomas Hardy* all had an unusually large head.

It was said that *Napoleon's* large head seemed to balance itself with difficulty on his shoulders.

William Thackeray was taken to the doctor on account of the large size of his head. He was described as an 'odd looking child like a pumpkin on a beanpole'.

Swinburne was said to have the largest hat at Eton. His head was unusually large, while the rest of his body was small. He was said to resemble 'a pumpkin balanced upon a forked radish'. His cousin, who was senior to him at Eton, expressed the fear that the little boy's head might snap off from the body and fall to the ground at any moment.

Various men of eminence were of unusually small stature. They included *Alexander the Great, Napoleon, Nelson, d'Annunzio* and *Christopher Wren. Alexander Pope* was 4 ft. 6 in. in height. *Lawrence of Arabia* suffered bitterly from his smallness, and tried to compensate for it by physical exploits—his fondness for feats of endurance and daring, rockclimbing, boating and difficult swimming. *Dollfus* was 4 ft. 11 in. in height.

Chang and Eng—Siamese Twins. The story of Chang and Eng is well documented. Numerous medical articles have been written about them, and many photographs of the twins are extant. Many of the articles have been brought together in the book by Hunter. In this section we have obtained some information from Hunter's book, some from a detailed medical article by Luckhardt, and some information from a variety of other sources.

The name Chang is Siamese for left, and the name Eng means right. The twins were born to a peasant woman in Siam in 1811; the father was a Chinese fisherman. The King of Siam, Rama II, ordered that the twins should be killed without delay, but he was persuaded to change his mind. When they were born the head of one was between the legs of the other. The twins were joined by a firm band or ligament which was twisted, so that they lay in opposite directions, but their mother turned them so that they both lay the same way, face to face with the heads and feet together, with the band straight. In the centre of the band was a single umbilicus, serving both babies. The ligament was for a long time so tight that they were always face to face. They could not turn in bed without being lifted up and placed in the desired position. Later, when they were older, and the ligament had been stretched, they could stand side by side, or back to back, and could turn themselves in bed by rolling one over the other.

It was extremely difficult for the twins to learn to crawl and walk, and they had to realise the necessity of moving together. By trial and error, and with the patient help of their mother, they learnt to do so.

Their mother must have been an intelligent and devoted woman. She set about stretching the band, so that instead of their being held face to face they could stand side by side. She taught them to sit and walk, and then to swim and handle a boat—for their home was on the river. The twins were first-born; later she had four more pairs of twins and four single-tons, all normal and well. Her husband died when Chang and Eng were eight. Chang and Eng acquired measles at the same time, and later they both acquired smallpox.

It soon became obvious that the twins had different person-alities. Chang was smaller and more feeble than Eng. Chang was more quick tempered, and inclined to be the leader. Eng would often give in to Chang rather than become involved in lengthy arguments, but there were many times when they could not agree. They first came seriously to blows when they were eight. Fights were not easily settled because they could not get away from each other. They had to learn self-control, and they were forced to accept the facts of their life.

Their first job was that of pedlars in the floating market. They started to breed duck eggs, and later to train performing ducks.

At twelve they could stand almost normally, apart from a slight outward tilt. For the sake of comfort they often stood with the inner arms round each other's shoulders. When one tripped, the band prevented him from falling completely, and he dangled from his brother, until either he could recover his balance, or was helped up by his twin.

Their fame was due to a remarkable stroke of luck. When they were thirteen, a merchant, Robert Hunter, saw them in the river, displaying their agility. He asked permission to take them to England, but the Siamese government would not allow it. Finally when they were seventeen their mother was persuaded to let them go to the United States, a lump sum being paid to her. On the voyage they learnt to play draughts, and became experts. They disliked playing with each other; if one made a bad move the other would correct him. On the boat they had a protracted argument about a bath, one wanting a cold bath on a cold day, and the other objecting; the captain had to come and make the peace.

In later years they frequently came to blows, and at one time were taken to court for fighting each other. They entered the show business in the United States.

The twins married, Chang having ten children, and Eng nine. The families lived in two homes, about a mile and a half apart, and it was an inflexible rule that they should pass three days alternately at each home.

There are many interesting medical facts about the twins. If one twin were touched when both were asleep, the other would awaken. They usually slept at the same time. They had a common liver, but when one was drunk, the other was unaffected. Chang drank heavily. They both had frequent bilious attacks, but at different times; when one had an attack the other was unaffected.

They had different tastes for food; what Chang liked, Eng detested. When one was feverish, the other had a normal temperature. The pubic hair of one was grey, and that of the other was black.

Chang had a stroke at the age of fifty-nine and never fully recovered. They both died at sixty-three, fortunately within a few hours of each other.

COMMENT

We have described a wide variety of ailments in these children —some of them probably representing nothing more than frequent colds and coughs, associated with marked parental anxiety, and some of them representing serious organic disease. The number of children who had epileptic fits was impressive, and the facts should encourage anxious parents of a child who has occasional fits.

Though a physical defect is obviously important, the attitude of parents and teachers to the handicap is of equally great importance. The handling of René Descartes and Edward

Gibbon, amongst others, was bad enough to make them neurotic for life.

The child's attitude to his appearance is well shown by the story of Leo Tolstoy and others. Children, and particularly young adults, want to be like others, and physical handicaps, or ugliness of features, may cause considerable emotional disturbance and unhappiness. It is obvious that parents can help such children by a healthy light-hearted and not oversolicitous attitude.

The well known story of Helen Keller is a challenge to all who have a handicapped child; and the lesser known story of Chang and Eng, apart from showing what a good mother from the poorest of homes can do for her children, provides much interesting information about a rare condition.

The physical ailments described are so diverse that it is difficult to draw conclusions from them. Perhaps the most important conclusion is the fact that handicaps, often severe and crippling for life, in no way prevented these children from going on to achieve success and fame. They may even have spurred them on to increased efforts to succeed. Coleridge, Dickens and others found that their physical weakness gave them more time than others had to devote to reading, thinking and similar pursuits.

One may conclude that if a child has the necessary intelligence, ambition and determination, together with wise management, help and encouragement by his parents, a serious physical handicap is no bar to the achievement of distinction.

CHAPTER 6

EARLY PERSONALITY

IN this chapter we have used the word personality in a
broad sense, to include aspects of behaviour and character.
It is of interest to observe these features in childhood and
their frequent persistence into adult life. We were impressed
by the small number of examples of what we now call 'behaviour problems'. We saw only one mention of nailbiting,
only one or two mentions of food refusal due to food forcing
(called by mothers 'poor appetite'), or of obesity, and none of
bed-wetting or the innumerable other problems which so
commonly worry mothers today.

For convenience we have divided the material up into
groups, dependent on the future career; they are men and
women of music and art, literature, science, religion, war,
and a miscellaneous group of people of eminence in a variety
of other fields.

MUSICIANS AND ARTISTS

We have little information about the childhood of *William
Blake*, who was later to combine poetry and art. We do
know that he was an imaginative child. When he was four
he was frightened by seeing God looking through the window,
and a little later he saw a tree at Peckham full of angels—and
received a sound thrashing for persisting in saying that he saw
them.

Beethoven was an 'ugly and unattractive child, headstrong
and obstinate to a degree'. When his father began to drink
heavily, Ludwig became bitter, sarcastic and morose. He was
rude and ill-mannered towards his friends and towards all
and sundry. He was described as being subject to wild fits of
rage and equally wild outbursts of remorse.

Cézanne was described by Perruchot as an odd child, even at the age of four, having inherited his father's obstinacy and temper. He would stamp his feet with hysterical rage when thwarted. When he was ten, he was a shy unstable boy, with violent shifts of moods from rudeness to friendliness, excessive quietness to noisiness, and with a stubborn and often intransigent nature. His father was overbearing and overprotective, and refused to allow him independence suitable to his age.

Van Gogh was rather a problem to his parents, in that they could not understand his rather odd ways and his independent mind. He was sensitive, abrupt in manner, with an intense curiosity.

Hanson described him as an arrogant prig when he was sixteen, looking 'like nothing so much as that depressing sight, a peasant out of his element. His clothes seemed not to belong to him, they sat stiffly on his awkward figure, unkempt reddish hair sprawled about his squared head, with light blue eyes set deep behind jutting brows, peering out small and suspicious from a freshly freckled face; with large hands and feet protruding awkwardly, a harsh voice speaking in bursts between strange silences, as if normal speech were throttled in him by feelings too violent for expression.'

Toulouse-Lautrec, as a little boy, was noisy, active, wilful and intensely curious. In his biography Perruchot wrote that 'in tables and pantry, in drawing room and kennels, the spoilt undisciplined child behaved like a tyrant, imposing his will and always his power'. He told the story of how one day in the cathedral of Saint-Cecile, oblivious to the horrified protests of his nurse, Toulouse-Lautrec suddenly announced: 'I want to pee—yes here'—and proceeded to do so on the cathedral's mosaic floor.

According to Hanson in his biography, Toulouse-Lautrec, as an older boy, 'had an impish charm, he was talkative in machine-gun fashion, he possessed a strong strain of schoolboy wit, he proved himself daring, mentally at least, and open to any lark, usually of his own inspiration, and when his wide mouth drew apart in its ready and attractive grin, and his dark eyes sparkled with fun, he was virtually irresistible'.

Toscanini was an obstinate and hardly an obedient boy. Once he had made his mind up not to do a thing, nothing could make him do it. His mother was constantly anxious about his appetite, and always had to coax him to eat.

WRITERS

John Bunyan had terrifying nightmares as a child. Lindsay wrote that John was 'scared and affrighted with fearful dreams'. 'The day of judgment, the horrible torments of hell fire, the presence of devils and wicked spirits, were with him as subjects of brooding from early childhood.' John said: 'These things did so distress my soul that in the midst of games I was liable to sudden depressions and premonitions.' Venables wrote that when John was nine years old he was 'racked with convictions of sin, and haunted with religious fears'.

These feelings did not last. At sixteen he became a soldier, and later served a prison sentence. Smiles described him as a 'swearer, tinker, reprobate and gaol bird'—before he repented, and wrote *Pilgrim's Progress*.

The insecurity of *Rousseau's* background is described in Chapter 1.

At the age of thirteen he was quite an expert at pilfering money and vegetables, and received whippings when caught.

At the age of sixteen, according to Green, he had a sudden impulse to exhibit his bare posterior to some women washing clothes in Turin. A few laughed, others shouted, and Jean Jacques was pursued by a man with a sabre; when cornered, he begged for mercy, claiming to be a young foreigner of princely rank who was mentally deranged and who had escaped from home.

William Cowper at Westminster School had fits of melancholy and delusions. He was convinced that he was suffering from tuberculosis. He was a shy diffident boy.

Goethe, as a boy, and to the end of his life, was subject to violent outbursts of temper, in which he lost all self-control.

William Wordsworth before his eighth year was a 'stubborn, wayward and intractable boy' (Legouis). He had an unmanageable temper. Legouis described how one day, when an undeserved indignity had been put on him, William went up to the attic with the firm intention of killing himself with one of the foils which were kept there. He took the weapon down, but his courage failed him.

His mother told a friend that the only one of her five children whose future caused her anxiety was William. 'He will be remembered', she added, 'for good or evil.'

At Cambridge he was not a good student, being impatient of advice and far from studious.

Samuel Taylor Coleridge described himself as a precocious and imaginative child. He wrote: 'I became fretful and timorous, and a tell tale, and the schoolboys drove me from play and were always tormenting me. Hence I took no pleasure in boyish sports and read incessantly. I became a dreamer, and acquired an indisposition to all bodily activity. I was fretful and inordinately passionate, and as I could not play at anything, and was slothful, I was despised and hated by the boys, and because I could read and spell, and had, I may truly say, a memory and understanding forced into almost unnatural ripeness, I was flattered and wondered at by all the old women. And so I became very vain, and despised most of the boys that were all near my own age, and before I was eight years old I was a character' (quoted by Campbell). He wrote that he had a deep and bitter contempt for others, even when a child. Owing to his inability to take part in sport, he took refuge in books.

Fausset wrote that Coleridge's inability to share in the physi-

cal activities of his older brothers and sisters made him feel
different from others. To them, Fausset wrote, he was either
an annoying oddity or a nuisance. He was spoilt by his father,
who showed him favouritism.

At nineteen he went to Jesus College, Cambridge. He won
a prize for a Greek ode, but left in his second year because of
a love affair. He became so poor that he decided to join the
army, and entered the fifteenth Dragoons under an assumed
name. An officer accidentally discovered his ability and
secured his discharge. He wrote *The Ancient Mariner* when
he was twenty-five.

Lord Byron was an unpopular boy at school. He described
himself as a little curly-headed good-for-nothing and mischief-
making monkey from his birth. He used to bite his nails,
much to the disgust of his mother, who boxed his ears or
hands for doing it.

He resolutely refused to allow his lameness to restrict his
exercise, and he rode, boxed, wrestled, fenced, fired pistols
and swam. When he was fifteen he mised a whole term at
Harrow, because of a love affair.

Byron said that as a boy, he could never bear to read any
poetry whatever without disgust and reluctance.

At Trinity College, Cambridge, he was thought to be somewhat eccentric, keeping a bear and several bulldogs.

Of all the eminent people mentioned in this book, one of
the most eccentric as a child was *Percy Bysshe Shelley*. With
regard to his parentage, Blunden wrote: 'by some inexplicable
chance or caprice of nature, he sprang in his single greatness
out of a family which apart from him continued through the
centuries without distinction, energy or noble error'.

One aspect of Shelley was his violent temper. Peck wrote
that 'the least circumstance that thwarted him produced the
most violent paroxysms of rage; and when irritated by other
boys he would take up anything, or even any little boy near
him, to throw at his tormentors'. His will was unbreakable.

The school regulations to him were nothing less than the scourge of oppression.

He was constantly teased and bullied by the other boys. At Eton the boys organised a 'Shelley baiting Society'. 'Whenever he sat down to read his Shakespeare or his Voltaire, his school-fellows would descend upon him like a pack of hunting dogs, chase their quarry over the meadows, and finally corner him into a hopeless fight against overwhelming odds' (Thomas). Blunden wrote that 'if he lay under a tree to dream of home and independence, his tormentors were at hand with some new invention to rouse and molest him. He poured forth vehement invective, and hootings were the answer.' He re-fused to take part in sport, he dressed oddly, and he would not conform. He was known as Mad Shelley. A contemporary wrote that 'he stood apart from the whole school, a being never to be forgotten'.

He carried out a variety of unusual experiments. In one he blew up the boundary palings of the playground with gun-powder. Another time he blew off the lid of his desk during a lesson, to the great surprise of the headmaster and the other schoolboys. He set fire to a willow tree by the use of gun-powder and burning-glass. He brewed strange fiery liquids and invoked departed spirits; he despatched fireballs; and in one experiment he killed some of the headmaster's pigs. Sir John Rennie, a schoolfellow, said that at times the boy was considered to be almost on the borders of insanity.

At eighteen he went to Oxford. There he was an anarchist. An acquaintance described his room there as follows: 'Books, boots, papers, shoes, philosophical instruments, clothes, pistols, linen, crockery, ammunition and phials innumerable, with money, stockings, paint, crucibles, bags and boxes, were scattered on the floor and in every place. An electrical machine, an air pump, the galvanic trough, a solar microscope, and large glass jars and receivers, were conspicuous amidst the mass of matter.'

Blunden wrote that 'no student read more assiduously; he was to be found, book in hand, at all hours; reading in season and out of season; at table, in bed, and especially during a walk; not only in the quiet country, and in retired paths, not only at Oxford, in the public walks, and High Street, but in the most crowded thoroughfares of London'.

When he was nineteen, he was expelled from Oxford on account of an essay on atheism.

He was drowned accidentally when he was thirty.

John Keats was an unusually pugnacious boy at school, and was always ready for a fight. He would fight anyone, morning, noon or night. Fighting was like meat and drink to him. Colvin described him as a violent and ungovernable child, but attractive and lovable when not fighting.

Alexander Dumas was teased for weeping so easily. At ten he was unpopular, because he was vain, over-confident and insolent.

George Borrow was described by Jenkins as a gloomy and introspective boy, who puzzled and worried his parents. He was slow of comprehension and almost dull witted, bursting into tears when spoken to, and a lover of solitude, retiring into odd nooks and corners, where he would sit for hours in thought.

Nathaniel Hawthorne lost his father as a child, and had an unusually solitary existence. His mother retired into solitude with Nathaniel and the two girls and completely cut herself off from the rest of the world. The three children kept to themselves, each of them eating, playing, reading and brooding in separate rooms.

Owing to a severe leg injury he was unable to play with other children. He stayed indoors all day and only went out after dark for a ramble through the fields or along the seashore.

As an adult he wanted to live entirely undisturbed, and strongly resented the intrusion of anyone into his solitude.

Hans Christian Andersen was described by Toksvig as 'a

strange dreamy child who carried his interior life so far that he often wandered around with his eyes shut, thus making his mother believe that his sight was bad'. In classroom he was such a day-dreamer that his teachers despaired of him. Paintings of Bible scenes were hanging in the classroom, and he would sit and stare at these, and dream himself so thoroughly into them that the voice of his teacher failed to penetrate his attention. He was an only child, and his parents always gave way to him.

Gogol was a difficult character. Magarshack, in his most interesting biography, wrote that Gogol was insolent to his teachers and despised them. 'At home', Gogol wrote in a letter, 'I am considered to be wilful, a kind of intolerable pedant who thinks he is cleverer than anybody else, that he is made differently from other people. At school they call me a meek fellow, the ideal of simplicity and patience. In one place I am modest, polite, in another sullen, dreamy, uncouth.' At school he was known for his childish and spiteful pranks, and for the biting epigrams he made about his fellows and teachers.

As a boy, he realised that he was different in his sexual outlook from others. Magarshack wrote that Gogol probably had his first sex experience with his mother's serf-girls, and this seemed to fill him with horror. Just before he died he admitted to his doctor that he had never felt any need for intercourse, and had never derived any pleasure from it.

Turgenev at nine showed hypochondriacal tendencies which plagued him throughout his life. Magarshack wrote that Turgenev imagined that the top of his head was covered only by skin and hair, and he had a morbid fear of anyone touching it. A mere touch with the finger would make him nearly faint. The boys at school soon discovered this, and insisted on pressing his skull, so causing him unbearable agony. He went to Moscow University at fifteen, and continued to be a hypochondriac. He was bed-ridden for several months. He had abdominal pain, like his father.

Flaubert was peculiar from the first. He was always in-terested in the morbid, and in lunatics. His father was a surgeon, and as a small child he climbed the wall of his father's hospital to see the corpses. Thomas, in his chapter on Flaubert, wrote that he went to a respectable school and 'for eight years he dreamed and observed and wrote, and ridiculed his fellow students and befriended them'.

When he was eighteen he spoke little, but when he did, 'his tongue was dipped in a cask of vinegar'. He showed utter contempt for the conventions, and looked upon everybody, including himself, as an utter fool. 'The very first nincompoop I see every day is myself in the morning, when I go to the mirror to shave, and the last one is whatever I happen to speak to before I go to bed.'

Swinburne is said by Thomas to have developed a trick, when excited, of jerking his arms down from the shoulders and vibrating his hands quickly like a spinning top. His mother was alarmed and took him to a specialist, who said that he was merely suffering from an excess of electrical activity and should be left alone.

Friedrich Nietzsche was an eccentric odd child. His father died when he was four, and his brother seven months later. His mother, a weak woman, was completely dominated by two of his father's sisters (his aunts) who took over the manage-ment of the home. His grandmother was also in the house. He lived in a world of women. His mother, not unnaturally, became overanxious about him and his sister Elizabeth. Lea wrote: 'Friedrich and Elizabeth, now being the object of her exclusive affection, she expected their exclusive affection in return; and this could only be shown by their acting just as she wished. Her sisters being conditioned by her fears, high in the scale of values stood security, respectability and piety. Any failure to conform to that was not merely wicked in itself, but a source of infinite suffering to her.' She stressed the ingratitude of inflicting such suffering.

Friedrich was very different from other boys, and an obvious butt for ridicule. Reyburn in his biography tells how Friedrich was 'serious, thoughtful and careful of his manners. He recited Bible texts and hymns with great feeling, and thereby impressed the young barbarians around him. They did not understand him or he them. They were in the majority, and constituted his environment, but he failed to adapt himself to them, so they teased him, and laughed at his priggish ways, but otherwise left him to his own devices. To Nietzsche the world was always a strange unsympathetic affair, not at all well behaved, not at all rational—in the sense in which he understood rationality; and even at this early stage we get a glimpse of the gap that existed for him between his outlook on life, his rules of life, and the needs of life itself.'

Reyburn describes how one day, just as school was over, there was a heavy downpour of rain, and the family looked out of the window to see where Friedrich was. All the boys were running like mad for their homes, but Friedrich was walking sedately along, with his cap covering his slate. His mother called out to him to run, and remonstrated with him on his arrival. 'But mama', he said, 'in the rules of the school it is written—on leaving the school boys are forbidden to jump and run about the streets, but must walk quickly and decorously to their homes.'

His mother was worried by his odd behaviour, and discussed him with her own father. He said that 'her ugly duckling might well turn out a swan; that he was an unusually able and talented boy, and should not be expected to conform too closely to the ways of more ordinary mortals'.

He played very few games, other than those of his own design, preferring solitude and the company of his own thoughts. As Reyburn said, he wished to lead, not to follow, to create, not to conform.

Reyburn wrote that as a young boy Friedrich took charge of his still younger sister and tried to mould her mind, prescribing her reading, helping her to reach after the ideal which he had set for himself.

At the age of nine to ten he wrote fifty-five poems. He had a profound conviction of his own ability.

In adolescence he began to have religious doubts, and his work deteriorated. When he was eighteen he became mildly drunk and made new resolutions, returning to his studies.

Oscar Wilde was different from other boys at his school. Pearson wrote that when Oscar was ten, he disliked exercise, loathed games and fighting, refused to climb trees, and had no spirit of adventure. He was careful of his clothes, loved flowers and solitude, and read avidly.

When he was thirteen he was clumsy and awkward, and was unpopular, partly because of his lack of interest in sport, and partly because he invented nicknames for boys, so clever that they stuck. He had no special friends.

At Trinity College, Dublin, he was described as an ungainly, overgrown, moping, awkward lad who was continually knocking things over when he moved about and at whom everybody laughed.

Conan Doyle was an aggressive boy, and always becoming involved in fights. His father was puzzled by his behaviour, though his mother was secretly pleased. The Fathers at Stoneyhurst were aware of his ferocious stubbornness; on the least suspicion that he was being intimidated, he would break rules deliberately so as to undergo the most savage punishment and show he could still look them in the eye afterwards (Carr).

Yeats worried his parents because he was so timid and wept too easily. At seven his father wrote: 'I am very anxious about Willy. He is never out of my thoughts.' The boy was shy, sensitive, nervous and easily rebuffed—a perfect target for bullying. He was ashamed of his own lack of courage.

G. K. Chesterton, would wander through the streets, muttering to himself. He wrote in his autobiography that he would wander about the streets of North Kensington, telling himself stories of feudal sallies or sieges. 'I can see him now', wrote Mr Fordham, 'very tall and lanky, striding untidily along Kensington High Street, smiling and sometimes scowling, as he talked to himself, apparently oblivious of everything he passed; but in reality a closer observer than most, and one who not only observed "but remembered what he has seen" ' (Ward).

SCIENTISTS

John Hunter was spoilt, because he was the youngest. His father was too ill to exert any discipline. John became stubborn, disobedient and a trial to everyone. When he could not get his own way he would cry for it, and keep on crying for hours until he could obtain what he wanted. At school he wept easily.

Charles Darwin said that he was much given to inventing deliberate falsehoods. 'For instance', he said, 'I once gathered much valuable fruit from my father's trees and hid it in the shrubbery, and then ran in in breathless haste to spread the news that I had discovered a hoard of stolen fruit.'

Edison as a child was quite intrepid, and was always becoming involved in scrapes. His father said that the boy was wanting in common sense, and he could make nothing of him. He set fire to his father's barn to see what happened (Chapter 1). He fell into a canal, and nearly drowned. On another occasion he was nearly smothered in a grain elevator.

On reading the autobiography of *Sigmund Freud*, it is difficult to disentangle the facts about his early personality from his own subsequent psycho-analytical interpretations. He describes how when he was seven or eight he deliberately urinated in his parents' bedroom. He was duly reprimanded by his father, who exclaimed: 'That boy will never amount to anything.' 'This must have been a terrible affront to my ambitions', he wrote, 'for allusions to this scene occur again and again in my dreams, and are constantly coupled with enumerations of my accomplishments and successes, as if I wanted to say "you see, I have amounted to something after all".' This is typical of his description of his early days. In fact he was a clever boy, and his father was fully aware of this and was proud of him. He had some justification for his often quoted outburst.

Freud in his early years had no doubt in his mind that fame lay ahead for him.

Maria Montessori spent her childhood in Ancona. She showed little promise at school. Standing, in his biography, describes how one day a teacher spoke disparagingly of the expression in her eyes. As a protest Maria never raised those eyes in the presence of that teacher again. In later years she attached great importance to treating even the smallest child with a respect that amounts almost to reverence.

As in the case of Sigmund Freud's story of his childhood, so in the case of *Carl Jung* it is difficult to separate fact from subsequent interpretation. If what he says is true, he must have been a very odd child indeed; but it is a matter of opinion whether the vivid descriptions of his dreams when he was three years old, written down when he was eighty-three, are likely to be factually correct. Having described a peculiar dream when he was three, he said that only later did he realise that what he had seen was a phallus.

He wrote that at twelve 'to my intense confusion, it occurred to me that I was actually two different persons. One of them was the schoolboy who could not grasp algebra and was far from sure of himself; the other was important, a high authority, a man not to be trifled with, as powerful and influential as a manufacturer. This other was an old man who lived in the 18th century, wore buckled shoes, and a white wig and went driving in a fly with high concave rear wheels from which the box was suspended on springs and leather straps.' This is reminiscent of schizophrenia.

At the same age he was bumped on the head by another boy, but was not seriously injured. Thereafter he had fainting spells, and stayed away from school for six months. He wrote: 'From then on I began to have fainting spells whenever I had to return to school and whenever my parents set me to doing my homework. I stayed away from school, and for me that was a picnic. I was free, could dream for hours, be anywhere I liked, in the woods, or by the water, or draw.' It was only when he heard his father saying that the boy tragically had epilepsy, that he decided to reform. 'I crept away', he said, 'went to my father's study, took out my Latin grammar, and began to cram with intense concentration.' The 'faints' ceased. He said that between the age of sixteen and nineteen his depressive state of mind improved.

Marie Stopes was described by Bryant as having an encyclopaedic brain as restless as mercury, and as being as arrogant, ambitious and peculiar as a female Napoleon.

SOME MEN OF RELIGION

Saint Francis as a boy was wild, extravagant and extremely generous. He was reckless and always gay, and was the leader of the men of Assisi in their sports, fashions, devilries and loves. He was very popular with his fellows.

George Fox, the founder of Quakerism, was said by Hodgkin in his biography to be different from other children: 'being more religious, inward, still, solid, and observing beyond his years, as the answers he would give, and the questions he would put upon occasions, manifested to the astonishment of those that heard him, especially in divine things. His mother, noticing his singular temper, and the gravity of wisdom and piety that very early shone through him, refusing childish and vain sports and company when very young, was tender and indulgent over him, so that from her he met with little difficulty.

'It so displeased him to see other persons behaving frivolously and lightly to one another, that he would say to himself: "If ever I come to be a man, surely I shall not do so, nor to be so wanton." "When boys and rude people would laugh at me", he wrote, "I left them alone and went my way; but people had generally a love to me for my innocence and honesty." '

He was grieved at the wickedness of the world, and at nineteen left his home to devote himself to a religious life.

Emanuel Swedenborg must have been an odd child. Writing in his old age he wrote: 'From my fourth to my tenth year my thoughts were constantly engrossed in reflecting on God, on Salvation, and on the Spiritual affections of man. I often revealed things in my discourse which filled my parents with astonishment, and made them declare at times, that certainly angels spoke through my mouth. From my sixth to my twelfth year it was my greatest delight to converse with the clergy concerning faith, saying that the life of faith is love, and that the love which imparts life is love to the neighbour; also that God gives forth to everyone, but that only those receive it who practise that love.'

White, in his biography, wrote that the bible and theology were the perpetual talk of his father's home. Emanuel and his brothers and sisters almost lived in the church, and were daily hearing or talking about services. He said that they were constantly questioned about what they had read and learned.

He acquired his Ph.D. at the age of twenty-one.

Charles Wesley was a serious thoughtful boy, who would do nothing without carefully weighing up the pros and cons. On rare occasions when he was offered something to eat between meals, he would say: 'Thank you, I will think about it.' His impetuous father once remarked to his wife that 'our son would not satisfy the most pressing needs of nature unless he would find a good reason for it'.

Dean Inge was described by Adam Fox as a wayward difficult child with a temper. He wrote that 'the wilful, affectionate, imaginative, unforthcoming little boy did not alter much except in wisdom for the next eighty years'.

Mary Baker Eddy, from the earliest childhood, had emotional outbursts, temper tantrums, and hysteria. When thwarted she would fling herself on to the floor, screaming and kicking, and often had convulsions and passed into semi-coma, or into 'the rigidity of cataplexy'. Her parents soon found that it was easier to let her have her own way than to try to appease her. Her father caused the authorities to cover the road in front of her house with a soft material, so that the noise of horses' hooves would not send her into convulsions. She continued to have hysterical convulsions in adult life.

From the age of eight she frequently 'heard voices', which she thought were divine.

SOME MILITARY LEADERS

Stories about *Oliver Cromwell's* childhood are conflicting, and some of them sound to us to be unlikely to be true. For instance, Lardner in his book on *Eminent British Military Commanders*, tells the story of how Oliver, then an infant, was snatched by a monkey from his cradle, carried through a garret window, and taken along the roof. There was great excitement and anxiety, but 'the monkey, as if conscious that she bore the future of England in her jaws, treated him very gently. After amusing herself for a time, she carried the infant back, and laid him safely on the bed from which she had removed him.'

There is probably more truth in subsequent scrapes which threw some light on Oliver's personality. He is said to have fallen into a deep pond, whence a clergyman rescued him. Many years later the clergyman was recognised by Oliver, now the republican general, when marching at the head of a victorious army through Huntingdon. The clergyman told him that he greatly regretted that he had not put Oliver into the pond to drown, instead of rescuing him from it.

It is not clear whether he was a clever boy at Huntingdon Grammar School, or an 'incorrigible dunce, as well as a rebellious and headstrong reprobate'. Lardner thought that Oliver took no interest in his work, but great interest in exploits of mischief. He wrote: 'There was not an orchard within seven miles of the town which failed to receive from him periodical visits, while the dovecotes of the neighbouring gentry were likewise laid under contribution, as often as a marauding party could be arranged. For those misdeeds, as well as for other delinquencies, he received, when detected, the most savage chastisement. Such excessive harshness produced no good effect on Cromwell. Of a bold and obstinate temper, he endured those merciless floggings without the utterance of a complaint, and returned to his former habits, not only with indifference, but with a dogged, and as it appeared, a triumphant hardihood.'

He received a flogging at the hands of his headmaster when he described a dream in which he himself was a gigantic figure, who would become the greatest person in the kingdom.

At seventeen he went to Sydney Sussex College, Cambridge. There he led a riotous life, sometimes working, at other times taking part in pastimes of violence. He excelled in football, cricket, cudgelling and wrestling. 'A contemner of the excessive requirements of polished life he undoubtedly was, nor any ways averse to drink first and afterwards to fight.' He had to leave Cambridge after a year, on the death of his father, and took up law in London. 'There he learned nothing but the follies and vices of the town, and became a debauchee and a boisterous and rude fellow.' He was now eighteen, and his mother gave him a serious talk about his bad behaviour: thereafter he became a model of virtue—for a time.

Clive at six was described by his uncle as 'out of all measure addicted to fighting' (*see* Chapter 1).

Napoleon Bonaparte described himself as a terror at home. 'I was an obstinate child', he said. 'I was extremely headstrong; nothing overawed me, nothing disconcerted me. I made myself formidable to the whole family. My brother Joseph was the one with whom I was oftenest embroiled; he was bitten, beaten, abused; I went to complain before he had time to recover from his confusion.' 'His anger was frightful', said his tutor, Madame Junot, 'and though I am no coward, I could never look at him in his fit of rage without shuddering.' He kept his elder brother Joseph in submission by beating and torturing him. His boisterousness and aggressiveness, even to boys bigger than he, earned for him the title of Rabulione—the little bandit. He was a thin, pale, unattractive boy. He said that as a boy he already had the feeling that all that pleased him must be his. Smiles wrote that nobody had any command over him except his mother, who found means, by a mixture of tenderness, severity and strict justice, to make him love, respect and obey her. From his mother he learnt the virtue of obedience.

Sokoloff described how Napoleon gathered the Ajaccio urchins together and organised them into gang battles with children from the suburbs. He wrote that he recognised no toys other than rifles, swords and drums. The walls of his room were covered with pictures of soldiers in battle formation. He stole white bread from his home in order to exchange it for black bread, the food of soldiers. 'His clothes were always torn and spattered with mud, and his body bore the scratches and black and blue bruises of many a fight.'

When seven he suddenly became enthralled with arithmetic, and forsaking all his aggressive pursuits, he sat for hours, poring over some problems. He covered the walls of his room with numbers, and arranged them into ranks. He liked solitude, and preferred the company of elders. Sokoloff said that when Napoleon was nine 'Ideas had so great a power over his mind, so omnipotent was his imagination, that the reality of everyday life became submerged in a world of fancy. But of a strange paradox this fiery brain had an insatiable hunger for figures, for absolutely exact facts, for mathematical calculations. This unbridled dreamer, even as a youngster, looked for precision in his actions, for clarity in his speech. It was as though nature wished to compensate for the supersensitivity of his unrestrained soul by a cold, powerful calculating intellect.'

He entered the Military Academy School of Brienne in France at ten. He became isolated and antagonistic, and was teased unmercifully. He built a retreat in the school vegetable garden and defended it against all. When they teased him he became more hostile and even contemptuous. It was only after many months that he began to earn their respect and acceptance, and subsequently became a gay friendly person, and leader of the school.

Bismarck even at the age of six, according to Jacks, was exerting authority and leadership over his schoolmates. He was a gloomy bad tempered youth, whom his teachers found difficult to manage. He got into trouble at school because of his lack of respect for them, and because of his pretentious arrogance.

When he was seventeen, at the University of Gottingen, he was a wild and reckless student, 'spending his time in jousting and carousals to the utter neglect of his studies. During his eighteen months' residence in the University he had fought and proved victorious in no fewer than twenty-seven duels, and soon became known as a brave and fearless youth, with a saucy tongue and a ready sword.' He neglected his studies, but when the examination drew near, worked hard, and after special coaching, passed successfully.

He then found it difficult to choose a profession, oscillating between the career of an estate owner and a government official.

General Gordon displayed features of his courageous personality at an early age. When on holiday in Corfu at the age of nine he flung himself into deep water while unable to swim. Lord Elton, in his biography, remarked: 'If during the siege of Khartoum the harassed Mr Gladstone had been informed of those early incidents, he would doubtless have found something symbolical in the confidence with which the child had relied on others to rescue him from an unauthorised venture out of his depth.'

He was one of eleven children, living at Woolwich arsenal where his father was an inspector of the carriage department. There he showed boisterous high spirits. He would release mice into the commandant's house, and spit into the top hats which visitors had left in the hall. He and his brother would push their young brother Freddy through the front door of Woolwich notables and hold the door handles to prevent his escape. He would keep the servants and neighbours at the door by constant bell ringing. He got workmen to make 'formidable squirts and crossbars firing heavy screws—thanks to which twenty-seven panes of glass in the Arsenal were broken on a single Sunday'.

He and his brother William planted their sister Helen on a chair in front of the window overlooking the main street, pinned her arms behind her, and made her grin and grimace in the window so that she would be taken by passing workmen for an imbecile.

When sixteen he became a cadet at Woolwich. He was nearly expelled when 'for some reason which Gordon considered inadequate the cadets were forbidden to leave their dining hall. A senior corporal, with arms outstretched, had been posted at the head of the narrow stairway which led up to it and the throng of cadets hung back, irritated but obedient in the doorway. It was more than Gordon could bear. Thrusting his way to the front, he lowered his head and charged. Butted violetly in the stomach the unfortunate representative of authority was precipitated head over heels down the stairway, to disappear through the door at its foot with the splintering crash of glass with which Woolwich was by now all too familiar.'

An exasperated instructor once told Gordon that he would never make an officer. Thereupon Gordon tore the epaulettes from his own shoulders, and flung them at his instructor's feet. Later he was sentenced to the loss of six months seniority for striking a newcomer on the head with a clothesbrush.

Lord Kitchener worried his mother because he was so exceptionally shy and reserved. Yet at Woolwich he was noted for his impulsiveness and rebellion against conformity.

Baden-Powell was a popular boy at school, not because he was particularly good at sport, but because of 'his good humour, his powers of mimicry, and wonder at his many quaint antics, which to the ordinary boy marked him out as being gifted with an admirable species of madness' (Hillcourt). Hillcourt wrote that he was different from other boys, who were puzzled by him and never quite knew whether he was joking or serious.

At times he felt a great desire for solitude, and he found an ideal spot for this in an untouched corner of a wood below the Charterhouse playing fields—a spot which had the additional appeal of being out of bounds. He wrote: 'The Copse Lore went beyond the development of health and body and mind—it helped me as a youngster to find my soul—it made one a comrade instead of an interloper in the family of nature.'

He was liked by his teachers. His school mistress at Tonbridge said that she would gladly have kept the boy on without fees of any kind, because his moral influence in the school was so good. At Charterhouse he joined the choir, the cadet corps as bugler, the orchestra as violinist, and played in the brass band. He showed talent as an actor, and sang and recited. Hillcourt wrote that the humorous monologue was his strong point, and that he would often make this up on the spot. He was skilled in making caricatures and in more serious painting.

Lord Montgomery seems to have been a normal determined popular boy, who early showed his powers of leadership and strength of character. Alan Morehead in his biography has supplied an interesting account of Bernard Montgomery's early days. He described Bernard as an active restless boy, who was forever plunging into some new project. He was more than ordinarily impatient of being thwarted, and showed an unusual eagerness to be leader in games. At St Paul's School he was said to tend to be argumentative and obstructive as an ordinary member of a sports team: his aim was to be captain, and to have the other boys obeying him—not so much because he wanted to be a leader *per se*, but because he thought that he could do the job better than they could.

His mother was a determined forceful woman, with a strong will, and Bernard possessed the same characteristics. The result was a considerable amount of conflict. As Morehead wrote, Bernard found himself battling with a will quite as strong as his own. He knew that he was being naughty, but something always seemed to be driving him on to the next conflict. His mother found it difficult to control his behaviour. He felt that he was not understood, and that everyone was against him.

At school he was good at sport, being captain of the first eleven and first fifteen, and a member of the swimming team.

Orde Wingate was a difficult eccentric boy. Some of the family background and influences are described in Chapter 1.

At Charterhouse, he would steal away to chapel and prayer when other boys were playing cricket or football. Sykes, in his book, told how when a friend mentioned to Orde that on Sunday his parents were going to take him to a concert, Orde said: 'If you go, you will bring your soul into danger of hell fire.'

Sykes wrote: 'The whole of his story from his early days to the end is one of conflict between the individual and the mass. In no action of his short life did he fail to assert the right of the exceptional man over the beliefs, conventions, expectations, hopes and even the morality of the "herd", the "mob", as he came to think of all majorities. That long conflict in which all that was admirable in him was to show, and in what he was frequently to be mistaken, in which he was to be both wise and foolish, began, as he admitted himself, at Charterhouse, with imagined wrongs.'

At the age of seventeen he passed with low marks into the Royal Military Academy at Woolwich. There he appeared to most people as a 'contrary, unsociable and dislikeable young man'. 'He was no more tidy than he had been as a schoolboy, making now something of a cult of slovenly clothes, well calculated to exasperate feelings in a military society.' He did as little work as he could without being expelled. He seemed to be a boorish youth with little prospect of future success.

OTHER MEN AND WOMEN OF EMINENCE

Thomas Arnold at Winchester School was shy and retiring. His manner was marked by 'a stiffness and formality, the very reverse of the joyousness and simplicity of his later years' (Stanley).

Stanley wrote that as a boy and young man Thomas was 'remarkable for a difficulty in early rising, amounting almost to a constitutional infirmity; and though his after life will show how completely this was overcome by habit, yet he often said that early rising was a daily effort to him'.

One of his schoolfellows said that 'he was stiff in his opinions, and utterly immovable by force or fraud, when he had made up his mind, whether right or wrong'. He was a clever boy, doing particularly well in history and geography. He became a Fellow of Oriel College, Oxford, when twenty.

Louis Thiers, French Statesman and President of France, had a reputation at school for his practical jokes, which, according to Smiles, made him the hero of his schoolfellows and the terror of his teachers. Amongst other tricks he stuck cobbler's wax on one of the seats, which held the master fast when he sat upon it. He was threatened with expulsion, but then settled down to work, becoming head of the class, and winning all the prizes.

Berlin, in his biography, wrote that the father of *Karl Marx* had early become aware that whilst his other children were in no way remarkable, in Karl he had an unusual and difficult son; 'with a sharp and lucid intelligence, he combined a stubborn and domineering temper, a truculent love of independence, exceptional emotional restraint, and over all a colossal ungovernable intellectual appetite.

'The timorous lawyer was puzzled and frightened by his son's intransigence, which in his opinion was bound to antagonise important persons, and might, one day, lead him into serious trouble. He frequently and anxiously begged him in his letters to moderate his enthusiasm, to impose some sort of discipline on himself, to cultivate polite civilised habits, not to neglect possible benefactors, above all not to estrange everyone by violently refusing to adapt himself.'

Florence Nightingale was an eccentric girl. Woodham Smith, in his most interesting biography, wrote that 'Florence was not an easy child. If she had been an ordinary naughty child, her mother would have understood her, but she was not naughty. She was strange, passionate, wrong headed, obstinate and miserable.'

Florence wrote that as a very young child she had an obsession that she was unlike other people. 'She was a monster. That was her secret which might at any moment be found out. Strangers must be avoided, especially children. She worked herself into an agony at the prospect of seeing a new face, and to be looked at was torture. She doubted her capacity to behave like other people, and refused to dine downstairs, convinced that she would betray herself by doing something extraordinary with her knife and fork.' She was overwhelmed with terror and guilt at the thought that she was different from others. These feelings were to be replaced by a feeling of discontent and restlessness. She wrote that as early as the age of six she was aware that the rich life of her home was utterly distasteful to her. 'She began, like many imaginative children, to escape into a heroine's past, and for hours at a time transferred herself completely to a dream world.' Her childhood was 'a series of passions', and she clung passionately to anyone who sympathised with her. She had an obsessional neatness, and was frequently upset and irritated by her sister's untidiness.

When she was seventeen, she felt unhappy in her environment, she felt that she had no one to confide in, and she 'poured herself out on paper'. She wrote scores of pages about her thoughts, writing on odd pieces of blotting paper, on the back of calendars, anything that she could lay hands on.

In a private note, when sixteen, she wrote: 'on February 7th, 1837, God spoke to me and called me to His Service'. The idea of nursing occurred to her later.

Her parents had no idea that Florence was unhappy and discontented. They thought that she was just a charming gifted young girl who was destined for a brilliant social success. Florence remained, however, thoroughly discontented and disturbed.

The turbulence of *Lord Curzon's* schooldays has been entertainingly described by the Earl of Ronaldshay in his biography. Curzon was a brilliant boy, who was able by rapid assimilation to outstrip all his fellows. He was constantly at odds with most of the masters at Eton. The Earl wrote: 'The spirit of rebellion was easily kindled by contact with authority, resulting in acts of insubordination and an impertinent demeanour, which made him anything but *persona grata* with the teaching staff. He was piqued by the inability of his masters to discount these ebullitions and to perceive beneath the surface the earnestness of the man. He took an unholy delight, consequently, in demonstrating to them in signal fashion this mistake. The capture of the French and Italian prizes was the outcome of an impish determination to score off the French and Italian masters with whom he had fallen out. He left the classes of both, read with fiery energy week after week far into the night, and won, first, the Prince Consort's prize for French by a larger percentage of marks and at an earlier age than had ever been done before, and subsequently to the surprise and annoyance of the Italian master, the Italian prize, his sardonic sense of satisfaction at this triumph being enhanced by the fact that among the vanquished was the favourite pupil of the latter. A history prize fell to him in similar circumstances. Stung to the quick by a disparaging remark from the lecturer on the subject, he withdrew from his class. In due course, to the astonishment of most people, he presented himself at the examination—and carried off the prize.'

He thought that some of the teachers had a special spite for him—and they probably had, in view of his behaviour.

The Earl continued: 'He was at once rampantly undisciplined and extraordinarily studious. To add further to the confusion aroused by those two antithetical characteristics was a tendency to conceal his virtues and represent himself as worse than he was. He shrank from being regarded wholly as a sap. Hence he committed wild exploits of insubordination. He made it a point of honour to proceed every year to Ascot races, not because he cared for racing, but because it was forbidden. For a similar reason he kept a stock of claret and champagne in the drawer of his room—not because he cared for drinking, but because he enjoyed the supreme effrontery of giving wine parties under the nose of his housemaster. But perhaps the most audacious of his escapades, at which, as he himself confessed in after years, he still stood aghast, was a sudden determination to play a game of tennis in upper school—the long panelled room adorned with busts and decorated with carved names innumerable, hallowed, if ever a room was, by a long tradition of decorous behaviour and bathed in a gentle atmosphere of learning. This wild idea was duly given effect to and for an hour the silence was broken by the boisterous laughter of four irreverent schoolboys, while tennis balls cannoned off the heads of Chatham and Canning and other giants of former days. The hour was well chosen, and the desecration escaped detection. And the heir of Keddelston and his accomplices flattered themselves, no doubt with justice, that they were the only persons who had ever played tennis in upper school.'

He proceeded to Oxford at the age of nineteen, and there his career was similar to that at Eton, but he acquired a considerable reputation for the brilliance of his speeches.

Gandhi's autobiography provides an interesting insight into his early personality. He wrote concerning his schooldays: 'I very jealously guarded my character. The least little blemish drew tears from my eyes. When I merited, or seemed to the teacher to merit, a rebuke, it was unbearable for me. I remember having once received corporal punishment. I did not so much mind the punishment as the fact that it was considered my desert. I wept piteously.'

He described how he and a relative became fond of smoking at the age of twelve. 'My uncle had the habit, and when we saw him smoking, we thought we should copy his example. But we had no money. So we began to pilfer stumps of cigarettes thrown away by my uncle. The stumps were not always available—so we began to steal coppers from the servants' pocket money in order to purchase Indian Cigarettes.' They became worried. 'At last, in sheer disgust, we decided to commit suicide.' They heard that Dhatura seeds were an effective poison, and went into the jungle to find them. They lost their courage and decided instead to stop smoking.

He married at the age of thirteen when still at school, an illiterate girl of the same age. He wrote that parents do not allow young couples to stay long together. The child wife spends more than half her time at her father's home. Gandhi wrote that in the first five years of his married life they did not live together more than an aggregate of three years.

Lord Birkenhead (F. E. Smith) was perhaps exaggerating when he described himself as a youth of incurable intellectual arrogance. He was foolish and prescient enough to tell a friend at school, 'before I die, I mean to be either Prime Minister or Lord Chancellor of England'.

Max Beaverbrook even as a child was an individualist. He tended to be a lone wolf, and frequently retired to some corner of the countryside for solitude. Driberg, in his biography, wrote that his closest friends were outside the family, and he rarely confided in his brothers and sisters. In church he often refused to sit in the Manse family pew. Those Christians, such as Baptists, who did not belong to the Presbyterian sect, were suffered to sit in the gallery, and not in the body of the church. Max would often cause his family embarrassment by sitting in the gallery, peering down on to his family below. Driberg wrote that when he went to the local school at five, he was remarkable chiefly for his ingenuity in mischief and his prowess as a fighter. He was a seasonal truant. 'In winter I attended school', he wrote, 'because it was warm inside. In summer I spent my time in the woods, because it was warm outside.'

He was twelve when he began his money-making career, by selling newspapers in the streets. Instead of selling them himself, he employed other boys to act as subagents, so that more papers could be sold. At this age he also started work in a drug store. Driberg described how he badly needed a bicycle for his out of school jobs, and his father could not afford the necessary money. A firm of soap makers offered a bicycle in exchange for wrappers from their soap tablets. Max borrowed sufficient money to buy several cases of soap wholesale, hawked the soap from door to door, selling at cost price, undercutting the local traders—on condition that the buyers gave him the soap wrappers. He sold enough to repay the debt and acquire the bicycle.

Sir Norman Birkett seems to have been a normal boisterous schoolboy at Ulverston and Barrow. Hyde, in his biography, tells how once, in the school at Barrow, he was caught daydreaming in the chemistry class and his master said: 'If you think you could give this lesson better than I can, Birkett, you'd better have my place.' 'I wouldn't mind having a shot at it,' he replied, and so they changed places. After questioning several of his schoolfellows, Birkett put a question to the master, and said the answer was wrong. He told him to come for the stick—but there the joke ended and Birkett was caned instead.

He had a riotous time on the daily train journey between Barrow and Ulverston. The carriages consisted of compartments connected by a lavatory between the two communicating doors. The boys would occupy adjoining compartments and rival factions, one led by Birkett, would raid each others' territory, armed with cans of water and other lavatory furnishings. On other occasions he would occupy a first-class carriage on a third-class ticket.

He was described by a contemporary as 'such a balanced boy, such a compound of mischief and responsibility, politeness and spirit, courage and compassion, charm and simplicity. He could behave himself without being a prig. He could assert himself and yet consider the feelings of others. He had intellect and yet could enjoy the rough and tumble of a boy's life.'

Nehru at Harrow School seemed to be just an ordinary boy with no particular characteristics and interest. He was probably never an exact fit, but was reasonably popular and his conduct was good. His housemaster later wrote that he was 'a nice quiet refined boy. He was not demonstrative, but one felt there was great strength of character. I should doubt if he told many boys what his opinions were, or the masters, with whom he had a good name, and he worked well, and seldom —almost never—gave trouble.'

In a letter he complained that his English colleagues were dull and uninteresting. He read more widely than they, and he was ahead of them in general knowledge.

He was sorry to leave school, in order to go to Trinity College, Cambridge, to work for a Natural Science Tripos in chemistry, geology and botany.

COMMENT

In this chapter we have ranged through a wide variety of personalities, which seemed to show no particular pattern. For instance, amongst the future men of religion, although George Fox and Emanuel Swedenborg were distinctly odd in childhood, because of their excessive piety, Dean Inge was a difficult short-tempered boy. Shelley, Nietzsche, G. K. Chesterton and Orde Wingate, amongst others, displayed notable eccentricities. Carl Jung, if the story was correct, was a psychological oddity as a boy, and long before him, John Bunyan was equally unusual. William Cowper, Schumann and Turgenev showed unusual hypochondriacal tendencies. Amongst literary men we saw the pugnacious Keats and Conan Doyle, and the timid lachrymose Yeats and Dumas.

Many of these children, because of their personalities, occasioned their parents considerable anxiety. Several of them, such as Cézanne, Goethe, Rimsky-Korsakoff, Bismarck and Napoleon, had an unbridled temper; Yeats was timid and refused to stand up for himself. Edison, Ferdinand De Lesseps and General Gordon worried their parents because of their boyish scrapes. William Wordsworth and Karl Marx were difficult to manage. George Borrow caused anxiety because of his gloominess, loneliness and tears.

Parents who are worried by the peculiarities of their children, and teachers who are baffled and perhaps infuriated by the odd or difficult behaviour of their charges, should take some comfort when they consider the achievements of these children. It may be that the eccentricities, like those of Florence Nightingale, and the more worrying aspects of their personality, are the very ones which are going to lead the child to fame.

We have to help our children with their personality problems. A child's personality is partly inherited, and partly the product of his environment at home and school—and he cannot be blamed for either of these. It is an unfortunate fact that difficult parents have difficult children—so that friction is likely. The most important way in which we can help difficult children is to accept them and to love them, remembering that all children are different, that it takes all sorts to make a world—and that it may well be that the difficult obnoxious child of today (who takes after one of his parents) will be one of the leaders of tomorrow.

CHAPTER 7

PRECOCIOUS CHILDREN

IN preparing this chapter it proved to be difficult to separate fact from fiction, and to separate the wheat from the chaff. We have discarded many stories which were intended to indicate unusual brilliance—in art, music or literature—but which to our mind did not necessarily point to anything unusual at all. We have tried to confine our remarks to children who did seem to show definite evidence of unusual advancement in their respective fields. Many of the examples were particularly well documented: examples are those of John Stuart Mill, Thomas Babington Macaulay, Lord Kelvin, James Crichton and Sir William Hamilton.

Several of these children went to University at what is by our present standards a remarkably early age. It was commonly the practice however, to go to University sooner than is the case now. Nevertheless, some of the children did go and graduated unusually early—and became appointed to a professorship at an unusual age by any standards. The following are some examples:

Hugo Grotius went to the University at eleven, obtained the LL.D. of the University of Orleans at sixteen, and was called to the Bar of the Provincial Court in Holland at the same age.

Leibnitz went to the University of Leipzig at fifteen and obtained his LL.B. at seventeen. He was offered the Chair of Law at Nuremberg at twenty.

David Hume went to the University of Edinburgh at eleven.

Lagrange became Professor of Mathematics in Turin at sixteen.

Monge became Professor of Physics at Lyons when sixteen.

Fourier and *Lobatchewsky* both became Professors of Mathematics at twenty-one.

Jeremy Bentham went to Oxford at twelve, took his B.A. at

fifteen, and his M.A. at eighteen. *Sir Humphry Davy* was offered the Chair of Chemistry at the Royal Institution at twenty-two, and was made a Fellow of the Royal Society at twenty-four.

Karl Witte obtained his Ph.D. at thirteen. *Lord Kelvin* went to the University of Glasgow at ten, and became professor there at twenty-two. *Turgenev* entered the University of Moscow at fourteen. *William Crotch* became Professor of Music at Oxford at twenty-two.

It will be recalled that *Richelieu* became a Bishop at twenty-three—but only because the Bishopric was in the gift of the family. The appointment aroused some local feeling.

Some bright children themselves became instructors at an early age.

George Eliot at the age of eleven held Sunday School classes at Nuneaton for boys and girls. *Philip Snowden* was a pupil teacher at the age of twelve (Chapter 12), and *John Dalton* opened his own school at the same age (Chapter 12). *Debussy* gave piano lessons when he was fourteen.

We have divided the rest of our material into subjects, as in other chapters, discussing the material under the headings Artists, Musicians, Scientists, Writers, Statesmen and Politicians, Men of Religion and Other Men of Eminence. We have concluded the chapter with a section on outstanding ability shown by these children in fields other than that chosen for their eventual career.

ARTISTS

As a rule, artists did not show their ability as early as musicians. There were, however, notable exceptions. *Titian* showed his genius in early childhood, and was a painter of celebrity at twenty. He continued painting until his death from plague at ninety-nine. His pupil *Tintoretto* was so skilful that Titian dismissed him from his class. *Rubens* was notable in childhood more for evidence of all-round intelligence than for artistic ability; he was always top of his form. *Joshua Reynolds'* drawings were the least promising of the Reynolds family: all the children were fond of drawing, and used burnt sticks on the walls of a long passage-way.

There are many stories of the early artistic precocity of *George Morland*. He spent many hours as a child in copying his father's pictures, and also those of Hobbema, Gainsborough and other artists.

Claude Monet showed very early artistic ability. Seitz, in his biography, wrote that Claude 'learned little at school, for he passed his time drawing the most irreverent caricatures of his teachers in his copy book: and he did not listen, for he longed to flee from his prison to the cliffs, beaches, jetties and water. Referring to the sea he declared later: "I should like to be always near it, or on it, and when I die to be buried on a buoy."' By the age of sixteen he was selling caricature portraits at 20 francs a sitting, and his talent was unmistakable.

Seitz wrote that Monet had some rather striking personality traits: 'he had little use for religion; he could be taciturn or irritable, with a tendency to vindictiveness and to craftiness with regard to money'.

At sixteen he was introduced to Eugène Boudin—a sailor's son who had a picture shop in Le Havre, and who did some painting himself. He taught Claude, though Claude detested Boudin's paintings. One day, however, he saw Boudin painting near Le Havre—and suddenly he saw the possibility of the art. 'Suddenly', he said, 'a veil was torn away. I had understood. I had realised what painting could be. By the single example of this painter devoted to his art with such independence, my destiny as a painter opened out to me.'

Toulouse-Lautrec was fond of sketching, and at eight filled page after page with pictures of horses, hounds, horsemen, birds and dogs. Perruchot, his biographer, described how 'whenever he took up pen or pencil he started to draw. He could scarcely open an exercise book without sketching. He would draw caricatures of the boys and masters; "not all of these were kind, but almost all were clever".'

Sickert as a boy was fond of acting and drawing. In class he drew clever caricatures. Once, when found out by the headmaster, his drawing was taken away and framed.

Epstein began drawing as a very young child. He wrote that he could not remember the time when he did not draw.

Pablo Picasso was said to be able to draw long before he could speak. When Pablo was ten, and his impoverished family had to move to Corunna, his father became an art master, and Pablo spent all his time painting and drawing under his father's instruction. He became particularly competent with charcoal drawings, and when he was fourteen he was so accomplished that his father presented him with his own palette and brushes and said that he would never paint again.

When his father acquired a post at the Barcelona School of Fine Arts, Pablo, now aged fourteen, was allowed to miss the initial stages and sit the examination to enter the next class —Life, Model and Painting. He completed the test in one day, though a month had been allowed for it. The boy felt that he had nothing to learn from the professors.

When he was sixteen he had taken all the tests at the Spanish schools. Penrose wrote that the life in the streets and the Prado were of much greater interest to him than the courses laid down by the professors at the academy in Madrid.

MUSICIANS

It is a remarkable fact that the great majority of men who achieved eminence as musicians had shown their musical gifts in early childhood. With the possible exception of genius in mathematics, this would not be so true of other subjects. On the other hand *Elgar* did not show any early precocity. *Christopher Gluck* showed no early evidence of his musical ability.

It is interesting that none of the geniuses were women,

though *Clara Schumann* achieved some reputation as a composer—perhaps largely because of her husband: and *Fanny Mendelssohn* was remembered because of her brother's name.

Below are some better known examples of early musical precocity.

Handel was famous by five. At eleven he had composed six sonatas for two oboes and a bassoon. He learned to play the harpsichord, violin, oboe and organ before he could talk. He played in public when fourteen. At sixteen he set *Almeria* to music, and at seventeen produced *Florinda and Nerone*.

Haydn showed early precocity, playing and composing at six. He composed a mass at thirteen. *Charles Wesley's* musical ability was recognised when he was two. When he was three he could play a tune on the harpsichord in time. His brother Samuel could play the organ at three.

Before *Wolfgang Mozart* was three, he had begun to pick out chords on the harpsichord and clavichord. When he was four, his father had begun to teach him minuets. He would take half an hour to memorise a short piece and an hour for a longer one, and then he would play them perfectly. By the time he was five he had begun to compose little pieces himself, and his father wrote them down for him. At six he composed a concerto for the clavier. His father, realising that Wolfgang was a musical prodigy, devoted his whole life to the boy's advancement.

His father set about displaying the boy's powers, and took him on a tour of the Courts of Europe when he was six, singing, playing the piano, the violin and the clavichord, 'dressed in his puce brown coat, velvet hose, buckled shoes, and with his long flowing curly hair tied behind'. Van Loon wrote that he 'took to these trips like a bear to honey and loved performing quite as much as most trained seals seem to do when catching fish and balancing soup plates on their noses'. He added: 'While living in stagecoaches and not over-comfortable inns and catching one cold after another, Wolfgang managed to pick up as much about counterpoint and composition as ordinary mortals, endowed with great application, may learn during some ten years spent in a conservatory of music with purple practice rooms for Debussy, blue ones for Brahms, and afternoon tea served by maids in waltz time.' Van Loon wrote that Wolfgang was always willing to show off and had no doubts of his own genius. He had no shyness or self-consciousness when performing in private or public, but could not bear to play to an audience which was not genuinely interested. At any lack of attention he would stop playing, often refusing to resume or bursting into tears. It is said that he wrote scores so quickly that they were blotted and untidy: he could not write quickly enough to keep up with his thoughts.

At twelve he composed his first opera *La Finta Semplice*. Smiles wrote that the professors of Europe stood aghast at a boy who improvised figures on a given theme and then took a ride-a-cock-horse round the room on his father's stick.

Carl Weber was taught to play and sing almost before he could talk, though serious lessons began when he was nine. When he was twelve, his talent and imagination greatly impressed his teacher. When he was eleven he published his first composition. His first six figures were published in Salzburg when he was twelve. His first opera *Das Waldmädchen* was performed in Vienna, Prague and St Petersburg when he was fourteen. At seventeen he was appointed conductor of the opera at Breslau.

Rossini played in public at fourteen.

Beethoven first played in public at eight. When *Schubert* was thirteen, the choirmaster said that whenever he tried to teach him anything new, he could do it already, and consequently he said that he gave him no actual tuition; he just talked to him and watched him with silent astonishment. Ruczizka, who gave him lessons in composition when he was fourteen, said that 'the lad knows everything already; he has been taught by

God.' Salieri said: 'He can do anything; he is a genius; he composes songs, masses, operas, quartets—whatever you can think of.'

Mendelssohn began to compose and play in public at nine. He wrote three quartets for the piano, violin and violoncello at eleven, and composed his first opera, *The Wedding of Comacho*, at sixteen. He wrote the Sonata in B flat at eighteen and the *Midsummer Night's Dream* at nineteen. *Berlioz* began to compose at twelve, *Chopin* in early infancy could not hear music without crying, and played the piano long before he could read or write. He began to compose at six. *Schumann* showed his genius in early childhood. *Verdi* played in public at ten; he begged to be allowed to study music. At the age of twelve he succeeded the village organist and earned £4 a year. He did not show early creative ability, and had to work hard to achieve what he did.

William Crotch was one of the most remarkable examples of musical precocity, ranking with Mozart, if not surpassing him, though lacking in originality. He had a remarkably sensitive ear for music, readily distinguishing any note struck. In his own memoirs he wrote that when he was six months old 'I would leave any diversion or my food to listen to my father; before I was able to name the tunes I wished to hear, I could touch the two or three notes with which they commenced'.

At two and a half he played the organ before a large company at Norwich. At three he was taken to Cambridge, where he played on all the college and church organs, 'to the astonishment of the gentlemen of the University'. He played at St James's Palace at three. At four he gave daily recitals in London, and toured the British Isles. He played at a concert of the Royal Artillery band at Woolwich.

At eleven he was organist at Trinity and King's College, Cambridge, and at fifteen was appointed organist of Christchurch, Oxford. At twenty-two he was appointed Professor of Music at Oxford.

Liszt played in public at nine. *Wagner* began to compose at fifteen—later than other musical geniuses. His first formal lessons began when he was eighteen. *César Franck* at fifteen entered the pianoforte competition at the Conservatoire. D'Indy tells how he played the work selected, Hummel's A minor concerto, in excellent style, and then, when it came to the sight reading test, took it into his head to transpose the piece which was put before him to the third below, playing it without the least slip or hesitation. The director of the Conservatoire was shocked, and withheld the first prize, but gave him a special reward—the Grand Prix d'Honneur, the only time it had been awarded there.

Brahms showed his precocity early, and became a bar room pianist. At thirteen he knew the inside of every tavern in the district. *Borodin* composed a polka at nine. *Dvorak* played and composed at twelve. *Sullivan* said that when he was not more than four or five, he knew that his career was to be music. It was the only thing he was interested in. When he was barely five he thoroughly enjoyed playing the piano, and showed that he had a wonderful memory for music.

Rimsky-Korsakoff at three or four would beat the drum in perfect time when his father played the piano. He learnt the piano at six, and attempted compositions at nine. His talent was recognised by his parents by the age of nine or ten.

Tchaikovsky very soon showed that he had a remarkable ear for music. His biographer wrote that no sooner had the boy acquired some rudimentary knowledge from his mother, than he could repeat on the piano all that he had heard on the orchestra. He delighted in playing, and often had to be dragged away from the piano. He would then drum tunes on the window panes. One day he did this to such effect that he broke the glass and cut his hand.

Brockway wrote that the boy's first recorded reactions to music were quite as neurotic as those of Chopin. 'He adored the pathetic melodies of Donizetti and Bellini, but would scream when being put to bed, saying that the tunes were still in his head and would not let him sleep.'

From earliest childhood *Arturo Toscanini* had an extraordinary interest in music. Sacchi, in his biography, described Arturo's pleasure when he heard anyone play any musical instrument. Medea Massoni, who had been sent to his father's workshop to learn tailoring, made him a primitive instrument out of the stalk of a corncob, and his delight was tremendous. The boy was sent to the Conservatory at Parma at nine, and was assigned to the cello. In his second year there he was given the high mark of 27 out of 30 for the cello.

Even as a child his great ambition was to conduct. He always tried to collect a group of boys and make them play music, and he ragged them until they agreed. He would re-arrange the scores and showed great attention to detail in the process.

Sacchi wrote that his exceptional musical gifts allowed him to grasp any technical problem, however abstruse, with the greatest of ease. He had an infallible ear and an astonishing memory. On one occasion he was taken to hear *Carmen*. Next day, without having seen a score, he wrote down a pot-pourri of the most beautiful passages, orchestrated for his few instruments, reproducing melodies with the fidelity of a gramophone.

In his final examination he obtained brilliant results with 160 out of 160 marks for the cello and 50 out of 50 for composition, with first place and a prize for the most promising graduate.

Debussy played and composed at eleven. *Sibelius* at ten composed a piece for the violin and violoncello, but could not be called an infant prodigy. His first indication of unusual talent was at the age of fifteen. *Richard Strauss* was a prodigy at five.

Arthur Schnabel, without any lessons or encouragement, played by ear the exercises which his sister Clara had learnt laboriously, and amazed the teacher, who thereupon began to teach him.

His biographer, Saerchinger, wrote that from a young age Arthur had shown himself to be extremely sensitive to sounds, the ringing of bells, music in the street, or the piano in the flat below. When he first heard the piano below 'he flung himself to the floor, pressed his ear to the boards, and listened in ecstasy'. A favourite occupation was to turn his back to the keyboard and guess the notes as his sister struck them. He showed that he had inherited his mother's gift of perfect pitch. When he was six it was obvious that Arthur was a musical prodigy, and he was given regular lessons. Everything else was subordinated to the aim of making him a pianist.

In one of his boyish pranks, he and his sister Freda, in his parents' absence, took the interior of a newly acquired grand piano apart so thoroughly that only an expert could put it together again.

He had a wonderful memory, and avoided the drudgery of learning things by rote. He had little interest in book learning or games, and had few friends.

Saerchinger wrote that 'it seems likely that the child's phenomenal musical comprehension and his avidity to express the essence of a work outran his patience in the effort to master it. There were times when he would play a piece almost perfectly the first time—with the perception of a mature artist—and then disappoint the teacher by not attaining the degree of finish that is expected to come after many hours of practice. All his life he revolted against the persistent practice that makes perfect.'

WRITERS

John Milton's father was determined that his son should devote his career to literature. John Milton wrote: 'my appetite for knowledge was so voracious that, from twelve years of age, I hardly ever left my studies or went to bed before midnight'. His ability and intelligence were highly regarded by his teachers.

It is said that *Molière's* quick intelligence distinguished him from all others at school. *Swift* could read any chapter of the Bible before he was three.

William Congreve wrote his *Incognita* when he was nineteen and all his plays before he was twenty-five.

Abraham Cowley was the youngest of seven children. His father died before Abraham was born. Nethercot, in his biography, described him as having 'extreme precociousness which stamped him as perhaps the most remarkable child in English literature'.

When he was nine he picked up a copy of Spenser's *Faerie Queene*—and it really fired his enthusiasm. He decided then and there to become a poet himself. Nethercot, in fact, wrote: 'He was thus made a poet as immediately as a child is made an eunuch.'

When he was ten or eleven he wrote his *Pyramus and Thisbe*, in 226 lines, which was published, and at twelve composed *Constantia and Philetus*. At thirteen he wrote and published *Poetical Blossoms*. He went to Westminster School, and at eighteen tried for a scholarship to Trinity College, Cambridge, without success, though he was later admitted as a scholar.

Pope at twelve was sent home for lampooning his teacher. He wrote his *Ode on Solitude* at twelve, his *Ode on Silence* at fourteen, and his *Pastoral* at sixteen.

Voltaire's ability was soon recognised by the Jesuits at his school. He could read the Bible when he was three. 'I wrote verses from my cradle', he said, and showed considerable promise in poetry. He won numerous prizes at school. It is said that his intelligence was 'like an arrow—an arrow which always went straight to the mark'. At twelve he satirised the Fathers of the Jesuit College, where he was educated. At nineteen he began the *Tragedy of Oedipus*—finishing it in the

Bastille, where he had been sent for writing satires on the King of France.

Samuel Johnson showed as a child that he had an excellent memory. It is said that he could read when he was two. He could recite the collect of the day from the prayer book after reading it once. He was inattentive, but learnt so rapidly and easily that he did well. Pearson wrote that after a single hearing or reading, Samuel could repeat verbatim whole pages of prose or poetry, English or Latin. Throughout his life, he could almost completely memorise a thing which he had read once. Like Rudyard Kipling, he had a knack of mastering the essence of a book in a very short time by judicious skipping.

As an example of his ready wit and quick thinking, one may cite the story of how one day his mother, when angry, called him a puppy. He immediately asked her whether she knew what they called a puppy's mother.

Rousseau acquired from his father his taste for reading novels. At eight he knew many 17th century French novels by heart. At nine he was reading Plutarch, and such works as Bosguet's *Discours Sur L'Histoire Universelle*, Ovid's *Metamorphosis*, and works by Molière, La Bruyère, and Fontanelle.

Jeremy Bentham could identify letters of the alphabet before he could talk. He taught himself to read when he was three. He was passionately fond of books, and before he was six he read so much that he could never find enough books to read. His parents soon discovered that the boy was a prodigy. At ten he wrote letters in Latin and Greek to his schoolmaster. At Westminster School, which he entered at eight, he excelled in Latin and Greek verse, and often wrote it for the other boys in his form. He went to Oxford at twelve, and Lincoln's Inn at sixteen.

Mack describes how when Jeremy was three he wrote apologetically to his grandmother concerning the imperfections in his letter. He wrote:

Honoured Madam, I have been very much troubled with Sore Hands, but the Greatest Trouble was their preventing me thus long from writing to my dear Grand-Mama, indeed if you knew how bad they are still, you would be surprised at my handling my Pen at all, having only the use of my Thumb and the Tip of my fore Finger, all the other Fingers of Each of my Hands being tied up together in a linnen Bag, otherwise I shod say a great deal more besides that I am Your dutiful Grandson.

Mills in his book, wrote that when Jeremy was three, he dismayed his elders, whom he was visiting in the country, by deserting them during a walk. When they returned they found that he had gone straight home, called for a footman to bring a light, and had reached down a folio of Rapin's *History of England* from the shelves and was busy reading it. Smiles wrote that 'hawked about by his father as a prodigy, the boy eventually conceived a disgust for society, and taking an aversion for law, his father all but abandoned him in despair of his ever achieving anything in that profession'. Jeremy, however, took refuge in books—and wrote about law, morals and religion, exerting great influence on legislation and education.

Goethe, when seven, learnt English, French, Italian, Latin, Greek and Hebrew, and read widely in history, secular and sacred. He was also taught music, drawing, dancing, riding and fencing. From his earliest youth he had a passion for nature. He showed particular interest in poetry, but did not show creative power until he was twenty.

Thomas Chatterton, according to Ellinger, when still four, would preside over his playmates as their master, and they his hired servants. He would stand before them on the church steps and hold them spellbound while he recited poetry and made speeches to them. He read incessantly, so that his parents feared for his health, and persuaded him to go out. As a young boy he spent many hours in the Church of St Mary Redcliffe, at Bristol, studying old parchments and documents. The office of Sexton was held by the Chatterton family, and Thomas's uncle fired his interest by showing him the church treasures. When he was eleven, a beautiful cross was destroyed by a church warden, and Thomas sent a satire on the parish scandal to a local journal. The first of his serious literary work—the *Duologue of Elinoure and Juga* was written when he was eleven. At fourteen he was apprenticed to an attorney, but he went unwillingly to work, because he wanted to study medicine. At seventeen he contributed to numerous London periodicals, writing political letters, eclogues, lyrics, operas and satires in prose and verse. Campbell, the poet, said: 'No English poet ever equalled Chatterton' at this age. His *Ode to Liberty* and *The Minstrels' Song* made him famous. At this age, however, he was faced with starvation. He was miserably paid for his writings, receiving a shilling for an article, and eightpence for each of his songs. Many of his writings were kept in reserve for publication, so that he did not receive payment. Finally, while still seventeen, he poisoned himself with arsenic and died. Smiles wrote that 'His fierce and defiant spirit, his scornful pride, his defective moral character, and his total misconception of the true conditions of life' had ruined him.

Coleridge was a precocious reader, and could read chapters of the Bible when he was three.

Thomas Moore, the Irish poet, had a gift for reciting verses when he was three, and was constantly encouraged to perform before admiring audiences in his home. He wrote love verses to Zelia when he was thirteen, and began his translation of *Anacreon* when he was fourteen.

His mother kept a strict eye on his studies. Sometimes, when he had been kept out late at a party, she would awaken the boy from his sleep in the small hours of the morning in order to get him to go over his lessons.

Byron when twelve broke into verse during a love affair with his cousin. At nineteen he published his *Hours of Idleness*.

Shelley, when at Eton at the age of fifteen, published a

romance, out of the proceeds of which he gave a party for his friends. At eighteen he published his *Queen Mab*.

Elizabeth Barrett Browning wrote verse and prose at ten, and published her first volume of verse at seventeen.

Walter Scott was a precocious child with a wonderful memory. Thomas wrote that 'his memory was like a sheet of blotting paper—he absorbed whatever he heard or read'. He ran round the house reciting poetry. It was difficult for anyone else to make himself heard in his presence, and a clergyman said that 'one might as well speak in the mouth of a canon as where that child is'. When he started school at eight he knew Shakespeare and Homer almost by heart. He was an avid reader, and had a vivid imagination.

Honoré de Balzac, though not a good scholar, had a brilliant memory, but he was bored with dull school work. He was convinced of his own ability, and when he was fourteen he confided to his sister and brother 'you shall see. I am going to be a great man.' *Shelley* was equally bored with class work, because he found it too easy. *Keats*, even as a tiny child, had the habit of adding a rhyming word to some word spoken, and then laughing.

Dumas was reading widely when he was five, and would join in the conversation of his elders, quoting information and ideas which he had read. Yet he did not do well at school.

Thomas Babington Macaulay, poet, statesman and jurist, the son of a Fellow of the Royal Society, a merchant, showed remarkable intelligence and precocity as a small child. The story of his early years has been told many times. For the account to follow we are indebted mainly to Trevelyan.

From the age of three Thomas read incessantly, for the most part lying on the rug in front of the fire, with his book on the floor, often with a piece of bread and butter in his hand. He had no interest in toys. On his walks he would tell his nurse or mother interminable stories out of his head. He was able to memorise without effort the exact phraseology of the books which he had read. He was described as a perfectly natural and altogether delightful child, always good tempered, always occupied and altogether without assumption.

It is recorded that at four, when a servant spilt hot coffee over his legs, he replied to an anxious enquiry: 'Thank you, madam, the agony is abated.'

His mother's old teacher recalled that when she called at the Macaulay's house, 'she was met by a fair, pretty, slight child, with abundance of light hair, about four years old, who came to the front door to receive her, and tell her that his parents were out, but that if she would be good enough to come in, he would bring her a glass of old spirits. When questioned as to what he knew about old spirits, he could only say that Robinson Crusoe often had some.'

When he was eight, his mother wrote: 'My dear Tom continues to show marks of uncommon genius. He gets on wonderfully in all branches of his education, and the extent of his reading, and the knowledge he has derived from it, are truly astonishing in a boy not yet eight years of age.' 'He took it into his head to write a Compendium of Universal History about a year ago, and he really contrived to give a tolerably connected view of the leading events from the creation to the present time, filling about a quire of paper. He told me one day that he had been writing a paper, which Henry Daly was to translate into Malabar, to persuade the people of Travancore to embrace the Christian religion. On reading it I found it to contain a very clear idea of the leading facts and doctrines of that religion, with some strong arguments for its adoption.' He was so inspired by reading Scott's *Lay of the Last Minstrel* and *Marmion*, the former of which he got entirely, and the latter almost entirely, by heart, that he determined on writing himself a poem in six cantos, which he called the *Battle of the Cheviot*. After he had finished about three of the cantos of about 120 lines each, which he did in a couple of days, he became tired of it.

Trevelyan wrote that 'the voluminous writings of his childhood, dashed off at headlong speed in the odds and ends of leisure from school study and nursery routine, are not only perfectly correct in spelling and grammar, but display the same lucidity of meaning and scrupulous accuracy in punctuation and the other minor details of the literary art, which characterise his mature works'. A remarkable feature of the boy was his extraordinary command of language.

At twelve he went to a private school. About school, it was said 'no one ever crept more unwillingly to school. Each afternoon he made piteous entreaties to be excused returning after dinner, and was met by the unvarying formula: "No Tom, if it rains cats and dogs, you shall go!"' Later he went to Trinity College. There, wrote Bryant, in his biography, he 'found himself at liberty to read all day and argue all night, which he generally did, supping in the small hours on roast turkey and milk punch, and ranging all history and philosophy till dawn flushed the grey balustrades and the pale faces of the disputants'.

When *Lord Lytton* was fifteen, his schoolmaster wrote that 'he had a mind of extraordinary compass. He has a physique, force and spirit which defy all competition here. Whoever lives to see him a man will find his mind employed not in the minor elegances of life, but in the higher branches of occupation and ambition. He can, and he will, if led on by a public school, highly distinguish himself there and in after life' (Terman and Oden). He produced his *Ismael* when he was fifteen.

Tennyson wrote an epic poem of 6,000 lines when he was twelve. He wrote his first volume of poems at eighteen, and at nineteen won the Chancellor's medal at Cambridge for his poem *Timbuctoo*. *Robert Browning* could read and write when he was four. At four he was removed from a dame's school because his proficiency in reading and spelling had roused the jealousy of the parents of other children. He began to improvise verses as soon as he could speak. At eight he knew much of Pope's *Homer* by heart.

Gogol at four could write words in chalk on the table and put them into sentences. He was writing poetry at five.

Victor Hugo was a clever boy at school, and his ability was very soon recognised. He wrote his first tragedy *Irtamene* when fifteen. He carried off three successive prizes at the Academy Des Jeunes Floreaux, winning the title of Master. It was said that 'he speaks little, but always to some purpose'.

Turgenev amazed everyone by his insatiable curiosity and interest in his surroundings. Magarshack wrote that he could sit for hours observing a branch of a tree or the leg of a horse, and would surprise people by the way he concentrated his entire attention on something which interested him. He had a prodigious thirst for reading.

Maria Brontë at six corrected the proofs of her father's manuscripts. At seven and a half she regularly read the newspapers and periodicals, giving her siblings an abstract of what she had read, and discussing them with her father. Her father said that long before her death at eleven he could converse with her on any of the leading topics of the day with as much freedom and pleasure as he could with any adult.

Christina Rossetti began to write verses when a child. Sandars, in his biography, wrote that without study or instruction, she became a poet, not only fully equipped with a metrical perfection which others have to struggle for many years to obtain, but with a freshness and originality which was striking. At eleven she presented her mother with a nosegay with the following verse:

> Today's your natal day
> Sweet flowers I bring
> Mother, accept I pray
> My offering
> And may you happily live
> And long us bless,

> Receiving as you give
> Great happiness.

Lewis Carroll (Charles Dodgson) lived in complete seclusion from the world in a farm parsonage almost two miles from a village near Warrington. Collingwood wrote that Lewis invented the strangest diversions for himself, making pets of the most unlikely animals, and numbering snails and toads among his intimate friends. He tried to encourage warfare among earthworms by supplying them with small pieces of pipe with which to fight. He invented games for his brothers and sisters and acquired the art of conjuring. With the help of various members of the family and a carpenter from the village he made a troupe of marionettes and constructed a theatre for them, writing the plays himself.

Collingwood wrote that the first report about Lewis Carroll from school read: 'I do not hesitate to express my opinion that he possesses, along with other and excellent natural endowments, a very uncommon share of genius. Gentle and cheerful in his intercourse with others, playful and ready in conversation, he is capable of acquirements and knowledge far beyond his years. You may anticipate for him a bright career.' He subsequently impressed his teachers at Rugby School.

Flaubert began to take notes of people and things which interested him as soon as he could write. He showed a high degree of intelligence in his earliest childhood.

Thomas Hardy had an intense interest in nature, and would identify himself with various objects and creatures. When he was nine he talked to wild animals. He was particularly interested as a child in watching human faces.

Robert Louis Stevenson was advanced in the age of walking and talking. He climbed a stair of 18 steps at nine months, walked unaided at eleven months, and referred to people by their names at thirteen months.

Oscar Wilde had a prodigious memory. It is said that in

class he would deliberately lead the master away on to more interesting topics by asking cunning questions about things which interested him.

George Bernard Shaw was top of his class at school. He learnt to read easily. He had a reputation for impertinence at school, because of his way of openly correcting the teachers if they said anything which differed from that which he had learnt at home. To keep him quiet they gave him stories to write, but Shaw, knowing that they never read them, used these to make fun of his teachers.

Sir Arthur Conan Doyle showed early promise in writing when he was at Stoneyhurst. He was awarded honours in his matriculation, and proceeded to a school at Feldkirch in Austria for a year. There he edited a school magazine. Carr, his biographer, quotes Arthur's uncle as writing: 'There can be no doubt of his faculty for that accomplishment' (poetry). 'In each one of his more serious inspirations I found passages of thoroughly original freshness and imaginative refinement. His "Feldkirch newspaper" gives capital promise.'

Rudyard Kipling was a clever boy. It is said that when he was only five years old he never forgot a face or name. When he was thirteen he read much more adult books than other boys of his age. He was able to extract the essence of a book in a very short time—while others might take a week to digest it.

The literary ability of *Rupert Brooke* was soon recognised at his first school and at Rugby. It is interesting to note, however, that in his first term at Rugby he was top in Latin and French, but nearly bottom in English. He secured a 'proxime accessit' for the school poetry prize when he was sixteen. Hassall, in his biography, wrote that in Rupert's last report from school, he was ninth in the upper bench of twenty-one boys. The report included the following comments: 'His work is more uneven than that of any boy in the form; he either dislikes details or has no capacity for them; but when he is good—on the purely literary side of his work and scholarship, he is capable of very brilliant results, and in English composition he *must* make a name.'

SCIENTISTS

Galileo was described by his father as an absent-minded little stargazer who saw strange visions and heard uncanny sounds. Even as a child he refused to accept explanations offered by others; he tried to prove things for himself. In his playtime he constructed all kinds of mechanical devices.

Robert Boyle as a boy wanted to study rather than play, and had to be forced to take recreation. When others were playing, he was constructing mechanical models and drawing.

Christopher Wren's father was Dean of Windsor—an intelligent widely read man, who was an accomplished orator, musician and mathematician. Christopher was one of eleven children, of whom two were boys. One of the boys died at birth.

Briggs, in his biography, gives an interesting account of Christopher's remarkable versatility in his later years of childhood and his adolescence. Little is known about his first nine or ten years, until he went to Westminster School. When he was nine he wrote a remarkable letter to his father in Latin. It was notable for the accuracy and composition and for the calligraphy, and was reproduced in *Parentalia*. At thirteen he invented a 'new astronomical instrument of general use'. At about the same time he invented a pneumatic engine. He went to Wadham College, Oxford, at fifteen to seventeen. There he made numerous inventions in astronomy, meteorology, geometry, mathematics, navigation and printing. He made a speaking organ, and useful surveying devices. There is a list of 53 inventions made during his stay at Wadham. He designed a ceiling, and a deaf and dumb alphabet. He translated a book on mathematics from Latin into English. When he was sixteen he wrote a theory of spherical trigonometry.

At the same age he helped to make moulds of human muscles and other anatomical preparations, explaining the function of human muscles by means of paste-boards.

He obtained his B.A. at nineteen, his M.A. at twenty-one, and at the same age was made a Fellow of All Souls College. At twenty-five he was appointed Professor of Astronomy at Gresham College, London. He took up architecture when he was about thirty years of age.

Isaac Newton had a slow start at Grantham, for a time being bottom of the class, but later reaching the top. His master said that it would be a great pity if such an able boy were to become a farmer. He showed a special interest in drawing and in the construction of mechanical devices. He drew innumerable charcoal sketches on the walls of his bedroom. He kept voluminous notebooks, with sections on arts, trades, science, botany and animals. He made models from wood, waterclocks, windmills, kites and lanterns. Sullivan described how Isaac observed the motion of the sun by driving in pegs on walls to mark hours and half hours.

Isaac Newton, like Marconi, displayed striking powers of concentration. He became completely absorbed in his work and oblivious of his surroundings. Newton said that if he differed from others, the difference lay in his capacity to pay his undivided attention to a problem. He would almost go into a trance for many hours at a time when pondering over something.

He liked solitude, and took little part in the games and amusements of his schoolfellows: he used all his leisure time in making things.

At twenty-one he discovered the binomial theorem.

Baron Gottfried Leibnitz was the son of a Professor of Moral Philosophy; he was largely educated at home by his mother until he went to the University at fourteen.

He was a remarkably methodical boy, classifying and systematising his knowledge, and applying principles and methods to his knowledge. Terman and Oden wrote that he was early concerned about the purpose, meaning and outcome of everything, striving to fathom the meaning of things, and relating one thing to another. At the age of eight he found a copy of Livy, and although he had no dictionary, he unhesitatingly set out to read it. He looked at the pictures, read what he could, and then re-read it until he had got the whole thing clear. When it was discovered at school that he had read the book, the teacher asked his mother not to let him read books he was going to read there; but he was examined on the book, and it was found that his knowledge of it was sound. He was then given the key to his father's library, and there he read Cicero, Quintilian, Seneca, Pliny, Herodotus, Xenophon, Plato, the Roman historians, and other Greek and Latin works. Long before he entered the University at fourteen, he was well acquainted with the science of mathematics and physics, and had read deeply ancient and scholastic philosophy and theology, including Plato, Aristotle and the Scholastics, the Lutherans, Jesuits, Jansenists, Thomists and Arminians.

Terman and Oden reported that in a University thesis presented at sixteen, he included examples from practical geometry and from mechanics, quoting and discussing the work of Bacon, Cardan, Campanella, Kepler, Galileo, Descartes, Aristotle, Plato, Archimedes, Hipparchus, Diophantus and others. He obtained his University degree at seventeen.

Voltaire later described Leibnitz as being 'in intellectual achievements perhaps the most erudite man in Europe'.

John Hunter, although late in learning to read, showed the greatest interest and curiosity in his surroundings. It is said that almost the first words which his neighbours could remember him uttering were what, how and why. At the age of twelve he would pester the shepherds, drovers and everyone else with 'questions about what nobody knew or cared about'.

Albrecht von Haller, Swiss physiologist, was an exceedingly delicate child, with severe rickets. He was of precocious intelligence, however. At nine he began to compose memoirs of great men. At ten he wrote a Chaldee grammar. At twelve he was composing verses in German. At sixteen he took up the study of medicine.

Muirhead tells how when *James Watt* was six, a visitor, seeing James bending over the hearth with a piece of coloured chalk in his hand, said: 'Mr Watt, you ought to send that boy to a public school and not allow him to trifle away his time at home.' James's father replied: 'look how my child is occupied before you condemn him'. The visitor then saw that James had drawn mathematical lines and circles on the hearth, and was marking in letters and figures from a calculation on which he was engaged. The visitor asked the boy several questions, and was astonished at the mixture of intelligence, quickness and simplicity which he displayed.

His parents were proud of his ability and gave him every encouragement.

William Herschel was soon found at school to have surpassed his teacher's knowledge, and he was used to instruct the younger boys.

Dr Edward Jenner, like Dr John Hunter, was fascinated by nature when a young boy. He made a collection of nests of the dormouse before he was eight, and collected fossils.

Lavoisier won several prizes at school, mostly in Greek and Latin, but otherwise little is known about his childhood.

John Rennie, the engineer, as a young boy showed his interest and ability in mechanical matters. At the age of six he was skilled in the use of the knife, hammer, chisel and saw.

When he was sixteen, an inspector of fisheries who attended one of the school examinations made a special note to the following effect: 'I must notice in a particular manner the proficiency of a young man of the name of Rennie. If this young man is spared, and continues to prosecute his studies, he will do great honour to his country.' In his examination in mathematics, after only six months teaching, he 'displayed such amazing powers of genius that one would have imagined him a second Newton'.

Sir Humphry Davy was said to have walked without help at nine months, and to have been advanced in other ways as an infant. He talked fluently before he was two. He was writing verses at five. He was a rapid reader throughout his life, and not long after he had learned to read, it was noted that he could read nearly as fast as the pages would turn. At school he excelled in Latin verse.

Isambard Brunel had begun to display his talent for drawing when he was four, and had mastered Euclid by the time he was six. At his school in Hove he amused himself by making a survey of the town and sketching its buildings.

Agassiz from his earliest childhood had had a passion for collecting fishes, birds, mice and rabbits. At ten he was fond of Greek, Latin, German and Italian, and proficient in them. At fourteen it was his aim with the help of his brother to memorise the Latin names of every known animal and plant. At fourteen he wrote to his parents: 'I have resolved as far as I am allowed to do so to become a man of letters. I should like to study at Bienne till the month of July, and afterwards serve my apprenticeship at Neuchatel for a year and a half. Then I should like to pass four years at a University in Germany, and finally finish my studies at Paris, where I would stay about five years. Then at the age of twenty-five, I could begin to write.'

Charles Darwin as a child was also an ardent lover of nature and a collector. He collected pebbles, shells, coins, birds' eggs, flowers and insects.

Thomas Huxley was an avid reader. Thomas wrote that every morning before dawn he would light his candle, pin a blanket round his shoulders, and sit up in his bed devouring all sorts of books on every conceivable subject. He would find an essay on geology as exciting as a novel, and a treatise on logic as invigorating as a drama.

The father of *Gregor Mendel* was a fruit grower. The Lady of the Manor, according to Iltis, Mendel's biographer, insisted that the village school children should be taught natural history and science, as well as the usual subjects. In the school garden the children were taught fruit growing and beekeeping. This background was highly relevant to Gregor's future career.

The teachers soon recognised Mendel's ability and spoke to his parents about it. His parents, who were ambitious for his future, sent him at eleven to a school in Leipzig. There he did very well, being marked 'Very Good' for diligence, and 'eminens' for his progress. He was top of the class. He then went to Troppau High School, where he was marked 'super-excellent' in all branches of study. His parents could not afford the fees, and he had to be entered as being on 'half-rations', and had to go hungry every day as a result. He worked very hard and made excellent progress.

At twenty-one, partly because of financial difficulties, he became a novice at the monastery of Brno—where later he was to become the Abbot. At twenty-seven he took up teaching duties as an unqualified teacher. He took examinations in Vienna when twenty-nine, to qualify him as a teacher, but he failed, failing again when thirty-four.

He was to make one of the greatest contributions to the science of life.

The life of *Sir Francis Galton* was described in three volumes by Karl Pearson. He declared that Francis knew his capital letters by twelve months, and his alphabet by eighteen months. At two he could sign his name, and at two and a half he could read a book called *Cobwebs to Catch Flies*. When he was nearly five, he wrote the following letter to his sister Adele:

My Dear Adele,
I am four years old and I can read any English book. I can say all the Latin Substantives and Adjectives and active verbs, beside 52 lines of Latin poetry. I can cast up any sum in addition and can multiply by

2, 3, 4, 5, 6, 7, 8, 10. I can also say the pence table. I read French a little and I know the clock.

Francis Galton   Febuary 15, 1827.

He went to school for three years. When he left at eight he had read and learnt the Eton Latin Grammar, Delectus, Eutropius, Phaedrus' fables, Ovid's *Metamorphoses* as far as the Medusa incident, and three quarters of Ovid's *Epistles*.

He took up the study of medicine in Birmingham when he was sixteen.

Sigmund Freud had a brilliant career at school, and was top of his classes in six out of eight years from the age of nine, and won numerous prizes. His father was proud of his precocity and did his best to help him. When he passed out with distinction at fourteen his father rewarded him with a promise of a visit to England.

He had a gift for languages, and was completely at home in Latin and Greek, French and German. He also learnt Italian, Spanish and Hebrew.

Chevalier Jackson, in his autobiography, gives an interesting account of his own early interests. It throws light on to his future career as a great surgeon. He wrote: 'As a boy I had no intimate friends and few companions. I seemed always so filled with incentive to do some particular thing that I had no desire for mere play; dancing, tennis, baseball and football had no more attraction in my later youth than hide and seek had in my childhood. I seemed unsociable because those things did not interest me enough to overcome an innate urge to make things, to create something, ornamental or useful or both. I began working with wood and sharp tools at four years of age. Thereafter I was never without a workshop; later it was called a laboratory, but it was always a place for constructive work. Play, as the term is usually understood, entered little if at all into my boyhood activities; it was more pleasure for me to make a sled than to coast on it.'

Charles Proteus Steinmetz, born with a severe hereditary spinal deformity (Chapter 5), lost his mother from cholera when he was one, and was brought up by his grandmother. Loki, his biographer, wrote that Charles led her a dreadful life, being thoroughly spoilt on account of his deformity, and highly intelligent, so that he rapidly learnt how to get his own way. Unlike Ruskin, he was not to be satisfied with a few bricks or other simple toys. He wanted to make things, and to experiment. Loki wrote that Charles did heroic deeds with candle grease and string. His grandmother would clean up the mess and gently beg him not to do it again. When the havoc was unusually serious she would threaten to tell his father. The boy would fly into an uncontrollable rage and challenge them to do their worst. The father could not bear to punish the boy because of the physical deformity—which was similar to his own.

Charles started the study of Latin at five, and at seven studied Greek, Hebrew, arithmetic, French, algebra, and geometry. Loki wrote: 'His mind was like a steel trap with a filing system attached. It caught everything and let go of nothing. Excluded by his deformity from the pleasant time-wasting occupations of childhood, he made learning his recreation. With breathless eagerness he hunted knowledge as other boys hunt sparrows. He was always at the head of his class, and his teachers began to look with wonder on this poor cripple, who had such a mighty intelligence locked up inside his poor misshapen head.'

He left the Gymnasium at seventeen. Loki tells how in order to receive his final degree the student had to appear publicly on a platform and submit to an oral examination. The only exception to this rule was in the case of a student whose work had been so remarkable that it seemed absurd to examine him with the rest. The examiners and candidate had to appear for the ceremony in formal dress. Charles had greatly looked forward to the ceremony—and was bitterly disappointed when it was announced that he had been excused from the oral. He thought a great deal about the matter, and began to realise that he was different from others and always would be.

He went to the University, and excelled in science and mathematics. He worked extremely hard, and his performance was brilliant.

Gugliemo Marconi went to school at twelve. He enjoyed school, and soon showed his ability. In his spare time he was constantly trying experiments with mechanical devices.

Gugliemo came into conflict with his father as much because of apparent wastefulness as anything else. Marconi's daughter in her biography tells how one incident precipitated a real crisis. He had borrowed a book by Benjamin Franklin, and inspired thereby, was making some experiments of his own. The boy was seen at the edge of a stream with a series of dinner plates which he had arranged in contact with a piece of string. When they were all in place he passed a high voltage electric current through the string, sending the plates crashing on to the stones. The spectators and his father thought that the boy was crazy. From that time onwards his father systematically ruined Gugliemo's apparatus whenever he saw it. His mother did her best to help her son to conceal it from his father. As a result of his mother's attitude and helpfulness, a very strong bond grew up between mother and son.

His daughter records that the boy was particularly liable to get into trouble at mealtimes, where he was expected to join in the conversation. Gugliemo would be absorbed in his thoughts, and then suddenly talk about the subject of his thoughts—much to the annoyance of his father.

At one stage his mother became anxious about him because of his extraordinary concentration on his work. She consulted a doctor as to whether he was going to damage his health, but he reassured her. She went out of her way to leave him in peace. She said: 'If only grown ups understood what harm they can do to children, they think nothing of constantly interrupting their train of thought.'

At Leghorn he was introduced to an old man, Nello Marchetti, who was going blind. Marchetti had been a telegraphist, and taught Marconi the morse code.

The real turning point in his career came when, at twenty, Gugliemo picked up an Italian journal on electricity, containing an article by Heinrich Hertz, which really fired his imagination. He then conceived the idea which was to make him famous. 'My chief trouble', he said later, 'was that the idea was so elementary, so simple in logic that it seemed difficult to believe no one else had thought of putting it into practice.' In fact Oliver Lodge had, but had missed the answer by a fraction. 'The idea was so real to me that I did not realise that to others the theory might appear quite fantastic.' His father deliberately deprived him of money, and the boy had to sell his shoes to buy some metal, wire and batteries. He completed his apparatus, but the Italians turned it down. He therefore took it to England.

STATESMEN AND POLITICIANS

Lord Macaulay once said that *Lord Clive* was a dunce, but a teacher said: 'If that child should live to be a man, and an opportunity be given for the exertion of his talents, few names will be greater than his.'

Burke's master wrote: 'his powers appeared not so much in brilliancy, as in steadiness of application, facility of comprehension and strength of memory'.

Warren Hastings was outstanding at Westminster School, especially in classics. When he was fourteen his guardian decided to remove him from school to prepare for a career in East India. His headmaster deeply regretted this, and offered to keep the boy at school without expense.

Thomas Jefferson mastered ancient and modern languages with great ease. Padover, in his biography, wrote that Thomas would study for fifteen hours a day and then run two miles for exercise. Everything seemed to interest him. 'His mind seized with equal avidity upon Greek grammar and Newtonian Physics. He mastered calculus with the same ease as Spanish. He learned to read Plato in Greek, Cicero in Latin, Montesquier in French. To get to the roots of the English Canon law he studied Anglo-Saxon. To read Ossian he learned Gaelic.'

Robert Peel's Tutor at Harrow once remarked: 'I shall not live to see it, but you boys will one day see Peel Prime Minister.'

Abraham Lincoln attended school for less than a year in his whole life, but when he was at school he was always at the head of his class. He read all books available, and carried books with him to work, so that he could read them in his spare moments.

William Gladstone at Eton was prominent as an essayist and debator, but was not a really outstanding pupil.

Bismarck was a clever boy at school, with quick comprehension, and a good memory.

William Pitt greatly impressed his father by his ability. When William was fifteen, at Cambridge, the Master of Pembroke wrote that 'he promises fair to be one of those extraordinary persons, whose eminent parts, equalled by as eminent industry, continue in a progressive state throughout their lives.'

Lord Rosebery wrote that William's tutor observed that the boy grasped the meaning of an author so readily that he never seemed to learn, but only to recollect. He wrote that although William had laboured under the disadvantage of chronic ill health, 'the knowledge which he then possessed was very considerable, and in particular his proficiency in the learned languages was probably greater than ever was acquired by any other person in such youth'. It was not uncommon for him when twelve, to translate into English, six or seven pages of Thucydides, which he had not previously seen, without more than two or three mistakes, and sometimes without one. He went to Cambridge when he was thirteen, took his M.A. at seventeen, and became Prime Minister at twenty-two.

Lloyd George had learnt to read and write long before he started school at four. He had a brilliant memory, and learnt his lessons without effort. He showed a particular aptitude for mathematics, and especially for mental arithmetic. He was convinced in his own mind that he was destined for a position of eminence.

Philip Snowden was consistently top of his class at school.

Though little is known about *Stalin's* childhood, it is known that he had a remarkable memory, and learned his lessons apparently without effort.

Aneurin Bevan was a prodigious reader, and would often stay awake until dawn reading books. He particularly enjoyed reading poetry. He would talk about politics, history or religion with ease.

Jan Christian Smuts had a remarkably retentive memory. His son, in his biography, tells how Jan tackled Greek for the first time during a six-day holiday before his final term, and locking himself up in his room, memorised the books and mastered the subject to such effect that he came out top in the subject. He could memorise large parts of books by reading them once. His examiners were inclined to accuse the boy of cheating, for many of the answers were verbatim from the text books. Jan Smuts said that at Stellenbosch his faculty for memorising was at its peak, and it had already waned somewhat by the time he reached Cambridge. Yet at the age of sixty or seventy, while working at botany, he could still memorise the thousands of Latin names of plants with the greatest ease. It is said that he memorised the whole of the contents of his library of 5,000 books and could immediately give chapter and verse for any quoted passage.

When Jan Smuts was seventeen, Cecil Rhodes heard him give an address of welcome. Rhodes remarked to a friend:

'Keep an eye on the young fellow Smuts, Jan will be the first man in South Africa.'

In *My Darling Clementine*, the story of Lady Churchill, by Fishman, the story is told of a Harrow master's first meeting with *Winston Churchill*. 'I was', he said, 'a young master lately from the University, with possibly a sufficiently full knowledge of the subject to be taught but with little knowledge of human nature, and least of all boy's nature. I entered a room where there were some twenty boys to find out what they knew and where to start. I tried this place and that in the textbooks, going back and forth, until in despair—*sotto voce*, as I thought, and certainly with no wish whatever to be answered, I said, "What am I to do with boys who know nothing?" Quick as a flash of lightning came the reply from a small fair-haired boy near me: "Please sir, teach us!" That boy was Winston Churchill.'

OTHER MEN AND WOMEN OF EMINENCE

A remarkable and well documented story of early genius is that of *James Crichton of Eliock*—later termed 'The Admirable Crichton'. There are several books about him, and many articles. He was born in 1560, the son of a Lord of Session and Lord Advocate in Scotland. His mother was a member of the Royal House of Scotland. It is uncertain where he attended school: it was probably in Perth or Edinburgh, and little is known of his early childhood. It is known, however, that he went to St Salvator's College at St Andrews University at the age of nine, took his B.A. at twelve and his M.A. at fourteen with the present day equivalent of first class honours. Part of the information which we have comes from a Centenary Volume of St Andrews University, in which there are brief accounts of some of the famous former students. The writer in this volume wrote as follows: 'Known to history as the Admirable Crichton for his universal accomplishments as scholar and man of action, the figure of James Crichton of

Eliock and Cluny stands out as one of the most remarkable and mysterious in that exceedingly interesting period of Italian life and letters towards the close of the 16th century.'

By the age of fifteen to sixteen he was a boy of extensive learning, 'having read through all the sciences, including political, rhetorical and philosophical subjects, and mathematics and other branches of science. He had learnt twelve languages by the age of sixteen and could answer his teachers in any of them. At seventeen he went abroad to display the extent of his erudition in the public disputations which were then common in the Universities of the Continent.'

Tytler, in his biography, described the public disputations, which were a feature of the day. The most learned men of the age contended with each other on the most abstruse questions of science and philosophy, in the presence of the public and University staff. James Crichton, on arrival in Paris at seventeen, in accordance with custom, 'affixed placards or challenges to literary and philosophical warfare, in the most conspicuous parts of the city, saying that in six weeks he would present himself at the College of Navarre to answer whatever subject should be proposed to him, in any science, liberal art, discipline or faculty, whether practical or theoretical, in any of the twelve specified languages—Hebrew, Syrian, Arabic, Greek, Latin, Spanish, French, Italian, English, Dutch, Flemish or Slavonic. He also undertook to write in prose or verse in any of these languages. He duly appeared in front of an immense concourse of spectators, and acquitted himself to the astonishment of all who heard him, receiving the public congratulations of the president and senior professors.'

James had become one of the most fearless swordsmen of the time, and 'rode with consummate grace'. He was also a brilliant dancer, and had a 'strong genius for music, with excellent performance on a wide variety of musical instruments'.

The day after his brilliant performance at the College of Navarre, he competed in a tilting match in the Louvre, and in the presence of ladies and princes of the Court of France, won from every competitor—and was given the title of the 'Admirable Crichton'.

Two years later he went to Italy, and in the presence of the Pope, many of the cardinals and most learned men of Italy, again astonished the spectators. He was publicly introduced to the Doge and Senate in Venice, and crowds flocked from all quarters to witness the exhibition of his talents in public disputations with the most learned men of the country.

An unknown writer, when James was twenty, wrote: 'He is a master of ten languages. These are Latin and Italian, Hebrew, Chaldaic, Spanish, French, Flemish, English and Scotch; and he is acquainted with German. He is deeply skilled in philosophy, in theology and astrology; he possesses a thorough knowledge of the Cabala. His memory is so astonishing that he knows not what it is to forget: and whenever he has once heard an oration, he is ready to recite it again, word for word, as it was delivered. He composes Latin verses upon any subject which is proposed to him, and in every different kind of metre. Such is his memory that although these verses have been extempore, he will repeat them backwards, beginning from the last word in the verse. His orations are unpremeditated and beautiful. His address is that of a finished gentleman, even to a wonder; and his manner, in conversation, the most gracious which can be imagined.

'He has attained a great excellence in the accomplishments of leaping and dancing, and to a remarkable skill in the use of every sort of arms. He is a remarkable horseman, and breaker of horses, and an admirable jouster. Upon the great question of the Holy Spirit, he has held disputations with the Greeks, and has exhibited an incalculable mass of authorities, both from the Greek and Latin fathers, and also from the de-cisions of the different councils. The same exuberance is shown when he discourses upon subjects of philosophy or theology, in which he has all Aristotle and the commentators at his finger ends, reciting not merely lines but pages in Greek. Saint Thomas and Duns Scotus, with their different disciples, the Thomists and Scotist, he has all by heart. He is a wonder of wonders.' Tytler quoted several other statements agreeing with the above.

He was killed by a drunken prince at Mantua when he was twenty-two.

Tytler names several other remarkable examples of intellectual precocity. They include *Pliny* the younger, *Tasso, Picus, Prince of Mirandula, Potitian, Alexander Cherubini, Lopez de Vega* (Spanish writer), *Melanchthon, Father Maignan, M. Petit* the elder, *Servin* the younger, *Anna Schurmann* and *Marchisetti. Anna Schurmann*, born in 1607, at ten distinguished herself by her productions in music, sculpture, painting and engraving, and her knowledge of languages, astronomy and philosophy. *Marchisetti* 'never was a boy': at thirteen he was master of the whole philosophy of Aristotle and at fifteen published a work containing 2,000 theological questions, which he undertook to defend against all who appeared to attack them in a public exhibition which was to last three days.

Lady Mary Wortley Montagu was clearly a girl of unusual intelligence. She lost her mother at four, and was brought up by a rather ineffective father, the future Marquess of Dorchester, and by her grandmother. She had a passion for reading. Halsbrand, in his biography, wrote that by the age of fourteen she had read widely, including the plays of Beaumont and Fletcher, Dryden, Lee, Otway, Congreve, Molière and Corneille. She was writing competent stories herself at that age. She taught herself Latin, by getting hold of a Latin Dictionary and Grammar, and hiding in her father's library every morning from 10 till 2 and in the evenings from 4 to 8 —and she acquired considerable proficiency in it.

She was greatly encouraged in her precocious learning by distinguished visitors to her home—including Joseph Addison, Richard Steele and William Congreve.

Christian Heineken was hardly an eminent man, for he died at the age of four years; he was famous, nevertheless. Born in 1721 in Lubeck, he was said to talk within a few hours of birth. Before he was twelve months old he could recite stories and verses. At fourteen months he knew the whole Bible. At two and a half years he had learnt ancient history, geography and anatomy, and knew 800 Latin words, learning over 150 new ones each week. He could read German, Latin and French fluently. At three years old he could add, subtract and multiply. In his fourth year he knew 220 songs, 80 psalms, 1,500 verses and sentences of Latin writers. He gave a demonstration before the King of Denmark in Copenhagen and died at the age of four years and four months.

David Garrick had a gift for imitating others in an uncanny way, and showed good powers of observation, but in general he did not excel at school. After a year at Lichfield Grammar School, when he was ten, he organised some of his schoolfellows to perform a play (*The Recruiting Officer*).

Lafayette, French patriot and soldier, at thirteen was instructed to write a Latin essay on the superiority of the spirit of man to brute force, as exemplified by horse and rider. With his usual recalcitrance, he wrote instead a paean of praise of the revolutionary spirit of freedom. His ability was recognised early.

Sir William Jones, oriental expert and jurist, was the son of an eminent mathematician, who died when William was three. He was a brilliant boy at Harrow School. Dr Thackeray, the headmaster, was greatly impressed by his intelligence and initiative. He once declared that 'If Jones were left naked and friendless on Salisbury Plain, he would nevertheless find the road to fame and fortune.' This, one feels, was an unusual compliment.

Thomas Young, natural philosopher, the first of ten children, lived most of his first seven years in the home of his maternal grandfather, who took great interest in his education. Wood, in his biography, wrote that at two years of age Thomas had learnt to read with considerable fluency, and went to the village school. At three he had read the Bible twice through, from end to end, and all Watts' hymns. When four he repeated the whole of Goldsmith's *Deserted Village*, with the exception of a word or two. He began Latin grammar when he was four. He went to a boarding school when he was six —but only stayed for eighteen months, making little progress there. When he was eight he greatly enjoyed the three-volume Dictionary of Arts and Sciences.

When twelve he committed to memory the greater part of the Westminster Greek Grammar, and read the whole of Beza's Greek and Latin testament.

He left school at thirteen, with a good knowledge of Greek, Latin, French, Italian, physics and optics, and was reading Hebrew, Chaldee, Syriac and Samaritan. At fourteen to fifteen he was writing specimens of the Bible in English, French, Italian, Greek, Latin, Hebrew, Chaldee, Syriac, Samaritan, Arabic, Persian, Turkish, and Aethiopic. From fourteen to eighteen he was reading and teaching himself mathematics, astronomy, philosophy and botany, especially Linnaeus, Newton's *Principia* and *Optics*, chemistry by Lavoisier and Black, and medicine by Boerhaave.

He took up the study of medicine at nineteen in London.

Hales wrote that the mother of *Mazzini* was convinced that her boy was a 'divine emanation destined to raise mankind to a high level'. Her cousin, Colonel Patroni, wrote when Guiseppe was eight: 'Believe me, Signora cousin, this dear boy is a star of the first magnitude, destined to shine with a true light and to be admired by the culture of Europe. Supreme geniuses, who in past epochs were the glory of their ages, generally showed in their infancy just those powers which can be seen in him.'

Alfred Nobel was a clever boy at school, and was first out of eighty-two in his class. Halasz, in his biography, wrote that

Alfred's report at the end of formal education, after one year
at school, read: 'A for general intelligence, A for industry,
A for conduct.' He would translate Voltaire into English,
German or Russian, and then re-translate them back into
French and compare the result with the original. He was able
later to speak many languages, easily and precisely. He was
very fond of Shelley's poetry, and wrote English verse.

The Earl of Birkenhead won every school prize for which he
entered. He gave a particularly good impression as a speaker
and essayist. When he was nine, his father assured him that
'There is no reason why you should not become Lord Chancellor.' He said that there was 'no ambition in life from which
he need shrink, no great office of state, no glittering prize
which was not vulnerable to the assault of industry, daring and
ability'. The boy was pleased with this, and was unwise enough
to tell the other boys, on his first day at school, that he proposed to be the future Lord Chancellor. He achieved his
ambition thirty-seven years later.

Lord Northcliffe was thought by his headmaster, Dr Milne,
to be one of the brightest boys and the most handsome, even
though he did not do so well in class.

Dean Inge's report read 'Excellent in all respects, work up
to a high standard. Ought to become a distinguished scholar.
I have nothing but praise for him.'

Lawrence of Arabia, when he was still two years old, learned
the alphabet by listening to his brother's lessons. His elder
brother said that by the age of five Lawrence could read the
newspaper upside down. He retained this gift. Aldington
wrote that Lawrence climbed a steep loft ladder at two.
When he was seven he was taken to see the Spithead review,
and was found reading Macaulay in the cabin. He did well at
the High School, Oxford, and became interested in archaeo-
logy. He was described as having an alert enquiring mind,
and as being clever with his hands. He loved anything mech-
anised and read widely.

Archbishop Temple learnt rapidly and easily at school. When he was twelve, he was top in classics and mathematics, and no pupil reached to within 50 marks of his total in the final examination. At thirteen he went to Rugby, and there had a distinguished record. Iremonger, in his biography, wrote that on his own initiative Temple had read in prep. periods the whole of seven English poets, the *Phaedo* and the whole of the *De Rerum Natura*. He was a frequent and fluent speaker in the debating society, and showed good musical appreciation. He left Rugby with a Major leaving exhibition. Iremonger wrote that 'his schoolfellows remembered him as a stout vigorous boy with a striking intelligent face, walking with a deliberate stride, a little uncertain what to do with his hands, but quite sure of himself in everything else, with a straw hat set at such an angle that he had to throw his head back in order to look straight ahead of him. He had an insatiable thirst for knowledge, and intense zest in enjoying everything. He was very friendly and kind to small boys, and above all, unswervingly loyal to his father, his school and his friends.'

Sir Norman Birkett was born in Ulverston. His father was a draper, who built up a flourishing business known throughout Furness. His mother died when he was three, and he wrote later that he had no memory of her. His father remarried next year. For details of his childhood we are indebted to Hyde.

Norman went to a new Infants' School when about four, but soon came home with a note to the effect that he had absorbed all they could teach him.

At eleven he went to a Higher Grade School at Barrow in Furness. There he did particularly well in chemistry. One of his school reports, when he was fourteen, showed him seventh out of thirty-one boys. He was given 'Excellent' in spelling and practical chemistry, while he was given 'Poor' for Euclid and algebra. He was 'Good' in penmanship, composition, French and physics. His conduct was 'Very good'; and he was described as a 'Very bright and intelligent student.'

OUTSTANDING ABILITY AND INTERESTS IN OTHER SUBJECTS

We have noted below some signs of unusual ability in subjects other than those which were chosen for the eventual career. There must be many more examples which we have not mentioned.

Galileo excelled at the lute, and played the organ and other instruments. He showed talent in drawing and painting.

Sir William Herschel showed musical precocity in childhood. At fourteen he was skilled with the oboe and the violin.

Gibbon wrote: 'in my childhood I was praised for the readiness with which I could multiply and divide, by memory alone, two sums of several figures; had I persevered in this line of application, I might have acquired some fame in mathematical studies'.

Alessandro Volta, genius of electricity, was one of nine children, five of whom became priests or nuns. He was born in Como, Italy. Alessandro was pressed by his family to enter the priesthood, like three of his brothers. By fourteen, however, he knew that he wanted to be a physicist. He acquired experimental equipment when he was sixteen, and at eighteen was in correspondence with a French physicist, the Abbé Nollet.

Giorgio de Santillana, in writing about Volta, said that Alessandro had considerable literary interest, and composed a long Latin poem on nature and science, discussing the researches of Joseph Priestley and James Watt. He said that the poem had considerable literary merit.

Mozart took an early and immense delight in mathematics. He would chalk sums all over available walls, furniture and staircases.

Carl Weber when eight was interested in oil, miniatures, pastel painting and engraving. He was not brilliant in them, though he did show competency. Gradually music supplanted the arts.

Both *Mendelssohn* and *Crotch* showed literary and artistic talent as precocious as their musical talent. *Schumann* showed a gift for literature as well as music. At thirteen he contributed articles to a local magazine. Between fifteen and eighteen he wrote two books, consisting mainly of poetry.

Richard Wagner showed outstanding talent for poetry. At thirteen, according to Thomas, he translated the first twelve books of the *Odyssey*, read Shakespeare in German, and knew Weber's opera *Der Freischütz* by heart.

Robert Browning was skilled in drawing and was known among his schoolfellows for his ability as a caricaturist. His father had serious hopes that he would become an artist.

Louis Pasteur was fond of drawing portraits. Experts believe that he might have become a great artist.

Borodin was fond of painting and at thirteen he was particularly interested in chemistry. He read widely.

Rimsky-Korsakoff was particularly fond of reading and arithmetic. 'Reading', he said, 'was child's play to me. I learned to read without being taught. My memory was splendid; whole pages of what my mother read to me I remembered word for word.'

George Bernard Shaw had a good ear for music, and although he could not play any instrument or read a note, he could sing and whistle from end to end the leading works of Handel, Haydn, Mozart, Beethoven, Rossini, Bellini, Donizetti and Verdi.

Renoir had musical talent. This was recognised by Gounod, who advised him to become a musician.

COMMENT

There are many features of the precocity of these children which are of interest. One is impressed by the number who were able to read at an unusually early age. Thomas Young and Francis Galton, for instance, were both reading well when they were two. Very many were intensely keen on reading, and they read widely. Many were remarkably precocious in the learning of languages. One of the most remarkable examples of this was William Hamilton (Chapter 8). Marconi and Newton and probably many others showed intense concentration. Several had an extraordinarily retentive memory. Perhaps the most remarkable in that respect was James Crichton, who had a vast encyclopaedic knowledge in several languages. Agassiz and Leibnitz both displayed features commonly seen in mentally superior children—the enthusiasm for collecting, classifying and systematising knowledge. Christopher Wren and Leonardo da Vinci (Chapter 12) were remarkable for the diversity of their interests and for their inventiveness. Crotch, though famous because of his musical precocity, lacked one of the hallmarks of true genius —creativity, so that his eventual achievements were slight. Several excelled in subjects other than that in which they were to acquire renown.

It is interesting to read about the attitudes of the parents to the outstanding qualities of their children. Marconi's father, probably not recognising his son's genius, did his utmost to prevent the boy's success, and might well have stifled his genius but for the boy's determination and his mother's help. The parents of Macaulay, fully recognising the boy's genius, displayed great wisdom in managing him—giving him every possible opportunity to learn, but doing nothing to show him off, and discouraging all forms of boastfulness.

The precocity of these children was an interesting contrast to the apparent lack of early promise in the children described in Chapter 3.

CHAPTER 8

MATHEMATICIANS

THERE is a vast difference between calculating ability, pure and simple, and creative mathematical genius. It seems that calculating ability bears little relationship to intelligence, for some of the boy calculators mentioned in this chapter were boys of low intelligence. Tredgold, in his book on *Mental Deficiency*, devoted a section to the so-called 'Idiots Savants'—idiots with remarkable abilities in certain fields, such as calculation, and painting of a repetitive type. Barlow, in his fascinating book entitled *Mental Prodigies*, has brought together some stories, most of them well authenticated, of remarkable calculating and mathematical ability.

Children with precocity in music tend to come from musical families; but children with precocity in mathematics tend to come from ordinary families without any evidence of a hereditary strain of mathematical ability. Exceptions are mentioned in this chapter. Some of the children mentioned—notably Hamilton, Gauss and Ampère, showed all-round ability.

In the first section we describe true mathematical geniuses. In the second section we give examples of boy calculators—all famous in their time, but totally lacking in creative ability. There was admittedly some overlapping between the two groups.

DISTINGUISHED MATHEMATICIANS

Gottfried Leibnitz was born in Leipzig, the son of a professor of moral philosophy, who died when his son was six. Gottfried was largely self-taught, by incessant reading in his father's library. At eight he began to study Latin, and at twelve had mastered it sufficiently to write good Latin prose. He later taught himself Greek. He became dissatisfied with classics, and took up logic. At the age of fifteen he entered the University of Leipzig to study law, and at seventeen entered the University of Jena to study mathematics. At twenty he took the LL.D. in Nuremberg, and was asked to accept the Professorship of Law, but he refused.

Bell wrote that mathematics was but one of the many fields in which Leibnitz showed conspicuous genius: he contributed to the knowledge of law, religion, statecraft, history, literature, logic, metaphysics and speculative philosophy, and his contributions in any one of them would have secured his fame and preserved his memory. He was interested in Economics, International Law, and the establishment of mining as a paying industry in Germany.

Bell wrote that it seems incredible that one head could have been responsible for all the thoughts, published and unpublished, that Leibnitz committed to paper. It is said that his skull was of less than average size.

Bell added: 'The harvest of all this ceaseless activity was a mass of papers, of all sizes and all qualities, as big as a young haystack, that has never been thoroughly sorted, much less publicised. Today most of it lies baled in the Royal Hanover Library, waiting the patient labours of an army of scholars to winnow the wheat from the straw.'

Bernoulli was another mathematical genius. Barlow noted that in three generations the family produced eight mathematicians of unusual ability, and that no fewer than one hundred and twenty of the descendants have been traced, and the majority achieved distinction: they included five Professors at Basel, and Professors at Groningen, St Petersburg and Padua. They included Daniel Bernoulli, born in Groningen in 1700, who was Professor of Mathematics at St Petersburg, and at other times was Professor of Anatomy, Physics, Botany, and Natural and Speculative Philosophy at Basel.

Léonard Euler, according to Bell, was the most prolific

mathematician in history, and was called by his contemporaries 'Analysis Incarnate'. It was estimated that 60 to 80 large quarto volumes would be required to publish his collected works. He is described as probably the greatest man of science that Switzerland has produced.

His father was a pastor and mathematician, and wanted his son to follow in his steps, but 'fortunately made the mistake of teaching the boy mathematics'. The boy knew what he wanted to do, but to please his father entered the University of Basle to study theology and Hebrew. In mathematics his ability was recognised by Johannes Bernoulli, who gave him private lessons.

The boy never lost his religious faith, and would conduct the family prayers for the household, often finishing up with a sermon.

Lagrange was described by Napoleon as 'the lofty pyramid of the mathematics and sciences'. He was probably the greatest mathematician of the 18th century.

His first interests were in classics. Bell wrote that it was more or less by accident that Lagrange became interested in mathematics, when an essay by Halley extolling the superiority of calculus over the synthetic geometrical methods of the Greeks fell into his hands. In an incredibly short time he had mastered entirely unaided the principles of modern analysis. At the age of sixteen he became Professor of Mathematics at the Royal Artillery School in Turin.

Gasford Monge was the son of a knife grinder and pedlar, who had a great respect for education, and sent his son to the local college, where he regularly won the first prize in all subjects.

When Gasford was fourteen he constructed a fire engine, much to the astonishment of the citizens. When asked how he did it, he replied: 'I had two infallible means of success: an invincible tenacity, and fingers which translated my thought with geometrical fidelity.' Bell described him as a born geometer and engineer with an unsurpassed gift for visualising complicated space relationships.

He was appointed Professor of Physics in Lyons at the age of sixteen.

Jean Baptiste Fourier lost both parents when he was eight, and was recommended to the Bishop of Auxerre by a charitable lady who had been impressed by the boy's good manners. The Bishop secured his entrance to the local military college.

Bell wrote that by the age of twelve the boy was writing magnificent sermons for the leading church dignitaries of Paris to preach as their own.

At thirteen he was a problem child, petulant and badly behaved. But then he became interested in mathematics, and changed completely. Bell wrote that to provide light for his mathematical studies after he was supposed to be asleep, Jean collected candle ends in the kitchen and the college.

The Benedictines of the College tried to persuade him to enter the priesthood, but he resolved to make mathematics his career. He became professor of mathematics at the age of twenty-one.

André Marie Ampère is famous for his measurement of electric current. He showed all-round precocity and had a brilliant memory. He learnt to count at the age of three or four, by means of pebbles. He read widely—including history, travel, poetry, romances and philosophy. His greatest interest was a twenty-volume encyclopaedia.

By the age of eleven he had mastered elementary mathematics and had studied the application of algebra to geometry.

At eighteen he studied the *Mechanique Analytique* of Lagrange, and repeated nearly all of his calculations (Barlow).

Carl Friedrich Gauss was described by Bell as 'The Prince of Mathematicians'. Bell wrote that in all the history of mathematics there was no one to approach the precocity of Gauss as a child.

He was born in a miserably poor cottage in Brunswick. His

father was an honest but uncouth ill-educated man, who was harsh and almost brutal to his sons. He did everything in his power to thwart Carl and to prevent his acquiring a suitable education. If the father had had his way, the boy would have become a gardener, or a bricklayer, as he was.

One day when Carl was two, his father was working out the weekly wages of the labourers under his charge, unaware that Carl was following the proceedings with a critical eye. Coming to the end of his long computation, he was startled to hear the little boy pipe up 'Father, the reckoning is wrong. It should be...' Carl was right. No one had taught him arithmetic. In later years he declared that he could reckon before he could talk.

He taught himself to read when he was two.

He started school when he was seven. 'This was run', Bell wrote, 'by a virile brute, one Büttner, whose idea of teaching the hundred or so boys in his charge was to throw them into such a state of terrified stupidity with his whip that they forgot their names.' When Carl was ten, Büttner gave the class an exercise which consisted of writing down all the numbers from 1 to 100 and adding them up. The pupil who finished first laid his tablet in the middle of the big table. Dunnington, in his biography, tells how the problem had scarcely been given when Carl threw his tablet on to the table and said in Brunswick dialect 'Ligget se' (There it is). Carl was right. He had calculated that

$$100 + 1 = 101$$
$$99 + 2 = 101$$
$$98 + 3 = 101$$

and so there are as many pairs as there are in 100. The answer, therefore, was $50 \times 101 = 5050$. Büttner was astounded, and obtained the best textbook of arithmetic available and presented it to Carl. 'He is beyond me', he said, 'I can teach him nothing more.'

Fortunately his mother, recognising the boy's genius, took

his part and defeated her husband's aim to keep the boy as ignorant as he was. She expected great things of him, and when he was nineteen she asked a mathematical friend whether Carl would ever amount to anything. He replied that 'he is the greatest mathematician in Europe'—at which she burst into tears.

When he was thirteen, according to Barlow, a new professor of mathematics handed back his first exercise to him, with the remark that it was unnecessary for such a mathematician to attend his lectures any more.

When he was fourteen the Grand Duke of the Duchy of Brunswick, hearing of his talents, sent for the boy, and was entertained by his calculations. He was so impressed that he paid for his school fees.

At nineteen he decided to take up mathematics as a career.

Richard Whateley was Archbishop of Dublin, and showed an all-round ability.

According to Barlow, Richard began to calculate at five, but the interesting thing is that he retained his power only for about three years. It left him when he started school, and thereafter, for the rest of his life, he declared that as far as numbers went, he was a perfect dunce.

Whateley said: 'There was certainly something peculiar in my calculating faculty. It began to show say between five and six, and lasted about three years. I soon got to do the most difficult sum, always in my head, for I knew nothing of figures beyond numeration. I did these sums much quicker than anyone could do on paper, and I never remember committing the smallest error. When I went to school, at which time the passion wore off, I was a perfect dunce at ciphering, and have continued so ever since.'

Augustin-Louis Cauchy was brought up in Paris during the bloodiest period of the Revolution. He was taught by his father.

Professor Lagrange, of the Polytechnique, heard of the boy's

genius, and advised his father to give the boy a literary education before he allowed him to touch any books of higher
mathematics. Laplace was also greatly impressed by the boy.
When the boy was eleven years old, Professor Lagrange
pointed to the boy, saying: 'You see that little man? He will
supplant all of us in so far as we are mathematicians.'

When Cauchy was thirteen, he went to the central school
and won first prizes in German, Latin and mathematics, and
a special prize in the humanities. When he was seventeen he
went to the Civil Engineering School, and was first of the
twenty students in his examination results.

Cauchy achieved fame for mathematical analysis.

The life of *Sir William Rowan Hamilton* has been described
by several authors. For most of the information below we
are indebted to the three-volume biography by Graves. We
have obtained other information from Bell's book on the biographies of mathematicians. Graves' book provides a great
deal of information, in the form of numerous letters. It is
not easy to read. Hamilton was described by Bell as 'By long
odds the greatest man of science that Ireland has produced.'
Graves wrote that Hamilton was universally acknowledged to
be one of the greatest mathematicians of his time.

William's father, a Dublin solicitor, was a man of great
energy, eloquence and intellect. Shortly after his first birthday
William was sent to live with his uncle and aunt at Trim. In a
series of letters this couple kept the parents informed about the
boy's progress. His mother died when he was twelve, and his
father when he was fourteen.

He was three years and one month when his uncle wrote
that he shamed other boys twice his age in reading the Bible,
though his uncle declared that he had no idea how he had learnt
to read. A month later he could read and spell the most
difficult words, and had spent a great deal of time in digesting
a dictionary. He was advanced in mathematics at this age.

When he was four years and two months he was good at

geography. He greatly impressed some visitors at his uncle's house by reading easily with books upside down. He not only read well, but understood perfectly what he had read. His teachers declared that they had never seen anything like it.

He was five when his mother received a letter saying: 'He is one of the most surprising children you can imagine: he is scarcely credible: he not only reads well, but with such nice judgment and point, that it would shame many who have finished their education. His reciting is astonishing, and his clear and accurate knowledge of geography is beyond belief. He reads Latin, Greek and Hebrew. He recites Dryden, Collins and Milton, and reads Homer in Greek and with the greatest of ease. He must have a reason for everything.' She was told that a Mr Montgomery tried him on Homer. 'To his amazement Willy read it with the greatest of ease. Mr Montgomery dropped the book and paced the room, but every now and then he would come and stare at Willy, and when he went away, he told Mr Elliott that such a thing he had never heard of, and that he really was seized with a degree of awe that made him almost afraid to look at Willy. He would not, he said, have thought so much of it had he been a grave quiet child; but to see him the whole evening acting in the most infantile manner and then reading all those things, astonished him more than he could express.'

When he was seven he mastered Italian and French, and read Homer in French. When he was eight he would amuse everyone by expressing his feelings with animation in Latin, or addressing an ode to Nature and Art in Latin.

At nine he could read Sanskrit and Arabic. His uncle reported: 'His thirst for the Oriental Languages is unabated. He is now master of most, indeed of all except the minor and comparatively provincial ones. The Hebrew, Persian and Arabic are about to be confirmed by the superior and intimate acquaintance with the Sanskrit, in which he is already proficient. The Chaldee and Syriac he is grounded in, and the

Hindoostanee, Malay, Mahratta, Bengali and others. He is about to commence the Chinese, but the difficulty of procuring books is very great.'

He wrote the following to his sister when he was ten: 'I have been for some time reading Lucian and Terence, the Hebrew Psalter on Sundays, and on Saturdays some Sanskrit, Arabic and Persian. I read at leisure hours Goldsmith's *Animated Nature*, and any new history or poetry that falls my way. I like Walter Scott very much. In arithmetic I have got as far as practice, and I have done near half the first book of Euclid with Uncle. I do the ancient and modern geography of the different countries together. I do the second lesson every morning in the Greek Testament, and on Sunday after church go over the scripture lessons of the past weeks with Doddridge's Notes and Improvement, and before church I read Secker on the Cathechism, and in the evening Wells' Scripture geography, a very entertaining book.' He made the practice of translating the classics and then retranslating them into Latin and Greek. When he was thirteen he boasted that he had mastered one language for each year he had lived.

At fourteen, he was introduced to Zerah Colburn, the American boy calculator (Chap. 8), and was fascinated by his methods, which they discussed together. As a result he became greatly interested in mathematics. At this time he was reading such authors as Aeschylus, Sophocles, Virgil, Sallust, Lucian, Horace and Blackstone's *Commentaries on Law*. In history he was reading Hooke, Vertot, Morgan's *France*, Smollett, Adam's *Manners and Customs of the Romans*, and in poetry Shakespeare, Milton, Blair, Young, Crabbe and Southey. He was studying arithmetical and geometrical progression, Euclid and the theory of eclipses.

By seventeen he had mastered integral calculus and had enough mathematical astronomy to calculate the eclipses, and he had now begun his career of fundamental discovery.

He did not attend any school before starting at the University at eighteen, into which he entered easily first out of a hundred candidates.

Bell wrote that 'To James Hamilton (his uncle), belongs whatever credit there may be for having wasted young William's abilities in the acquisition of utterly useless languages and turning him out, at the age of thirteen, as one of the most shocking examples of a linguistic monstrosity in history. That Hamilton did not become an insufferable prig under his misguided parson-uncle's instruction testifies to the essential soundness of his Irish common sense. The education he suffered might well have made an ass of even a humorous boy, and Hamilton had no humour.' Reading Graves' biography, one feels that this judgment was perhaps a little hard. The boy must have been a difficult one to manage, because of his thirst for knowledge.

He won almost all available prizes at the University, and obtained the highest honours in both classics and mathematics. At the age of twenty-one he became Professor of Astronomy at the University of Dublin.

The techniques devised by him are today indispensable in mathematical physics.

Though *Galois* died at the age of twenty, he had established his name and genius in mathematical circles. He was born near Paris, his mother coming from a long line of distinguished Jesuits. There was no sign of mathematical talent on either side.

Bell, in his biographies of mathematicians, wrote that Galois' mathematical genius came on him like an explosion, probably at early adolescence.

At twelve, having had no teaching except that given to him by his mother, Galois went to the Lycée in Paris, his first school, and hated it. 'He was shocked into unappeasable rage', and saw 'tyranny in action'. He became bored with classics and was moved to a lower class. He did not work at the subject. Mathematics were given a place very subsidiary to classics in the school curriculum.

He was suddenly fired by the subject of mathematics, and made incredibly rapid headway. At fourteen he absorbed masterpieces of algebraical analysis—though his class work in mathematics was mediocre. He had the gift of being able to perform the most difficult mathematical calculation entirely in his head—and this upset his teachers and examiners, who insisted on details, which to him were obvious or trivial, and he repeatedly lost his temper with them as a result.

According to Bell, a teacher remarked: 'The mathematical madness dominates this boy. I think his parents had better let him take only mathematics. He is wasting his time here, and all he does is to torment his teacher and get into trouble.'

At sixteen he was thoroughly embarked on his career of fundamental discovery. He was implored by his teacher to be systematic, but the advice was ignored. He took the entrance examination for the Polytechnic in Paris—but failed, because of the stupidity of the examiners—and he was embittered for life.

When he was seventeen, his teacher in advanced mathematics, Louis Richard, recognised the boy's genius. The boy was making discoveries of epochal significance in the theory of equations, and published his first paper. He persuaded Cauchy to present one of his discoveries to the French Academy—but Cauchy lost the paper.

He tried a second time to secure entrance into the Polytechnic, but finished up by throwing his eraser in the face of the examiner—and entrance was refused, largely because of his habit of calculating in his head.

At nineteen he was admitted to the University. He composed three papers on the theory of algebraic equations, far in advance of anything done before by others, and submitted it for a prize in the Academy of Sciences. The secretary received it but died before it could be submitted, and the manuscript could not then be found.

When he was nineteen, the Revolution occurred, and he

joined the National guard. He died in a duel when he was twenty.

Truman Safford was the son of a Vermont farmer. His mother was a teacher. He showed all-round precocity. Barlow states that at six he could calculate mentally the number of barley corns in 1,040 rods (617,760). He began to study books on algebra and geometry at the same age.

Barlow gives a good description of a test by the Rev. H. W. Adams, who asked the boy to multiply in his head

$$365,365,365,365,365,365 \text{ by } 365,365,365,365,365,365.$$

'He flew round the room like a top, pulled his pantaloons over the tops of his boots, bit his hands, rolled his eyes in their sockets, sometimes smiling and talking, and then, seeming to be in an agony, in not more than one minute, replied

$$133,491,850,208,566,925,016,658,299,941,583,225.'$$

He went to Harvard and graduated at eighteen. He spent several years in the observatory and made many important astronomical calculations. He had an encyclopaedic memory, loving chemistry, botany, philosophy, geography, history and astronomy. He became Professor of Astronomy in the Williams College at twenty.

His calculating ability lasted only for about six years. Barlow remarked that his loss of calculating power was remarkable. Whereas at ten years he could calculate correctly in his head in 60 seconds a multiplication sum whose answer consisted of 36 figures, some six or seven years later he was no better at calculation than his neighbours.

When *Bertrand Russell* was asked who was the greatest man produced by France in modern times, he replied '*Henri Poincaré*'.

Poincaré came from a good family. He first became seriously interested in mathematics when he was fifteen. Long before that he had shown a precocious intelligence. He read with incredible speed, and could always remember the page and line on which a particular subject was discussed. He had a very good memory of things which he had heard; he just sat and listened and remembered. He was never disturbed by others talking while he worked. He was absent-minded, and often forgot his meals, and could not say whether he had had breakfast or not. He was outstanding in classics at school.

His mathematics, Bell wrote, were done in his head, as he paced restlessly about, and were committed to paper only when he had thought the calculation out in detail.

At the Polytechnic, Poincaré was distinguished not only for his brilliance in mathematics, but for his brilliance in physical exercise. Nevertheless, he had certain spatial difficulties (Chapter 4) making him awkward in certain skills, such as drawing.

Bell wrote that when Poincaré was acknowledged as the foremost mathematician and leading man of science in his time, he submitted to the Binet intelligence tests, and made such a disgraceful showing that, had he been judged as a child instead of as the famous mathematician he was, he would have been rated as an imbecile.

CALCULATORS

Jedediah Buxton was a man of little intelligence who was born in Derbyshire. It is said that at maturity his mental age was ten.

He had a remarkable though slow calculating ability. Barlow states that on one occasion he squared mentally a number of 39 figures, taking two and a half months to do it.

Apart from one visit to the Royal Society, where he demonstrated his ability when he was fifty-two, he never left his birthplace.

In a sermon he paid no attention to the preacher's meaning, but would amuse himself by counting the words spoken.

He died at the age of seventy.

There are several other stories of calculating ability in mentally defective persons. Bell mentioned one *Jean Fleury*, an unteachable refractory inmate of Armentières asylum, who could give the square root of four figures in four seconds, and the cube root of six figures in six seconds. One day in 1912 he was told the date and the day of the week and asked what day 22nd May 1908 had been. He gave the correct answer in five seconds.

Zerah Colburn was the son of a 19th-century Vermont farmer. At six he gave public demonstrations in Boston, Mass. Barlow wrote that at the age of seven he was asked: 'What number multiplied by itself will produce 998,001?' He answered in less than four seconds 999. At the same age he was asked in Portsmouth, U.S.A.: 'Admitting the distance between Concord and Boston to be 65 miles, how many steps must I take in going this distance, allowing that I go three feet at a step?' He answered 114,400 in ten seconds.

He was asked how many seconds there are in eleven years, and answered 346,986,000 in four seconds, excluding leap years.

At the age of eight, he raised the number 8 to the 16th power in his head—281,474,976,710,656. He was asked the square root of 106,929, and before the number could be written down he immediately answered 327. He was then asked to name the cube root of 268,336,125, and with the same ease and promptness he replied 645. He was asked to give the cube root of 413,993,348,677 and gave the correct answer, 7,453, in five seconds.

Barlow wrote that there is a great deal of factual information about his mathematical feats. He was examined by Laplace and others at the French Academy. In his early years his calculations were accompanied by bodily contortions. Colburn declared that he was quite unable to tell how the answers came into his mind. Barlow wrote that his process of operation was unusual, for he was entirely ignorant of the common rules of arithmetic at the time, and could not perform on paper a simple sum of multiplication or divison.

As a result of the efforts of Washington Irving, he obtained admission to the Lyceum Napoleon. He became deacon of a

Methodist Church, and later an itinerant preacher. He became a professor of Latin, Greek, French and Spanish languages and English classical literature in a seminary styled the Norwich University, and died at the age of thirty-five.

It is of interest that Colburn had a great influence on William Hamilton, arousing in him enthusiasm for mathematics, and so was indirectly the instrument which caused Hamilton to take up his distinguished career of astronomy.

George Parker Bidder was born in Moreton-Hampstead, the son of a stonemason.

His achievements are described by Barlow. At four George showed an extraordinary ability for calculation, and was exhibited as a prodigy. Nevertheless, he had no formal instruction in figures; the only instruction which he had was given him when he was six, by his brother who taught him to count to 100.

At ten he was asked: 'What is the compound interest on £4,444 for 4,444 days at 4½ per cent per annum?' In two minutes he gave the answer £2,434 16s. 5¼d. At eleven he was asked to divide 468,592,413,363 by 9,076. In one minute he answered 51,629,838. At thirteen he was asked to find the number whose cube less 19 multiplied by that cube shall be equal to the cube of 6. He answered instantaneously 3.

His father took him round the country to give public exhibitions, and found it highly profitable. As a result his education was neglected.

When he was twelve, Sir William Herschel, the astronomer, came to see the boy calculating. Later the boy went to the University of Edinburgh, winning mathematics prizes. On graduating, he went into the Ordnance Survey. He is said to have founded the London Telegraph system, to have constructed the Victoria Docks, London, and to have become the President of the Institute of Civil Engineers. He never lost his ability to calculate and to remember figures.

An interesting feature of Bidder's genius is the fact that his brother was an excellent mathematician, while another brother (a minister) could quote almost any text in the Bible and give chapter and verse. One of Bidder's sons became a Q.C., and was distinguished in mathematics at Cambridge. Another son became a Fellow at Oxford. A nephew had remarkable mechanical ingenuity. Two of his grandchildren showed unusual mathematical powers.

Johann Dase, born in Hamburg, resembled Jedediah Buxton, in being little more than a calculating machine, who was able to carry out enormous calculations in the head, but was almost incapable of understanding the principles of mathematics. His ability in other fields was very limited. He never mastered any language. He began giving public exhibitions when he was fifteen.

When he was thirteen he reckoned the natural logarithms (7 places) of the numbers from 1 to 1,005,000. Bell wrote that, when being studied by Schumacher, he multiplied 79,532,853 by 93,758,479 in 54 seconds. He could multiply two numbers each of 20 figures in 6 minutes. He could extract mentally the square root of a number of 100 figures in 52 minutes. He retained his powers throughout his life.

Vito Mangiamele was a shepherd boy who had a remarkable calculating ability, which he lost after childhood. Both his brother and sister had a similar power. He had had no education. At the age of ten he demonstrated his ability before the French Academy, and supplied the cube root of 3,796,416 (156) in 30 seconds.

Jacques Inaudi, an Italian shepherd boy, had very little education, and did not learn to read or write until he was twenty. His memory except for figures was poor. He lived by public exhibition, and demonstrated his gifts before large audiences in almost every capital in Europe and in the United States. At the age of seven he could multiply five figures by five figures instantaneously. His powers continued throughout his life (Barlow).

COMMENT

The difference between mere calculating ability and creative mathematical genius was mentioned at the beginning of this chapter. While some persons of low intellect are able to calculate in a remarkable way, creative mathematical genius is associated with a high level of intelligence. The most remarkable example of all-round intellectual brilliance is that of Sir William Hamilton, who showed outstanding ability in the classics and languages, as well as in mathematics and astronomy. Leibnitz and Cauchy, amongst others, showed high ability in other subjects.

A most peculiar feature of Richard Whateley's genius, and that of Truman Safford, was the way in which the calculating ability was lost after a few years.

The story of Galois is one of a genius whose full potentiality was impeded by a difficult personality and by appalling misfortune.

CHAPTER 9

PUNISHMENT AND BULLYING AT SCHOOL

THIS is a disturbing chapter. It describes some of the miseries which young boys had to tolerate when they went to school. Although the corporal punishment inflicted by the masters was a problem different from that of bullying by their pupils, the end result was the same—and the two evils were so constantly combined in one school, that we felt that we could reasonably combine a discussion of both in one chapter. It would indeed not be surprising if boys, so cruelly treated by their masters, were to be equally cruel to each other.

In the Book of Proverbs XIII, 24, it is written 'He who spares the rod hates his son, but he who loves him is diligent to discipline him' and XXIII, 13, 'Do not withhold discipline from a child; if you beat him with a rod, he will not die.' The person or persons responsible for those words had much to answer for. Many have rationalised their brutality by means of those words. For centuries, whippings were the order of the day, and regarded as an essential part of good teaching.

Many were the famous men who as children suffered from tyrannical teachers. In the case of young *Edison*, the Rev. Engle, his headmaster, 'imprinted lessons with the leather strap'. *Yeats* wrote that he 'remembered little of childhood but its pain'. *H. G. Wells* was caned at the slightest provocation. Dr Richard Busby, the famous whipping master of Westminster School, in 1738, boasted that sixteen of the Bishops then on the bench had been birched by him. *James Watt*, *Thomas Carlyle*, and many others were bullied and tormented at school.

It is interesting that at the Lyceum School, Moscow, which *Pushkin* entered at the age of twelve, corporal punishment was absolutely prohibited. Mirsky wrote that the best and most beneficient feature of the Lyceum was the warm friendship which united all the schoolfellows.

We came across two accounts of particularly unpleasant activities, in which boys were deputed to spy on other boys.

In *Martin Luther's* school, boys were appointed spies. It was their responsibility to mark down the names of those who spoke German, swore, or otherwise acted against the rules. At the end of the week the teacher would apply one stroke of the cane for each point of bad behaviour. Martin often received fifteen strokes at a time.

In *John Hunter's* school, pupils from the age of nine were permitted to speak no other tongue but Latin either during classes or in conversation among themselves, and in order to ensure compliance two or three scholars were selected by the teachers to act as eavesdroppers. First offenders were warned, but repeaters were whipped. 'Whippings were given impartially to good and bad students alike—to the bad for forgetting their lessons, to the good so that they would remember them' (Kobler).

In the pages to follow we have described some of the unpleasant experiences of boys who were later to achieve eminence in life.

In his biography of *Thomas Cranmer*, Ridley wrote: 'His schoolmaster was marvellous severe and cruel. It is clear that his teacher was one of those ignorant and brutal schoolmasters who were so strongly condemned by Erasmus and Cranmer's colleague, Sir Thomas Elyot. It was an age in which religious leaders impressed upon their flock that their chief duty as parents was to punish their children, because scripture taught that by striking their child with a rod they would deliver his soul from Hell. Not only were the children beaten for trivial offences; they were sometimes flogged when they had committed no offence at all in order to mortify and humble them. Cranmer said later that the schoolmaster had dulled the wits of the scholars in his charge, and had made them hate rather than appreciate good literature; and he said that in his own case, the treatment which he had received at school had permanently damaged both the good memory and the natural audacity with which he had been endowed as a child.'

Samuel Johnson was thrashed unmercifully by the Rev. John Hunter, the headmaster at Lichfield Grammar School. He would thrash the boys without bothering to find out whether they were ignorant or negligent. If any boy failed to answer a question, he was whipped. Johnson called him 'so brutal that no man who had been educated by him ever sent his son to the same school'. He told Boswell that in English schools many boys had been maimed by excessive chastisement.

William Cowper at six went to a boarding school. Wright, in his biography, wrote: 'The timid little fellow suffered in no common degree from the brutality of his schoolfellows. Here, he says in his memoir, I had hardships of different kinds to conflict with, which I felt more sensibly in proportion to the tenderness with which I had been treated at home. But my chief affliction consisted in my being singled out from all the other boys by a lad about fifteen years of age as a proper object upon whom he might let loose the cruelty of his temper. I choose to forbear a particular recital of the many acts of brutality with which he made it his business continually to persecute me. It will be sufficient to say that he had, by his savage treatment of me, impressed such a dread of his figure upon my mind that I well remember being afraid to lift up my eyes upon him, higher than his knees; and that I knew him by his shoe buckles better than any other part of his dress.' Cowper records that the boy was subsequently expelled.

Gibbon, in his autobiography, wrote that he 'purchased the knowledge of the Latin Syntax at the expense of many tears and some blood'. He had entered the Kingston-upon-Thames School when he was nine. He wrote that 'there is not, in the course of life, a more remarkable change than the removal of a child from the luxury and freedom of a wealthy home, to the frugal diet and strict subordination of a school; from the tenderness of parents and the obsequiousness of servants, to the rude familiarity of his equals, the insolent tyranny of his seniors, and the rod of a cruel and capricious pedagogue.'

He added: 'My timid reserve was astonished by the crowd and tumult of the school; the want of strength and activity disqualified me from the sports of the playfield; nor have I forgotten how often I was reviled and buffeted for the sins of my Tory ancestors.'

Pitt, having suffered much ill treatment, told Lord Shelbourne that 'he scarcely observed a boy who was not cowed at Eton'. Henry Fielding was one of the many sufferers there. Dudden, in his biography, wrote that 'As in all public schools of the period, discipline at Eton was maintained by the traditional Orbilian method. Boys who were idle, boys who broke bounds, boys who were guilty not merely of grave offences, but even of quite trivial faults, were alike subjected to correction at the flogging block.' 'With true Spartan devotion, he sacrificed his blood at the famous Birchen altar, whereat the exuberances of the foremost youth of England were regularly chastened.'

Both *Samuel Coleridge* and *Charles Lamb* suffered under the rod of Rev. James Boyer, the Upper Master at Christ's Hospital. Coleridge even dreamt about him in later years. James Boyer caned the boys until he drew blood. He was subject to violent rages. As Charpentier wrote: 'the lust to strike used to come in gusts upon this half-possessed teacher'. Lucas, in his biography of Charles Lamb, wrote: 'Nothing was more common than to see him make a headlong entry into the schoolroom, from his inner recess, or library, and with turbulent eye, singling out a lad, roar out "Od's my life, Sirrah, I have a great mind to whip you"—then, with as sudden a retracting impulse, fling back into his lair—and, after a cooling lapse of some minutes, drive headlong out again, piecing out his imperfect sense, as if it had been some Devil's litany, with the expletory yell "and I will, too".

'In his gentler moods, when the rabidus furor was assuaged, he had to resort to an ingenious method, peculiar, for what I have heard, to himself, of whipping the boy, and reading the Debates, at the same time; a paragraph, and a lash between; which, in those times, when parliamentary oratory was most at a height and flourishing in these realms, was not calculated to impress the patient with a veneration for the diffuser graces of rhetoric.'

When Boyer died, Coleridge expressed the hope that his soul was now in heaven, 'borne by a host of cherubs, all face and wing, and without anything to excite his whipping propensities'.

Francis Thompson, the poet, wrote feelingly about the torments and bullying to which he was subject at school. After spending a happy time at home, where he was perhaps somewhat overprotected, he went to the Catholic College of St Cuthbert, at Ushaw, near Durham. He wrote: 'Fresh from my tender home, and my circle of just-judging friends, these malignant schoolmates who danced round me with mocking evil distortion of laughter were to be devilish apparitions of a hate now first known; hate for hate's sake, cruelty for cruelty's sake.'

Reid pointed out in his biography that although Francis escaped actual bodily harm, 'It is the petty malignant annoyance recurring hour by hour, day by day, month by month, until its accumulation becomes an agony; it is this which is the most terrible weapon that boys have against their fellow boy, who is powerless to shun it because, unlike the man, he has virtually no privacy. His is the torture which the ancients used, when they anointed their victim with honey and exposed him naked to the restless fever of the flies.'

Shelley entered the Sion House Academy at Isleworth. Peck

describes the principal, the Rev. Dr Greenlaw, as 'a choleric man of a sanguinary complexion, in a green old age, not wanting in good qualities, but very capricious in his temper, which, good or bad, was influenced by the daily occurrences of a domestic life not the most harmonious, and of which his face was the barometer and his hand the index'.

Ralph Emerson at the age of nine went to the Boston Public Latin School, where the headmaster was William Biglow. Rusk, in his biography, wrote that the headmaster 'would flourish his cane as he demanded of a backward pupil what an active verb expressed'. 'I'll tell you what it expresses,' he would say, bringing the stick down upon the boy's haunches with decided emphasis— 'it expresses an action and necessarily supposes an agent (flourishing the cane, which descends again as before), and an object acted upon; as Castigo Te, I chastise thee: do you understand now, hey?'

Edward Bulwer, Lord Lytton, was so bullied at school (when he started at nine) that his health, spirit and happiness were all lost. He became so ill after a fortnight that his frightened mother took him away for good. Escott wrote that one wholesome lesson learned at this juvenile hotbed of cruelty and vice was a lifelong loathing of meanness and tyranny.

Richard Cobden went to a school in Yorkshire. Lord Morley wrote: 'Here he remained for five years, a grim and desolate time, of which he could never afterwards endure to speak. The unfortunate boy from his tenth to his fifteenth year was ill-fed, ill-taught and ill-used. He never saw parent or friend; and once in each quarter was allowed to write home. It was not until he was fifteen that this cruel and disgusting mockery of an education came to an end'.'

After leaving school he became a clerk in his uncle's warehouse, and later a traveller for his uncle, collecting orders for muslins and other fabrics.

Gogol, in order to escape punishment at school, pretended to be mad.

In his biography Magarshack, describing the episode, wrote: 'His face became distorted, his eyes blazed savagely, his hair seemed to stand on one end, he gnashed his teeth, foamed at the mouth, threw himself down on the floor, and began to smash the furniture. The headmaster approached cautiously, but Gogol seized a chair and drove him to cover. He was seized by four school porters and taken to the school sanatorium, where he spent two months in the company of his friend Vysotsky, his attacks of simulated madness returning everytime he had a visit from the school doctor.'

Alfred Lord Tennyson was brutally treated by the headmaster of the school at Louth, the Rev. Waite. Lounsbury, in his biography, wrote that the boy could not hold his knife and fork for days after a caning. He was so brutally flogged for not knowing his work that he had to stay in bed for six weeks. Lounsbury added that the school was presided over by a man whom it 'would be a compliment to call a ruffian'. The system of education was thoroughly bad, and everything had to be learnt by rote: it did not matter whether or not it was understood. He wrote that the school was further characterised by the methods prevailing and the belief which was firmly held and carried out in practice that nothing could be expected to stay permanently in a boy's brain until it had been effectively driven in by blows on his body. The teachers would walk up and down the room with canes. They would box ears and rap knuckles on every pretext. In front of the schoolboys and in full view of them was the inscription in Latin: 'Who spares the rod, hates the child.'

When *Gladstone* went to Eton, the headmaster was Dr Keate, with whom, according to Lord Morley, 'the appointed instrument of moral regeneration in the childish soul was the birchrod'. Dr Keate on occasions was known to have flogged over eighty boys on a single day, and his one regret in the evening of his life was that he had not flogged more.

It is said that Dr Keate admonished his students to be pure

in heart, 'and if you're not, I'll flog purity into you through your hides'.

John Bright went to the Friends School at Ackworth. Trevelyan wrote that 'even this great school, maintained by a religious society, in many things in advance of public opinion in gentleness and kindness and justice, was in many respects grievously mismanaged. In the matter of food, it was insufficient in quantity and quality. In the matter of punishment, it was harsh if not barbarous, and the comforts and health of the children were very inadequately attended to.'

Anthony Trollope's autobiography provides a sad story of an unhappy childhood. He wrote: 'my boyhood was, I think, as unhappy as that of a young gentleman could well be, my misfortunes arising from a mixture of poverty and gentle standing on the part of my father, and from an utter want on my part of that juvenile manhood which enables some boys to hold up their heads even among the distresses which such a position is sure to produce.'

He went to Harrow School when he was seven, and had a thoroughly unhappy time there. He wrote: 'I was never spared: I was not allowed to run to and fro between our house and the school without a daily purgatory. No doubt my appearance was against me. I remember well, when I was still the junior boy in the school, Dr Butler, the headmaster, stopping me in the street and asking me, with all the clouds of Jove upon his brow, and all the thunder in his voice, whether it was possible that Harrow school was disgraced by so disreputable dirty a little boy as I. He was in the habit of flogging me constantly.'

He went for a time thereafter to a private school in Surrey, and thence to Winchester. After three years there his father had to bring him back to be a day boy at Harrow, because of financial difficulties. Trollope, writing about this second period at Harrow, declared: 'Perhaps these eighteen months were the worst of my life. I was now over fifteen, and had come to an age at which I could appreciate at its full the misery of expulsion from all social intercourse. I had not only no friends, but I was despised by all my companions. The indignities I endured are not to be described. As I look back it seems to me that all hands were turned against me—those of masters as well as boys. I was allowed to join in no play. Nor did I learn anything, for I was taught nothing.

'I was never a coward, and cared for a thrashing as little as any boy, but one cannot make a stand against the acerbities of 300 tyrants without a moral courage of which at that time I possessed none.

'At last I was driven to rebellion, and there came a great fight—at the end of which my opponent had to be taken home.'

He wrote that he felt convinced that he had been flogged more often than any human being alive. It was just possible, he said, to obtain five scourgings in one day at Winchester, and he often boasted that he obtained them all.

Sir Oliver Lodge, in his autobiography, described the cruelties of his schooldays, which he said were undoubtedly the most miserable part of his life.

Firstly, he was subjected to a great deal of caning by his teachers. Secondly, he was bullied by other boys.

With regard to canings, he wrote that 'I was so small at the time that I was given a bath by the housemaid every Saturday night, and I remember the kindly girl weeping when she saw my scars'—which had been inflicted for grammatical mistakes.

'The book called Ellis's exercises was perfectly hateful in this connection. It was merely a collection of English sentences that had to be turned into Latin. The copybook containing your version was sent up, and you sat watching to see when the master would come to your copybook. You saw his pen underlining the mistakes, and shuddered when you saw a double mark being made—for that the cane was the only recompense.'

The teacher's cane, he said, had a curved handle, and he brought it down on the hand with some vigour, so that a weal instantly appeared on the hand, and the tears came to the eyes. 'After two blows of this kind the smart was unendurable; your hand curled up and writing was impossible.' 'The cane was part of the system of instruction, sometimes because you did not know your lesson, but most often for mere grammatical mistakes.' He added that the whole instruction was kept on dull and dispiriting lines, for though they read the works of famous authors, they were never told anything about them.

He wrote that he was much the smallest boy in the school, and he was subjected to a great deal of bullying. 'Once', he said, 'I remember having gone to Chetwynd Church for the afternoon service with some of the other boys. Some servants from the hall occupied the same pew; and in going out I opened the door for them to go out first. This was considered an offence, and for it I was ordered fifty lashes.'

He described how a delicate boy was given a hundred lashes with a rope end. He was tied to an overturned chair. The result was 'not so much that blood was drawn, but that his skin went like a rotten apple'.

He wrote that his memory of school was largely coloured by the various kinds of thrashings which he received.

Canings in the process of teaching music were less common —or at least we did not come across many records of them. *Puccini* had reason to hate music as a child. According to Thomas, whenever he struck a false note at practice he received a vigorous kick on the shin, so that ever afterwards, the sound of a false note sent his reflexes into action and his foot into the air with a jerk.

There are many other stories of excessively strict discipline at school. *Sir Arthur Conan Doyle* was at Stoneyhurst, where the Fathers exerted an iron discipline. Punishment with a flat rubber weight called a Tolley, made the hands blacken and swell up to twice their size.

Lord Northcliffe (then Harmsworth) at the age of eleven went to the Grammar School at Stamford. There, according to Pound and Harmsworth, he was 'constantly picked on by the master, a fork-bearded clergyman named Edward Musson, who caned him three times a week for two years, and instilled Latin grammar with the cane'. A school contemporary remembered Harmsworth being given 'four on each hand, and as many strokes from the nape of the neck to the calf of the leg as could be given without overlapping'. When he was stripped for a bathe the boys saw the blue-black marks all down his back.

Eventually Harmsworth was removed from the school after having to be kept off school for a term because his thumb had been split by a cane.

Chevalier Jackson's autobiography described a shocking story of bullying and misery at school. He wrote: 'In my memory the tearfulness of my childhood and boyhood hangs like a pall over everything. Looking backward now, from the impartial analytic viewpoint of later life, I do not see that I had more than my share of the usually recognised causes for sorrow; but some of the tears were justified, and all the troubles were very real to me then. One cause of grief arose from an unusual degree of hypersensitiveness to the suffering of human beings or animals. Other boys could look on, enjoy looking on, and seek opportunities to look on, at bloody cockfights, dog fights, boy fights, man fights and all similar contests. I always ran away crying, and hid until it was all over. The greatest of all causes of sorrow of my tearful boyhood was cruelty to horses. Bull terriers were bred for the purpose of fights: they always fought to the death. The tearfulness and terror of my childhood seem to have been concerned with the cruelty and my helplessness to stop it, rather than with the gruesomeness of the "sights".'

Concerning his own experience of bullying, he wrote: 'It seems strange that in the latter half of the 19th century, the life of a schoolboy could be a nightmare of persecution and torment. Yet such was the case with me. There was no persecution by the teachers. I never had any trouble with them. The persecution, torment and abuse came from a group of older pupils. Almost always I was waylaid, tormented and tortured. Physical torture was cunningly planned so as to leave no tell tale marks. A favourite torture was to hold me by the feet, first suspending me and then swinging me round and round with my head at the periphery of the circle until I would cry because of pain and fall with vertigo when released. Another torture was to choke me with both hands round the neck until unconsciousness approached. Many times I felt I should never come home alive. A favourite torture was to say: "Now we are going to kill you".'

'The little tin luncheon bucket was often the means of torment—the boys filling it with sand, coal ash or rotten eggs. Hunger to the point of faintness became my usual afternoon condition.

'Another form of torturing was to take off my cowhide boots, fill them with snow, and throw them over the fence into a snow covered field. By the time they were recovered, emptied of wet, icy slush, and put on, my feet were very nearly frozen, and they remained cold and wet in school all day.' He had severe chilblains, and suffered great pain from this form of bullying.

He went on: 'Dipping me into the watering trough, suspension over the precipice of the quarry, were never to be forgotten ordeals.' Another time he was led blindfolded into the workings of a coal mine and left in total darkness. By good fortune he was found.

He wrote that at last came the day of deliverance, one of the happiest days of his life, when he left school, and at seventeen entered the University of Pittsburgh to study medicine.

In his book he meditated on the causes and nature of bullying. He wrote that he never on a single occasion told anyone about it. He had frequent nightmares because of it, and was miserably unhappy throughout his entire school career.

Gilbert Murray, in his *Unfinished Autobiography*, refers to the severe bullying and teasing to which he was subjected when at school in Australia. He wrote: 'We were at Southey's (School) a very foul mouthed crew of young ragamuffins. I was once or twice criticised for not swearing, and felt myself something of an outcast in consequence. Pretty soon I made a bargain with the powers above. I had a strong objection to obscene language, but I thought I mighty satisfy popular feeling by swearing. I did it entirely as a matter of calculation; I got little or no pleasure from it, but in order to be less unpopular I deliberately swore at every second sentence.'

He wrote that all through his school life he was more upset by mental torment and teasing than by bullying. He frequently thought of running away, though he was not bullied much. He was greatly disturbed by the terrible cruelty to animals shown by some of the boys.

One bully, he said, would at the beginning of term select a particular victim and arrange that he would never see him without making him cry.

He was so unhappy that he decided to commit suicide, and went to a tree with a rope. He was just about to complete the act when he was stung by a bulldog ant. During the succeeding delay, he was found and stopped.

Paul Nash, in his autobiography, wrote a terrifying account of the teaching methods in his school—the Planes, at Greenwich. 'The system of education at the Planes was easy. You were there to be got into the Navy. The place was a crammer's, a place where they stuffed you with knowledge against time. If you didn't absorb the mental food quickly enough, they beat it into your head. There was no caning. That was too elaborate. Punishment was swift and direct. If you were slow or stupid, you were cuffed till your head sang.

'Each master had a different style. The Latin and History

masters, both cultured men, preferred a deliberate slanting slap across the side of your cheek. It could sting damnably, yet somehow it was a fair blow. But upstairs was a class taken by a tall half-caste, who obviously enjoyed himself. He hit cruelly and viciously, his dark lips writhing back from his little pointed teeth. The commander hit with his clenched fist, generally in a blind growling rage.

'I should not like to live over again the first three weeks I spent at the Planes. As a new boy I endured not only the terrors of the classroom, but out of school, an ordeal of bullying far more than anything I had known at Colet Court. Here you were hit with the blackboard compass for choice. It had a metal stud, and you were lucky if it hit only your bottom.

'By the beginning of the second week I was desperate. It did not take long to find me out. Fright and constant cuffing made me more stupid. I became the butt of the class and even the other boys looked on me as a kind of moron. A crisis came one cold Monday morning when the Commander was taking us in arithmetic. Monday was his bad morning, when he was invariably in a state of hardly suppressed irritation, ready to explode at any minute. We were all cold; most of us had chilblains on our fingers. We stole uneasy glances at the Commander, who was going round almost in silence, but breathing too heavily to be safe. We knew that ominous quiet and we saw that he was gripping his ivory ruler. Suddenly there was a sharp tap and a yelp of pain somewhere behind me. I did not need to look round, even had I dared. The Commander had found a mistake and had rapped some wretched boy across his chilblains with the ivory ruler, a well-known trick of his winter term technique. I could hear him swearing and stabbing at the sums with a bit of pencil. He was coming near and he was in a black temper. I couldn't get my sums to come out. I knew there was an obvious fault, but I was paralysed with fear, as in a bad dream. I heard the Commander's heavy hurried breathing by my ear and I smelt his breath. The next moment I was knocked sideways out of my desk. With a roar of fury he began to shout questions at me, cuffing my head with heavy blows on the ears. I remained dumb and impotent. He yelled at me to sit down and correct my sum. A few minutes later there was a kind of half strangled screech followed by a resounding slap, and the Commander's voice, hoarse and nearly inarticulate with passion. Two boys were whimpering and someone was crying rather wildly and blowing his nose in a noisy way. Everyone was now in a state of nerves. Even the clever boys began to make mistakes and get hit and cursed at. In the next classroom which was visible through the glass partition I could see the History master dealing out his cool judicious slap. Then the far door burst open and a small fair boy from the half-caste's form hurried across to the lavatory. I couldn't think. I knew the Commander was coming back, but I was dazed and becoming desperate. In a moment he was on me again. Half way through the morning he always went into his private house for ten minutes, presumably for a drink of some sort. He had just come back, straight to my desk, by now quite beside himself with rage, bellowing or almost whispering, choked, literally with fury, and his first blow was such a wild swing that all his rings flew off and rolled over the floor. I was past caring what happened and I think this exasperated him even more. He fell on me without mercy. When he had done I escaped to the lavatory. My ears were bleeding and I could not stop crying. I wrote to my father imploring him to take me away. I described what we had to go through. I don't know whether he took any action, but it was quite clear to me in his letter that I had to stay on.'

Suddenly, he wrote, everything was changed—when he scored the winning goal at football, and much of the bullying and caning stopped. He failed to pass the Naval Examination.

He added: 'I was seventeen when the long and complicated purgatory of my school life came to an end. I emerged from it impaired in body and spirit, more or less ignorant and equipped for nothing. It took at least three years to build up my self-respect, and my education only began when I was at liberty to learn for myself. I think it is fair to say that in those years I suffered greater misery, humiliation and fear than in all the rest of my life.'

Aneurin Bevan stood up to his master, who was a snob and a bully. Michael Foot tells how when the teacher, Mr Orchard, hit him on the chin, Aneurin retaliated by stamping on his corns. When the headmaster mocked a boy in the class, Aneurin threw an inkwell at him.

Many years before *Sir Humphry Davy* had retaliated to punishment in a somewhat different way. He was a happy little boy, with some courage. Treneer wrote that when the teacher pulled Humphry's ears, the boy would come next day with his ears in plaster, replying, when asked the reason, that it was 'to prevent mortification'.

COMMENT

These were certainly days of what seems to us today to be the most shocking cruelty. Apart from the misery and unhappiness which the canings and bullyings caused, one wonders how many behaviour problems resulted from them, and how many scars were left on the personality.

The description by Paul Nash of his terror during his punishment at school shows clearly the mental impotence, almost paralysis, which can result from fear.

Teachers of those days would indeed have been astounded if they could have looked into the future, and seen teachers being taken to court for caning a child or cuffing him on the ears.

We cannot say how much the various stories of cruelty and bullying were exaggerated. Some children suffer more than others because of a particularly sensitive nature. Some men may retain a vivid memory of childhood unhappiness, while others with similar experiences would tend to minimise the unpleasantness of the past—perhaps in a deliberate effort to forget it. The picture which we gather from the accounts in this chapter is not necessarily an altogether accurate one.

One of us has discussed elsewhere* the theory and principles of punishment. The following comment summarises the main principle: 'Much punishment would be avoided if teachers and parents would realise that children learn far better from praise and encouragement for good behaviour, than from threats of punishment, discouragement, and the weapons of fear, sarcasm and ridicule. Children learn more by being shown the reasons for good conduct, by being treated as individuals who will co-operate if given a chance, and by being given increasing opportunities to exercise decision and self-control. As one writer put it, too many parents and teachers still place great faith on rules and regulations, in demanding unquestioning respect for authority, obedience without question, freedom from annoyance for themselves, and still cling to retaliatory theories.'

One of the many reasons why punishment is usually wrong is that it is meted out for things which are in no way the fault of the child—features such as poor concentration, overactivity, difficulty in reading or arithmetic, or clumsiness.

As George Bernard Shaw once wrote: 'To punish is to injure. You can't mend a person by damaging him.'

* Illingworth R. S. (1964). *The Normal School Child. His Problems, Physical and Emotional.* London: Heinemann.

CHAPTER 10

OPINIONS ABOUT SCHOOL AND UNIVERSITY

MOST of the opinions expressed by a variety of eminent men in this chapter are far from complimentary to the schools in which they spent their early days. The methods of teaching used were for the most part very different from those used now. Little was known about motivation. Teaching tended to be by rote, and the cane was an essential part. It would not be surprising if more intelligent boys had later to criticise the teaching methods from which they suffered. Many of them yearned for more freedom to read, and longed to study those subjects which interested them, instead of those ordained by the rigid school syllabus.

Critical comments on school are more likely to be recorded in biographies than are comments of the opposite kind—probably because it is thought that the critical comments will be of greater interest to the reader.

It is impossible to determine what harm was done by the teaching methods experienced by these children. No one can say what those children would have achieved in life if the methods had been different. Perhaps they would never have achieved eminence at all.

The criticisms in the pages to follow came from a wide variety of men, who acquired renown in the fields of religion, literature, medicine, teaching, and the arts. The most scathing came from George Bernard Shaw, who must certainly have thoroughly deserved his description of himself as 'a disagreeable little beast'. We were particularly interested in the apt and discerning comments made by Winston Churchill about his instruction at school.

Samuel Johnson disliked formal instruction. He did well at school, not because he liked learning but because he disliked punishment, while his excellent memory made learning easy. According to Hesketh Pearson, Johnson said that he never worked willingly in his life as man or boy, and never made a real effort to do his best, except when fear of the rod or desire to excel made him try. He was convinced that children resented being taught what they did not want to know and that such teaching was valueless. He felt that nothing could be learnt unless the child was interested. It is noteworthy that in spite of the canings which he experienced himself, he declared that 'no attention can be obtained from children without the infliction of pain'.

John Hunter loathed his school at East Kilbride. According to Kobler, Hunter described education as consisting of 'a little reading and writing, a great deal of spelling and figures, geography which never got beyond the dullest statistics, and a little philosophy and chemistry, which were dry as sawdust, and as valuable for deadening purposes'. Latin he detested. Kobler said that Hunter skipped his classes as often as he dared, and when he did attend, it was in body only, not in spirit. He refused to settle down and study his lessons, and no one succeeded in making him do so. The only mark which Kilbride left on him was a hatred of book learning which lasted the rest of his life.

Gibbon spoke of his time at Oxford as 'the fourteen months the most idle and unprofitable of my whole life'.

Jeremy Bentham hated Westminster School, where he was not even provided with a bed to himself. He described the school as his 'Special Hell'. He went to Oxford at twelve, and hated it. His three undergraduate years there, he said, were a dreary waste. He made few friends and learned little.

Goethe expressed the opinion that the object of education should be to foster taste rather than to communicate knowledge. *Sir Humphry Davy* wrote (to his mother): 'learning is a true pleasure; how unfortunate it is that in most schools it is made a pain'.

Sir Walter Scott, to use Thomas' words, found the soulless routine of lessons at the High School, Edinburgh, both tedious and meaningless. He could not learn by rote. Unless a subject interested him, his mind wandered. He was an inattentive pupil.

Carlyle thought that the University presented a picture of the blind leading the blind.

Lord Byron hated Harrow School in his first years there, and referring to Trinity College, Cambridge, said 'the place is the devil'.

In his autobiography, *Benjamin Haydon*, the artist, wrote: 'I do not think that any man left his school without lamenting the time lost in getting a little of everything, without knowing correctly the principles of anything.'

De Quincey went to Manchester Grammar School at fifteen, and experienced increasing misery there, running away when seventeen for a holiday in Wales. He complained of the lack of exercise, lack of time to eat dinner, the lack of an opportunity to take a walk. 'Every day, and every day, with scarcely a moment's variation, returns the same dull routine of stupid employment.'

In his autobiography, *Froebel* wrote that 'Latin was miserably taught and still worse learnt.' Concerning physical geography, he wrote: 'we repeated our tasks parrot-wise, speaking much and knowing nothing, for the teaching on this subject had not the very least connection with real life, nor had it any actuality for us'. Froebel disliked dry formal instruction.

A few months before leaving school, *Gogol*, according to Magarshack's biography, wrote to his mother that what really surprised him was that he had learnt so much at that 'stupid institution'. 'If I know something', he declared, 'I owe it entirely to myself.' As for his life at school, 'hardly anyone', he wrote, 'has endured so much ingratitude, injustice, and contempt'. He added that he was 'sick to death of the hateful school'.

Ferdinand de Lesseps was always resentful of school discipline and routine.

Charles Darwin found his lectures in the medical course at Edinburgh intolerably dull. His lectures on Materia Medica were 'something fearful to listen to'. He said that there were no advantages and many disadvantages in lectures as compared to reading.

When passing his old playground *Robert Browning* spoke of 'the disgust with which he always thought of the place', and 'the vindictive misery of the hapless childhood' which he spent there.

Disraeli said that he found the mouths of teachers to be full only of words, while great books delighted him because they were written by great men with feelings like his.

Lord Tennyson hated his school at Louth so bitterly that in after life he would never go down the street in which it was situated.

In a letter to his mother, *Thackeray* wrote: 'I like my school, there are so many good boys to play with. There are 370 in the school. I wish there were 369.'

From the first *George Borrow* disliked the routine of school life. Jenkins wrote that in a thousand ways George was different from his fellows. He longed to wander in the country. At fifteen he conspired with three of his fellows to make a dash for life—and they tramped to Great Yarmouth. They were all caught.

Sir James Paget said that the best that could be said about the education which he received was that it was fair for what it cost—eight guineas a year.

We mentioned in Chapter 9 the unhappiness experienced by *Anthony Trollope* at school. Concerning the teaching he received at his various schools, notably Winchester and Harrow, he said: 'during the whole of these twelve years, no attempt had been made to teach me anything but Latin and Greek, and very little attempt to teach me those languages. I do not remember any lessons either in writing or arithmetic. French and German I was certainly not taught.'

Thomas Huxley entered school at eight and left at ten, and had no further regular schooling. He had bitter memories of his school. He said: 'the society I fell in with at school was the worst I had ever known. The people who were set over us cared as much for our intellectual and moral welfare as if they were baby farmers.'

Henry Adams had a passionate hatred of school. In his autobiography, he said that he always reckoned his schooldays, from ten to sixteen years, as so much time thrown away. 'He hated it because he was here with a crowd of other boys and compelled to learn by memory a quantity of things that did not amuse him. His memory was slow and the effort painful. He was a slow thinker, and efforts to hurry him made him slower still.'

William Booth complained that his school provided no stimulation. His headmaster, he said, never woke up to William's ambition to learn until he was about to leave the school.

At thirteen *Lord Northcliffe* left school, after what he described as the two unhappiest years of his life.

Edvard Grieg, the Norwegian composer, had a strong distaste for school at Bergen. Monrad-Johansen described how Edvard, knowing the rule that boys who were late for school had to stand outside until the end of the lesson, would place himself under a nearby rain spout, until he was soaked to the skin. His master would then send him home to change his clothes—and Edvard solved the problem of badly prepared homework. He did this once too often, for his teacher, thinking that he was more wet than seemed reasonable, had him watched—and a thrashing resulted.

Edvard wrote in later years: 'School life was to me deeply unsympathetic; its materialism, harshness and coldness was so contrary to my nature that I would think out the most in-

credible things to be quit of it, even if only for a little while.'
'I saw in school life only a boundless unhappiness, and I could
not explain to myself the necessity for all those child agonies.
I have no doubt at all that school developed the evil in me and
let the good lie fallow.' He told about his discouragement at
school when one day at the age of twelve or thirteen he
arrived with a sheet of music written by him, and entitled in
large letters 'Variation on a German Melody for the Piano by
Edvard Grieg—opus 1'. His teacher, seeing it, ridiculed him,
pulled his hair, and shouted: 'Another time he will have the
German Dictionary with him as he should, and leave such
trash at home.'

George Bernard Shaw made several derogatory remarks about
the education which he received. Concerning his school he
wrote that 'my inurement in that damnable boy prison
effected its real purpose of preventing my being a nuisance to
my mother for at least half the day'. 'Lessons were set us
which I had to learn on pain of punishment not cruel enough
to effect its purpose with boys like me who were free enough
at home to have something more interesting to do than poring
over unreadable school books; but I was not taught manners
or loyalties nor held to any standards of dress or care of my person. Discipline was confined to silence or sitting still, which
did not prevent me from carrying on furtive conversations or
fights with the boy sitting next, who might be friend or foe.'
'School is the most damnable purveyor of lies ever invented.'

At one school he formed a secret society sworn to give
topsy-turvy answers to questions asked by the teachers, and to
compete for the bottom places in the class. A teacher called
him 'The Devil Incarnate'.

Elsewhere he wrote: 'My verdict is that proletarian children
should be sent to really public proletarian secondary schools,
and that their contact with young Etonian, Harrovians, Wyke-
ham boys and Rugbeians, should be limited to street fights
with them.'

He also confessed: 'I instinctively saved my brains from destruction by resolute idleness, which, moreover, made school meaningless and tedious to me.'

In Louis Simon's *Shaw on Education* there are many interesting Shavian comments. Shaw said that he forgot what Latin he had learnt (from his uncle), primarily because he was kept in a class where the master never called on him to recite 'because he knew I could, and therefore devoted himself to trapping the boys who could not', and also because the 'teaching method consisted mainly of asking a boy once a day in an overcrowded class the Latin for a man on a horse or what not'.

In his *Everyman's Political What's What* Shaw wrote: 'My school was conducted on the assumption that knowledge of Latin is still the be all and end all of education. I was given no reason why I should learn Latin instead of some living language. There was, in fact, no reason, as there were plenty of translations of all the classics that have any survival value. The method of teaching was barbarous; I was ordered to learn the declensions and conjugations and instalments of the vocabulary by rote on pain of being caned or kept in after school hours if I failed to reel off my paradigms without prompting. When I could do this, Caesar's commentaries and Virgil's famous epic were thrust into my hands, and without a word of explanation as to what these old commentaries had to do with me. Why, if I was to have a dead language forced on me, they should not have begun with Greek instead of the culturally inferior Roman, I was not told, perhaps because the reason was too silly, being that the school had not yet advanced from the Norman conquest to the Renaissance.'

He related that he was confronted with algebra without a word of explanation that would have made it interesting to him. Although Euclid gave him no trouble, he failed in examinations because the questions stated not the problem, but their numbers in the book, of which he knew nothing, having picked up all the solutions in class. He never forgave his teachers for failure to explain the practical value algebra and geometry may have. 'Not a word was said to us about the meaning or utility of mathematics, we were simply asked to explain how an equilateral triangle could be constructed by the intersection of two circles, and to do sums in a, b and x, instead of pence and shillings, leaving me so ignorant that I concluded that a and b must mean eggs and cheese, and x nothing, with the result that I rejected algebra as nonsense, and never changed that opinion until in my advanced twenties Graham Wallace and Karl Pearson convinced me that instead of being taught mathematics I had been made a fool of' (Self Sketches).

He was interested in literature at school, and once received a 'first class' for an essay.

In the Preface to *Misalliance* he stated that he was a confirmed idler, and so failed disgracefully in examinations. 'None of my school masters really cared a rap whether I learnt my lessons or not, provided my father paid my schooling bill, the collection of which was the real object of the school.' Examinations were never a source of anxiety to him, and he said that he could not understand the boys who prepared their lessons and studied for examinations. Again and again he insisted that 'my schooling did me a great deal of harm and no good whatever: it was simply dragging a child's soul through the dirt'.

He recalled with horror and indignation the evil things he picked up in the schools in Ireland. In *Misalliance* he said: 'I was taught lying, dishonourable submission to tyranny, dirty stories, a blasphemous habit of treating love and maternity as obscene jokes, hopelessness, evasion, derision, cowardice and all the blackguard's shifts by which the coward intimidates other cowards.'

With respect to the teaching of history, he told (in *What's What*) of a class of about fifty boys seated in alphabetical order. Each day a chapter in *The Students' Hume* was assigned, and the teacher would go through the chapter and through the alphabet asking questions about facts and dates. 'As my name began with the letter S, I could calculate within ten lines or so what question would fall to me.' He emphasised the impossibility of learning history from a collection of bare facts in the order in which they actually occurred, and that it is only through the medium of works of art that history can best be understood.

In *Biographers' Blunders Corrected* (Self Sketches) Shaw pointed out that in *The Quintessence of Bernard Shaw*, Duffin is mistaken about Shaw being unteachable. 'You say I was an unschoolable boy at a bad school. But what is an unschoolable boy? I was greedy for knowledge, and interested in everything, and if school taught me nothing except that school is a prison and not a place of teaching, the conclusion is that pedagogy is not yet a science.'

Oscar Wilde hated mathematics and was disinterested in science. He made many scathing comments on education. According to Pearson, Wilde thought that school education of any sort was valueless, and that nothing that is worth knowing can be taught. 'We teach people how to remember —we never teach them how to grow. Everybody who is incapable of learning has taken to teaching—that is really what our enthusiasm for education has come to. How appalling is that ignorance which is the inevitable result of the fatal habit of imparting opinions. How it wearies us and must weary himself, with its endless repetition and sickly reiteration. How lacking it is in any element of intellectual growth. In what a vicious circle it always moves.'

The routine of school was distasteful to *Joseph Conrad*. Jean-Aubry, in Conrad's biography, wrote that Joseph disliked most of the school subjects. He liked geography, but the 'marks awarded to that subject were almost as few as the hours apportioned to it in the school curriculum by persons of no romantic sense for the real, and ignorant of the great possibilities of active life, with no desire for struggle, no notion of the wide places of the world—mere bored professors in fact, who were not only middle aged, but looked to me as if they had never been young. And their geography was very much like themselves, a bloodless thing with a dry skin covering a repulsive armature of uninteresting bones.'

Though more or less happy at Hodder House and Stoney-hurst (apart from the beatings), *Sir Arthur Conan Doyle* was impressed by the intolerable dryness of his lessons. Carr wrote in his biography that history was made like dry powder in the mouth—all dates and places without any people: it had no more appeal to the imagination than the hated $x^2 + 2xy + y^2$.

When four years of age, *Steinmetz* was sent to a kinder-garten, but according to his biographer, 'to the spoiled little cripple it was a fearful prison with no grandmother to yield to his whims'. 'When he returned home at noon he raised such a fearful and tearful row that his father did not send him back for another year.'

Ekman wrote that *Sibelius* discussed his schooling as follows: 'If I am asked what interested me most at school, I can say with a clear conscience "Nothing". I must, however, make an exception in favour of natural science, which coincided with my love of nature. History was able to engross me at times, if it dealt with periods that appealed to the imagination; then I read the dry schoolbook as if it were a novel. I must not forget the classical languages, that opened up a new ex-alted world of beauty. Homer and Horace had a significance in my development that I cannot value highly enough.'

Lord Birkenhead (F. E. Smith) never forgave Harrow School for failing him in a scholarship examination when he was thirteen. 'In these days', he said bitterly, 'the examiners re-jected what were known as the half wits after two days' ex-amination, making it plain that those who were so rejected were cumbering up the ground to the embarrassment of really promising youngsters.' He added: 'I was among the half wits.' Among the fellow half wits were A. B. Ramsay, afterwards Master of Magdalene, Cambridge, and Leo Amery, Cabinet Minister. When in later years Birkenhead encountered the headmaster, he gave full vent to his grievance.

In his book *My Early Life*, in addition to describing his own unhappiness at school, *Winston Churchill* made many important comments on education in general.

He hated his preparatory school, where, he said, he made very little progress at his lessons and none at all at games. Floggings were severe and frequent. Looking back on his school days as a whole, he wrote: 'I was considerably discouraged. All my contemporaries were better both at games and lessons. It is not pleasant to feel oneself so completely outclassed and left behind at the very beginning of the race.' 'In retrospect these years form not only the least agreeable, but the only barren and unhappy period of my life. This interlude of school makes a sombre grey patch upon the chart of my journey. It was an unending spell of worries that did not seem petty, and of toil uncheered by fruition; a time of discomfort, restriction and purposeless monotony.'

He wrote: 'where my reason, imagination or interest were not engaged, I would not or I could not learn. In all the twelve years I was at school, no one ever succeeded in making me write a Latin verse or learn any Greek except the alphabet.

'Examinations were a great trial. The subjects which were dearest to the examiners were almost invariably those I fancied least. I would have liked to have been examined in history, poetry and writing essays. The examiners, on the other hand, were partial to Latin and mathematics, and their will prevailed. I should have liked to have been asked to say what I know. They always tried to find out what I did not know. When I would willingly have displayed my knowledge, they sought to expose my ignorance.'

He said that he was always glad that he learnt English at Harrow. The clever boys studied Latin and Greek, and the dullards English.

Igor Stravinsky wrote: 'I picture the first years of my adolescence as a series of irksome duties and the perpetual frustration of all my desires and aspirations. The constraint of the school to which I had gone filled me with aversion. I hated the classes and the tasks and I was but a very poor pupil, my lack of industry giving rise to reproaches which only increased my dislike for school and its lessons. Nor did I find any compensation for all this unpleasantness in those school friendships which might have made things easier. During all my school life, I never came across anyone who had any real attraction for me.'

G. K. Chesterton described the time at school as 'the period of what is commonly called education, that is the period during when I was being instructed by somebody I did not know, about something I did not want to know'.

Lawrence of Arabia declared that apart from reading, writing and French (which he already knew), all he learned at school came from the books he read for himself. 'School was usually an irrelevant and time consuming nuisance which I hated and contemned.' He declared that he was educated 'very little, very reluctantly and very badly'. Nevertheless, he won prizes each year.

The things that *Einstein* hated most about school were the rigidity of the school curriculum and the garrison atmosphere (Michelmore). It is bad, he said later, for a school to work with methods of fear, force and artificial authority. They destroy the sincerity and self-confidence of the pupil.

Aneurin Bevan hated school and felt that boys and girls should educate themselves, as he had done.

COMMENT

Comment is superfluous in that the chapter is a collection of comments made by distinguished people about their schooling. One feels much sympathy for most of the persons mentioned in their criticisms.

CHOICE OF CAREER

THE choice of career commonly depends on a concatenation of circumstances, but some people ascribe
their decision to a particular event. This section is
concerned with men and women of eminence in whom there
was a turning point in their life, and one significant factor,
such as the suggestion of a friend, a chance contact, or the loan
of a particular book, which fired the child's interest, and which
seemed to determine the future. It would be idle to claim
that these were the only factors involved; but they seemed to
be important factors which were responsible for the course of
their careers.

ARTISTS

It was said that *Giotto* at the age of ten, when watching
sheep, was drawing on flat stones which lay in front of him,
when Cimabue saw Giotto's drawings, stopped in amazement,
and asked him to stay with him in Florence, in order to have
lessons from him. Thomas recounts a similar story about
Goya. A monk saw him sketching in the fields and asked
to be taken to his home, a farm. There he persuaded the boy's
parents to let him take him and have him taught. At fifteen
Goya was apprenticed to the artist Don José Lujan Martinez,
and worked with him for five years, learning much about
colour and design.

George Romney left school at eleven and assisted his father
in his workshop, doing wood carving. The boy's mind
turned to art when he was lent a copy of Leonardo's treatise
on painting. It was not, however, until twenty-one that he
seriously decided to make art his career, and became apprenticed to an artist.

The genius of *Antonio Canova* as a sculptor was discovered when he modelled a lion out of a roll of butter, for the Senator Falieri of Venice. The Senator recommended him to the artist Bernardi Torelti, who took him into his studio—and was soon completely surpassed by his pupil.

It was Dr Johnson who suggested to *Joseph Turner's* parents that they should let Joseph become an artist, instead of a butcher or barber. It is not clear how Dr Johnson became interested in the boy.

Joseph had always been interested in drawing, and it was said that he could draw before he could spell. When he was nine, according to Falk, his teacher paid numerous visits to the nearby public house during class time, and Joseph would spend the time sketching birds and trees which he could see through the school windows.

In his autobiography, *Frith* tells how at the age of twelve, when looking through some of his father's engravings, he asked for a pencil and paper and began to copy an engraving of a dog. He wrote: 'what impelled me to the deed which actually determined my future life I cannot tell. If I might guess at the motive, I think it was merely that I thought it would afford me a chance of sitting up later than the hour of the children's bedtime, rigorously fixed at nine o'clock; as it did, for I was allowed to finish my wonderful production there and then. If I had doubt as to what prompted me to my first work, I have none whatever as to what induced me to undertake the second. I received 6d. for the dog, with a promise of a similar reward for another effort. From that moment I was considered the genius of the family, and school-masters were informed that all other learning must be considered secondary to the cultivation of this great gift. And very secondary indeed it became.' In fact, apart from a little French, he learned practically nothing at school.

It is said that *Cézanne's* life was transformed by the advent of a new boy, Émile Zola, to his school. Cézanne had not been working hard, but he and Zola had similar interests, and began to read everything they could. Cézanne took up law to please his father, but gave it up to devote all his time to painting.

Sickert's father did not want his son to be a painter, like himself. He wanted him to be a solicitor. It was a chance meeting with Whistler which decided the boy. He joined Whistler.

Renoir's introduction to art began when he had to be apprenticed to a manufacturer of glazed ware, because of the poverty of his parents. He decorated porcelain and china cups. He then painted designs for ladies' fans, covered restaurant ceilings with frescoes, and it was only later that he went to a studio to learn the principles of art.

MUSICIANS, ACTORS AND ACTRESSES

Haydn's ability was recognised by a schoolmaster cousin, at the age of six, and he was put into the choir of the catholic church at Hainburg. There he amused himself by snipping off the tails from the wigs of the choristers in front of him and received a thrashing. At eight he came to the attention of Reutter, Kapellmeister of St Stephen's Cathedral, Vienna, who furthered his training there.

Franz Liszt had shown great musical promise as a small boy, and at ten was taken to Czerny, in the hope of receiving lessons. According to Thomas, Czerny said that he was sorry that he could not take any more pupils. Suddenly he stopped, for Franz had slipped over to the piano and had began to play the most difficult of Czerny's 'Études'. Czerny listened in silence—and then said that he was amazed; he had not heard such talent since Schubert. He then agreed to take Franz at a reduced fee.

The insecurity and unhappiness in the early life of *Jenny Lind* have been described elsewhere (Chapter 1). It may be claimed that her grandmother was the first to discover Jenny's musical ability. Joan Bulman, in her biography, relates that 'When she was four years old, a military band was passing down the street in Stockholm on the way to the palace. Jenny was at the piano, picking out the tune of the fanfare, finding the notes with such fluency and ease that her grandmother thought it was her elder sister practising.' When Jenny heard her approaching, she thought that she had done wrong, and hid under the piano, where she exactly fitted.

The turning point in her career occurred when she was nine. She would sit in the window singing. One day the maid of Mademoiselle Lundberg, a dancer at the Royal Opera House, was passing, and stopped to listen. She told her mistress that she had never heard such a beautiful voice. Mademoiselle Lundberg asked the maid to find out who the girl was and asked the mother to let Jenny sing to her. Mademoiselle Lundberg heard the girl sing, and said: 'The girl is a genius,' and told her that she should be educated for the stage, offering her an introduction to the directors of the Royal Theatre at Stockholm. The mother first scoffed at the idea, but Jenny's grandmother supported it. Mademoiselle Lundberg was not easily put off, and persuaded Jenny's mother to let the girl have singing lessons. Jenny was introduced to the singing master at the theatre, with the result that the authorities offered to take her at once into the singing and dramatic school, taking complete responsibility for her maintenance, education and training. The girl was wildly happy, but was later boarded out at her own home, to her bitter disappointment. When she was fourteen she ran away from home, and was found a room by the matron of the opera school. Her mother went to law to recover her daughter, and won her case, so that when Jenny was sixteen she had to return home again. When she was eighteen she left home for good.

At fifteen *Sarah Bernhardt* decided to be a nun. It was a visitor at dinner, the Duc de Morny, who suggested that she should become an actress. The suggestion was agreed to, and she went to the conservatoire.

Anna Pavlova's father died when she was two years old, and left his wife almost penniless. Anna wrote later that she and her mother had nothing to eat for days apart from rye bread and cabbage soup.

When she was eight she was taken as a special Christmas treat to see a performance of *The Sleeping Beauty* by the Imperial Russian Ballet. She wrote later: 'I was spell-bound. I gazed and gazed, and wild plans began to circulate in my brain. It was the second act and the corps de ballet were waltzing together. "Anna", said my mother, amazed at my excitement, "wouldn't you like to join these people and dance with them?" "No" I replied without hesitation, "I would rather dance by myself like the lovely Sleeping Beauty. One day I will and in this very theatre." My mother laughed, but I was lost in my dream and did not heed her. At eight years old I had found the one unchanging ambition of my life.' Franks, her biographer, described how her mother at first hardly listened to her entreaties, and then attempted to temporise by promising that she would be allowed to go to ballet later. Anna said that she did not mean that sort of dancing: she wanted to be a Ballet Dancer, like the Sleeping Beauty. She found that she had serious difficulties to contend with—not only her mother's opposition, but the fact that the director of the academy said that she was too young, and must wait another two years.

When ten she passed the entrance examination for the academy, and then, she said, 'My toil and suffering had begun.' Frank wrote that 'Discipline and exercises, work and yet more work, became not merely the governing factors of Pavlova's life, from the time until her death, but the best part of life itself—just as they are for every dedicated dancer.'

She soon made her mark as a student, and a brilliant future was prophesied for her. She made her first public appearance four or five years later. At the end of her training she was thought to be too thin, 'meagreness being considered an enemy of good looks', and she was told that she must fatten herself up. This she did, with the help of codliver oil.

After her passing out examination at the age of eighteen, she made her first appearance in the *False Dryads*. Valerian Svetlow in his biography wrote that 'It was her first public appearance, and she at once caught the eyes of all. She was delicate, svelt and pliant like a reed, with the open expression of a little Spanish girl; ethereal and fleeting, she was as graceful and fragile as a piece of Sèvres porcelain.' At twenty-one she was promoted to the rank of second soloist, at twenty-two to first soloist, and at twenty-six to ballerina.

Stravinsky's father was an opera singer and his mother was musical, but they refused to allow Igor to have piano lessons. He went to the University to study law, but by good fortune came into contact with the son of Rimsky-Korsakoff. This really started him on his musical career.

WRITERS

When *Metastasio*, future Italian poet, was improvising verse at eleven and declaiming to a crowd in the street, Gian Gravina, a critic of repute, overheard him. Gravina was so impressed that he adopted him, altered the boy's name to Metastasio, and gave him a good education, leaving him a fortune when he died. Metastasio showed great promise, writing verses at ten, at twelve translating the *Iliad* into octave stanzas, and at fourteen composing his *Tragedy of Guistino*. He lived to the age of eighty-four, writing poetry and drama to the end of his life.

The turning point in the career of *Jean de la Fontaine* came when he was twenty-two. He had decided on an ecclesiastical career, but at twenty-two according to Terman and Oden, he experienced his first awakening to the beauty of verse when an officer staying at the Chateau Thiery happened to read to him an ode by Malherbe. Jean listened with rapt joy and admiration, and became a completely different person—full of enthusiasm and happiness.

Sir Walter Scott entered college to prepare for a legal career, like his father; he would have preferred to be a soldier, but the effects of poliomyelitis made this impossible. It was because of this physical disability that he began to write.

Charles Dickens 'had always the belief that his early sickness had brought to himself one inestimable advantage, that it strongly inclined him to reading'.

Gogol, according to Magarshack, said that an important turning point in his life, when he was sixteen, was the arrival at his school, of a new teacher Nikolai Belousov. He was the idol of his pupils, and a rare person who treated his pupils as friends. He was an educated man of liberal views, and brought about a revolution in Gogol's writings and in his whole outlook on life.

Belousov was in sympathy with a secret revolutionary society, and this, together with his critical attitude to the government, had a deep influence on Gogol. Belousov was eventually reported by a rival for spreading subversive and free-thinking ideas among his pupils, and was banished—to Gogol's great regret.

It was the discovery of Rousseau which, according to Thomas, reconciled *Leo Tolstoy* to his ugliness and opened his eyes to the beauty of nature. Tolstoy worshipped Rousseau like a God and wore a medallion portrait round his neck. He was inspired by the philosophy of Rousseau to write his first novel.

The same author, Thomas, tells how *Émile Zola* began to write. His mother wanted him to be an engineer, like his father. Émile was in despair about the choice of career, having reached the age of twenty. Later, when wrapping books in the shipping department of a publishing house, he spent his spare time writing reviews of the books for his own interest.

His employer, finding him doing this, saw his potentiality and promoted him to the advertising department. He now began to write assiduously, and turned from poetry to fiction.

Thomas Hardy was unable to go to University, because his father could not afford it. He was apprenticed to an architect, but disliked the work. He qualified in architecture, and began to write poetry. It was his wife who persuaded him to change from poetry to prose.

James Barrie said that it was a puppet show in his bedroom which awoke his liking for the stage, and led him to resolve to become a dramatist.

At thirteen he went to Dumfries Academy, devouring 'penny dreadfuls, magazines containing exclusively sanguinary matter, largely tales about heroic highwaymen and piracy on the high seas' (Roy).

At eighteen he went to Edinburgh University.

SCIENTISTS

The famous French surgeon, *Ambroise Paré*, was acting as stable boy to an abbé at Laval, when a surgical operation was performed on one of the brethren of the monastery. He was asked to assist, and he was so interested that he decided to become a surgeon. He never attended any University, but served as an apprentice to a master barber-surgeon.

Thomas told the well known story of how *Galileo*, as a medical student, was kneeling in a service at the cathedral in Pisa, when he saw an oil lamp, left swinging by the sacristan, who had filled it. Galileo suddenly jumped up, to the amazement of other worshippers. He noted that the rhythm was regular, and that the pendulum of the rattling chains was taking exactly the same time in each of its oscillations, although the distance of the oscillations was constantly becoming less. He went home and tried the experiment with two pendulums of different lengths, and found that the total swings were the same.

He flirted with the idea of becoming a monk, but his father removed him at twelve from the monastery school, and wanted him to become a cloth merchant. The boy then wanted to study mathematics, but instead was sent to the University of Pisa to study medicine. He was refused the doctors' diploma, and left the University.

M. Petit, famous French surgeon, as a boy first attracted the attention of Littré, the anatomist, by performing a vivisection on a rabbit. From the age of seven he regularly attended Littré's lectures. By nine he was so proficient in anatomy that he was given sole charge of the anatomy theatre. Smiles described the remarkable sight of a nine year old boy, standing on a chair, delivering lectures to students and able professional men.

It is easy to see how *Linnaeus* became interested in botany, for both his parents had a great love for flowers. There was an outstanding rectory garden, with several hundred different foreign plants. The rector of the school was also a plant lover, and exerted considerable influence on Carolus. His parents wanted him to follow his father's footsteps, and become a priest; but he chose a scientific career.

John Hunter, destined to be a famous physician, and easily the most famous member of his family, caused his parents bitter disappointment, for his two elder brothers were doing well at their work, his brother William in anatomy in London, and his other brother in law in Glasgow. John was the black sheep of the family. He stayed at home to work on the farm until he was seventeen, having showed no particular aptitude in anything. He went to join his brother in Glasgow, but the brother became bankrupt. At twenty, with no future in front of him, he wrote to his brother William in London, and joined him, taking two weeks to ride there. He began to help his brother in dissections, and then embarked on his medical career by studying medicine at Barts.

Telford, designer of the Caledonian Canal, the Menai and Conway bridges, and the Birmingham and Liverpool canal, among many other engineering feats, was brought up in extreme poverty in a Dumfriesshire cottage, and worked as a farm labourer. He then became apprenticed to a stonemason. While working at stonemasonry, an elderly lady lent him books, and soon friends and neighbours also lent him reading matter. He read in all his spare time. He later became a stonemason in Edinburgh.

Sir Astley Cooper was stimulated to take up surgery because of his success in stopping a haemorrhage from a torn femoral vessel in a man who had been run over by a cart. He improvised a tourniquet and saved the man's life.

Michael Faraday was brought up in a home of great poverty, and at the age of thirteen was put to work as an errand boy to a bookseller. He was promoted to be an apprentice bookbinder—and this gave Michael access to books, which he read avidly in his spare time. He particularly enjoyed reading books on electricity. He was allowed to attend a series of lectures on science, at a shilling a time, paid by his employer and brother. He expected to be a bookbinder for the rest of his life.

The turning point in his career came when he copied out Sir Humphry Davy's lectures and bound them, sending them to Sir Humphry and asking for a job in the laboratory. He was given a job washing bottles, polishing desks, cleaning the inkwell and sweeping the floor. He helped Sir Humphry, and began to work with him. At twenty-two he was invited to accompany his master as assistant on a lecture tour in Europe (Thomas).

Niels Abel, famous Norwegian mathematician, and one of the principal founders of modern mathematics, seemed to have no talent for anything when he was fifteen; but when the teacher flogged a fellow student so unmercifully that he died, the teacher was dismissed, and a new teacher took over. This man was a mathematician, and sparked the genius in young Abel, and fired his interest in mathematics.

Claude Bernard entered employment at the age of eighteen with a pharmacist. It was his job to sweep the pavement, rinse bottles and serve at a shop. His chief supplied drugs to a nearby veterinary school, and Claude enjoyed the visits there, and developed his interest in physiology.

Truax tells how *Joseph Lister*, aged ten, was waiting for his father to inspect his lessons, when he happened to look out of the window. He was startled by a remarkable sight; owing to a defect in the glass, a kind of bubble had formed, and when he looked through the bubble he could see everything outside much more clearly than he could when he looked through the rest of the glass. He asked his father for the explanation. His father told him that the bubble was acting as a magnifying glass, and could not explain it, but promised to look it up in a book of optics. This aroused Joseph's interest in optics. He was to invent the achromatic lens and to become a Fellow of the Royal Society.

Robert Mayer, German scientist, was described by Kretschmer as being extremely passionate and temperamental in his early years. He was outstanding at school because of his effervescent wit and the remarkable flight of ideas, which made it almost impossible to keep him to one train of thought in conversation. He was also notorious for his absent-mindedness.

When he was ten, the sight of a mill at work raised in his mind the question of the conservation and transportation of energy, and the problem of perpetual motion. He pondered a great deal about the matter, but it was not until he was a ship's surgeon on the way to the Dutch East Indies, that he suddenly stumbled on the law of the conservation of energy, and the function of food in providing human energy.

Sir Thomas Clifford Allbutt went to St Peter's School at York (where another boy destined for fame, Guy Fawkes, had been a pupil). Thence he went to Caius College, Cambridge, with a scholarship in Classics. Sir Humphry Rolleston wrote that the almost accidental reading of Auguste Compte's *Philosophic*

Positive transformed Allbutt's outlook and determined his future life by turning his thoughts to science. He then went to St George's Hospital to study medicine.

Edison's interests in science began at nine when his mother gave him books on physical science.

The parents of *Sigmund Freud* were determined to let their boy choose his own career—so differently from many of the parents mentioned in this section. He was inclined to study law, because of the influence of a schoolfriend. It was Goethe's essay on Nature that decided him to become a medical student, and he entered the University of Vienna to study medicine.

The father of *Arthur Conan Doyle* wanted Arthur to be a business man and mathematician—but Arthur loathed arithmetic. His mother suggested that he should become a doctor.

A deciding factor in his life was a friend's gift of Macaulay's *Lays of Ancient Rome*. He was enthralled with this, and searched for more books by Macaulay. When he was invited to spend a holiday in London his first ambition was to see Macaulay's grave in Westminster Abbey. Later Edgar Allen Poe really excited his mind and shaped his literary tastes.

It is said that a serious illness at the age of four aroused in *Alfred Adler* the desire to become a physician, and nothing would make him change his mind. He studied in the University of Vienna, and at twenty-eight started in private practice as an eye specialist—becoming a psychiatrist later.

Albert Einstein's father wanted him to become an electrical engineer, but at sixteen the boy was allowed to enter for the Zürich Polytechnic Academy. He failed the examination. He tried again later, and was successful, obtaining a teacher's certificate, but was refused an appointment. He then took up a clerical post in the Swiss Patent Office in Berne.

His interest in mathematics was aroused not by the school, but by his uncle, who gave him his first understanding of algebra.

OTHER PERSONS OF EMINENCE

The father of *St Francis of Assisi* was a tailor, and expected his son to succeed him in the business. This was not to his son's liking. He led a normal somewhat riotous life, typical of the times, and was taken prisoner when fighting for his city in one of the numerous inter-city fights. He became ill, and had occasion to meditate on his way of life. He suddenly changed, and became 'like a man in a trance, from that time onwards living the life of the poorest of the poor—to work for the poor and needy'.

Joan of Arc claimed to have heard the voice of the Archangel Michael—and later the voices of St Marguerite and St Catherine. She was told by the Archangel to leave her home and go to the aid of the King against the English. She raised an army of 8,000 and defeated the English at the Battle of Orleans.

Martin Luther had a vision when he was twenty-two. There was a severe thunderstorm, and lightning struck the ground near him. He was terrified, and called: 'Help me, St Anne—I want to become a Monk.'

The story of *Saint Bernadette's* vision at Lourdes is told by Margaret Trouncer. Bernadette was an ill-educated girl, who had scarcely any schooling and could not read or write. She had troublesome asthma. At the age of thirteen she had a vision at the grotto—hearing first a rushing sound, and then seeing a light brighter than the sun, followed by the appearance of a very young girl, of her own size, with a face as white as wax. The girl talked to Saint Bernadette, who was unable to call out to her sisters who were near, because she had lost her voice. Later, in the presence of others, she had the same vision, but no one else could see anything.

Mazzini was a doctor's son, born in Genoa. He received his early education at the Royal College in Genoa, which, according to Hales, was a place where boys were principally preoccupied with the problem of how to overthrow authority.

Both inside and outside the classroom they learnt how to do this if they were brave enough. According to King, another biographer, the boy lived a quiet studious life until one day, when he was fifteen years old, he saw the despairing faces of the abandoned and defeated Piedmontese liberals after the collapse of the Carbonaro revolutions. He longed to follow them, 'neglected his lessons, and sat moody and absorbed, interested only in gleaning news of the exiles and learning the history of their defeat'. He insisted on dressing in black. In time he returned to his books and worked hard again. When still fifteen he was arrested by the police for helping to lead a tumult in the University Church.

He took up medicine, but fainted at his first attendance in the operation room, and decided to take up law. King described him at this stage as a troublesome scholar, always rebelling against authority. He persistently refused to attend the compulsory religious observances, just because they were compulsory, but the authorities ignored his insubordination. He became a revolutionary leader among the undergraduates.

In later years he was to be feared by rulers of many countries.

Thomas Erskine, famous advocate, brought up in poverty, had little education and never went to a University. Lord Birkett wrote that Thomas became a midshipman on a war-ship and served in the army. His regiment moved to a town where a court was in session under Lord Mansfield, who was presiding as judge. Thomas attended the court and was so impressed that he asked to see the judge, and thereupon decided to take up law.

Sir Edward Marshall Hall, advocate, decided to go to the Bar because of one morning which he spent in the Magistrate's Court at Brighton. Lord Birkett described how Marshall was so captivated by the story which he heard that he decided then and there to study law himself.

Margaret Murray, Egyptologist, had had no interest in the subject at all until the day her elder sister, reading the weekly

edition of *The Times*, saw a note that Sir Flinders Petrie was
going to hold a series of classes at University College, London.
She told Margaret to apply for admission to the classes, and
persuaded her mother to write a letter of introduction.
Margaret attended them—and so began a profitable partner-
ship with Sir Flinders, which led to her international fame as
an Egyptologist.

Winston Churchill claimed that his collection of about 1,500
toy soldiers was the factor which guided him to take up a
military career.

Lord Beaverbrook showed his money-making propensity
when twelve years old, when he sold newspapers in the street.
Driberg, in his biography, tells how Max, instead of selling
all the papers himself, employed other boys to act as subagents, so that the papers could be sold more rapidly and
extensively.

He stayed at school until fourteen, but in addition worked
in a drug store. He had to be up in the morning in time to
collect the shop key from the head clerk's house to open the
shop at 7 a.m. He then swept the floor, washed medicine
bottles and went to school. After school he returned to the
shop, selling goods till ten or eleven o'clock at night. For this
he was paid a dollar a week.

When he left school he was entered for a local bank. He
had no intention of taking such a job, and took good care to
fail the entrance examination. He then became a correspondent
for one of the papers he was selling, earning a dollar for a
column. After this, he took preliminary law examinations,
and later went to Calgary, with Richard Bennett who was
destined to be Prime Minister of Canada. He and a friend
borrowed money to start a bowling alley, and later set up
business collecting and delivering cargoes of meat. For a time
he was an expert at poaching, with some less reputable members of the community.

At twenty he was drinking heavily and gambling. Suddenly,

on his twenty-first birthday, while fishing on a lake in Nova Scotia, 'he experienced a sort of conversion which was as sudden, as blindingly intense and as lasting in its effect as those of Saul of Tarsus and John Wesley'. He decided then and there to work hard and save money. It was the turning point of his life.

COMMENT

We are conscious of the possibility and indeed likelihood that we have unwittingly placed wrong emphasis on some features which seemed to us from our reading to have been milestones in the life of the men and women in question. It could hardly be otherwise. Nevertheless, the story could be greatly elaborated. In other parts of this book we have told about the turning points in the career of other famous men and women—such as John Bunyan, William Penn, William Booth and Florence Nightingale. It is probable that most men of eminence could think of some event, perhaps of little apparent significance at the time, which was the really deciding factor in their choice of career.

CHAPTER 12

EARLY STEPS TO FINAL CAREER

IN this chapter we have attempted the difficult task of
bringing together stories from the childhood and adolescence of famous men and women, in order to illustrate
the early vicissitudes which they experienced in the establishment of their careers.

We believe that the very many parents who wrangle with
their children about the choice of their life's work, or whose
children cannot make up their minds as to what career to
choose, will find something of interest in this chapter.

We were particularly interested in the many changes of
mind with regard to career. Law, for instance, was for a long
time one of the most favoured careers for men of the middle
social class, and numerous boys were persuaded to study law
against their wishes. *Petrarch, Voltaire* and *Molière* forsook the
law for literature. *Bunyan, Cervantes, Chaucer, Coleridge, Dante,
Descartes, Ben Jonson* and *Loyola* were soldiers and forsook
this occupation to enter science, the arts or literature. Many
of the children destined for fame changed from one profession
to another.

Sidgwick, in his biography of *William Herschel*, wrote:
'The underlying patterns of men's lives make a fascinating
study, for they are as various as man himself. Some describe
a course from the cradle to the grave as direct and unswerving
as the flight of an arrow. The life lines of others are dis-
jointed, contorted, diverted by chance encounters and accidents
till any semblance of pattern is lost beneath a tangle of apparent
irrelevancies.' The early life of Sir William Herschel was
certainly a fascinating story of a circuitous route to the final
career and so to fame.

ARTISTS

Leonardo da Vinci early decided to be an investigator, teacher and artist. He begged his father to apprentice him to a painter, but his father refused, because painters were regarded as inferior, and his father wanted him to be a lawyer. At eighteen, however, Leonardo became apprenticed to Andrea del Verrocchio, the Florentine painter, sculptor and architect. Leonardo painted an angel in a picture by his master, 'The Baptism of Christ' so beautifully that Verrocchio gave up his own painting in despair. Leonardo then came under the influence of Toscanelli, naturalist and mathematician, who had theories about the earth being round. Leonardo became interested in geography, astronomy, natural history, physics and engineering, inventing labour saving tools, drawing maps, designing machines for turning and grinding, and filling his notebooks with dozens of scientific and artistic sketches (Vallentin).

Michelangelo's father was annoyed at his boy's repeated requests to be allowed to become an artist. He had displayed his passion for drawing from the earliest years. The father intended his five sons to go into business and become bankers. He beat Michelangelo and scolded him, but failed to shake him out of his ambition. The boy was sent into the country to be looked after by the wife of a stonemason. There Michelangelo covered the walls of the stonemason's house with sketches. With great reluctance the father apprenticed him to Ghirlandajo. The boy was set the task of grinding colours and copying bits of drapery from sketches for paintings on the walls of Santa Maria Novella, but, when his paintings were better than the originals, Ghirlandajo became jealous. The boy was then taught sculpture in the garden of the Medici, and while working there, Lorenzo the Magnificent happened to see his work. He was fourteen years old at the time—and was taken into the Palazzo Medici, where he met many artists.

At one time he thought of renouncing his art to enter a

monastery, having heard the teachings of Savonarola; but decided to continue with it. The 'Battle of the Centaurs' was done when he was seventeen, and the 'Sleeping Cupid' when he was nineteen.

The autobiography of *Benvenuto Cellini* described his early struggles to achieve his ambition to be an artist. His father began to teach him the flute when he was five, wanting him to be a musician. The boy hated it, and became apprenticed to a goldsmith. The father wanted him to continue to play the flute, but Benvenuto asked whether he would be allowed to draw for so many hours one day, if he sacrificed the next day to the flute.

He wrote that he had the utmost aversion for the flute, and played it merely in obedience to authority. His father said: 'I am determined to make a great musician of him, in spite of those who would fain prevent such a genius from shining in the world.'

The father of *Sir Joshua Reynolds* was undecided whether the boy should become a painter or an apothecary. Joshua wanted to become a painter and was apprenticed to Thomas Hudson, the leading portrait painter in London. He soon proved to be better than his master, and left after two years.

Corot's father was a hairdresser. The boy was much loved by his parents, who disapproved of his painting but let him have his own way. They hoped that he would become a business man, and after school the boy took up a job as drapery salesman. After six unhappy years at this he took up painting. He settled down outside Paris, but did not sell his first painting until his fifth decade.

Edouard Manet's father, a judge, was determined that his son should become a magistrate. Edouard thought otherwise. Perruchot, in his biography, indicated that it was Edouard's uncle Fournier who really stimulated and encouraged the boy to study art: certainly Edouard's father thought this, and never forgave the uncle for it. This uncle was impressed with

the boy's talent for drawing and gave him every encouragement, taking him to the Louvre, and suggesting that he
should take drawing at the Collège Rollin. The father objected strongly, but yielded, and at the age of fourteen Edouard
went there for classes. Edouard had strong views about painting, and the work at the college bored him. He drew what
interested him, instead of the model which he was supposed to
be drawing. His neighbours, including Proust, copied him.
He was reprimanded for this, and also for being idle and inattentive. This was reported to his father, who was extremely
angry with him.

His father was seriously disturbed at the boy's determination
to be a painter, and told him never to mention the word
again. Edouard threatened to run away if he was made to
read law. At last his father said he could do anything he liked,
apart from painting, and Edouard decided to go to sea,
joining the navy at sixteen. He sat the entrance examination,
but the results were so bad that he was told that it would be
useless to take the oral.

He took a voyage to Rio and back, as a means of securing
admission to the École Navale, but his father then decided that
it was hopeless to expect Edouard to pass any examinations,
and suggested that he should go to the École des Beaux Arts.
The boy refused, but was sent at the age of eighteen to work
under Thomas Couture—a daring and revolutionary painter.
This was just to Edouard's liking, and he worked really hard
under his master.

Gauguin wanted to be a sailor when he left school, and made
two voyages to South America as apprentice on a cargo boat.
He was promoted to be second mate, and sailed round the
world on a thirteen-month voyage. At nineteen he did his
military service as a stoker in the navy.

After five years at sea, which he described as the most bitter
years of his life, he joined the stock exchange. He started to
paint as an adult.

Vincent Van Gogh left school at sixteen to learn the trade of salesman in the Goupic gallery at the Hague. From there he travelled to Brussels, London and Paris. Laprade, in his biography, wrote that Vincent then became obsessed with the idea of devoting his life to religion, and seriously considered going into the church. He returned to England and became a schoolmaster at Ramsgate. After this he spent some time working for a clergyman in London. Subsequently he went to a missionary school in Brussels and was sent out as a lay preacher. He nursed the sick and taught children. At twenty-six he was tramping along roads in Holland and Belgium, selling his paintings to peasants.

Toulouse-Lautrec, whose full name was Henri-Marie-Raymond de Toulouse-Lautrec-Monfa—came from a distinguished family, and a life of affluence awaited him. He was determined, however, to be an artist, to the dismay of his parents. At eighteen he left for Paris to study art.

At a very early age *Jacob Epstein* showed his interest in drawing and has written: 'I cannot recall a period when I did not draw.' He wrote that 'I was a tremendous reader, and there were periods when I would go off to Central Park, find a secluded place far away from crowds and noise, and there give myself up to solitary reading for the day.' He added: 'What chiefly concerned my family was why I did things which could not possibly bring me any money, and they deplored this mad or foolish streak in me. They put it down to perversity that made me a lonely boy, going off on my own to the woods with a book, and not turning up to meals, and later making friends with negroes and anarchists. My parents did not discourage me, but could not understand how I could make a living by Art. Their idea of an artist was that of a person who was condemned to starvation.'

Nevertheless, it was a happy home, and his parents, though worried about his future, did nothing to impede the fulfilment of his ambitions.

Paul Nash had considerable difficulty in deciding on a career. He wrote that before he left St Paul's school his parents tried to get him to become an architect, but a difficulty with mathematics made this impossible. Paul said that he now had to face the fact that so far he had been a failure—and that in the opinion of a good many people he was practically doomed to remain a failure. His father suggested that he should enter a bank, but this hardly seemed rational in view of his difficulties in mathematics. Paul then suggested that he should become an artist, and in despair his parents agreed.

MUSICIANS

Handel's father wanted his boy to become a barber, as he himself was, and later wanted him to become a lawyer. His father forbade him to touch a musical instrument, and even avoided sending him to a public school, for there he would be taught music. Smiles described how Handel found means to procure a dumb spinet, concealed it in a garret, and went to practise on the mute instrument when everyone was asleep. Handel took up law at the University of Halle, to please his father. He deputised for the organist at the cathedral, and was offered the post when the organist left. The Duke of Saxe-Weissenfels heard of his keenness and interceded with his father. One month after qualifying, Handel abandoned law to devote his life to music.

Beethoven's regular schooling ceased when he was eleven. Although he had been practising music from the age of five, his first good teacher, when he was eleven, was Christian Neefe. Beethoven deputised for Neefe as court organist in Bonn at the age of twelve, and became part organist, part conductor, in the rehearsals at the court there. His life's work as a serious musician began when he was thirteen, when told to play in the Electoral orchestra. At seventeen he went to Vienna, where Mozart asked him to improvise for him, and gave him some lessons free of charge.

Rossini was the son of the town trumpeter and inspector of slaughterhouses at Pesaro, on the Adriatic coast. He had practically no education, and was described as no more than a street-arab. He became a blacksmith's apprentice. A priest then taught him to sing. At thirteen Rossini played a child's role in an opera at Bologna. He sang, and played the horn. He was greatly helped by Cavaliere Gusti, engineer at Bologna, who took a liking to the boy and taught him. He composed some pieces, one of which was performed in public when he was sixteen. When he was eighteen he was invited to compose an opera for a theatre in Venice.

The father of *Franz Schubert* was a desperately poor school-master. When he was seven his father began to teach him the violin and piano. At eleven he became choirboy in the Court Chapel, and so was admitted to the Royal Seminary in Vienna. There he impressed everyone by his musical ability.

His father intended him to become a schoolmaster too, but was deeply upset and angry when he discovered that his son intended to make music his career. Brockway wrote: 'For some years his father regarded his son's talent as pleasant and harmless, but when it began to interfere with the boy's studies, and he began to fear that Franz was not the stuff of which schoolmasters are made, he blew up.' He almost turned him out of the house when Franz refused to abandon his interests.

When his voice broke he accepted a post as assistant to his father in the school. He loathed this work. He fell out with his father again, and for three years was not on speaking terms with him.

He composed his first masterpiece when seventeen. By the age of nineteen he had written more than 150 songs.

The father of *Louis Berlioz* was determined that Louis should follow in his footsteps and take up medicine. Louis disapproved of the idea, and quarrelled with both his parents about it—but agreed to do more work at the subject if they obtained a new flute for him. To this his father agreed.

Louis, however, hated the work. His first experience in the dissecting room was a nightmare, and it is said that he escaped through the window and ran back to his lodgings as if chased by the devil. At twenty-one he dropped all pretence of doing medicine, and took up music.

The life of *Mendelssohn* was described by Brockway as the happiest in musical history. He was brought up in a happy cultured household, in which the parents did everything they could to foster their boy's musical ambition.

Robert Schumann left school at eighteen, and was persuaded with great reluctance to go to the Law School at Leipzig, because his mother was determined that he should become a lawyer. It is said that he did not attend a single lecture there, completely neglecting his studies, though composing several musical pieces. At twenty he decided to devote himself to music.

Johannes Brahms was born in the slums. His father was a musical jack of all trades, who had married a woman seventeen years his senior—an ugly, crippled, bad tempered person.

Johannes was taught music by his father, and at eight was sent to a music teacher to learn the piano. Within a year, according to Brockway, 'he was much in demand at the brothels, where he was the darling of the prostitutes, who thought it fun to try to arouse his immature emotions'. Brockway wrote that it is impossible to overestimate these odd experiences on the boy's makeup: he depended all his life on prostitutes for physical satisfaction.

Borodin at seventeen took up medicine at St Petersburg, to please his parents, and graduated as a doctor. At twenty-six he went abroad as delegate of the Academy of Physicians. He had always been interested in music, however, and subsequently decided to make it his career.

Tchaikovsky's parents planned to send their boy to a School of Mining Engineers, but finally decided to send him to the School of Jurisprudence at St Petersburg. Prior to this he had to go to a boarding school for preparatory work, at the age of twelve. In his biography, Tchaikovsky wrote a vivid description of his parting from his parents. 'When the actual moment of parting came, he completely lost his self-control, and clinging wildly to his mother, he refused to let her go. Neither kisses, nor words of comfort, nor the promise to return soon, were of any avail. He saw nothing, heard nothing, but hung upon her as though he was part and parcel of the beloved presence. It became necessary to carry off the poor child by force, and hold him until his mother was driven away. Even then he broke loose, and with a cry of despair, ran after the carriage, and clung to one of the wheels, as though he would bring the vehicle to a standstill. To his life's end Tchaikovsky could never recall this hour without a shiver of horror.'

He showed no special interest in music until he was nineteen. He qualified in Jurisprudence, and entered the Ministry of Justice as a clerk at the age of twelve. He joined music classes and finally embarked on his musical career at twenty-three.

Dvorak's father was a butcher, and wanted his son to follow in his footsteps. He became apprenticed to his father, but did not like the work. At sixteen he went to an organ school in Prague—to begin his musical career.

Rimsky-Korsakoff said that until he was an adult he never dreamed of becoming a musician. He wanted to go to sea, and at twelve joined the Naval College at St Petersburg, staying for six years—though meanwhile receiving some instruction in the cello and piano. At seventeen a contact with Balakirev, leader of the new Russian school of music, finally decided him about his career. At the age of eighteen he went to sea for a three-year period, during which time he composed a symphony which was later performed in St Petersburg.

Elgar left school at fifteen and joined a firm of solicitors at

Worcester. He soon gave up all thought of a legal profession and joined his father in the music shop.

Delius, after leaving Bradford Grammar School, went to the International College at Isleworth to learn office work. After three years he joined the family business in the wool trade at Bradford. He was interested in music and it was some years later, after a fairly long period in Scandinavia, that he left business to take up music as a career.

Like Schumann and Tchaikovsky, *Sibelius* was expected by his parents to take up a legal career, and enrolled at the University of Helsingfors. After two terms he gave up law for music.

Sir Henry Wood was the son of an optician, who was also a book lover, with a great interest in art and music, and who owned a shop for model railway engines in Oxford Street. Henry's father sang as a tenor in church, and sometimes sang in St Paul's Cathedral and Westminster Abbey. Henry's mother taught him the notes on the piano. He did not attend school until he was nearly nine. Henry said in his autobiography that he spent a large part of every day strumming triads on an excellent Broadwood cottage piano, and studied music in his bedroom till late at night. At ten he became deputy organist at St Mary's Church, Aldermanbury, at thirteen deputy organist at St Sepulchre's Church, Holborn, and at seventeen organist at St John's Church, Fulham. He had his first serious experience of conducting when he was twenty, and the following year was engaged by Sullivan and D'Oyly Carte to superintend the rehearsals of *Ivanhoe*.

WRITERS

Giovanni Boccaccio was the son of a Florentine merchant, who was determined to make his son a lawyer. At ten Giovanni was apprenticed to a Parisian business man, and a few years later became a commercial traveller for his father. He loved reading, and disliked trying to sell his wares. His father complained that he spent more on books than he made from selling his goods. Giovanni was sent to the University of Naples to study law, but he refused to work at this, being determined to become a writer.

He bitterly reproached his father for insisting on his going into business, writing: 'If my father had dealt wisely with me, I might have been among the great poets.' In fact, he became famous for the *Decameron* and other works.

Ben Jonson, after leaving school, became a bricklayer, like his stepfather, but disliking the job, took up military service, and later became a writer.

Before he was eighteen *John Bunyan* had begun to assist his father at the forge. He had had the most scanty education, learning only to read and write. At twenty he had a religious awakening, and also came under the influence of a religious girl, whom he married. He renounced pleasure and decided to live a sober religious life.

Daniel Defoe was told by his father: 'I want you to be a minister, and if not a minister, a merchant. But in any event I want you to be a successful gentleman.' Daniel decided to enter on a business career. He had a mixed and adventurous time. His book, *Robinson Crusoe*, appeared when he was fifty-nine.

Voltaire was persuaded by his father to study law, but he disliked it and soon gave it up.

The story of the insecurity of *Jean Jacques Rousseau's* early life has been told elsewhere (Chapter 1). He had little formal schooling. On leaving school, he was put into a notary's office. This was unsuccessful, and at thirteen he was apprenticed to an engraver. This job, he said, did nothing but transform him into a lazy and furtive oaf. In his *Confessions* he said hard things about his master, but as Green wrote in his biography: 'One suspects that he' (the master) 'had good reason to be enraged at an apprentice who broke into his office, abstracted his materials and ruined his best tools by engraving medals for an imaginary order of chivalry.' Jean Jacques was offended at being considered on a par with his less intelligent workmates. He was soundly and frequently whipped, and grew taciturn, moody and apprehensive. In his lifetime he embarked upon and abandoned twelve different trades.

At sixteen, after an expedition with friends outside the walls of Geneva, he found the city gates shut and ran away. Broome, in his biography, then describes how a catholic priest of a small village sent Jean to Annecy, with an introduction to Baronne de Warens who was to get him into the Church. She seemed to be somewhere between 'mother and mistress' to him.

Thomas Gray considered a career in medicine, but then decided to go into law. After travelling abroad he settled in Cambridge for the rest of his life.

On leaving school, *William Cowper* became a clerk in a law office. 'After three mis-spent years', to use his words, he embarked on his literary career when he was twenty-three.

Alfieri was so thrilled when he first saw the sea at Genoa, that he decided to be a poet. He worked hard at school, and then travelled extensively. According to Smiles he 'drowned ennui and melancholy in dissipation', and at nineteen fell violently in love. He was almost heartbroken when his love was not reciprocated and resolved to die, but his valet saved his life. He fell in love again, was again disappointed, cut off his hair, and in his loneliness began to write verses, and found his life's work.

Johann Goethe ascribed his first interest in drama to the gift of a set of puppets when he was seven. His biographer, Brown, described the struggle and friction between father and son concerning Johann's choice of career. His father was determined from the beginning that his own son should become a lawyer, and the boy's desire to be a writer was ignored. Johann wanted to go to the University of Göttingen, but his father overrode his desires and entered him for the University of Leipzig.

Johann said later that he left his home at Frankfurt with 'joy as intense as that of a prisoner who has broken through his gaol window and finds himself a free man'. He never lost his dislike of his native city. Before departing he confided to his sister Cornelia that he had not the least intention of becoming a lawyer. He left with the deliberate intention of following his own inclinations, to study literature.

He told his professor about his intentions, and the latter tried to discourage the boy. Johann refused to attend the lectures, and his attendance became a joke. It was the professor's wife, Frau Böhme, who saw the promise in the boy—and advised him about clothes and manners, guided him in his reading and criticised his poems.

Chateaubriand was sent to a Jesuit school at Rennes to study mathematics, in order that he could enter the Royal Navy. The boy had no enthusiasm for such work, however, and devoted his time to reading and later to writing.

William Wordsworth had two sets of verses published when he was sixteen. At seventeen he went to Cambridge—devoting most of his first year to writing his *Evening Walk*.

He was undecided about his future, though his guardians expected him to go into the Church. He thought of studying law, but because of his violent headaches decided against a sedentary occupation.

Wordsworth claimed that he obtained little profit from his time in Cambridge, where 'the manners of the young men were very frantic and dissolute'. At twenty-one he went to France to learn the language—and spent more and more time writing.

Thomas Carlyle was mathematics master at Annan Academy for two years. He disliked the work, and took up the study of law, before finally deciding on literature as a career.

George Borrow was articled at sixteen to a firm of solicitors, but spent his spare time learning Welsh, Danish, Arabic, Armenian, and the Saxon languages, before devoting his time to writing and travelling.

At eleven *Charles Dickens* had to leave school to earn money, and made a few pennies by singing comic songs in Limehouse. He then began a job pasting labels in a factory. Determined to become a writer, he attended Wellington House Academy for odd periods between jobs, and founded and edited a newspaper there, selling copies for marbles and pieces of slate pencil. At fifteen he was sent to work in a lawyer's office.

He eventually became one of the richest men in Europe.

Alexandre Dumas had many difficulties in the choice of a career. Thomas tells how his mother tried to make a scholar out of him, but he hated learning. She tried to make him into a violinist, but he hated music. Finally she tried to interest him in the priesthood, but he ran away from home and for several days lived in the woods. His mother gave him up in despair, saying: 'The only thing he can do is to write a good hand—but any idiot can do that.' Yet he was a good fencer and wrestler, and a first-rate shot.

At fifteen he became a copy clerk in a notary's office, but spent more time in reading than copying. He wanted to go to Paris, and being an expert billiards player, he made enough money to go there. There he met an actor in the Théâtre François, and confided that he wanted to be a writer. The actor jokingly touched his forehead and said: 'I hereby baptise thee poet, in the name of Shakespeare, Corneille and Schiller.' He went home with a deep determination to make the jest come true—and succeeded.

Hans Christian Andersen's father, an impoverished cobbler, intended to apprentice Hans to a tailor, but Hans refused. Hans was determined to become an opera singer. He was thought to be mad when at fourteen he walked to Copenhagen and visited the Royal Theatre to state his ambitions. He achieved no success. He tried to become a dancer, but failed.

However, he was sent to school and subsequently to University. He wrote his first book (*A Journey on Foot*) at twenty-four, and it was an immediate success.

Flaubert's father was very much against his son embarking on a literary career. He wanted him to follow his own footsteps and become a doctor. When the boy was eighteen he utterly refused to become a doctor, and was sent to study law in Paris. He showed no interest in this either, being determined to be a writer. In despair his father let him have his own way.

Guy de Maupassant was sent in his early teens to a clerical seminary, but he had no intention of becoming a priest, and was expelled. Later he entered the Lyceum and worked for the bar. When the Prussian invasion occurred, he joined the supply section of the army. He published his first volume of poems when thirty.

One of the most bitter struggles in connection with the choice of career was that of *Samuel Butler*. It was a struggle which, as in the case of Goethe, led to permanent estrangement between father and son. Samuel's father was determined that his son should follow in his footsteps and be ordained. Canon Butler practised what his son called 'will-shaking—the use of money power as a means of attempting to bring his son to heel whenever he tried to go his own way': and Canon Butler threatened to cut off Samuel's allowance if the boy did not go into the Church. No threats, however, would make Samuel agree. Canon Butler, according to Cole, Samuel's biographer, thought that there were only two possible alternatives for a son of his who was so misguided as to reject the Church as a career—that of teacher or lawyer. Samuel looked on both these careers with equal abhorrence. He wrote to his mother: 'I would migrate, learn to farm in England, turn homeopathic doctor, or learn to paint, in which I have strong reason to believe I should succeed. But "No", from my father. To the other two courses, namely the law or a schoolmaster's life, I say "No", no less decidedly. You would, with the best intentions in the world, make me a bed that I know very well would not fit me. I know that when I am in, escape is impossible, and knowing that I have duties to myself to perform even more binding on me than those to my parents, with all respect adopt the alternative of rejecting the pounds, shillings and pence and going in search of my own bread my own way.'

Samuel had thought seriously of becoming a painter, but, as Cole put it, this roused the strongest opposition at home, on the ground that 'painting was not respectable and artists were known to be an immoral lot'. Eventually his mother persuaded her husband to give Samuel enough capital to emigrate to New Zealand. Canon Butler concluded that this was the least evil course open to him.

The father of *Robert Louis Stevenson* was a civil engineer, and dearly wanted Robert to follow in his footsteps. When Robert left school at seventeen he was entered for a science degree at the University of Edinburgh, against his wish, because he wanted to study literature. Balfour, his biographer, described how Robert 'acted upon an extensive and highly rational system of truancy, which cost him a great deal of trouble to put in exercise'. 'No one ever played truant with more deliberate care, and none ever had more certificates of attendance for less education.' The art of writing was his only concern, and he devoted his whole time to this end.

When he was fifteen *Joseph Conrad* announced that he wanted to go to sea—though he had never even been to the seaside. His relatives were amazed, and did their best to dissuade him. They sent him to Switzerland with a tutor, but Joseph persisted in his plea, and at sixteen set off for Marseilles to embark on a ship. He served for two years on French ships in the Mediterranean and on the South American coast. At nineteen he came to Lowestoft and became able seaman on a coaster.

He wrote his first novel at about thirty-five, when suffering from an illness, probably malaria, in the Congo, and published it when he was thirty-eight.

Edgar Wallace was the illegitimate child of a small-part actress called Polly Richards. Edgar Wallace (a fictitious name, designed to secure secrecy of the birth), was handed over to one Mrs Freeman, a Billingsgate fish-porter's wife, recommended after discreet enquiries by the midwife. It was a good home, though poverty was severe.

After two years Polly Richards came back, having decided that her son should be placed in an institution. Mrs Freeman objected strongly, and offered to adopt the boy. The offer was accepted.

The Freemans insisted on his remaining at school until he was twelve, although their own boys had left when they were ten.

Margaret Lane, his biographer, described how Edgar was initiated into the world of crime. He joined a gang of boys whose favourite exploit was stealing type from a typefounders. Though he did not take part in the raids, he received a little of the loot, and later was to embroider the exploits, with a fine disregard for the truth, and to make them into hair-raising stories.

By the time he was eleven, the theatre was almost an obsession with him. At the Sunday School he discovered the pleasures of fiction, in the form of 'penny dreadfuls' and the like.

He began to sell newspapers, but this was stopped when the Freemans found out. At twelve he found a job in a print-ing firm, but disliked it, and thereafter had a long series of jobs. He worked one trip on a trawler, and later worked as a plasterer and road maker. He then joined the West Kent Militia, and at eighteen joined the Royal West Kent Regiment. He had time to read, and began verse writing, and story telling. He was sentenced to a spell of imprisonment with hard labour for being absent without leave, and then went to

South Africa. There he met Kipling, who advised him against a literary career, but Edgar was encouraged by a missionary's wife. When he was twenty-three he finally decided that he would take up writing as a career, and leave the army as soon as possible.

SCIENTISTS AND ENGINEERS

It was intended when *Isaac Newton* was sixteen that he should follow his father's footsteps and become a farmer, but he showed no interest in the farm work. Sullivan, in his biography, tells how Isaac, when set to watch the cattle or the sheep, would pass the time reading, or making models with his knife; and while he was thus engaged the animals strayed at their pleasure. When he was sent to market, he would leave a servant to barter while he spent the day in an odd corner with his books. It soon became obvious that he was not going to make a farmer, and he was sent back to school. At eighteen he went to Cambridge to study mathematics.

The designer of the Manchester Liverpool Canal, *James Brindley*, was born in a humble cottage in Buxton, and was entirely self-taught. He never learnt to read and write properly. He began as a jobbing labourer, and at seventeen became apprenticed to a millwright in Macclesfield. He then set up as a millwright on his own.

He was later to become famous for designing some 260 miles of canals in England.

William Herschel, astronomer and scientist, was born at Hanover, the son of an obscure military bandsman. He himself started as a professional musician. Sidgwick, who wrote the biography, described the steps in William's career. He wrote: 'Each step in his development followed logically from his predecessor in a progression which seems to have been unalterably determined. His work as a practising musician demanded that he should learn the theory of music. To do this he had to study and improve his grasp of mathematics: this captured his imagination and led him on far beyond the point that his musical understanding required: it led him, in fact, to the study of optics. This in turn led to the construction of a telescope, and later to his becoming one of the world's greatest astronomers and the discoverer of Uranus.

His father exerted a good influence on him, in encouraging him to learn.

At nineteen, after a brief military career, which he disliked, he went to England, where he arrived practically penniless. He applied to a music shop for copying work, and did this well. At twenty-four, he became a concert manager in Leeds, at twenty-eight an organist at Bath, and a widely known musical authority. He studied astronomy in his spare time, constructing his first telescope when thirty-eight.

It was a slow tortuous route to distinguished astronomy.

It is not surprising that there are several biographies of *John Dalton*, the eminent scientist, because of the interest of his early days and his slow but steady rise from the humblest of beginnings to eminence.

Dalton's father was a Quaker, and was hand loom weaver at Eaglesfield, Cumberland. Dalton attended the village school until he was eleven, and came under the influence of Elihu Robinson, a skilled instrument maker and meteorologist. Roscoe considered that Robinson had an important influence on John Dalton's future career. He helped John in his studies, and taught him mathematics.

When he was twelve, Dalton nailed a large notice on the door of his father's cottage to the effect that he, John Dalton, was to open a school for both sexes on reasonable terms, and that paper, pens and ink would be obtainable within. School was held first in an old barn, then in the father's cottage, and later in the Quakers' Meeting House. The pupils were of all ages, from infants to boys and girls of sixteen or seventeen. Roscoe describes how Dalton felt it necessary to chastise offenders against discipline, and how the boys who were older than John rebelled and offered to fight him in the graveyard. When he locked them in for misbehaviour they broke the schoolroom windows. In his spare time John did some farming.

When he was fifteen he went to Kendal to join his older brother in his school. His sister went too, and kept house for the boarders. The fee was ten and sixpence per quarter. There, according to Brockbank, John was 'a severe disciplinarian, exacting order, silence and faithful adherence to prescribed rules'. He frequently used the cane, and got into trouble on one occasion for its overzealous use. He kept records of the weather, and measured the rainfall. Dalton taught English, French, Latin, Greek, writing and arithmetic. He stayed there for twelve years, before going to Manchester to teach philosophy and mathematics.

He was to become a renowned scientist, the founder of the atomic theory, a chemist and mathematician.

The story of *George* and *Robert Stephenson* is one of the most remarkable accounts of the rise to world renown from the meanest beginnings and from dire poverty. George Stephenson served as a cowherd, and later drove the 'Gin Horse' at the colliery. At fourteen he assisted his father as fireman at a shilling a day. He had no education whatsoever, and had not learnt to read by the age of eighteen, but had learnt how the pit engine worked by taking it to bits and cleaning it. George realised that he would have to learn to read, and so he took lessons in spelling, three nights a week, paying threepence a week for his lessons. Later he took lessons in mathematics, at fourpence a week. Smiles, in his *Lives of the Engineers*, tells how George worked at sums during his spare time in the mine. At twenty-one he became engineman at Willington Quay.

His son Robert went at twelve from the village school to a school in Newcastle. He acquired a donkey to take him there. Smiles wrote that '... he was a shy unpolished country lad, speaking the broad dialect of the pitman, and the other boys would tease him for the purpose of provoking an outburst of Killingworth Doric'. The other boys laughed at him at first, but he soon earned their respect for his ability. After four years at school in Newcastle he became an apprentice in the Killingworth pit, but at nineteen went to the University of Edinburgh to attend science classes.

The parents of *Louis Agassiz* wanted him to join his uncle's business in Neuchatel. His teacher, however, had recognised his remarkable ability and persuaded the parents to let the boy stay on at school.

He started a two year course at Lausanne at the age of fifteen, and at nineteen went to the University of Heidelberg. As his parents wanted him to take up medicine, he took his M.D. to please them, but later changed to natural history. Amongst other achievements he founded the Museum of Comparative Zoology in Boston.

Charles Darwin had early shown an interest in science, and had a secret laboratory in his father's garden. He was sent to the University of Edinburgh to study medicine, but found that the lectures there were intensely boring. His father then decided that Charles should instead go into the Church, and Charles spent three long years at Christ's College, Cambridge, as divinity student—years, he said, which were sadly wasted, in praying, drinking, singing, flirting and card-playing. Thomas tells, however, that a contact there with Professor Henslow was an important point in Darwin's career. The professor suggested that Charles should sail as a naturalist on the *Beagle*. Thomas wrote that Captain Fitzroy, who commanded the *Beagle*, hesitated to take Charles because he judged from the shape of his nose that he had neither the mentality nor the energy to become a good scientist. However, the captain changed his mind and took him.

David Livingstone at the age of ten was put to work in a cotton factory. At thirteen he attended evening classes and learned Latin. He worked in the factory from six o'clock in the morning to eight o'clock in the evening, and after his classes studied till midnight.

Before he was twenty he decided to study medicine in order to be a missionary in China. His father first opposed this, because he feared that David might want to practise medicine for the purpose of gain, but finally gave way and granted the boy his wish.

The mathematical genius *Karl Weierstrass* was born in Münster. Bell, in his biographies of famous mathematicians, wrote that Karl's father was a man of uncompromising righteousness, domineering authority and Prussian pigheadedness, and nearly wrecked Karl's life by attempting to force him into a career which was not to his liking.

The boy deliberately decided to neglect the work chosen for him, and eventually took up mathematics, having shown his outstanding ability at the Catholic School at Münster when he was fourteen.

Cantor, another mathematical genius, had a similar experience. His father was determined that the boy should become an engineer, and nearly succeeded in wrecking his life. Eventually the boy had his own way, and entered the University of Zürich at seventeen.

Louis Pasteur was the son of a tanner living in the Jura mountains near the Swiss frontier. His father hoped that his boy would become a teacher, and at seventeen Louis became an usher in the Lyceum at Besançon. He did not teach himself, but had to see that the boys had learnt their lessons, and keep order in the dormitory. On Sundays he would accompany them to Mass, and on Thursdays he had to take them for a walk. In his spare time he was able to study.

A pupil at the Lyceum allowed Louis to use his microscope. On Thursdays Louis would take this with him and examine insects with it. This really determined his future career.

Lord Nuffield at fourteen saved up sufficient money to buy a second-hand solid-tyred bicycle. This, the first machine of his own, was almost constantly being taken to pieces and put together again. He hoped to become a surgeon, but at fifteen when his father became ill, he was the breadwinner, and he entered employment with a bicycle firm. He opened a garage in Oxford, and then began to make motor cycles. When he was thirty-five, he made his first motor car, and so developed the vast Morris Car Industry. When he was sixty-six he founded the Nuffield Foundation with a donation of ten million pounds' worth of stock in Morris Motors.

Maria Montessori had to maintain a determined struggle to secure the career of her choice—but her choice was not always the same. When she was fourteen she was particularly interested in mathematics, an interest which she always retained. In his biography, Standing described the struggle which followed. Her parents suggested that Maria should become a teacher, because that was almost the only career open to women. She categorically refused to consider it. Instead she decided to apply her interest in mathematics to the study of engineering. There was no course open to girls, and so she attended classes at a technical school for boys. She felt attracted towards biology, and later decided to become a doctor.

The idea that a woman should become a doctor was unheard of in Italy. She went to see Dr Bacelli, head of the Board of Education, but he said that such a career was quite impossible for a woman. Maria shook hands and quietly remarked: 'I know I shall become a doctor of medicine.'

In the end she had her way and was admitted to the medical faculty of the University, as the first woman medical student in Italy. She distinguished herself by winning a series of prizes and scholarships.

Warsaw was the birthplace of *Madame Curie*. She became involved in a students' revolutionary organisation and had to leave the city. After a time she went to Paris, where she and her older sister both wanted to go to the Sorbonne. Marie suggested that she, Marie, should obtain a post as governess and help her sister to get through college, and then when she, the sister, had got her doctor's degree, she should help Marie in return. The scheme was carried through.

Henry Ford was the son of a farmer in comfortable financial circumstances. Henry went to school at seven, and did well there except in spelling. Nevins, in his interesting biography, remarked that agriculture in those days required great resourcefulness and a wide variety of skills—a background which had an important bearing on Henry's future career: for Henry was from the earliest years of a highly mechanical turn of mind, and soon learnt how to make running repairs on the farm machinery. Apart from his pleasure in the mechanical aspect of farm life, he disliked farming. He said once: 'I have followed many a weary mile behind a plough, and I know all the drudgery of it.' His earliest recollections were of too much work being done for too few results. His mother exerted a deep influence on his life. Nevins described how she implanted in him a deep sense of obligation. 'You must learn the right of play', she would say, 'life is not all fun.' 'The best fun follows a duty done.' She taught her children that unpleasant jobs call for courage, patience and self-discipline. When Henry grumbled about doing a particular job, she would say: 'Life will give you many unpleasant tasks to do: your duty will be hard and disagreeable and painful to you at times, but you must not pity yourself, do what you find to do, and what you know you must do, to the best of your ability.' She never whipped the children, but exerted a firm loving discipline. She died when Henry was twelve.

Nevins described how Henry became involved in various mechanical experiments at school. When he was ten he directed the construction of a water-wheel, which was hooked on to an old coffeemill, with a rake handle as connecting rod, and used by the boys for grinding clay, potatoes and gravel. In another experiment he made a steam turbine, the boiler of which blew up, blowing a bit through Henry's lip, knocking out anther boy, and setting the school fence on fire. He made a device for opening and closing the farm gate from a farm wagon without leaving the seat. He sharpened the saws, mended hoes, reapers and mowers, reset handles of tools, and repaired wagons. He liked nothing more than working with tools. These, he said, were his toys.

Nevins described how one day, Henry at the age of twelve, was driving with his father to Detroit, when they encountered a steam engine going along the road under its own power. Nevins wrote: 'It was a sight almost as astounding to the boy as if Elijah's chariot of fire had suddenly appeared.' 'I remember that engine', Ford said forty-seven years later, 'as though I had seen it only yesterday.' It was the first road vehicle, not drawn by horses, which he had ever seen. Henry jumped off the wagon and started to talk to the engineer before his father knew what had happened. He was later allowed to fire the engine and run it. The idea of an engine being used for propelling a vehicle firmly planted itself in his mind.

When he was thirteen another important event occurred— he was given a watch. He immediately took it to bits and put it together again. By the age of fifteen he was an expert watch repairer.

He was most anxious to leave the farm, and at sixteen left for Detroit. After six days he lost his job because he got into trouble for rapidly mending a machine which his workmates had spent many hours trying to repair. He then got a job in a machine shop at two dollars fifty a week. As his board was costing three dollars fifty weekly, he sought additional work, and repaired clocks and watches every evening for an additional two dollars a week. He thought seriously of mass-producing watches, but considered that the difficulties were too great. His next job was in a power plant in a dry dock company.

MEN OF RELIGION

William Penn had his first religious experience when he was eleven. His father had heard that an itinerant Quaker Preacher, one Thomas Loe, was in the region, and decided to invite him to the home in order to form a first-hand assessment of his ideas. Loe duly appeared, and spoke to the family and domestic staff. William was greatly impressed. Some time later, while alone, 'he had a sudden sense of the reality of God and of the possibility of the soul's communion with the Divine Spirit'. From that moment he decided that his calling in life was religion.

In course of time he went to Christchurch, Oxford, and described it as a place of 'hellish darkness and debauchery'. At Oxford, William and his friends held religious meetings. He drew on himself the displeasure of the college authorities. When, however, he deliberately absented himself from chapel, and refused to wear the prescribed surplice, he was expelled (at the age of eighteen). On return home he was thrashed by his father, the Admiral, and turned out of the house. He was forgiven and sent to Paris, in the hopes that he would lose his Quaker beliefs. Subsequently he was imprisoned for them. William went to America and founded Pennsylvania, having inherited land there in settlement of a debt to his father.

The childhood of *William Booth* was an unhappy one. He had little help or encouragement from either of his parents, and was brought up in an atmosphere of severe poverty. Although his grandfather had started religious services in the slums of Nottingham, his parents had little interest in religion.

William soon became a ringleader among his fellows, and earned the nickname of 'Captain'. He had to leave school at thirteen, because of the poverty of his parents, and went into a pawnbroker's business—a job which he hated.

Harold Begbie, in his interesting biography of William Booth, describes the sudden change which occurred in William when he was fifteen. The boy had been impressed by seeing children crying for bread in the streets. 'The visual memory of ragged children weeping bitterly for food in the streets of the town was a picture printed on his soul with a sharpness that could not be blurred.' He decided that he wanted to change the whole character of his life. 'I felt', he said, 'that I wanted, in place of the life of self-indulgence to which I was yielding myself, a happy conscious sense that I was pleasing God, living right, and spending all my powers to get others into such a life. I had no disposition to deny my instincts, which told me that if there was a God his laws ought to have my obedience and his interests my service. I felt that it was better to live right than to live wrong; and as to caring for the interests of others instead of my own, the condition of the suffering people around me, people with whom I had been so long familiar, and whose agony seemed to reach its climax about this time, undoubtedly affected me very deeply.'

The deciding factor in his life, however, was the episode of the pencil case. Begbie quotes William Booth's story of the affair. William said: 'The moment came one night at 11.00 p.m. in the streets of Nottingham. It was in the open street that the great change passed over me. The entrance to the Heavenly Kingdom was closed against me by an evil act of the past which required restitution. In a boyish trading affair I had managed to make a profit out of my companions whilst giving them to suppose that what I did was all the way of a generous fellowship. As a testimonial of their gratitude they had given me a silver pencil case. Merely to return their gift would have been comparatively easy, but to confess the deception I had practised was a humiliation to which for some days I could not bring myself. I remember as if it were but yesterday—the spot in the corner of the room under the chapel, the hour, the resolution to end the matter, the rising up and the rushing forth, the finding of the young fellow I had wronged, the acknowledgment of my sin, the return of the pencil case—

the instant rolling away from my heart of the guilty burden, the peace that came in its place, and the going forth to serve my God and my generation from that hour.'

Begbie wrote that 'No conversion could be simpler, less dramatic and more natural; few in the long history of Christianity have brought a richer harvest to the whole world.' He added: 'Happiness had come to him; he had escaped from the wretchedness of unrest by confessing to a sin that haunted his conscience, and by deciding to live henceforth in the knowledge and service of God.'

He was at first shy and self-conscious about speaking in the open. He joined in the services but would neither preach nor pray. He gave his first sermon at seventeen, in Kid Street, Nottingham. An Evangelist from Scarborough was the first to realise his power as a preacher. Begbie described the event as follows: 'The meeting was held in a small cottage. He had come straight from work. There was a box placed upside down on the table for a desk, with two candles burning, one each side of the Bible. The door stood open, and poor women came into the tiny parlour, bringing their own chairs with them. In the doorway was a group of men, afraid to come in lest they should be converted, but interested in this new way of preaching religion. They filled up the doorway, a dark little crowd that extended into the street. His sermon was very gentle and tender. He talked of young children learning to walk. He described how they toddled, and swayed and came near to falling: he said how difficult a thing it was for little babies to learn the use of their legs, to trust their tiny feet, and to advance with courage. Then he asked if any mother, watching her child's first efforts to walk, would be cross with her infant's failure, would shout at it when it swayed, would sit still unmoved when it fell and hurt itself. Then he said it was just as difficult to live a true Christian life, and that we should always be on the lookout for helping people, especially those who were only just beginning to live that life. He said it was wrong to judge them when they failed, and just as wrong to sit idle when they fell. We should run, and lift them up and help them. Hard words would not help them; sitting still would not help them; we must go and do something to make it less hard for them to walk straight.'

STATESMEN AND POLITICIANS

Benjamin Franklin was one of seventeen children, all of whom survived. He was the youngest son. His father was a tallow-chandler and soap-boiler. After Benjamin had had two years at the local school, he was taken into the business. He disliked the work and wanted to go to sea, but his father would not agree, putting him instead into the cutler's trade. Later, Benjamin's interest in books led his father to apprentice him at twelve to a printer. When he was sixteen he decided to leave his father and go to New York. His father forbade it, and Benjamin ran away from home and embarked on a sloop bound for New York. There he arrived with no recommendation, knowing no one, and with very little money in his pocket. Thence he secured a place on a boat to Philadelphia, helping to row. He arrived there with one dollar and a shilling. He gave the shilling to the boatman and slept in the street. There he was picked up by a Quaker, and obtained a job with a printer. He went to London when he was eighteen, and again secured a job with a printer, returning to Philadelphia when he was twenty.

He wrote: 'From the poverty and obscurity in which I was born, and in which I passed my earliest years, I have raised myself to a state of affluence and some degree of celebrity in the world.'

His autobiography is a fascinating account of his struggle from poverty to the Presidency of Pennsylvania and to international renown.

It seems surprising that *Benjamin Disraeli's* formal education ended when he was fifteen, when he left school. Even at that time he had great ambitions, and was obsessed with the idea that he was to be a great man. He wanted to be an orator, but his father wanted him to be a lawyer and articled him to a firm of solicitors. Benjamin was thoroughly unhappy in this role. Clarke, in his biography, wrote that 'Demosthenes and Cicero inspired him to emulation. He too, would be an orator. In the solitude of his room he poured forth speeches and grew intoxicated with his own eloquence. He began to ponder over the music of language. He studied the collocation of sweet words, and constructed elaborate sentences in solitary walks. The boy's ambition was stirred. He longed for a life of activity and fame: and he saw that the faculties he had so sedulously cultivated could only find the fit arena for their exercise in political controversy and Parliamentary debate.'

At twenty Benjamin Disraeli had a long way to go before he was to satisfy his ambition. He hated his work in the solicitor's office. He was seriously in debt as a result of unwise speculation. His colossal plans for success had come to nothing. He began to write novels—the first, *Vivian Grey*, being highly successful. After travelling abroad on the proceeds of his writing he settled down in politics, entering Parliament at thirty-four.

Abraham Lincoln rose to the heights from the depths of poverty. Though not much is certain about his childhood, it is known that he was born in a log cabin in an obscure corner of Kentucky, and that in such cabins the floor was earth, and the whole family, including hired labourers and guests, slept in one room. His father was a labourer, and his mother died when he was nine. He attended school for less than a year in his whole life.

He worked as a farm labourer. It is said that he sometimes held up the harvest operations by making burlesque speeches or sermons from some tempting tree stump. At the age of seventeen he would read everything he could find, but books were rare luxuries. When he was nineteen he was employed in helping to take goods by boat to New Orleans, where he saw Negroes working as slaves. He then became a village shopkeeper and later a surveyor. Finally he took up law.

He became President of the United States when fifty-two.

Another fascinating account of a rise from the depths of poverty to fame is that of *James Keir Hardie*, as described by Stewart and Lowe in their biographies. Keir was born in a one-roomed house in Lanarkshire; his father was a ship's carpenter, who had long spells of unemployment. His mother was a farm labourer, a dauntless woman of spirit, who left James in charge of his grandmother while she worked.

When he was six, Keir was earning a few coppers weekly as a barefoot boy. His father had an accident at his job, and was incapacitated for many weeks. There were no wages or income of any kind, and there was no compensation act or insurance. The family had to sell most of their goods, and Keir, at seven, became the breadwinner, often working twelve to fourteen hours a day. At home he was a clumsy boy, spilling his porridge and milk.

He had no education except for a few months, when he did not even complete his only copy book, which had cost three halfpence. Before he could read he would gather odd bits of newspaper and printed matter off the streets, packing them into his pockets, and when he got home he would pretend to read them. His mother eventually taught him to read, and he took advantage of the skill after working hours by studying placards and the open pages of books in the windows of bookshops. Though he could read he could not write his name until he was seventeen—having taught himself in the pit during spare time.

At ten he became a message boy for the Anchor Line, and later he worked for a baker, making three and sixpence a week. He was now the only breadwinner, for there was a lockout on the Clyde, and the benefits for the unemployed, which included his father, were two shillings a week. In the baker's shop he worked from 7 a.m. to 7.30 p.m. He was the eldest of a family of three, and his brother was seriously ill with a fever. One day, having lost a lot of sleep in looking after his brother, he reached the shop fifteen minutes late. He was told that if he were late again, he would be punished.

Next morning he was late again. Lowe describes the day. 'It was a wet morning, and when he reached the shop, he was barefooted, drenched to the skin, cold and hungry. There had not been even a crust of bread in the house that morning. The girl behind the counter told him that he was wanted by the master. Outside the dining room door a servant bade him wait till "master had finished prayers". The baker was much noted for his piety. At length the girl opened the door, and the sight of that room was fresh in the memory of Hardie when he told the story nearly fifty years afterwards. Round a great mahogany table sat the members of the family with the father at the top. In front of the father was a very wonderful looking coffee boiler, in the great glass bowl of which the coffee was boiling. The table was loaded with dainties. The master looked at Hardie over his glasses and said "Boy, this is the second morning you have been late. I therefore dismiss you, and to make you more careful in future I have decided to fine you a week's wage. Now you may go." Keir wanted to tell him about his home, but he was sent out of the room.

'The master continued to be a pillar of the church and a leading light in the religious life of the city.

'Keir went out into the rain, and wandered through the streets most of the day. He knew that his mother was waiting for his wages. Eventually he went home and told his mother what had happened. He also gave her a wet roll which the girl at the counter in the baker's shop had given him. That night the mother gave birth to another baby.'

Keir then got a job in a coal mine. He said: 'for several years I rarely saw daylight during the winter months'. He went down the pit by six in the morning and did not leave it till five-thirty at night. He began to attend a night school. Pupils had to take their own candles, because no lights were provided. His mother encouraged him to learn, and he took up shorthand.

He later joined a trade union, and began his life as an agitator, beginning as a propagandist for temperance. He was the founder of the British Labour Party.

Sir James Sexton was born in a Newcastle upon Tyne slum, in abject poverty. His father had been a member of a band of Irish gipsies, and had migrated to England. In his autobiography he told how one day when his mother had gone out to buy the Sunday dinner (butcher's fragments, or a hambone with which to flavour the pea soup), leaving James in the charge of a neighbour, she came back to find James missing. His bed folded up against the wall to save space, and James had been on the bed when it was folded up. He was found in the nick of time, black in the face, and in urgent need of resuscitation.

The family moved to St Helens, where his parents set up a stall in the market. He wrote: 'How dear old mother managed is still beyond my comprehension. She was up with the lark in the summer, and long before daylight in winter preparing the meagre morning meal of oatmeal and skimmed milk in the huge earthenware vessel which served also for sundry other purposes (including the family washing), stirring the mixture with the stick which she also used to stir the dirty clothes, and sometimes applied to our backs when we tried her patience beyond endurance. Afterwards she would set out with her husband, bearing, like him, a pack as big as Christian's, containing the very miscellaneous collection of goods which they hoped to sell to provide the next day's food for their brood. To tide us over the day she would leave what she called "the heel" of a loaf, thinly plastered with dripping skimmed from the pot in which now the clothes and now the scraps of bacon were boiled. That had to serve as dinner for

those of us who were attending school. If trade was exceptionally good, Mother might bring back a sheep's head, but
that was an exceptional and luxurious feast for the family
which grew larger with every passing year.'

'We attended school, for which the fee was three pence a
week, with sixpence a month for the coke stove.' He tells
how he and a friend defaulted in the payment of the sixpence,
in order to buy some Nelson cakes, to assuage their hunger.
They were found out, and placed nearest the door, where they
would not feel the benefit of the stove. He decided to have
his revenge, and obtained some rock-blasting powder from
the coal mine, and put it in the stove while helping to lay the
fire for the following day. When the schoolmaster lit
the fire in the morning there was a violent explosion, which
split the stove from top to bottom, and drove the flue through
the wall into the yard. School was dismissed for the day.
Fifty-five years later, when standing as Parliamentary candidate for St Helens, he revealed for the first time the true explanation of the explosion.

When he was nine he was promised one and sixpence a
week for punching holes in clog irons with a hand machine,
but never got it, for he was told that as a learner he should
work for two weeks without wages. He downed tools and
went home. He then got a job in a glass works at two and
sixpence a week, working a twelve hour shift; this paid the
rent of the family slum dwelling.

He told of his father's part in the Irish Republican Brother-
hood, or Fenian Agitation, and the smuggling of guns and
ammunition which went on from his home.

The boy developed the wanderlust and he set off for Liverpool, tramping all the way, sleeping under hedges. Just outside Ashton-under-Lyne, he was found by a policeman, who
instead of arresting him, fixed him up for a night in the
work-house. In later years he was to be parliamentary candidate for Ashton. He then stowed away on a boat bound

for San Francisco. He was found out and thrashed, and then enrolled on the ship's company at a salary of a shilling a month.

James Sexton left his sea life when his father died, and became an agitator in Liverpool's dockland—and at sixty-five, a member of the House of Commons.

Philip, Viscount Snowden, was born in a two-roomed cottage at Ickornshaw in Yorkshire. In his autobiography he tells how he went to the local school, where the fee was twopence a week for the younger boys, and threepence a week for the older ones, with extra for the copy-books.

His first experience of speech making was in the Band of Hope, where he gave a recitation. His father was interested in elocution, and trained him.

When Philip was twelve years old—like John Dalton—he became a teacher. He was put in charge of a class of forty boys and girls, not much younger than he was. He wrote that he would have remained a schoolmaster for the rest of his life if the firm in which his father and sisters worked had not become bankrupt, with the result that he had to look for a different career. His father wanted him to become a lawyer, but could not afford it and Philip was put into an insurance company office. He became a Labour Member of Parliament at forty-two.

Ramsay MacDonald was born in the direst poverty in Lossiemouth. His mother had no house of her own and he was born and brought up in his grandmother's two-roomed thatched cottage. His mother worked as a servant in a large house and his grandmother looked after him.

He had no father, and was the only male in the household, and according to Weir, his biographer, he was idolised by his mother and grandmother. This environment led him to expect ready sympathy all his life, and was probably responsible, Weir suggested, for the vanity, huffy jealousy and petulance of which he has been accused.

He went to a small local school, and his ability was soon recognised by his teacher, who was a particularly good and understanding man exerting a wise discipline and earned the respect of his pupils. At eighteen Ramsay went to London, working as a clerk at twelve and sixpence a week. He continued his own education by evening classes. A serious illness caused him to become a journalist. At twenty-eight he joined the Independent Labour Party, and later became Prime Minister.

Feiling, in his biography, told how *Neville Chamberlain*, when at Rugby, was asked to speak in the debating society. He refused, saying 'No, I don't take any interest in politics and never shall.' When asked for his reason he replied: 'you don't know what our house is like for days before my father makes one of his big speeches. Everybody has to be quiet, and even at meals conversation is subdued. Wretched man, he never knows what he is going to say.' Nevertheless, he yielded to pressure and did speak, and went on to become Prime Minister.

Ernest Bevin was the son of a farm labourer. Before he was seven he had lost both mother and father, and was left in great poverty. His formal education consisted of nothing more than the essentials of reading, writing and arithmetic. He had to earn his living when he was eleven as a farm boy, working ten hours a day for sixpence a week, paid in a lump sum of six and sixpence every quarter. At thirteen he became a kitchen boy in a bakehouse in Bristol. For six shillings a week and his meals, he worked twelve hours a day for a seventy-two hour week. One of his jobs was to push a barrow loaded with pies and pastries to the refreshment rooms at Temple Meads Station in Bristol. He later became a van boy at ten shillings a week, and subsequently a conductor on the horse-drawn trams.

He joined a mission as Sunday School teacher, and it was this which led him to discover his ability to argue, think and speak. He began to read and study, and soon read extensively any books which he could find.

Aneurin Bevan in his last months at school took a job as a butcher's boy, earning two and sixpence a week, for long hours. He spent some of it on the *Magnet*, the *Gem*, and other boys' magazines. His mother banned them from the house, and he had to hide them under a nearby bridge. Eventually she stopped him doing the job.

At the age of fourteen he went into the pit, bringing home ten shillings a week, all of which he gave to his mother, who gave him occasional tuppences.

Michael Foot, in his biography, tells how a group from the Sunday School class in Tredegar contacted the Independent Labour Party in Merthyr and formed a Tredegar branch. Aneurin became a regular attender and speaker there, in spite of his stammer.

In his early teens he made himself a nuisance by spreading unrest among the pits and earned the title of 'that bloody nuisance Bevan'. Foot wrote that 'he moved from pit to pit, provoking the curses of the overmen and the mingled alarm and admiration of his brother William. After a dispute with an undermanager he was dismissed from the pit, and he took the complaint to the Lodge, proving victimisation, and securing reinstatement.' He was sent to a pit which fellow miners regarded as a bad one, and there too he stirred up unrest, developing hatred of private ownership and of the inefficiency of the mine owners. At nineteen he became Chairman of the Lodge.

The future Chancellor of Austria, *Engelbert Dollfuss*, was an illegitimate baby, probably the son of a farm labourer. He had a happy childhood in a good home, where poverty was considerable, but management was wise. He wrote later about his home: 'This was when I saw, from my childhood onwards, the battle against want. And if today I take such an interest in these things, it is because I learned it all there. We never had anything to spare, and always had to slog away for what we got. That gave me an understanding and sympathy for the economic troubles of the people.'

Brock-Shepherd, in his biography, wrote that the only sign of anything of exception in the boy was his insatiable appetite for reading. 'The moment he had mastered the mysteries of print, he lived with a book in his hand, either tending the cattle in the meadows during the long summer days, or squinting under a petroleum lamp in his room during the long winter months.'

He announced that he was going to be a priest, but his parents could not afford the money for the training involved. The local priest persuaded the Bishop to offer the boy a free place in the seminary near Vienna. Engelbert failed his first year's examination and had to repeat it. He was not outstanding there. His teacher said 'Dollfuss was certainly among the good students, but I cannot remember him ever standing out especially in his work. He was an industrious scholar, even very industrious, and he made steady progress, yet he never threw off any sparks.'

He developed a great interest in people, and displayed a notable strength of character. He was very small in stature—and as an adult only reached 4 ft. 11 in. Brock-Shepherd wrote that it was at the seminary that Engelbert 'first proved to himself and others that his strength of character and his sunny nature were more than enough to make up in the world for his lack of inches. Without arrogance, and apparently almost without effort, the smallest pupil in the school soon commanded respect from the biggest.'

'The picture which most of his comrades will have taken away is of Dollfuss, standing on tiptoe or upon a chair to make himself seen or heard, organising petitions or protests, reconciling two heated disputants in an argument, or drawing the essentials out of some general debate. The politician in him was, in fact, already awakened.' He became distinguished as a speaker in debates.

He moved to Vienna to complete his studies in the University, at the age of twenty-one, but it was then that he lost interest in a theological career. His stepfather was very upset, but said 'There's only one thing that matters—grow up to be a decent person and not a rogue.' He took up law.

OTHER MEN OF EMINENCE

The parents of *Hernando Cortez* were bitterly disappointed when the boy gave up his law studies at the University of Salamanca. He was their only son, and they had put all their hopes in him. He determined to sail for the Indies, and after several vicissitudes achieved his ambition.

The Duke of Wellington caused much anxiety to his parents with regard to his future career. When he left school as a result of his failure in classics his mother had no idea what to do with him. She announced that he was 'good for powder and nothing more'. She said that it was a matter of indifference to her what commission he got as long as he got one soon. In fact he was appointed Ensign in the 73rd Highland Regiment in India (when he was eighteen).

Froebel did badly at school, and was regarded as a dunce. At fifteen he became apprenticed to a forester, and worked at this for two years. He then went to the University of Jena. His career ended when he was imprisoned for a debt of thirty shillings. He had phases as surveyor, accountant, secretary and architect, before taking up teaching under Pestalozzi. After studying in Göttingen and Berlin, he acquired world wide renown for his novel teaching methods.

Sir Edward Clarke, one of the most famous of British advocates, is cited by Lord Birkett as a striking example of a rise to fame against great odds. At the age of thirteen, Clarke had left school and was helping his father in a silversmith's shop in London. He was an avid reader, and attended evening classes, taking the examination of the Society of Arts and the external examinations of the University of Oxford. He began to speak in local debating societies, and practised public speaking. 'He had no money, no influential friends, no connection with the law, and no social standing.'

Norman Birkett was always expected to go into his father's drapery business, and at fifteen he became an apprentice in it, working at the job for seven years. Hyde, in his biography, wrote that Norman's brother and the other apprentices would listen to his sales talk with admiration. His cousin declared that 'It was an anticipation of modern advertising methods, with much imagination mixed with the description of the goods, not all of it strictly true.'

He attended night school classes, studying a variety of subjects from shorthand to physiology. He won a prize at seventeen in a local newspaper competition for an essay. He became a local preacher in the Ulverston Methodist circuit and rapidly became a success, preparing his sermons with great care, and practising the delivery in his room at home. When he was twenty-one, he entered a Local Preacher's examination, and was bracketed first out of 150 candidates from the whole of England. He then decided to train for the Methodist Ministry, and studied theology. He also joined the local Liberal Party, campaigning for the local Liberal candidate. The latter, greatly impressed by his speeches, suggested that he should practise at the Bar. Norman continued, however, to train for the Ministry. He secured entry to Emmanuel College, Cambridge, and only later took up law.

Lawrence of Arabia, as a student of history at Oxford, decided to study the castles of Palestine and the Lebanon. He announced that he intended to go to the Levant, touring on foot, and living on milk, bread and fruit. In June 1909 he set off with £100, a camera and a revolver, along with a pass from the Turkish Government.

COMMENT

We believe that many will find inspiration in the stories of men's rise to eminence from the humblest of beginnings. The stories include the rise of Ben Jonson, the bricklayer; James Brindley, the totally uneducated jobbing labourer; Frederick Delius, the office boy; Joseph Conrad, the able seaman; Henry Ford, the farmer's boy; Benjamin Franklin, the soap boiler; Gauguin, the ship's stoker; Abraham Lincoln, the farm labourer; Rossini, the blacksmith's apprentice; George Stephenson, the cowherd; Van Gogh, the schoolmaster and Edgar Wallace, the newspaper boy. We have given many other examples. We were particularly impressed with the rise of some of the great socialist leaders in this country, from the poorest of origins. Examples are Keir Hardie, James Sexton, Ramsay MacDonald, Ernest Bevin, the kitchen boy in a bakehouse, and Aneurin Bevan, the butcher's boy. Perhaps it was this very poverty which acted as the spur to ambition.

Let us hope that in this country and others it will always be possible for children to rise to world-wide fame like this— even though they have lacked every possible help at home, even though they have not been to the best schools, and even though they were never able to go to a University.

Some of the stories, like those of Benvenuto Cellini and Michelangelo, illustrate the folly of a father insisting that his child should take up a particular career of parental choice. How right Handel was to object to becoming a barber, as his father wanted, Schubert to object to becoming a school-master, Dvorak to object to being a butcher! The severe estrangement between father and son, resulting from such parental insistance on choice of career, was well shown by the story of Goethe, and of Samuel Butler. Such insistance may be basically due to parental selfishness and obstinacy. Children may well need guidance in the choice of career, as when a child is thought by his parents to be eminently capable of entering a profession, and yet wants to be a manual labourer, or to take up semiskilled work. Nevertheless, children should normally be encouraged to take up the career of their choice.

CHAPTER 13

SOME EVIL MEN

FOR the purposes of this chapter we have collated all the interesting information which we could obtain concerning some of the less pleasant characters and events of history—ranging from Nero to the Spanish Inquisition, the French Revolution, and Adolf Hitler and his friends. We hoped that we might be able to demonstrate a pattern in the childhood environment and behaviour of these people, or relevant features in the attitude of their parents and their management of their children.

In some ways this chapter is disappointing—partly because of the dearth of information about the childhood of some of the men—such as Judge Jeffreys and Torquemada, and partly because of the absence of a consistent pattern in the childhood of these villains of the future. Some, like Judge Jeffreys, Marat, Torquemada and Himmler, came from good homes; Hitler, on the other hand, had an unpleasant cruel father, though a good mother.

No fewer than five of our selected group had what psychiatrists would term emotional deprivation in their early years—the loss of a parent. These were Nero, Ivan, Robespierre, Danton, and Goering. Danton, Robespierre, Laval and Goebbels were clever boys: Marat, Laval and Himmler were well behaved boys at school. Ivan, Titus Oates, Danton, Goering, Mussolini and Laval all showed features commonly seen in boys who will be future delinquents.

There is no regular pattern in these stories. Perhaps in that lies their main interest. Nevertheless all we know about them is superficial and distant. It might be that with deeper knowledge, on a personal level, there would be—if not one pattern—at least a trend.

The Emperor Nero was born feet first—and this was said to be an evil omen. When he was two he lost both his parents —his father by death, and his mother by banishment, and he was brought up by an aunt Domitia.

At eleven he was a boy of lively intelligence and quick wit, fond of carving, painting, riding and diving. He wrote verses.

He was not a vicious or sullen boy, but a boy with artistic and literary tastes, clever with his fingers, affectionate and fond of home.

He was adopted by the Emperor Claudius when he was thirteen. He married at fifteen and became the Prince Successor. Claudius died when Nero was seventeen, poisoned by Agrippina's order, and Nero was made the new Emperor. In the first years of his rule he showed liberality and clemency. Later, however, he had his mother murdered by soldiers. He then killed his wife, in order to marry another woman. He had innumerable Christians massacred after the great fire which destroyed half of Rome: and he avenged a conspiracy with frightful bloodshed. He committed suicide at the age of thirty-one.

We have obtained much of our information concerning *Thomas de Torquemada*, the scourge of the Jews, from the biography by Hope.

'Thomas was born in Torquemada near Valladolid, the son of a nobleman, Pero Fernandez de Torquemada. There is a significant and important fact about his ancestry. Thomas was not 'clean'. The blood purity of which he as a high born Spaniard was so proud, largely because it was so rare, had been polluted at the end of the 14th century by Alvar Fernandez de Torquemada, Thomas' grandfather, who had married a Jewess recently converted to Christianity. At this time, when the Jews were living in peace in Spain, before the hideous outbreaks of murders and pogroms, it was a common thing for impoverished Spanish nobles to marry the daughters of rich converted Jews, the dowry being assessed high for the stain on the blood. This factor undoubtedly contributed to Thomas' maniacal hatred of the Jews, and particularly of the Christian sons of Jewish parents.'

Very little is known about the childhood of Thomas de Torquemada, or even about the first fifty-eight years of his life. In fact prior to the age of fifty-eight he was a nonentity. While still a boy he took the habit of a Dominican—a grave step as it doomed his family and estate to extinction. His decision was justified by his scholastic brilliance. He studied theology and philosophy, took his doctor's degree, and went into a monastery, becoming noted for his piety and austerity.

As the highest official in the Spanish Inquisition, he was responsible for some 1,000 people being burnt at the stake, and some 100,000 being imprisoned or disgraced. He died at the age of seventy-eight.

We found very little of interest concerning the childhood of *the Borgias*. Very little indeed is known about the childhood of Pope Alexander VI (Rodrigo Borgia), who was notorious for his sexual orgies and perversions, or about Lucretia Borgia. We gathered only a little about Lucretia's brother, Cesare, the son of Alexander VI.

When Cesare was a child, many privileges and honours were heaped upon him. At the age of six, he was granted all the revenues from the prebends and canonries of the cathedral of Valencia, and at seven he was given another canonry. At the age of nine he became Treasurer of Cartagena. When he was sixteen he passed his examinations at the University of Pisa with distinction, and at seventeen he was appointed to the See of Pamplona and at the same age was appointed Bishop of Valencia.

All that we can say with certainty about him was that he was brought up in affluence, and that his father set him the worst possible example of licentious living, taking no care at all to conceal his sexual orgies from his children.

Cesare committed many murders by the sword, by poison-ings and by the hands of his accomplices, and was well known for his sexual debauchery. He was murdered at the age of thirty-one.

Ivan the Terrible. Waliszewski, in his biography, described how young Ivan was brought up in an atmosphere of insecurity and violence. He lost his father when he was five and his mother was killed by poisoning when he was eight. The affairs of state were carried on by regents until Ivan was old enough to take control himself. There were violent struggles for power in Moscow, with much violence and carnage. The regents, while subjecting the country to a most intolerable tyranny, were teaching their future master the most odious and undesirable lessons. Thanks to them, violence in every form took hold of the boy's feelings and imagination, and inspired him, body and soul. 'Violent he was to be, like them, growing up as he did in an atmosphere of perpetual battle, ready to give blow for blow, desperately nervous, cruel and irritable.' His earliest pleasures shared with the companions chosen for him, were hideous. Seeing men tortured under his eyes, he tortured beasts until he should be old enough to torture human beings. His great amusement, long before puberty, was to throw dogs down from the top of one of the castle terraces and enjoy their anguish.

When he was thirteen he caused one of the regents to be carried off and strangled. When he was sixteen, on a hunting expedition, he found his way barred by Novgorod musketeers. There was a scuffle, and the young Prince was alarmed, but not hurt. He was angry, and showed his wrath by having several put to death.

He became Czar and Emperor when he was seventeen and commenced a reign of terror. He had large numbers of the landowners tortured and executed. He was ruthless in dealing with any opposition—having his opponents killed. He killed his own son in a quarrel and died in Moscow four years later, at the age of fifty-four.

Judge Jeffreys became Lord Chief Justice of England at thirty-eight, the youngest occupant of the woolsack in history.

Little is known about his childhood. He was born in Wrexham, and had a long line of distinguished ancestors. He had a good father, who 'had always studied the welfare and happiness of his children, and had never been guilty of an unkind or unjust act to any of them'. His mother was a good pious woman. The family was a particularly united one, and the parents devoted themselves to the welfare of their children.

All that can be said with certainty of his boyhood is that he was considered by those who knew him to be a boy of exceptional talents and charm, and that he received the best education possible. He went to a school near Wrexham when he was three, at seven to Shrewsbury School, and at fourteen to St Paul's School for two years. He then went to Westminster School, under the famous Dr Busby, who was famed for his canings. George was flogged here for idleness and impudence. At fourteen he went to Trinity College, Cambridge and thence to the Inner Temple.

The Judge was described by Irving as 'one of the most vehemently detested memories in the history of his country'. Hyde wrote that his reputation for bloodthirstiness is probably unrivalled in our judicial annals. 'If there is one name which is more hated than any other in English history, and which has been made to stink in the nostrils of his fellow countrymen, it is that of George Baron Jeffreys, commonly known as Judge Jeffreys.' He had 320 executed for high treason and 800 sold into slavery in the West Indies. Much to the relief of his countrymen, he ended his days in the Tower of London, dying as a result of the kidney stones (which were said to have been responsible for his bad temper). Keeton, in a more recent book, has brought forward evidence to the fact that he was not such a bad man as had been popularly supposed.

Titus Oates was the son of an ex-weaver, later a parson, who had been tried for his life when a young woman was drowned in a 'baptism'. His biography was written by Jane Lane, to whom we are indebted for the information below.

Born in 1648 he had repeated convulsions when a toddler, and there were small hopes for his life. In later childhood he had a repulsive and persistent nasal discharge, earning him the nickname of 'filthy mouth' among his playmates. 'I thought that he would have been a natural', his mother said, 'for his nose always ran, and he slobbered at the mouth, and his Father could not endure him, and my husband would cry "Take this snotty fool away!"'

At sixteen he went to the Merchant Taylor's School in London. Concerning his entry into the school, his master said: 'I was sent to receive him into the school, which I did in an unlucky hour. Truly, the first trick he served me was that he cheated me of our entrance money which his father sent me.' He was expelled in the following year, and was sent to a village school. He was dull and backward at school, and was a hopeless dunce, but at nineteen went to Cambridge—and was expelled from there after two terms. He pretended he wanted to to become a Roman Catholic, and was sent to study in Spain. His only purpose in this move was to discover secrets from the catholics so that he could make money out of them. Later he invented details of a catholic plot to murder Charles II and massacre the protestants. A wave of anti-catholic feeling spread over the country, and it was for this reason that over thirty catholics were executed and many more imprisoned. He became a national hero, and was granted a pension and a bodyguard. Soon, however, he was found to be guilty of perjury, and was flogged, pilloried and imprisoned, dying in ignominy at the age of fifty-six.

The Marquis de Sade was born in 1740 into a noble family. His father, the Compte de Sade, was a cold, restrained, formal man, a soldier and diplomat. The Compte's wife spent most of her married life separated from him, and had nothing to do with her son, the Marquis, after his earliest childhood. Little then is known about the boy's early years. When he was four or five, he was given into the care of his uncle, the Abbé Francois de Sade, whose sexual life was notoriously irregular, and who did not disguise the fact he had a mother and daughter as contemporary mistresses, living permanently at his chateau.

When the boy was ten he was placed in charge of another tutor, the Abbé Amblet, at a Jesuit College.

At fourteen he was sent to his regiment, at the outbreak of the seven years' war with Germany. As a young soldier he was frequently in trouble. His earliest surviving letters contain promises to abstain from debauchery and gambling.

At thirty-two he was condemned to death for unnatural sexual offences and poisoning. He escaped but was rearrested and imprisoned. He escaped again but was found and imprisoned in the Bastille, where he wrote obscene novels.

Geoffrey Gorer, in his biography of this remarkable Marquis, wrote: 'By the standards of almost any known society De Sade was in some ways a bad man, for some of his life nearly a mad man, and always a profoundly sad man.' The Marquis was a writer and sexual pervert, who showed a remarkable psychological insight into the minds of other perverts. It is from his name that the word 'sadism' is derived. He died in a lunatic asylum.

Jean Paul Marat was by birth a Swiss: his father, a physician, was born in Sardinia. Jean received a thorough education at home, 'thus escaping "all the vicious practices of childhood which degrade and enervate the man" when he is educated at the local school'. Little otherwise is known about his childhood. He wrote that from his earliest years he had been devoured by the love of glory, which never left him for a moment. 'At the age of five', he wrote, 'I wished to be a schoolteacher, at fifteen a professor, at eighteen an author, at twenty a creative genius.'

He said that at school he was docile and diligent, and that his masters could obtain anything from him by kindness.

LFC Y

At sixteen he went to the University of Bordeaux to study medicine. There 'his capacious mind readily absorbed learning. He had a keen perception and his memory was marvellously retentive.'

He practised as a physician in Soho Square, London, for ten years, and was given the honorary degree of Doctor of Medicine of the University of St Andrews. He returned to France and became a leader of the French Revolution.

Jean Paul Marat was perhaps the most bloodthirsty of the leaders of the French Revolution. He was described by a French historian as 'the apostle of assassination en masse'. He calculated that with proper organisation, 260,000 men could be put to death in one day. He declared in the assembly that there would be no peace in France until 286 traitors had been brought to the scaffold. Some thought that he was insane. He was murdered at the age of fifty.

The father of *Maximilien Robespierre* was a lawyer. Maximilien lost his mother when he was seven. His father was devastated by his wife's death, threw up his practice, and deserted his children. He died during purposeless wanderings through Germany. Various relatives rallied to the needs of the four children and looked after them. Maximilien was brought up by Godfearing aunts to become a good Christian.

He entered the college at Arras, and soon became head of his class. He was highly intelligent and worked hard. He was one of the best pupils and received a scholarship for work at the college in Paris. He said: 'Endowed with intelligence enough, but above all with a perseverence in work rarely found in a youth, I was able to gain and keep the first rank in my class.' Examinations meant nothing to him; he had no difficulty in doing well in them.

He was a prig at school, and none of the other boys liked to play with him. He was boastful about his abilities, and made himself unpopular as a result. Van Loon wrote: 'Maximilien withdrew into a little dream castle of his own construction, a little castle on a little hill, but dominating the entire landscape. There he could feel himself superior to everybody else. He knew what was being said about him, that he was not a legitimate child, that he had been the reason why his lawyer father had been forced to marry his plebeian mother.' He was described as a pale unattractive looking boy, with manners which were awkward, provincial and lacking in charm.

Van Loon tells how one day Louis and Marie Antoinette were to visit the college. Maximilien, as the cleverest boy in the school, was chosen to compose the ode of welcome. He was fitted out with a new suit of clothes, and excitement was great. Unfortunately it rained, and the Royal Procession was delayed. The Queen told her husband that she did not want to proceed with the visit. Maximilien was furious and never forgot. Some thirteen years later he demanded the guillotine for Louis and his wife.

He died under the guillotine himself at the age of thirty-six.

The father of *George Jacques Danton* was a lawyer: he died when George was two years old.

George was an ugly child and an ugly man. According to Beesly, when George was an infant being suckled by a cow, a bull interfered, and severely gashed George's lip with its horn. When he was older he was said in retaliation to have provoked an encounter with a second bull, and he was the victor at the expense of a mutilated nose. He subsequently acquired smallpox, which left his face further disfigured.

He went first to a girls' school, later to a boys' school, and then to an ecclesiastical boarding school at Troyes. At the last school he was 'bored to death' he said. 'If', he wrote, 'I have to listen much longer to that bell, it will toll my funeral.'

Warwick, in his book on the French Revolution, wrote that at school George took badly to discipline, and was best remembered for insubordination. He was described as 'a robust, rollicking lad, meddlesome, high spirited, somewhat rebellious, but most affectionate and generous'. Lamartine said that 'he was of an open communicative disposition, and was beloved in spite of his ugliness and turbulence, for his ugliness was radiant with intellect, and his turbulence was calmed and repented of at the least caress of his mother'. He was in no way vicious as a boy. In spite of his idleness, his resistence to discipline, and his not infrequent truancy from school (to swim in the Aube), he was popular both with scholars and teachers. He showed rapid comprehension and he kept up in work with the hardest workers. 'His instinct sufficed without reflection. He learned nothing; he acquired all.' 'He sometimes organised rebellions and riots at school, which he excited or calmed by his harangues, as if he were rehearsing for events of his future career.' He won several prizes at school, and distinguished himself in declamation. Beesly wrote that his class was always eager to hear his themes read, because they were sure to contain something original and striking. His compositions, when he was fourteen, were already of a high standard.

When he was sixteen he played truant to see the coronation of Louis XVI at Rheims, some eighty miles away, walking all the way there and back. He received only minor punishment on his return to school.

On leaving school he commenced the study of law and was called to the Bar when he was twenty-six.

It was Danton who inaugurated the reign of terror in the French Revolution—ending his days under the guillotine at the age of thirty-five.

Grigori Rasputin. Maria Rasputin, who wrote a biography about her father, remarked that few men have been hated as much as he was.

Maria Rasputin writes that as a child Rasputin was no different from any other child. She says, however, that even as a child he had a remarkable insight into the minds of his friends, and had an uncanny way of knowing the good and bad things which they had done out of his sight. Rasputin said: 'I used to play with the children of Pokrovskoie and quarrelled with them, but I never dared to steal or pilfer the smallest thing. I used to believe that everybody would at once see that I had stolen something since I myself was aware of it as soon as one of my comrades had stolen.' This gift of 'second sight' was to remain with him throughout his life, and be the source of terror in his associates.

He had a happy childhood, though his mother died when he was twelve. He had little formal education.

His daughter wrote that even as a child Rasputin also showed a remarkable magnetism. 'From his childhood he possessed an incontestable power of magnetism such as first gave him a certain authority over his comrades of the village, and later gave him considerable empire over hundreds of people who approached him.' According to Colin Wilson, it was at this time, at about fifteen, that he discovered his sexual attractiveness. Wilson added that all his many biographers agree about his sexual prowess. It was to be a feature of his life to the end.

From the age of fifteen he was greatly interested in religious matters. He took part in prayer meetings and evening gatherings in the village, and amazed people by his religious and philosophical learning as well as by his clairvoyance. One day when the peasants had met in order to discuss the theft of a horse and the steps to be taken to discover the culprit, Grigori Rasputin, then twelve years old, interrupted and told them who the thief was. The peasants were astounded, knowing that he could not have seen anything of the crime; and they found that he was correct.

He became employed at fifteen as a wagon driver, and had to deliver goods to many parts of Siberia. At sixteen he was asked to take a young novice to a monastery, a hundred miles away. This led to his entering the monastery and staying there for four months. Later he frequently visited the monastery, where he received religious instruction. The peasants began to come and submit to him their religious difficulties; he would talk about them in the meetings and then a hymn or psalm would be sung. The village priest became concerned about Grigori's growing influence and denounced him to the authorities. The police were asked to determine what sort of witchcraft was taking place. His daughter wrote: 'the perquisition fully exonerated my father, and one of the policemen who went to get Grigori Rasputin in the little oratory where he was at his prayers, was so struck by the mystic fervour that emanated from him, that he fell at his knees asking for his benediction, and became in the future one of his most faithful participants'. This was before Grigori was nineteen years of age.

At nineteen he was flogged and imprisoned for claiming that a load of furs had been stolen from him after he had been attacked by robbers. In fact it was shown that he had left the wagon untended, and it was then that the furs had been stolen.

He married at nineteen. At twenty he saw a vision of the Virgin in the sky. He sought the advice of a hermit at the monastery, and was advised to go on a pilgrimage to Mount Athos in Greece. This he did, walking the 2,000 miles with a friend. From Greece he went to the Holy Land.

The reader may feel that his daughter was not quite right when she wrote that Grigori was the same as any other child. As she said herself, he had certain unusual qualities which were to have a considerable bearing on his career.

Through the Czarina he became virtually ruler of Russia, and was murdered at the age of forty-five.

Robert Shaplen, in his biography, provides an interesting account of the childhood of *Ivan Kreuger*. As Shaplen said, it is easy with hindsight to read into Ivan's childhood escapades the early signs of the world swindler, though most of them might have been passed off as no worse than the behaviour of many other normal schoolboys.

On his mother's side, there was one case of insanity and one of suicide which was ascribed to general paralysis of the insane (a late manifestation of syphilis). After death, it was suggested that many aspects of Kreuger's life could be explained by general paralysis and he did, in fact, contract syphilis, but was thought to have been cured of it. His father was the owner of a successful match factory at Mömsterås on the Baltic. He was the third child, and three more followed him.

At school he clearly possessed high intelligence, and seemed to be constantly intent on demonstrating it. He seemed to be fearless, and had no thought of the consequences of what he did. He learned to swim at seven by accepting a challenge to jump into a deep pool. When another boy dared him to jump off a tall tree, he did, and narrowly escaped serious injury.

In innumerable ways in childhood he showed that he lacked completely a sense of right and wrong—just as he did in adult life. Shaplen wrote that 'he was surely one of the most astonishingly amoral men who ever lived'. The first thing which he stole was an envelope of pressed flowers belonging to a schoolfellow.

At school he was remarkably adept at taking short cuts— even though they were not quite honest, and he had no sense of guilt about it: in later years he was to do the same on a colossal scale. Shaplen wrote that in place of remorse, he felt pride at his own ability. Ivan said in later years: 'I guess I wasn't quite like the other boys: I thought things through for myself.' One of his schoolmates said: 'It isn't that he cheated more than the rest of us, but that he just did it better.'

He had a spectacularly retentive memory. He was said, at the age of five, to recite word for word a sermon he had heard in church, and then he recited it backwards. As an adult he could recite verbatim the numerous fictions in the balance sheets.

He could read a book rapidly and absorb everything in it —and tended to become lazy as a result. He would wait until examination time without working, and then rely on expert cribbing—and he was never caught. One of his schoolfellows later said that if anything dangerous was undertaken, Ivan always had a part in it. He forged a set of keys to enter the headmaster's office in order to obtain the final examination marks before they were announced—and sold them. Another time he tried to obtain the examination papers in advance, but was foiled because they had been locked up in a safe.

He was clever enough to recognise the important things and the principles, and to ignore side issues. As Shaplen said, he learnt to obtain the maximum results with the minimum of effort. He was an expert at systematisation—a quality which he never lost.

He had a knack of appraising his teacher's weakness, and consequently knowing what he could and could not do. He was an expert at cheating, and so was enabled to pass his examinations much younger than the other boys.

He went to the Technical University in Stockholm, to study engineering, and here too he became recognised for his intellect. A fellow student said that he took pleasure in using his agile mind 'for the deception of everyone with whom he came into contact'. He was admired by his fellows for his tricks—and in later years he was to charm astute financiers into giving him their clients' money without keeping track of what he was doing with it.

He did not want to settle down in the match business, and went off to America, a penniless Scandinavian. He struggled for a foothold there, and eventually built up an immense financial empire. When he was fifty-two he was murdered or committed suicide, and it was found that his empire was one of the greatest frauds ever perpetrated.

Some may legitimately feel that the account of *Pierre Laval* should not be included in this chapter. It is not for us to argue about the rights or wrongs of the verdict which led to his being shot for collaboration with Hitler. It is said that he did save many thousands of Jews from extermination. However, we decided to include him in the chapter, as being one of the less desirable of eminent men. His biography was written by Cole.

Laval's father owned a butcher's shop and inn. His mother was a placid devout woman.

He was a clever boy, who was consistently top of his class at the village school. He was a strong willed child, who dominated his fellows and in games was determined to win —altering the rules where necessary to enable him to achieve this. In spare time he served in the bar and delivered meat.

He had a violent temper, and was stubborn and rebellious. He delighted in crude practical jokes. He once caught a fox and let it loose on his uncle's poultry farm. He led a gang of children which was a constant source of trouble to the police. In order to please his mother he became a choirboy, but scandalised the priest by drinking the communion wine when he was supposed to be polishing the communion plate.

Hoping to reform him by kindness, where severity had failed, the priest gave him the honour of carrying the crucifix in the ceremonial procession through the village. It was a blustery showery day, and the boy forgot his dignity in the delight of stepping into every large puddle which was near. The splashes of dirty water brought a sharp reproof from Sister Angelique. 'Furious at receiving a scolding in public, and from a nun, he kept a sharp lookout for the next big puddle in the road and then jumped into it with both feet.' Sister Angelique boxed his ears. Laval, flushed with anger, propped the crucifix against the wall and yelled 'carry it yourself then' —and walked off.

He left school at eleven, and worked very hard for his Baccalaureat to qualify for the University. He succeeded in gaining entry to the Lycée at Moulins, and qualified in natural science. He then decided to be a lawyer.

He was shot for collaboration with the Nazis.

The father of *Benito Mussolini* was a blacksmith, a politically-minded man who had never been to school, but who was intelligent, and contributed articles to socialist journals. His views were violently expressed, and he had been in prison for them. Benito's mother was a schoolmistress, a quiet religious woman. She was gentle and kind and a woman of intelligence. We have obtained much of the information in this section from the book by Hibbert.

The family lived in poverty in two rooms on the second floor of a house at Dovia. Meals often consisted only of vegetable soup, wild radishes and chicory, and flat cakes made of flour and water.

Benito was a difficult child. He was disobedient, quarrelsome and moody, readily losing his temper. He often came home with his clothes torn and his face scratched and bleeding after a fight over the proceeds of poaching expeditions. Although he was surly, aggressive and obstinate, his brother and sister adored him, and he was quite popular among the children of the village. He was a dreamer, and would sit for hours on end watching the birds and gazing over the valley. 'One day', he told his mother, 'I shall astonish the world.'

At school he was difficult to manage. He would crawl under the desks and pinch the bare legs of the children. He refused to stay long in church services, and threw stones at children on their way to the Sunday School.

At nine he was sent away to school at Faenza, where it was hoped that the strict discipline imposed by the Fathers would control him. He hated the school, he hated the Fathers, and he hated the other boys, particularly the rich ones who sat at a different table and ate better food. He became more and more arrogant, and refused to work. When a Father hit him, he threw an inkwell at him. He stabbed a boy in a fight, and was almost expelled, but was allowed to stay until the end of the school year. The Fathers were delighted when he left, saying that they had never had such a difficult pupil.

At his next school he was just as unhappy and intractable. There too he stabbed a boy in a fight and this time was expelled. At fifteen he was subsequently readmitted as a dayboy, and at eighteen passed his final examinations and was given a teaching diploma.

In spite of his difficult behaviour his unusual intelligence was recognised at school. He had developed a thirst for knowledge and a passion for declamation.

He subsequently became head of the Fascist party and dictator of Italy, leading his country to a disastrous war at Germany's side. When Italy collapsed, he escaped into hiding near Lake Como, but was found and killed by Italian partisans at the age of sixty-two. His body was hung head downwards from a girder at a petrol station in Milan for all to see.

Little is known about the childhood of *Julius Streicher*. He was born in the Swabian village of Fleinhausen, one of nine children of an impoverished elementary schoolteacher. He went to a teachers' training college and became an elementary school teacher in Nuremberg. It was thought that his intelligence quotient was low average.

He was renowned for his ruthless persecution of the Jews through his newspaper *Der Stürmer*. He was hanged at Nuremberg as a war criminal.

Adolf Hitler was the son of a minor Austrian customs official, who was illegitimate. The parents were second cousins. The mother had had a very unhappy childhood, and she was not happy in her marriage. Four of her six children died. She told Kubizek (one of Hitler's biographers): 'What I hoped and dreamed of as a young girl has not been fulfilled in my marriage'—and added resignedly, 'but does such a thing ever happen?' Adolf's father was a hard, unsympathetic, bitter and short tempered man, who had had three wives and an illegitimate child—and another child immediately after his wedding.

Adolf's performance at school was wretched. At the Linz

Realschule he did so badly that he had to be moved to another school, and there he failed to achieve the customary leaving certificate. His school reports had been uniformly bad, and his mother regularly wept over the reports which he brought home. He said, when sixteen, that he hated school, hated the teachers and hated his schoolmates. As a boy he was always against everyone, and at odds with the world.

On leaving school he wanted to be an artist or an architect, but he failed the entrance examination to the Vienna Academy of Fine Arts. He would also have liked to make music his life work.

His mother used to say 'our poor father cannot rest in his grave because you will blast his wishes. Obedience is what distinguishes a good son, but you do not know the meaning of the word. That's why you did so badly at school, and why you are not getting anywhere now.'

His friend Kubizek described his early speeches, which Adolf practised on him, at the age of sixteen. 'These speeches', he said, 'used to be like a volcano erupting. It was as though something quite apart from him was bursting out of him. This was not acting, not exaggeration: this was really felt, and I saw that he was dead earnest. Again and again I was filled with astonishment at how fluently he expressed himself, how vividly he managed to convey his feelings, how easily the words flowed from his mouth when he was completely carried away by his own emotions. It was not what he said that impressed me most, but how he said it. This to me was something new and magnificent.' He said that there was no doubt that his friend Adolf had shown a gift for oratory from his earliest youth, and Adolf knew it. He would emphasise his words by measured and studied gestures.

Kubizek went on to describe a paradoxical quality. Hitler was always full of deep understanding and sympathy, and always knew what Kubizek needed and wanted.

As Führer, Hitler was responsible, through his assistants, for the death of millions of Jews. He led his country into a world war, which was responsible for the death of some fifteen million soldiers, sailors, airmen and civilians. He committed suicide in an air-raid shelter at the age of fifty-six.

Goering's mother travelled from Haiti to Bavaria, for the birth of Hermann, and then left him with a family friend, returning to Haiti. He did not see his mother again until he was six, and at school. His biography was written by Frischauer.

He hated school—and expressed a hearty wish that it would be burnt down. He refused to accept punishment there without retaliation. When punishment was imminent, he went to bed and demanded to be sent home. For four weeks his tutor sent letters of protest to his parents. He was examined by doctors, but they were apparently unable to deal with him, and his strike continued.

He was moved to another school, at Ansbach. After a few weeks he gave his schoolbooks to some wandering gipsies and told them to pawn them if they wished. He ran away and returned to his home, refusing to go back to Ansbach. He then went to a military college, where he was much more happy.

He did return to the school at Ansbach, at the age of forty-two. The Headmaster then made a glowing speech, saying how Ansbach school was proud to count the Prime Minister of Prussia among its boys. He asked nothing of his present pupils except that they should model themselves on the great man who was the product of the school.

Goering founded the Gestapo and set up the concentration camps, becoming Marshal of the Reich. He was condemned to death by Hitler, captured by the Americans, condemned to death at Nuremberg, but committed suicide a few hours before he was due for execution.

Joseph Goebbels' father was a manual worker, a stern devout catholic with an austere manner. His mother was of Dutch origin, a woman of great strength of character. We are indebted to the biography by Manvell and Fraenkel for much of the information below.

At the age of four Joseph developed poliomyelitis, with residual weakness of a leg, which was made worse by an operation. His parents were greatly worried by this, and transmitted their anxiety to Joseph—who became bitter about his handicap, his poverty, and later about his smallness of stature (five feet as an adult). Owing to his handicap, he was unable to take part in sport. It is said that his earliest recollections were of unhappiness and abnormality. He had a habit of shutting himself up in his room after school to brood or read. He read a great deal, and had a taste for music and amateur acting. He was greatly upset at being rejected for military service on account of his physical disability.

He was a good scholar, and was often top of his form, but was unpopular with his fellows and teachers because of his habit of boasting about his knowledge. He was subsequently described by Sir Neville Henderson as the most intelligent of all the Nazi leaders.

When he matriculated at twenty the examination results were very good, and he was invited by his headmaster to give the end of term farewell speech on behalf of those leaving school. His speech was described as stilted and pompous, and the headmaster, who disliked him because of his supercilious manner, remarked that one thing at least was certain: Goebbels would never make an orator.

Both his parents fully expected him to become a catholic priest: he was interviewed for the priesthood, but was rejected.

He was Minister for Propaganda in Hitler's régime. He committed suicide at the age of forty-eight.

Heinrich Himmler, a professor's son, was brought up in a calm and cultured home. He was baptised as a catholic and was a regular attender at church. We are indebted to the biography by Frischauer for the information below.

Before Heinrich was ten, he showed a special interest in

history. He knew the dates of famous battles, the wars of the Middle Ages, and tales of the Red Indians. By the time he entered High School, he could match his teacher's knowledge of Germany's past.

At school he was described as a good pupil, and a diligent boy, but he had special difficulty with languages. However hard he tried to learn a foreign language, he never achieved success. Neither did he show musical ability. It is said that for many months he tortured himself with attempts to learn the piano, but his father began to realise that the attempt was hopeless.

As a boy he developed an almost morbid interest in tracing his ancestry, the first symptom, his biographer remarked, of a morbid inclination to look into the past. In later years he was to insist on a complete record of the ancestry of the S.S. men as far back as 1750. Apart from this interest, we could find nothing else about his childhood and his environment which threw light on his subsequent history as a Nazi leader. He became Reichsführer of the S.S. and set up the Dachau concentration camp. He committed suicide at the age of forty-five.

Adolf Eichmann was born at Solingen in the Rhineland, the eldest of five children (four boys and a girl). His father was an accountant in the Tramways and Electricity Company at Solingen, but later rose to be chief of an electrical construction company. He was a deeply religious man, and twice each Sunday attended the Protestant Church. Adolf's mother died in childbirth when he was four. His father was heartbroken and decided to leave for Linz in Austria—where Hitler spent his boyhood days. Adolf did not seem to be unduly upset at the loss of his mother. He and his brothers were looked after by two aunts. The neighbours were exceptionally kind to the children. When he was eight, his father remarried. Adolf's stepmother was a harsh, domineering woman. His childhood was not a happy one.

Quentin Reynolds, in his biography of Eichmann, wrote that Adolf suffered from his semitic appearance, and his school-mates often called him 'Der kleine Jude', the little Jew. His teachers remembered him as a boy who disliked school and school work. They said that he was a strange withdrawn boy, who sat at the back of the class and day-dreamed. He had few friends, and took little part in games; he was something of a problem child.

Reynolds wrote that when Adolf was thirteen, and at school in Thuringia, his name was mentioned in a local newspaper as a leader of a gang which had cruelly tormented a Jewish class-mate. The children had beaten up the Jewish boy and torn his clothes. Adolf told each one when it was his turn to beat the boy. Twenty years later the Jewish boy died in a con-centration camp on Eichmann's orders.

Reynolds tells that subsequently, when Eichmann was at school in Linz, there were two Jewish boys in his class, and one of them was a constant victim of Adolf's bullying. One day Adolf and his friends, encouraged by the antisemitic attitude of their teachers, beat up the Jewish boy in the school yard. As he lay on the ground, battered and bleeding, Eichmann placed his foot on the boy's chest, as a conqueror. When the boy was finally able to get on his feet, he jumped up and bit Adolf on the arm. The boy never returned to school—and ten days later hanged himself.

Adolf was the least clever of the children, and he alone was unable to finish at the High School, or even graduate from the vocational school for engineering to which he was then sent (at sixteen). He had been lazy at school, and had not shown ability. His father put his unpromising boy to work as an ordinary mining labourer, but then found him a post in the sales department of an electrical company, a post held by Adolf for two years. In 1925, when he was nineteen, he was out of work, with no prospect of a career in front of him—walking the streets of Linz, unemployed and disillusioned.

As an adolescent, he was frequently invited into Jewish homes. Clarke wrote: 'Many times in the warmth and friendliness of old Vienna he was invited as an educated and honoured guest into the humble Jewish homes he was later to turn into ghettoes. He was happy among his new found friends and they would wine and talk together long into the night. He liked their warm way, enjoyed their light hearted family squabbles, their voluble way of life.'

He came under the influence of Adolf Hitler, and at twenty-five joined the illegal Austro-German Veterans Association and then the Nazi party. He subsequently became responsible for the death of six million Jews—and finally met his death in Israel at the hands of the Jews whom he had tried so hard to exterminate.

COMMENT

We know of no studies of the background of evil-doing such as that which characterised the twenty men described in this chapter. There are many books and papers concerning the background of delinquency, and their findings may be of some interest in the present study. The most common factors found in the case of juvenile delinquency are as follows: A bad home, a low social class, a large family, a bad neighbourhood, with the influence of gangs: a weak, alcoholic, punitive father, who shows little interest in his children and is hated by them; emotional deprivation—rejection by the parents, or loss of parents by bereavement or divorce; lack of discipline at home; insecurity; a bad example set by the parents, a family history of delinquency; and the presence of a physical handicap—such as poor eyesight, deformity of a limb, or a stutter. Delinquents (who are mainly boys), retain the immaturity of earlier years; they lack a conscience (they have 'superego lacunae' to use a psychiatric term). The level of intelligence, though often average or above average, is more often somewhat low.

Such is the common background of the young delinquent. It is easy to see some of these features in the early life of Ivan the Terrible, or of Cesare Borgia. They were brought up in an atmosphere of evil doing, were set the worst possible example, and did not experience the firm loving discipline which is so necessary for the normal child. Five of the twenty evil men lost one or both parents in early childhood, but others, as we stated earlier in this chapter, had a good home, which, as far as we can tell from the slender evidence available, was all that it should have been. It is regrettable that our information is so incomplete.

The evil deeds of these men probably arose from a concatenation of factors and circumstances—features of their personality, some of which they had inherited from their parents; probably subtle errors of management as children, of which we have no information; and then the force of circumstances and friendships developing in later years. We must admit that in the case of many of the men whom we have described, there were no discoverable factors which made these men what they were.

It is interesting to note that of these twenty men, ten were murdered or otherwise put to death, five committed suicide, one (Sade) died in a lunatic asylum, another (Judge Jeffreys) in the Tower of London, and Titus Oates died in disgrace. The remaining two, Ivan and Torquemada, died a 'natural death'.

CHAPTER 14

PATHWAYS TO FAME

IT is interesting to speculate about the factors which led the men and women we have described to the fame which they eventually achieved.

Many can reasonably be said to have been men and women of genius—but that is a word which is difficult to define. We would not apply it to some of the men whom we have described, and certainly not to the 'evil men'.

Various attempts have been made to define the word 'genius', though most of them are more descriptive than definitive. Carlyle described genius as 'an infinite capacity for taking trouble'. F. W. Meyers regarded genius as 'a power of utilising a wider range than other men can utilise of faculties to some degree innate in all'. Schopenhauer wrote that genius consists of the ability to see a pattern in things, and to see the general in the particular. Cyril Burt remarked that the man of genius does not merely think of new solutions; he perceives new problems, and sees the familiar in a new light.

William James wrote that the essence of genius is to know what to overlook; the genius can separate the wood from the trees, can pick out that which is relevant and discard the rest. It is not clever merely to be sceptical. The genius does not merely feel sceptical; he sets about proving whether an idea is right or wrong.

Buffon declared that the genius of great men consists of their superior patience: nothing repels or tires them. Smiles wrote that men of genius are not only laborious and persevering, but they are enthusiasts too.

According to Emerson, genius is one-third inspiration and two-thirds perspiration. Yet no man by hard work alone can become a genius; though one essential to achievement is the willingness to work hard, and the ability to concentrate, without mental fatigue. The tremendous enthusiasm for reading, and the devotion of many long hours to the work in hand, was a feature of the lives of many of the men described by us.

One factor, found in most men of genius, is creativity. This is by no means synonymous with a high degree of intelligence. Arnold Gesell wrote, many years ago, that a high degree of intelligence is often associated with a meagre degree of creativity. Many of the famous people described by us had a remarkable degree of originality and of creativity.

Many make the mistake of thinking that a high degree of intelligence is the most important prerequisite to eminence and fame. Terman and Oden, in their book *Genetic Studies of Genius*, provided a great deal of evidence that many of the famous men of the past did not possess a really high level of intelligence, but had other qualities which led to success. Terman and Oden wrote that 'a high, but not the highest intelligence, combined with the greatest degree of persistence, will achieve greater eminence than the highest degree of intelligence with somewhat less persistence'. Many writers have emphasised the high degree of persistence shown by men of eminence—a persistence against great odds, and particularly against the wishes of teachers and of parents. We have given many examples of the child's persistence in his choice of career, against great opposition at home. We have told how frequently parents were greatly disappointed with their children as a result—and how these children, because of this determination, achieved fame never dreamt of by their parents. Germant referred to the tenacity of purpose shown by many men of genius, with a high degree of perseverance, bordering on obstinacy, which overcame all the obstacles in their path.

Samuel Smiles wrote that 'The clever and diligent boy often fulfils the promise of his youth; though if wanting in application, he may turn out to be a very indifferent man; whereas the boy of no promise at all, may achieve distinction and eminence, especially if he possesses patient application and perseverance.'

Other factors commonly important for the achievement of success include various personality traits, such as the ability to get on with people: the ability to profit from one's own experience and the experience of others; and ambition, with the desire to accomplish.

Lord Birkett, in his book *Six Great Advocates*, discussed the qualities which led *Sir Edward Clarke* to fame. Clarke was brought up in poverty, leaving school at thirteen, and never went to a University, but became one of Britain's greatest lawyers. Lord Birkett suggested that the qualities were his energy, his wonderful memory, his willingness to work hard, his gift of eloquence, and his sense of purpose that could not be moved or beaten down or disheartened. 'But above all these things, and this is the secret of Sir Edward Clarke's tremendous career—he had that inward urge, born in the secret places of the heart, to excel, to triumph over circumstances, and to become a famous and distinguished man.'

We were particularly interested in the circumstances which led various men to the final career of their choice. These circumstances were often quite fortuitous. In other cases children were given every opportunity from the earliest months of life. Some enjoy serendipity—the gift of finding valuable or agreeable things without seeking for them.

Success often depends on an opportunity; but it depends even more on the willingness, intelligence and foresight to take the opportunity when it is offered. As Brutus said to Cassius in Julius Caesar:

> There is a tide in the affairs of man
> Which, taken at the flood, leads to fortune;
> Omitted, all the voyage of their lives
> Is bound in shallows and in miseries.

One thinks of the difficulties which many writers experienced in securing a publisher for their first book: Edgar Wallace is a good example. One will never know how much potential genius has been nipped in the bud by lack of opportunity, by bad schooling, or by a poor home environment. We shall never know how many were stifled by lack of motivation at home or school, by poor teaching, by unwise choice of career, by frank discouragement.

By no means all the men described were blessed with good health, and in fact a surprisingly large number had quite troublesome handicaps of one sort or another. It has even been suggested that a physical handicap acted as a spur to achievement—as in the case of Lord Byron, Charles Dickens, Sir Walter Scott and Lawrence of Arabia. Samuel Smiles wrote that misfortune was often a stepping stone to genius; and that many men of possible distinction and brilliance had been lost to the world simply because nothing interrupted the course of their prosperity. Many people, Smiles wrote, owe their good fortune to some disadvantage under which they laboured; it is in struggling against it that their best faculties are brought into play. In this connection it is interesting to note the very large number of eminent people who suffered the loss of a parent in early life.

The stimulating effect of a good home is an invaluable asset in the life of a child. It is thought that much of the backwardness of intelligent children from lower social classes may be ascribed to lack of stimulation at home, lack of books, lack of intelligent conversation, the parents' lack of interest in their child's achievement, and even doing discouragement from homework. Yet a surprisingly large number of men of fame came from the poorest of poor homes. They included Abel, Bevin, Brahms, Brindley, Bunyan, Burns, Copernicus, Dickens, Dollfuss, Faraday, Franklin, Keir Hardie, Ben Jonson, Laplace, Lincoln, Luther, Ramsay MacDonald, Mussolini, Anna Pavlova, Rossini, Sexton, Stalin, George Stephenson, Telford and Turner, amongst many others. Perhaps the poverty with which they started life acted as a stimulus to endeavour. Ralph Waldo Emerson suggested this when he wrote: 'I cannot help saying to poverty "Be welcome, provided only that thou comest not quite too late in life." Riches fetter talent rather than poverty: many an intellectual giant may be stifled under thrones and golden mountains. When the oil of wealth is poured on the flames of youth, and especially of the more ardent stronger youth, there will little more be left of the Phoenix than the ashes; only a Goethe has the power to keep his Phoenix wings unsinged in the sun of prosperity.'

It would be tedious to list the employment of the fathers of the men whom we have discussed. Some, however, may be mentioned. Martin Luther's father was a miner. John Bunyan's father was a tinker. The fathers of Copernicus, Handel and Turner were bakers. Kant's father was a harness maker. Rousseau's father was a watchmaker. The father of Gauss was a bricklayer. Michael Faraday's father was a blacksmith. The fathers of Thomas Telford, of Brindley, Alexander Murray, Rennie, Burns and Ernest Bevin were farm labourers. These men had great difficulties at the onset of their life, and many of them had little or no education, with no background of learning at home. George Stephenson, for instance, had had no education at all, and had to learn to read and write when he was eighteen.

Several started with the disadvantage of illegitimacy. They included Boccaccio, Erasmus, Leonardo da Vinci, Borodin, Cézanne, Edgar Wallace, Ernest Bevin, Sarah Bernhardt, Lawrence of Arabia, and Chancellor Dollfuss.

Many others came from wealthy homes, or homes of learning and culture. They include Alfieri, Bacon, Boyle, Byron, Cavendish, Cowper, Dante, Descartes, Cesar Franck, Galileo, Hume, Lafayette, Linnaeus, Lytton, Rembrandt, Scott, Shelley, Toulouse-Lautrec, Beatrice Webb, Wellington, Christopher Wren, and very many others. Napoleon was disturbed by the wealth of his fellows. He wrote: 'At Brienne I was the poorest of my schoolfellows. I was proud, and most careful that nobody should perceive this. I could neither laugh nor amuse myself like the others.' He disliked the luxury and wealth of the cadets in the Military School in Paris, and thought it was bad for them.

Quite a number were sons of doctors. They included Berlioz, Robert Boyle, Ramon Y. Cajal, Miguel de Cervantes, Clemenceau, Dostoevsky, Flaubert, Handel, Marat, Sir Edward Marshall Hall, Mazzini, Sir John Moore, Poincaré, Proust and Oscar Wilde. There are probably many others of whom we are not aware.

It is a common misconception that men of genius are more likely to be mentally unstable than others who are less intelligent. Kretschmer, in his book *The Psychology of Men of Genius* gave strong arguments in favour of the idea that genius is akin to madness. On the other hand, Terman and Oden, in their follow up study of 1,528 children with an intelligence quotient of 140 or more, showed that they were more stable, had fewer neurotic symptoms, fewer nervous breakdowns, a lower divorce rate, and a lower suicide rate, than children of average intelligence. It may well depend on one's definition of genius. In our series of famous men, a few did eventually become insane: they included Dostoevsky, Galton, Maupassant, Julius Mayer, Conrad Meyer, John Stuart Mill, Newton, Nietzsche, Rousseau, Ruskin, Schumann and Van Gogh.

Several of the men made half-hearted or genuine attempts to commit suicide in their early years: they include Thomas Chatterton (who died of poisoning), Chateaubriand, Gandhi, Gilbert Murray and Tolstoy. Alfieri at the age of eight attempted to poison himself in a fit of melancholy by eating what he thought was hemlock. It made him sick, and he was shut up in his room, after which he was taken in his nightcap to the neighbouring church. 'Who knows', he said, 'whether I am not indebted to that blessed nightcap for having turned out one of the most truthful of men?' He made another attempt on his life when he was nineteen. Mark Twain attempted suicide when he was thirty. Not having studied the later history of the famous men included in our book, we cannot say how many attempted suicide in later years.

Success and fame in one's vocation by no means indicates similar success in other aspects of life. A man may be highly successful in his business career, and a total failure in his relationships with his wife, or in the upbringing of his children. The remarkable upbringing to which John Ruskin was subjected may well have contributed to his achievements as a writer and critic; but it is very likely that they were responsible for his disastrous sex life. We have discussed the factors which might well have led to the sexual difficulties of Leonardo da Vinci, Proust, Gogol, Oscar Wilde, Nobel and Lawrence of Arabia.

That there is commonly a genetic factor in genius can hardly be denied. Sir Francis Galton studied the careers of relatives of judges, statesmen, commanders, writers, poets, scientists, musicians, painters, divines and athletes, and found strong evidence of a genetic factor. He found that 977 eminent men had 535 eminent relatives, while 977 ordinary men had only 4 eminent relatives. He wrote that it would be inconceivable that various geniuses would not have achieved equal eminence in a different environment. Havelock Ellis, Samuel Smiles and others have studied the same question.

Well known examples of hereditary genius include the Darwin family, which produced Fellows of the Royal Society in five generations; the Bach family which was actively musical for seven or eight generations; and the Bernoulli family, nine members of which attained eminence in mathematics or physics.

It would be undesirable to study the genetic background of genius in all the many famous men mentioned in this book. We have much sympathy with the remark by Hanson, in his biography of Toulouse-Lautrec, that 'it is customary for a biography to open with a sketch of the subject's family and ancestors. Often enough this section is of necessity the most tedious in the book, and there are times when the tedium also seems profitless.' We certainly found many prolonged and verbose accounts of the family background in some of the biographies which we read—though we would not deny the interest in some of those accounts. Karl Pearson in his biography of Sir Francis Galton devoted 99 pages to the ancestry.

Though in many instances there were obvious indications of brilliance in one or other parent of a famous person, there were many other examples in which no sparks or signs of genius could be found. Some of the remarks of biographers are mentioned below.

The parents of Isaac Newton and those of Keats were in no way distinguished. It was said of Handel that 'through some unknown strain in his blood, from heaven knows what forgotten ancestor, the seeds of music found its way into Handel's heart, and refused to be dislodged'. Hudson described Joshua Reynolds' father in the following terms: 'His neat handwriting reveals him as a learned man of little consequence, and in the worldly sense, a failure of great respectability.' Concerning George Washington, Weems wrote: 'Where George got his great military talent is a question which none but the happy believers in a particular providence can solve: certain it is, his earthly parents had no hand in it.' Turner was described by Thomas as 'the insignificant son of an insignificant father and a host of insignificant ancestors'. Blunden, writing of Shelley, said that 'Shelley, by some inexplicable chance or caprice of nature, sprang in his greatness out of a family which apart from him continued through the centuries without distinction, energy or noble error'.

Freud had five uncles, of whom only one was healthy. One was a hydrocephalic idiot. One became insane at fifteen, and an aunt became insane at twenty. A cousin died of epilepsy.

Vallentin wrote concerning Einstein, that 'there was nothing in this middle class milieu to explain an outstanding destiny'. With regard to Franklin Roosevelt, Burns wrote that 'one looks in vain for any foretoken of Franklin Delano Roosevelt in these Delano or Roosevelt lives'.

Several workers have studied the relationship between genius and the place in the family. Like others, Francis Galton, in his book *English Men of Science*, found that the elder sons were almost twice as likely to achieve fame as younger sons. Galton suggested that they are more likely to become possessed of independent means, and therefore to be able to follow the pursuits of their choice: they are treated more as companions by their parents, and have earlier responsibility, and so develop greater independence of character. In infancy the first-born has more attention from his parents.

There must be many other factors which we do not understand. It has been shown repeatedly that more children with mental deficiency, mongolism, certain forms of cerebral palsy and certain congenital defects are born at some seasons of the year than at others.

Van Loon wrote: 'I am beginning to suspect that genius is rather like wine, in that there are certain regions which are apt to raise a much better crop of genius than others, and there are definite years during which the genius harvest in all parts of the world will be much greater than during other years or numbers of years.' In this connection the year 1809 is outstanding. In that year were born Braille, Darwin, Gladstone, Gogol, Oliver Wendel Holmes, Lincoln, Mendelssohn, Poe and Tennyson. (The year 1769 produced Mohammed Ali, Brunel, Viscount Castlereagh, Baron Cuvier, Napoleon and the Duke of Wellington.)

Smiles remarked that in Italy groups of great artists appeared almost simultaneously; he cited, as examples, Leonardo da Vinci, Michelangelo, Perugino, Raphael and Titian.

The fact is that at present there are so many variables which affect a child's life and future career, that we are unable to modify them in such a way that we could say, like Watson of Baltimore: 'Give me a dozen healthy infants, and my own specified world to bring them up in, and I'll guarantee to make any one doctor, lawyer, artist, merchant, chief, beggarman or thief.'

Perhaps one day we shall learn how to translate all the various facets of the personality, intelligence and aptitudes of child, parent, siblings and teachers, into figures: we shall isolate in detail the various factors which affect a child before conception, and during pregnancy: we shall learn more about the exact effect of the innumerable features of the management and environment of the child from the moment of birth to the time of starting school—and their influence when he is at home from school: we shall learn more about the sensitive or critical period at which he should be taught each subject of the curriculum, and about the particular method of teaching which is most suitable for him as an individual: and then we can feed all this into a computer, with details of his physical status and weaknesses, the social circumstances of his family, and all the other factors which will affect him, and find out how much opportunity he should be given, and when: to how much thwarting he should be subjected, and when: how much opposition should be offered to his choice of career, or how much support should be given: what sort of a wife he should have to spur him on, or to oppose him—and then we can enable him to achieve distinction and fame. Then, perhaps, we shall learn what circumstances lead to the transition of a newborn baby to the rebel, critic, poet or scientist of the future. The variables at present are too great for the human mind to encompass. Only a computer could handle the variables: but only the human mind can supply the computer with the necessary data—and that we are not ready to do.

CONCLUSION

Perhaps the most striking feature of the early days of all

these men of fame (and infamy) is the absence of a pattern; they came from the widest variety of home backgrounds, ranging from the direst poverty to affluence and prosperity, from ignorance and a total absence of intellectual stimulation, to the best of homes which provided every opportunity for learning and advancement. Some were brought up by wise and loving parents who devoted their lives to their children; others were left to bring themselves up, were beaten and maltreated, or were brought up by cranks with the most extraordinary ideas of child management. Some had intensive home education, some went to the best schools in the country, some had the most shockingly bad education, or no education at all. Some at school were lazy; many played truant; several were expelled; many failed to gain entrance to a University. Some had poor health, physical handicaps, convulsive disorders, and psychological problems. Some displayed an early intellectual precocity which was obvious to all; many were apparently just ordinary children, with no suggestion of any unusual ability, and many were definitely backward. Some were the despair of their teachers, and were given up as beyond hope. Many of them had serious disagreements with their parents over the choice of their career, and many caused their parents the bitterest disappointment—not only because of their refusal to fall in with their parents' wishes with regard to career, but because of their poor progress at school. Some knew from the earliest years exactly what they wanted to do in life: others reached their final career by a circuitous and tortuous route until finally they found the work in which they were to excel.

We thought that the stories were fascinating. They provide many important precepts for parents and teachers. They indicate the great difficulty and virtual impossibility of forecasting achievement, the difficulty of detecting a child's potential, and the difficulty of determining the best home and scholastic background for enabling a child to develop his potential to the full. We cannot possibly say how much genius has been nipped in the bud by an unsuitable home environment, by poor teaching, or by wrong choice of subject for study at school or for career. We cannot possibly say whether the men described by us achieved their fame in spite of their homes and their schools or because of them—even when the homes were thoroughly deplorable, and the education was as unsatisfactory as it could be.

Boys who had the unhappiest childhood because of their homes, or who were bullied and derided at school, or were beaten unmercifully by their teachers, might never have achieved what they did if they had been brought up differently. Life is so complex that no man can say.

We would like to feel that this book will help parents and teachers to be more tolerant of their charges. Children may reach fame in spite of, or because of, the unusual and perhaps difficult features of their personality. The child who is backward today (unless he is mentally subnormal) may be the genius of tomorrow. Whether he will reach eminence or not, he certainly deserves sympathy, encouragement and help to make the most of what he has, whatever his social class, creed or colour.

REFERENCES

SECTION A

Abel, N. *See* Bell (Section B).

Adams, H. (1961). *The Education of Henry Adams.* (*An Autobiography*). Boston: Houghton Mifflin.

Addison, J. Lord Macaulay (1898). *The Life and Writings of Joseph Addison.* London: Macmillan.

Adler, A. Orgler, H. (1963). *Alfred Adler.* London: Sidgwick & Jackson.

Agassiz, L. *See* Thomas (Section B).

— *See* Terman and Oden (Section B).

— Lurie, E. (1960). *Louis Agassiz—A Life in Science.* Chicago: Univ. of Chicago Press.

Alfieri, V. *See* Smiles (Section B).

Allbutt, T. C. Rolleston, Humphry (1929). *The Right Honourable Sir Thomas Clifford Allbutt.* London: Macmillan.

Ampère, A. *See* Barlow (Section B).

Andersen, H. C. Toksvig, S. (1934). *Hans Christian Andersen.* London: Macmillan.

— *See also* Van Loon (Section B).

Arnold, T. Stanley, A. P. (1880). *The Life and Correspondence of Thomas Arnold.* London: Murray.

— Worboise, E. J. (1885). *The Life of Dr Arnold.* London: Isbister.

Austen, Jane. Johnson, R. B. (1930). *Jane Austen.* London: Dent.

Bach, J. Terry, C. S. (1928). *Johann Sebastian Bach.* London: Oxford Univ. Press.

— *See* Smiles (Section B).

— *See* Thomas (Section B).

Baden-Powell, R. Hillcourt, W. with Olave, Lady Baden-Powell (1964). *The Two Lives of a Hero.* London: Heinemann.

Baldwin, S. Young, G. M. (1952). *Stanley Baldwin.* London: Rupert Hart Davies.

Balfour, A. J. Young, K. (1963). *Arthur James Balfour.* London: Bell.

Balzac, H. *See* Thomas (Section B).

Barrie, J. M. Roy, J. A. (1937). *James Matthew Barrie.* London: Jarrolds.

Beaverbrook, Lord. Driberg, T. (1956). *Lord Beaverbrook.* London: Weidenfeld and Nicolson.

Beethoven, L. *See* Brockway (Section B).

— *See* Thomas (Section B).

— *See* Van Loon (Section B).

351

— In *Grove's Dictionary of Music and Musicians*. London: Macmillan.
— Dickinson, A. E. F. (1941). *Beethoven*. London: Nelson.
— Riezler, W. (1938). *Beethoven*. London: Forrester.
— Scott, Marion (1934). *Beethoven*. London: Dent.
Bentham, J. Mack, M. P. (1962). *Jeremy Bentham*. London: Heinemann.
— *See* Smiles (Section B).
— *See* Terman and Oden (Section B).
Berlioz, L. Elliott, J. H. (1938). *Berlioz*. London: Dent.
— *See also* Brockway (Section B).
Bernadette, Saint. Trouncer, M. (1958). *A Grain of Wheat*. London: Hutchinson.
Bernard, C. Olmsted, J. M. D. (1939). *Claude Bernard*. London: Cassell.
Bernhardt, Sarah. Richardson, J. (1959). *Sarah Bernhardt*. London: Reinhardt.
Bernoulli, J. *See* Barlow (Section B).
Berzelius, Johann. Holmyard, E. J. (1931). *Makers of Chemistry*. Oxford: Clarendon Press.
Bevan, A. Foot, Michael (1962). *Aneurin Bevan*. London: McGibbon & Kee.
Bevin, E. Bullock, A. (1960). *The Life and Times of Ernest Bevin*. London: Heinemann.
— Williams, F. (1952). *Ernest Bevin*. London: Hutchinson.
Bidder, G. *See* Barlow (Section B).
Birkenhead, Earl of. The Earl of Birkenhead (1959). *The Life of F. E. Smith, First Earl of Birkenhead*. London: Eyre & Spottiswoode.
Birkett, Sir Norman. Hyde, H. M. (1964). *Norman Birkett*. London: Hamish Hamilton.
Bismarck, O. Jacks, W. (1899). *The Life of Prince Bismarck*. Glasgow: Maclehose.
— Ludwig, Emil (1929). *Bismarck*. Boston: Little Brown.
Blake, William. Margoliouth, H. M. (1951). *William Blake*. London: Oxford Univ. Press.
Bland—Sutton. Bland—Sutton, J. (1930). *The Story of a Surgeon*. London: Methuen.
Boccaccio, G. *See* Thomas (Section B).
Booth, W. Begbie, H. (1920). *The Life of William Booth*. London: Macmillan.
Borgia, Cesare. Sabatini, R. (1926). *The Life of Cesare Borgia*. London: Stanley Paul.
— Woodward, W. H. (1913). *Cesar Borgia*. London: Chapman & Hall.

— Yriarte, C. (1947). *Cesare Borgia*. London: Aldor.

Borodin, A. Dianin, S. (1963). *Borodin*. London: Oxford Univ. Press.

Borrow. G. Jenkins, H. (1912). *The Life of George Borrow*. London: John Murray.

Boyle, R. Saunders, L. (1885). *Robert Boyle, Inventor and Philanthropist*. London: Wood.

Brahms, J. *See* Brockway (Section B).

— *See* Thomas (Section B).

Braille, Louis. Roblin, J. (Undated). *Louis Braille*. London: Royal National Institute for the Blind.

— Henri, Pierre (1952). *La Vie et l'Oeuvre de Louis Braille*. Paris: Presses Universitaires de France.

Bright, J. Trevelyan, G. M. (1913). *The Life of John Bright*. Boston: Houghton Mifflin.

Brindley, J. *See* Smiles (Section B).

Brontë, Branwell. Gerin, Winifred (1961). *Branwell Brontë*. London: Thomas Nelson.

Brontë, Charlotte. Gaskell, E. *Charlotte Brontë*. London: Oxford Univ. Press.

Brooke, R. Hassall, C. (1964). *Rupert Brooke*. London: Faber & Faber.

Browning, Elizabeth Barrett. *See* Thomas (Section B).

Browning, R. Griffin, W. H. (1910). *The Life of Robert Browning*. London: Methuen.

— Chesterton, G. K. (1957). *Robert Browning*. London: Macmillan.

Brunel, I. Rolt, L. T. C. (1957). *Isambard Kingdom Brunel*. London: Longmans Green.

Bunyan, John. Lindsay, J. (1937). *John Bunyan*. London: Methuen.

— Venables, E. (1888). *Life of John Bunyan*. London: Scott.

Burke, E. *See* Terman and Oden (Section B).

Burns, R. *See* Terman and Oden (Section B).

Butler, Samuel. Cole, G. D. H. (1947). *Samuel Butler and the Way of all Flesh*. London: Home & Van Thal.

Buxton, J. *See* Barlow (Section B).

Byron, Lord. Marchand, L. A. (1957). *Lord Byron*. London: Murray.

— Moore, T. (1833). *Lord Byron*. London: Murray.

— *See also* Smiles (Section B).

— *See also* Thomas (Section B).

Cajal, Ramon Y. Haymaker, W. (1953). *The Founders of Neurology*. Springfield: Charles Thomas.

Canova, A. *See* Smiles (Section B).

Cantor, J. *See* Bell (Section B).

Carlyle, T. Garnett, R. (1887). *Life of Thomas Carlyle*. London: Scott.
— *See also* Terman and Oden (Section B).

Carroll, Lewis (Rev. C. L. Dodgson). Collingwood, S. D. (1898). *The Life and Letters of Lewis Carroll*. London: Nelson.

Castlereagh, Viscount. Hassall, A. (1908). *Viscount Castlereagh*. London: Pitman.

Cauchy, A. *See* Bell (Section B).

Cellini, Benvenuto (1906). *Memoirs*. London: Dent.

Cervantes, Miguel de. *See* Thomas (Section B).

Cézanne, H. Perruchot, Henri (1961). *Cézanne*. London: Perpetua Books.

Chamberlain, J. Garvin, J. L. (1932). *The Life of Joseph Chamberlain*. London: Macmillan.

Chamberlain, N. Feiling, K. (1946). *The Life of Neville Chamberlain*. London: Macmillan.

Chang and Eng. Luckhardt, A. B. (1941). Report of the autopsy of the Siamese twins together with other Interesting Information covering their Life. *Surg. Gynec. Obstet.*, **72**, 116.
— Hunter, K. (1964). *Duet for a Life Time. The Story of the Original Siamese Twins*. London: Joseph.

Chateaubriand, F. Sieburg, F. (1961). *Chateaubriand*. London: Allen & Unwin.

Chatham, Lord. Lord Rosebery (1910). *Chatham*. London: Humphreys.

Chatterton, T. Ellinger, E. P. (1930). *Thomas Chatterton, The Marvellous Boy*. Philadelphia: Univ. of Pennsylvania.
— Meyerstein, E. H. W. (1930). *Chatterton*. London: Ingpen & Grant.
— *See also* Smiles (Section B).

Chekhov, A. Magarshack, D. (1962). *Chekhov*. London: Faber & Faber.

Chesterton, G. K. Ward, M. (1944). *Gilbert Keith Chesterton*. London: Sheed & Ward.

Chopin, F. Niecks, F. (1890). *The Life of Chopin*. London: Novello, Ewar & Co.
— *See also* Brockway (Section B).
— *See also* Thomas (Section B).
— *See also* Van Loon (Section B).

Churchill, W. Cowles, V. (1953). *Winston Churchill*. London: Hamish Hamilton.
— (1959). *My Early Life*. London: Odham Books Limited.
— Fishman, J. (1963). *My Darling Clementine. The Story of Lady Churchill*. London: Allen.

Clarke, Sir Edward. Lord Birkett (1961). *Six Great Advocates*. Penguin Books.

Clive, R. Minney, R. J. (1957). *Clive of India*. London: Jarrolds.
— *See also* Smiles (Section B).
Cobden, R. Morley, J. (1881). *The Life of Richard Cobden*. London: Chapman & Hall.
Colburn, Z. *See* Barlow (Section B).
Coleridge, Samuel Taylor. Campbell, J. D. (1896). *Samuel Taylor Coleridge*. London: Macmillan.
— Fausset, H. I. (1933). *Samuel Taylor Coleridge*. London: Cape.
— Charpentier, J. (1929). *Coleridge*. London: Constable.
— Chambers, E. K. (1938). *Samuel Taylor Coleridge*. Oxford: Clarendon Press.
Confucius. *See* Thomas (Section B).
Congreve, W. Gosse, E. (1924). *Life of William Congreve*. London: Heinemann.
Conrad, J. Jean-Aubry, G. (1957). *The Sea Dreams*. London. Allen & Unwin.
Constable, J. Leslie, C. R. (1845). *Life of John Constable*. London: Longmans.
Cooper, Sir Astley. *See* Hale-White (Section B).
Copernicus, N. *See* Thomas (Section B).
Cortes, H. Salvador de Madariaga (1954). *Hernan Cortes*. London: Hollis & Carter.
Cortez, H. Prescott, W. H. (1929). *History of the Conquest of Mexico*. London: Allen & Unwin.
— *See also* Terman and Oden (Section B)
Cowley, A. Nethercot, A. H. (1931). *Abraham Cowley*. London: Milford.
Cowper, W. Wright, T. (1892). *The Life of William Cowper*. London: Fisher Unwin.
— *See also* Terman and Oden (Section B).
Cranmer, T. Ridley, J. (1962). *Thomas Cranmer*. Oxford: Clarendon Press.
Crichton, J. Tytler, P. F. (1823). *Life of the Admirable Crichton*. Edinburgh: Tait.
— in *Votiva Tabella*. A memorial volume of St Andrews University (1909). St Andrews: Maclehose.
— *See also* Barlow (Section B).
Cromwell, O. Ashley, M. (1957). *The Greatness of Oliver Cromwell*. London: Hodder & Stoughton.
— *See also* Lardner (Section B).
Crotch, W. In *Grove's Dictionary of Music and Musicians*. 1954. London, Macmillan.

Curie, M. *See* Thomas (Section B).

Curzon, Lord. Earl of Ronaldshay (1928). *The Life of Lord Curzon.* London: Benn.

Cuvier, L. Lee, R. (1833). *Memoirs of Baron Cuvier.* London: Longman.

Dalton, J. Brockbank, E. M. (1906-1923). *Medical Pamphlets.*

— Hendry, W. C. (1854). *John Dalton.* London: Cavendish Society.

— Roscoe, H. E. (1895). *John Dalton.* London: Cassell.

— *See also* Thomas (Section B).

Dante Alighieri. *See* Smiles S. (Section B).

Danton, G. Beesly, A. H. (1899). *Life of Danton.* London: Longmans Green.

— Warwick, C. F. (1909). *Danton and the French Revolution.* London: Unwin.

— *See also* Terman and Oden (Section B).

Darwin, Charles. Darwin, F. (1908). *Charles Darwin.* London: Murray.

— *See also* Thomas (Section B).

Dase, J. *See* Barlow (Section B).

Davy, Sir Humphry. Holmyard, E. J. (1928). *The Great Chemists.* London: Methuen.

— Treneer, A. (1963). *The Mercurial Chemist.* London: Methuen.

Debussy, C. O'Brien, M. and G. O. (1933). *Claude Debussy.* London: Oxford Univ. Press.

— *See also* Thomas (Section B).

— *See also* Brockway (Section B).

Defoe, D. *See* Thomas (Section B).

Delius, F. Beecham, Sir Thomas (1959). *Frederick Delius.* London: Hutchinson.

De Quincey, T. Eaton. H. A. (1936). *Thomas De Quincey.* New York: Oxford Univ. Press.

Descartes, R. *See* Bell (Section B).

Dickens, Charles. Forster, G. (1872). *Charles Dickens.* London: Chapman & Hall.

— Pearson, H. (1949). *Dickens.* London: Methuen.

— *See also* Thomas (Section B).

Disraeli, B. Clarke, E. (1926). *Benjamin Disraeli.* London: Murray.

— Jerman, B. R. (1960). *The Young Disraeli.* London: Oxford Univ. Press.

Dollfuss, E. Brook-Shepherd, G. (1961). *Dollfuss.* London: Macmillan.

Dostoevsky, F. Coulson, J. (1962). *Dostoyevsky, A Self Portrait.* London: Oxford Univ. Press.

— *See also* Thomas (Section B).

Doyle, A. Conan. Carr, J. D. (1949). *The Life of Sir Arthur Conan Doyle.* London: Murray.

Dumas, A. *See* Smiles (Section B).

— *See* Terman and Oden (Section B).

— *See* Thomas (Section B).

Dvorak, A. Hoffmeister, K. (1928). *Antonin Dvorak.* London: Lane.

Eddy, Mary Baker. *See* Thomas (Section B).

— Dakin, E. F. (1929). *Mrs Eddy.* New York: Scribners.

Edison, T. Josephson, M. (1961). *Edison.* London: Eyre & Spottiswoode.

Ehrlich, P. Marquardt, M. (1949). *Paul Ehrlich.* London: Heinemann.

Eichmann, A. Arendt, H. (1963). *Eichmann in Jerusalem.* London: Faber & Faber.

— Clarke, C. (1960). *Eichmann. The Savage Truth.* London: World Distributors.

— Reynolds, Quentin (1961). *Minister of Death.* London: Cassell.

— World Jewish Congress (1961). *Dossier of Eichmann.* London.

Einstein, A. Frank, P. (1948). *Einstein.* London: Cape.

— Michelmore, P. (1963). *Einstein.* London: Muller.

— *See also* Thomas (Section B).

— Vallentin, A. (1954). *Einstein.* London: Weidenfeld & Nicolson.

Elgar, E. Dunhill, T. F. (1938). *Sir Edward Elgar.* London: Blackie.

Eliot, G. *See* Thomas (Section B).

Emerson, R. W. Rusk, R. L. (1949). *The Life of Ralph Waldo Emerson.* New York: Scribners.

Epstein, J. (1955). *An Autobiography.* London: Hulton Press.

Erskine, T. Lord Birkett (1961). *Six Great Advocates.* Penguin Books.

Euler, L. *See* Bell (Section B).

Faraday, M. *See* Thomas (Section B).

Flaubert, G. *See* Thomas (Section B).

Fontaine, J. Hamel, F. (1911). *Jean de la Fontaine.* London: Paul.

— *See* Cox (Section B).

Ford, H. Burlingame, R. (1957). *Henry Ford.* London: Hutchinson.

— Nevins, A. (1954). *Ford, The Times, The Man and The Company.* New York: Scribners.

Fourier, J. *See* Bell (Section B).

Fox, G. Hodgkin, T. (1896). *George Fox.* London: Methuen.

— *See also* Terman and Oden (Section B).

Francis, St. Sabatier, P. (1901). *St Francis of Assisi.* London: Hodder & Stoughton.

Franck, C. D'Indy, V. (1910). *Cesar Franck.* London: Lane.

Franklin, B. (undated). *Autobiography*. London: Hutchinson.

Fresnel, A. *See* Smiles (Section B).

Freud, Sigmund (1950). *An Autobiographical Study*. Translated by J. Strachey. London: Hogarth.

— Jones, E. (1953). *Sigmund Freud*. London: Hogarth.

— Lauzon, G. (1962). *Sigmund Freud*. London: Souvenir Press.

Frith, W. P. (1888). *My Autobiography*. London: Bentley.

Froebel, F. Bowen, H. C. (1893). *Froebel and Education by Self Activity*. London: Heinemann.

Galileo, G. Fahie, J. J. (1903). *Galileo, His Life and Work*. London: John Murray.

— *See also* Thomas (Section B).

Galois, E. *See* Bell (Section B).

Galton, Sir Francis. Karl Pearson (1914). *The Life, Letters and Labours of Francis Galton*. 3 volumes. Cambridge: The Univ. Press.

Gandhi, M. (1949). *An Autobiography*. London: Phoenix Press.

— Fischer, L. (1951). *The Life of Mahatma Gandhi*. London: Cape.

Garrick, D. Oman, C. (1958). *David Garrick*. London: Hodder & Stoughton.

Gauguin, E. Perruchot, H. (1963). *Gauguin*. London: Perpetua Books.

Gauss, C. F. Dunnington, C. W. (1955). *Carl Friedrich Gauss*. New York: Hafner.

— *See* Barlow (Section B).

— *See* Bell (Section B).

Geddes, P. Boardman, P. (1944). *Patrick Geddes, The Maker of the Future*. Chapel Hill: Univ. of N. Carolina Press.

Gibbon, E. (1907). *Autobiography*. London: Oxford Univ. Press.

Giotto. *See* Thomas (Section B).

— *See* Vasari (Section B).

Gissing, G. Korg, J. (1963). *George Gissing*. Seattle: Univ. of Washington Press.

Gladstone, W. E. Magnus, P. (1954). *Gladstone*. London: Murray.

— Morley, J. (1904). *The Life of William Ewart Gladstone*. London: Macmillan.

Gluck, Christoph W. (1954). *Grove's Dictionary of Music and Musicians*. London: Macmillan.

— *See* Brockway (Section B).

— *See* Terman and Oden (Section B).

Goebbels, J. Manvell, R., Fraenkel, H. (1960). *Doctor Goebbels*. London: Heinemann.

Goering, H. Frischauer, W. (1950). *Goering*. London: Odhams Press.

Goethe, J. Brown, P. H. (1913). *The Youth of Goethe.* London: Murray.

Gogol, N. Magarshack, D. (1957). *Gogol.* London: Faber & Faber.

Goldsmith, O. Freeman, W. (1951). *Oliver Goldsmith.* London: Jenkins.

— Moore, F. F. (1910). *The Life of Oliver Goldsmith.* London: Constable.

— *See* Smiles (Section B).

Gordon, General. Lord Elton (1954). *General Gordon.* London: Curtis Brown.

Gorky, M. (1953). *Autobiography.* London: Elek Books.

— (1961). *Childhood.* London: Oxford Univ. Press.

Gosse, E. (1907). *Father and Son. A Study of two Temperaments.* London: Heinemann.

Goya, L. *See* Thomas (Section B).

Gray, T. Ketton-Cremer, R. W. (1955). *Thomas Gray.* Cambridge: Cambridge Univ. Press.

Grieg, Edvard. Monrad-Johansen D. (1938). *Edvard Grieg.* London: Curtis Brown.

Grotius, Hugo. Knight, W. S. M. (1925). *Hugo Grotius.* London: Sweet & Maxwell.

Hall, Marshall. Lord Birkett (1961). *Six Great Advocates.* Penguin Books.

Haller, A. *See* Smiles (Section B).

Hamilton, W. Graves, R. P. (1882). *Life of William Rowan Hamilton.* London: Longmans Green.

— *See* Bell (Section B).

Handel, G. *See* Brockway (Section B).

— *See* Smiles (Section B).

— *See* Thomas (Section B).

Hardie, James Keir. Lowe, D. (1923). *From Pit to Parliament. The Story of James Keir Hardie.* London: Labour Publishing Co.

— Stewart, W. (1921). *J. Keir Hardie.* London: Cassell.

Hardy, Thomas. Hardy, F. E. (1928). *The Early Life of Thomas Hardy.* London: Macmillan.

— Holland, C. (1933). *Thomas Hardy, O.M.* London: Jenkins.

— *See also* Thomas (Section B).

Hastings, Patrick. Hastings, Patricia (1959). *The Life of Patrick Hastings.* London: Cresset Press.

Hastings, W. *See* Terman and Oden (Section B).

Hawthorne, N. *See* Thomas (Section B).

Haydn, F. *See* Brockway (Section B).

— *See* Thomas (Section B).

Haydon, B. R. (1926). *The Autobiography and Memoirs of Benjamin Robert Haydon.* London: Davies.

Heineken, C. Strauch, A. (1924). Christian Heineken. *Amer. J. Dis. Child.*, **27**, 163.

Herschel, W. Sidgwick, J. B. (1953) *William Herschel, Explorer of the Heavens.* London: Faber & Faber.

Himmler, H. Frischauer, W. (1953). *Himmler.* London: Odhams Press.

— Manvell, R., Fraenkel, H. (1965). *Heinrich Himmler.* London: Heinemann.

Hitler, A. Bullock, A. (1952). *Hitler.* London: Odhams Press.

— Kubizek, A. (1954) *Young Hitler.* London: Wingate.

Holmes, Oliver W. Morse, J. T. (1896). *Life and Letters of Oliver Wendell Holmes.* London: Sampson Low & Marston.

Hugo, Victor. Duclaux, Madame (1921). *Victor Hugo.* London: Constable.

— *See also* Smiles (Section B).

— Marois, André (1956). *Victor Hugo.* London: Jonathan Cape.

— *See also* Thomas (Section B).

Humboldt, A. Bruhns, K. (1872). *Life of Alexander Van Humboldt.* London: Longmans Green.

Hume, J. Mossner, E. C. (1954). *The Life of David Hume.* London: Nelson.

Hunter, John. Gloyne, S. R. (1950). *John Hunter.* Edinburgh: Livingstone.

— Kobler, J. (1960). *The Reluctant Surgeon.* London: Heinemann.

— Paget, S. (1897). *John Hunter.* London: Fisher Unwin.

— Young, A. (1961). *The Men who made Surgery.* New York: Hillman Books.

Huxley, T. H. *See* Thomas (Section B).

Inandi, Jacques. *See* Barlow (Section B).

Inge, Dean. Fox, A. (1960). *Dean Inge.* London: Murray.

Ivan. Waliszewski, K. (1904). *Ivan the Terrible.* London: Heinemann.

Jackson, Chevalier (1938). *An Autobiography.* New York: Macmillan.

James, H. Jefferson, D. W. (1960). *Henry James.* London: Oliver & Boyd.

— Matthiessen, F. O. (1961). *The James Family.* New York: Knopf.

Jefferson, T. Padover, S. (1942). *Jefferson.* London: Harcourt, Brace & World, Inc.

Jeffreys, Judge. Hyde, H. M. (1940). *Judge Jeffreys.* London: Harrap.

— Irving, H. B. (1898). *The Life of Judge Jeffreys.* London: Heinemann.

— Keeton, G. W. (1965). *Lord Chancellor Jeffreys and the Stuart Cause.* London: Macdonald.

Jenner, Doctor. Fisk, D. (1959). *Doctor Jenner of Berkeley.* London: Heinemann.

— *See* Hale White (Section B).

Joan of Arc. *See* Thomas (Section B).

Johnson, Samuel (1934). *Boswell's Life of Johnson.* Oxford: Clarendon Press.

— Clifford, J. L. (1955). *Young Samuel Johnson.* London: Heinemann.

— Pearson, H. (1958). *Johnson and Boswell.* London: Heinemann.

Jones, William. *See* Smiles (Section B).

Jonson, B. *See* Terman and Oden (Section B).

Jung, C. Jaffe, A. (1963). *Carl Jung, Memories, Dreams and Reflections.* London: Collins.

Kant, I. Paulsen, F. (1902). *Immanuel Kant.* London: Nimmo.

Keats, John. Colvin, S. (1917). *John Keats.* London: Macmillan.

— Erlande, A. (1929). *Life of John Keats.* London: Cape.

— Amy, Lowell (1924). *John Keats.* London: Cape.

Keble, J. Battiscombe, G. (1963). *John Keble.* London: Constable.

Keller, H. Harrity, R. and Martin, R. (1964). *Helen Keller.* London: Hodder & Stoughton.

Kelvin, Lord. King, A. G. (1925). *Kelvin the Man.* London: Hodder & Stoughton.

— King, E. (1910). *Lord Kelvin's Early Home.* London: Macmillan.

— Thompson, S. P. (1910). *The Life of William Thomson, Baron Kelvin.* London: Macmillan.

— *See also* Thomas (Section B).

Kepler, J. *See* Smiles (Section B).

Kipling, R. Carrington, C. (1955). *Rudyard Kipling.* London: Macmillan.

Kitchener, Lord. Magnus, P. (1958). *Kitchener.* London: Murray.

Knox, Ronald. Waugh, E. (1959). *Ronald Knox.* London: Chapman & Hall.

Kreuger, I. Shaplen, R. (1961). *Kreuger, Genius and Swindler.* London: Deutsch.

Lafayette, Marquis de. Latzko, A. (1936). *Lafayette, A Soldier of Liberty.* London: Methuen.

Lagrange, J. *See* Bell (Section B).

Lamb, Charles. Lucas, E. V. (1905). *Life of Charles Lamb.* London: Methuen.

Laval, P. Cole, H. (1963). *Laval.* London: Heinemann.

Lavoisier, A. Turnbull, H. W. (1929). *The Great Mathematician.* London: Methuen.

— *See also* Thomas (Section B).

Lawrence of Arabia. Aldington, R. (1955). *Lawrence of Arabia*. London: Collins.

— Villers, Jean B. (1958). *T. E. Lawrence*. London: Sidgwick & Jackson.

Lear, E. Davidson, A. (1938). *Edward Lear*. London: Murray.

Leibnitz, G. Carr, H. W. (1929). *Leibnitz*. London: Benn.

— *See also* Bell (Section B).

— *See also* Terman and Oden (Section B).

Leonardo da Vinci. Vallentin, A. (1952). *Leonardo da Vinci*. London: Allen.

— *See also* Smiles (Section B).

— *See also* Van Loon (Section B).

Lesseps, F. de. Beatty, C. (1956). *Ferdinand de Lesseps*. London: Eyre & Spottiswoode.

Lincoln, A. Barton, W. E. (1925). *The Life of Abraham Lincoln*. London: Arrowsmith.

— Masters, E. L. (1931). *Lincoln, the Man*. London: Cassell.

— Nicolay, J. G., Hay, J. (1890). *Abraham Lincoln*. New York: Century.

Lind, Jenny. Bulman, Joan (1956). *Jenny Lind*. London: Barrie & Rockliff.

Linnaeus, C. Jackson, B. D. (1923). *Linnaeus*. London: Witherby.

Lippi, Fra L. *See* Vasari (Section B).

Lister, Joseph. Truax, R. (1947). *Joseph Lister*. London: Harrap.

Liszt, F. *See* Thomas (Section B).

Livingstone, D. Gelfand, M. (1957). *Livingstone the Doctor*. Oxford: Blackwell.

Lloyd George. Thomson, M. (undated). *David Lloyd George*. London: Hutchinson.

Lobatchewsky. *See* Bell (Section B).

Lodge, Sir Oliver (1931). *Past Years—an autobiography*. London: Hodder & Stoughton.

Luther, Martin. Boehmer, H. (1957). *Martin Luther*. London: Meridian Books.

— Erikson, E. H. (1958). *Young Man Luther*. London: Faber & Faber.

— *See also* Thomas (Section B).

Lytton, Lord. Escott, T. H. S. (1910). *Edward Bulwer, First Baron Lytton of Knebworth*. London: Routledge.

— *See also* Terman and Oden (Section B).

Macaulay, Lord. Bryant, A. (1932). *Macaulay*. London: Davies.

— Trevelyan, G. O. (1932). *Lord Macaulay*. London: Oxford Univ. Press.

— Trevelyan, G. O. (1932). *The Life and Letters of Lord Macaulay*. London: Longmans, Green and G. M. Trevelyan.

MacDonald, Ramsay. Weir, L. M. C. N. (no date). *The Tragedy of Ramsay MacDonald.* London: Secker & Warburg.

Mackenzie, J. Power, Sir A. D'Arcy (1936). *British Masters of Medicine.* London: Medical Press and Circular.

— Wilson, R. M. (1926). *The Beloved Physician.* London: Murray.

Manet, E. Perruchot, H. (1962). *Manet.* London: Perpetua Books.

Mangiamelli, V. *See* Barlow (Section B).

Manson, P. Manson-Bahr, P. (1962). *Patrick Manson.* London: Nelson.

Marat, J. Roche (1964). *Famous People and Their Illnesses.* London: Roche Products.

— Warwick, C. F. (1909). *Danton and the French Revolution.* London: Unwin.

— *See* Terman and Oden (Section B).

Marconi, G. Jacot, B. L., Collier, D. M. B. (no date). *Marconi.* London: Hutchinson.

— Marconi, D. (1962). *My Father, Marconi.* London: Muller.

Marx, K. Berlin, I. (1939). *Karl Marx.* London: Thornton Butterworth.

— Carr, E. H. (1934). *Karl Marx.* London: Dent.

Maugham, William Somerset. *British Medical Journal* (1965). Vol. 2, p. 1552.

Maupassant, Guy de. *See* Thomas (Section B).

Mayer, R. *See* Kretschmer (Section B).

Mazzini, G. Hales, E. E. Y. (1956). *Mazzini and the Secret Societies.* London: Eyre & Spottiswoode.

— King, B. (1911). *The Life of Mazzini.* London: Dent.

Mendel, G. Iltis, H. (1932). *Life of Mendel.* London: Allen & Unwin.

— *See also* Thomas (Section B).

Mendelssohn, F. *See* Smiles (Section B).

— *See* Thomas (Section B).

Metastasio, P. *See* Smiles (Section B).

Meyer, C. F. Fray, A. (1925). *Conrad Ferdinand Meyer.* Stuttgart: Cottasche Buchhandlung Nachfolger.

— Hohenstein, L. (1957). *Conrad Ferdinand Meyer.* Berlin: Athenaum.

— Sadger, J. (1908). *Konrad Ferdinand Meyer. Eine pathographisch-psychologische Studie.* Wien: Bergmann.

— Zach, A. (undated). *Conrad Meyer.* Bern: Verlag Paul Haupt.

Michelangelo. *See* Smiles (Section B).

— *See* Thomas (Section B).

Mill, J. S. Packe, M. St. J. (1954). *John Stuart Mill.* London: Secker & Warburg.

— *See also* Freehill (Section B).

Milton, J. Fletcher, H. F. (1956). *The Intellectual Development of John Milton.* Urbana: Univ. of Illinois Press.
— *See* Thomas (Section B).
Mirabeau, G. Vallentin, A. (1946). *Mirabeau.* London: Hamish Hamilton.
Mohammed. *See* Thomas (Section B).
Molière, J. *See* Terman and Oden (Section B.)
Monet, Claude. Seitz, W. (1960). *Claude Monet.* London: Thames & Hudson.
Monge, G. *See* Bell (Section B).
Montagu, Lady M. Halsbrand, R. (1956). *The Life of Lady Mary Wortley Montagu.* London: Oxford Univ. Press.
Montessori, M. Standing, E. and M. (1957). *Maria Montessori.* London: Hollis & Carter.
Montgomery, Lord. Morehead, Alan (1947). *Montgomery.* London: Hamish Hamilton.
Moore, Sir J. *See* Lardner (Section B).
Moore, Thomas. Gwynn, S. (1905). *Thomas Moore.* London: Macmillan.
— Strong, L. A. G. (1937). *A Portrait of Thomas Moore.* London: Hodder & Stoughton.
Morland, G. Baily, J. T. H. (1906). *George Morland.* London: Otto.
Mozart, W. John, O. (1882). *Life of Mozart.* London: Novello, Evans.
— Haldane, Charlotte (1960). *Mozart.* London: Oxford Univ. Press.
— Scarlett, E. P. (1964). The Illness and Death of Mozart, *Arch. intern. Med.,* **114,** 311.
— *See also* Brockway (Section B).
— *See also* Van Loon (Section B).
Murillo, B. *See* Terman and Oden (Section B).
Murray, Alexander. *See* Smiles (Section B).
— *Also, Dictionary of National Biography.*
Murray, Gilbert (1960). *An unfinished Autobiography.* London: Allen & Unwin.
Murray, Margaret (1963). *My First Hundred Years.* London: Kimber.
Mussolini, B. Hibbert, C. (1962). *Benito Mussolini.* London: Longmans.
Napoleon. Ashton, J. (1884). *English Caricature and Satire on Napoleon.* London: Chatto & Windus.
— Sokoloff, B. (1938). *Napoleon.* London: Selwyn & Blaunt.
— *See* Cox (Section B).
— *See also* Van Loon (Section B).
Nash, Paul (1948). *Outline—an Autobiography.* London: Faber & Faber.
Nehru, J. Moraes, F. (1956). *Jawaharlal Nehru.* New York: Macmillan.

Nelson, H. *See* Terman and Oden (Section B).

Nero. Henderson, B. W. (1903). *The Life and Principate of the Emperor Nero.* London: Methuen.

Newton, I. Brewster, D. (1855). *Sir Isaac Newton.* Edinburgh: Constable.
— More, L. T (1962). *Isaac Newton.* New York: Dover Publications.
— Sullivan, J. W. N. (1938). *Isaac Newton.* London: Macmillan.
— *See also* Thomas (Section B)

Nietzsche, F. Lea, F. A. (1957). *The Tragic Philosopher.* London: Methuen.
— Reyburn, H. A. (1948). *Nietzsche.* London: Macmillan.

Nightingale, F. Woodham-Smith, C. (1950). *Florence Nightingale.* London: Constable.

Nobel, A. Halasz, N. (1959). *Nobel.* London: Hale.

Northcliffe, Lord. Pound, R., Harmsworth, G. (1959). *Northcliffe.* London: Cassell.

Nuffield, Lord. Andrews, P. W. S., Brunner, E. (1955). *The Life of Lord Nuffield.* Oxford: Blackwell.

Oates, Titus. Lane, Jane (1949). *Titus Oates.* London: Dakers.

Osler, W. Cushing, H. (1925). *The Life of Sir William Osler.* Oxford: Clarendon Press.

Paderewski, I. Landau, R. (1934). *Paderewski.* London: Ivor Nicholson & Watson.
— Phillip, C. (1934). *Ignace Paderewski.* New York: Macmillan.

Paget, Sir James. *See* Hale White (Section B).

Paré, Ambroise. Paget, S. (1897). *Ambroise Paré.* London: Putnam.

Pascal, B. Bishop, M. (1937). *Pascal. The Life of Genius.* London: Bell.
— Fletcher, F. T. H. (1954). *Pascal.* Oxford: Blackwells.
— Mortimer, E. (1959). *Blaise Pascal.* London: Methuen.
— *See* Terman and Oden (Section B).

Pasteur, L. Grant, M. P. (1960). *Louis Pasteur.* London: Benn.
— Vallery-Radot, R. (1902). *The Life of Pasteur.* London: Constable.
— *See* Smiles (Section B).

Pavlov, I. Babkin, B. P. (1951). *Pavlov.* London: Gollancz.

Pavlova, A. Franks, A. H. (1956). *Pavlova.* London: Burke Publishing Co.

Peel, R. Parker, C. S. (1891). *Sir Robert Peel.* London: Murray.

Penn, W. Dobrée, B. (1932). *William Penn—Quaker and Pioneer.* London: Constable.
— Peare, C. O. (1956). *William Penn.* London: Dobson.
— *See* Terman and Oden (Section B).

Pestalozzi, J. Green, J. A. (1913). *Life and Work of Pestalozzi.* London: Clive.
— Silber, K. (1960). *Pestalozzi.* London: Routlege & Kegan Paul.
Petit, J. *See* Smiles (Section B).
Picasso, P. Penrose, R. (1958). *Pablo Picasso.* London: Gollancz.
Pitt, W. Gibson, E. (1898). *Pitt.* London: Longmans Green.
— Lord Rosebery (1918). *Pitt.* London: Macmillan.
— *See also* Terman and Oden (Section B).
Poincaré, H. *See* Bell (Section B).
Pope, A. Roche (1964). *Famous People and Their Illnesses.* London: Roche Products.
— Sherburn, G. (1934). *The Early Career of Alexander Pope.* Oxford: Clarendon Press.
— *See* Thomas (Section B).
Proust, M. Barker, R. H. (1958). *Marcel Proust.* London: Faber & Faber.
Puccini, G. *See* Thomas (Section B).
Rabelais, F. *See* Thomas (Section B).
Raphael, S. *See* Thomas (Section B).
Rasputin, G. Rasputin, Maria (1934). *My Father.* London: Cassell.
— Wilson, C. (1964). *Rasputin and the Fall of the Romanovs.* London: Barker.
Rembrandt. *See* Thomas.
Rennie, J. *See* Smiles (Section B).
Renoir, P. Renoir, Jean (1962). *Renoir, my Father.* London: Collins.
— *See* Thomas (Section B).
Reynolds, J. Hudson, D. (1958). *Sir Joshua Reynolds.* London: Bles.
— *See* Thomas (Section B).
Rhodes, C. Lockhart, J. G, Woodhouse, C. M. (1963). *Rhodes.* London: Hodder & Stoughton.
Richelieu, Duc de. Belloc, H. (1930). *Richelieu.* London: Benn.
— Perkins, J. B. (1904). *Richelieu.* London: Putnam.
Rimsky-Korsakoff, N. A. (1924). *My Musical Life.* London: Secker.
— *Also in* Grove's Dictionary of Music and Musicians. London: Macmillan.
Robespierre, M. Morley, J. (1923). *Biographical Studies.* London: Macmillan.
— *See* Terman and Oden (Section B).
— *See* Van Loon (Section B).
Romney, G. Gower, R. S. (1904). *George Romney.* London: Duckworth.
Röntgen, C. Glasser, O. (1933). *William Conrad Röntgen.* London: Bale & Danielsson.

Roosevelt, Eleanor (1962). *Autobiography.* London: Hutchinson.

Roosevelt, F. Burns, J. M. (1956). *Roosevelt. The Lion and the Fox.* London: Secker & Warburg.

Ross, Sir Ronald. *See* Hale White (Section B).

Rossetti, C. Sandars, M. F. (1930). *The Life of Christina Rossetti.* London: Hutchinson.

Rossetti, D. G. Waugh, E. (1928). *Dante Gabriel Rossetti.* London: Duckworth.

Rossini, G. *See* Brockway (Section B).

Rousseau, Jean-Jacques (1931). *Confessions.* London: Dent.

— Broome, J. H. (1963). *Rousseau.* London: Arnold.

— Green, F. C. (1955). *Jean-Jacques Rousseau.* Cambridge: Cambridge Univ. Press.

Roussel, A. Deane, B. (1961). *Albert Roussel.* London: Barrie & Rockliff.

Rubens, P. *See* Thomas (Section B).

Ruskin, J. (1899). *Praeterita.* London: Allen.

— Cook, E. T. (1911). *John Ruskin.* London: George Allen.

— Evans, J. (1954). *John Ruskin.* London: Jonathan Cape.

— Harrison, F. (1902). *John Ruskin.* London: Macmillan.

— Leon, D. (1949). *Ruskin.* London: Routledge & Kegan Paul.

— Wilenski, R. H. (1933). *Ruskin.* London: Faber & Faber.

Sade, Marquis de. Gorer, G. (1964). *The Life and Ideas of the Marquis de Sade.* London: Panther Books.

— Lely, G. (1961). *The Marquis de Sade.* London: Elek Books.

Safford, T. H. *See* Barlow (Section B).

Schnabel, A. Saerchinger, C. (1957). *Arthur Schnabel.* London: Cassell.

Schubert, F. Duncan, E. (1905). *Schubert.* London: Dent.

— In *Grove's Dictionary of Music and Musicians.* London: Macmillan.

— *See* Brockway (Section B).

— *See also* Thomas (Section B).

Schumann, R. Chissell, J. (1948). *Schumann.* London: Dent.

— In *Grove's Dictionary of Music and Musicians.* London: Macmillan.

— *See* Thomas (Section B).

Schweitzer, A. (1924). *Memoirs of Childhood and Youth.* London: Allen & Unwin.

— Seaver, G. (1955). *Albert Schweitzer.* London: Black.

Scott, Walter, Grierson, H. H. (1938). *Sir Walter Scott.* London: Constable.

— Pearson, H. (1954). *Walter Scott.* London: Methuen.

— *See* Thomas (Section B).

Sexton, Sir James (1936). *Agitator, The Life of the Dockers' M.P. Autobiography.* London: Faber & Faber.

Shaw, G. B. (1949). *Sixteen Self Sketches.* London: The Society of Authors.

— Churchill, Winston S. (1962). *Great Contemporaries.* London: Fontana Monarchs.

— Ervine, St John (1956). *Bernard Shaw.* London: Constable.

— Henderson, A. (1932). *George Bernard Shaw.* New York: Appleton.

— Simon, L. (1958). *Shaw on Education.* New York: Columbia Univ. Press.

— Winsten, S. (1946). *Aspects of Shaw's Life and Work.* London: Hutchinson.

— Winsten, S. (1956). *Jesting Apostle.* London: Hutchinson.

Shelley, Percy Bysshe. Blunden, E. (1946). *Shelley.* London: Peters.

— Dowden, E. (1886). *The Life of Percy Bysshe Shelley.* London: Kegan Paul.

— Peck, W. E. (1927). *Shelley.* London: Benn.

— White, N. I. (1947). *Shelley.* London: Secker & Warburg.

— *See also* Thomas (Section B).

Sheridan, R. Moore, T. (1825). *Life of Sheridan.* Paris: Galignani.

Sibelius, J. Ekman, K. (1935). *Sibelius.* Helsingfors: Holger Schilotts Forlag.

— *See* Thomas (Section B).

Sickert, W. Browse, L. (1960). *Walter Sickert.* London: Rupert Hart-Davis.

Smellie, W. Johnstone, R. W. (1952). *William Smellie. The Master of British Midwifery.* Edinburgh: Livingstone.

Smuts, J. C. Smuts, J. O. (1952). *Jan Christian Smuts.* London: Cassell.

Snowden, Philip Viscount (1934). *An Autobiography.* London: Ivor Nicholson & Watson.

Socrates. Taylor, A. E. (1932). *Socrates.* London: Davies.

Stalin, J. Deutscher, I. (1949). *Stalin: a Political Biography.* London: Oxford Univ. Press.

— Trotski, L. (1947). *Stalin.* London: Hollis & Carter.

Steinmetz, C. P. Leonard J. N. (1929). *The Life of Charles Proteus Steinmetz.* New York: Doubleday Doran.

— *See* Thomas (Section B).

Stephenson, R. Rolt, L. T. C. (1960). *George and Robert Stephenson.* London: Longmans, Green.

— *See also* Smiles (Section B).

Sterne, L. Cross, W. L. (1909). *The Life and Times of Laurence Sterne.* New York: Macmillan.

— *See* Thomas (Section B).

Stevenson, R. L. Balfour, G. (1901). *Robert Louis Stevenson.* London: Methuen.

Stopes, M. Bryant, K. (1962). *Marie Stopes.* London: Hogarth.

Strauss, J. *See* Brockway (Section B).

Stravinsky, Igor (1936). *Chronicle of my life.* London: Gollancz.

— *See also* Brockway (Section B).

Streicher, Julius. Kelley, D. M. (1947). *22 cells in Nuremberg.* London: Allen.

Sullivan, A. Wyndham, H. S. (1926). *Arthur Seymour Sullivan.* London: Kegan Paul.

Swedenborg, E. White, W. (1867). *Emanuel Swedenborg.* London: Simpkin Marshall.

— *See* Terman and Oden (Section B).

Swift, J. Collins, J. C. (1893). *Jonathan Swift.* London: Chatto & Windus.

— Craik, H. (1894). *The Life of Jonathan Swift.* London: Macmillan.

— *See* Thomas (Section B).

Swinburne, A. *See* Thomas (Section B).

Talleyrand, P. Duff Cooper (1932). *Talleyrand.* London: Cape.

Tchaikovsky, P. Tchaikovsky, M. (1906). *The Life and Letters of Peter Ilich Tchaikovsky.* London: Lane.

— *See also* Brockway (Section B).

Telford, T. *See* Smiles (Section B).

Temple, Archbishop. Iremonger, F. A. (1948). *William Temple.* London: Oxford Univ. Press.

Tennyson, A. Lounsbury, T. R. (1915). *The Life and Times of Tennyson.* London: Humphrey Milford.

— Tennyson, C. (1949). *Alfred Tennyson.* New York: Macmillan.

Thackeray, C. Melville, L. (1927). *Thackeray.* London: Benn.

— *See* Thomas (Section B).

Thiers, L. *See* Smiles (Section B).

Thompson, Francis. Reid, J. C. (1959). *Francis Thompson, Man and Poet.* London: Routledge & Kegan Paul.

Tintoretto. *See* Smiles (Section B).

Titian, T. *See* Thomas (Section B).

Tolstoy, L. Maude, A. (1908). *Leo Tolstoy.* London: Constable.

— *See* Thomas (Section B).

Torquemada, T. Hope, T. (1939). *Torquemada, Scourge of the Jews.* London: Allen & Unwin.

Toscanini, A. Sacchi, F. (1957). *The Magic Baton.* London: Putnam.

Toulouse-Lautrec. Hanson, L. and E. (1956). *The Tragic Life of Toulouse-Lautrec.* London: Secker & Warburg.

Trollope, A. (1947). *An Autobiography.* Univ. of California Press.
— Walpole, H. (1928). *Anthony Trollope.* London: Macmillan.
Turgenev, I. Magarshack, D. (no date). *Turgenev.* London: Faber & Faber.
— Yarmolinsky, A. (1959). *Turgenev.* New York: Orion Press.
Turner, J. Falk, B. (1938). *Turner the Painter.* London: Hutchinson.
— Finberg, A. J. (1961). *The Life of J. M. W. Turner.* Oxford: Clarendon Press.
— *See* Thomas (Section B).
Twain, Mark. *See* Thomas (Section B).
Van Gogh, V. Elgar, F. (1958). *Van Gogh.* London: Thames & Hudson.
— Hanson, L. and E. (1955). *Portrait of Vincent.* Toronto: Clarke, Irwin.
— Laprade, Jacques de (1953). *Van Gogh.* London: Heinemann.
Verdi, G. Hussey, D. (1963). *Verdi.* London: Dent.
— *See* Brockway (Section B).
Volta, A. Giorgio de Santillana (1965). Alessandro Volta. *Scientific American* Vol. 212, p. 82.
Voltaire, F. Brandes, G. (1930). *Voltaire.* New York: Tudor Publishing Co.
— Chase, C. B. (1926). *The young Voltaire.* London: Longmans, Green.
— Noyes, A. (1936). *Voltaire.* London: Sheed & Ward.
Wagner, R. Hight, G. A. (1925). *Richard Wagner.* London: Arrowsmith.
— Jacobs, R. L. (1935). *Wagner.* London: Dent.
— *See* Brockway (Section B).
— *See also* Thomas (Section B).
Wallace, E. Lane, Margaret (1938). *Edgar Wallace.* London: Hamish Hamilton.
Walpole, Horace. Stuart, Dorothy (1927). *Horace Walpole.* London: Macmillan.
Warburton, E. *See* Smiles (Section B).
Washington, G. Weems, M. L. (1962). *The Life of Washington.* Cambridge: Harvard Univ. Press.
Watt, James. Dickinson, H. W. (1935). *James Watt.* Cambridge: Cambridge Univ. Press.
— Muirhead, J. P. (1859). *James Watt.* London: Murray.
— Smiles, J. (1904). *Lives of the Engineers.* London: Murray.
Webb, B. Cole, Margaret (1945). *Beatrice Webb.* London: Longmans, Green.
Weber, K. Saunders, W. (1940). *Weber.* London: Dent.
— *See* Terman and Oden (Section B).
Weierstrass, K. *See* Bell (Section B).

Wellington, Duke of. Guedalla, P. (1937). *The Duke.* London: Hodder & Stoughton.
— Petrie, C. (1956). *Wellington.* London: Barrie.
— Wright, G. N. (1841). *Duke of Wellington.* London: Fisher.
Wells, H. G. (1934). *An Experiment in Autobiography.* London: Gollancz.
Wesley, C. *See* Barlow (Section B).
Wesley, J. Green, V. H. H. (1961). *The Young Wesley.* London: Arnold.
— Laver, J. (1932). *Wesley.* London: Davies.
— *See* Thomas (Section B).
Whateley, R. *See* Barlow (Section B).
Whistler, J. *See* Thomas (Section B).
Whittier, J. *See* Thomas (Section B).
Wilberforce, W. *See* Terman and Oden (Section B).
Wilde, Oscar. Pearson, H. (1949). *The Life of Oscar Wilde.* London: Methuen.
Wingate, Orde. Sykes, C. (1959). *Orde Wingate.* London: Peters.
Witte, Karl. Pastor Witte (1913). *The Education of Karl Witte; or The Training of the Child.* Translated by L. Weiner. London: Harrap.
— *See* Carmichael (Section B).
— *See also* Freehill (Section B).
Wood, Sir Henry (1938). *My Life of Music.* London: Gollancz.
Wordsworth, W. Legouis, E. (1897). *The Early Life of William Wordsworth.* London: Dent.
Wren, C. Briggs, M. S. (1951). *Christopher Wren.* Falcon Educ. Books.
— Briggs, M. S. (1953). *Wren the Incomparable.* London: Allen & Unwin.
Yeats, W. B. (1955). *Autobiography.* London: Macmillan.
— Hone, J. (1942). *W. B. Yeats.* London: Macmillan.
Young, T. Wood, A. (1954). *Thomas Young. Natural Philosopher.* Cambridge: Cambridge Univ. Press.
Zola, E. *See* Thomas (Section B).

SECTION B

Baker, H. J. (1953). *Introduction to Exceptional Children.* New York: Macmillan.
Bakwin, H. (1949). The gifted child. *J. Pediat.*, **35**, 260.
Barlow, F. (1951). *Mental Prodigies.* London: Hutchison.
Bell, E. T. (1937). *Men of Mathematics.* London: Gollancz.
Bereday, G. Z. F., Lauwerys, J. (1962). *The Gifted Child.* London: Evans.

Bloom, B. S. (1964). *Stability and Change in Human Characteristics.* New York: Wiley.

Brain, Russell (1960). *Some Reflections on Genius.* London: Pitman.

Brockway, W., Weinstock, H. (1939). *Men of Music.* London: Methuen.

Burt, C. (1962). The psychology of creative ability. (Book Review), *Brit. J. educ. Psychol.,* **32**, 292.

Carmichael, L. (1954). *Manual of Child Psychology.* New York: Wiley.

Cruikshank, W. M. (1956). *Psychology of Exceptional Children and Youth.* London: Staples.

Ellis, Havelock (1904). *A Study of British Genius.* London: Hurst & Blackett.

Freehill, M. F. (1961). *Gifted Children.* New York: Macmillan.

Galton, Francis (1874). *English Men of Science.* London: Macmillan.

— (1962). *Hereditary Genius.* London: Fontana Library.

Germant, A. (1961). *The Nature of the Genius.* Maryland: Charles Thomas.

Gesell, A. (1948). *Studies in Child Development.* New York: Harper.

Hale-White, W. (1935). *Great Doctors of the Nineteenth Century.* London: Arnold.

Hollingworth, L. S. (1929). *Gifted Children. Their Nature and Nurture.* New York: Macmillan.

— (1942). *Children above 180 I.Q.* Yonkers: World Book Co.

Kretschmer, E. (1931). *The Psychology of Men of Genius.* London: Kegan Paul.

Lardner, D. (1832). *Eminent British Military Commanders.* The Cabinet Encyclopedia.

Lennox, W. G. (1960). *Epilepsy and Related Disorders.* London: Churchill.

Pascal, R. (1960). *Design and Truth in Autobiography.* London: Routledge & Kegan Paul.

Roucek, J. (1962). *The Unusual Child.* London: Owen.

Smiles, Samuel (1887). *Life and Labour.* London: Murray.

— (1904). *Lives of the Engineers.* London: Murray.

Stedman, L. M. (1924). *Education of Gifted Children.* New York: World Book Co.

Terman, L. M. (1947). *The Gifted Child Grows Up.* Stanford: Stanford Univ. Press.

Terman, L. M., Oden, M. H. (1925-1959). *Genetic Studies of Genius.* Stanford: Stanford Univ. Press.

— (1959). *The Gifted Child at Mid-Life.* London: Oxford Univ. Press.

Thomas, H., Thomas, D. L. (1959). *Living Biographies of Great Composers.* London: Allen.

— (1959). *Living Biographies of Great Poets.*
— (1959). *Living Biographies of Great Painters.*
— (1959). *Living Biographies of Great Novelists.*
— (1959). *Living Biographies of Great Philosophers.*
— (1959). *Living Biographies of Great Religious Leaders*
— (1959). *Living Biographies of Famous Women.*
— (1959). *Living Biographies of Great Scientists.*
   Tindall & Cox.
Tredgold, A. F. (1949). *Textbook of Mental Deficiency.* (Re idiots savants).
   London: Baillière,
Van Loon, H. W. (1943). *Lives.* London: Harrap.
Vasari, Giorgio (1927). *The Lives of the Painters, Sculptors and Architects.*
   London: Dent.
Witty, P. (1951). *The Gifted Child.* Boston: Heath.
Yoder, A. H. (1894). The study of the boyhood of great men. *Pedagogical Seminary,* vol. 3, No. 1.

SECTION C

Sources of information referred to by others, but not seen by us:

Biographie Universelle.
Alphonse de Candolle (1873). *Histoire des Sciences et des Savants Depuis deux Siècles.* Geneva.
Comte's Positivist Calendar.
Dictionary of National Biography.
Lives of the Saints, by the Bollandist Fathers. Paris. First Volume, 1643.
   Sixty-first Volume, 1875.
Lombroso, Man of Genius.

INDEX OF PERSONS

SUBJECT INDEX

ROBERT CUNNINGHAM AND SONS LTD., LONGBANK WORKS, ALVA